Baseball's Most
Outrageous Promotions

Baseball's Most Outrageous Promotions
From Wedlock and Headlock Day to Disco Demolition Night

Joseph Natalicchio

McFarland & Company, Inc., Publishers
Jefferson, North Carolina

ISBN (print) 978-1-4766-9512-9
ISBN (ebook) 978-1-4766-5599-4

Library of Congress cataloging data are available

Library of Congress Control Number 2025036627

© 2026 Joseph Natalicchio. All rights reserved

No part of this book may be reproduced or transmitted in any form or by any means, electronic or mechanical, including photocopying or recording, or by any information storage and retrieval system, without permission in writing from the publisher.

Cover image: Fans in attendance at the Grandstand Managers Night promotion by the St. Louis Browns on August 24, 1951, at Sportsman's Park (National Baseball Hall of Fame and Museum, Cooperstown, New York)

McFarland & Company, Inc., Publishers
Box 611, Jefferson, North Carolina 28640
www.mcfarlandpub.com

To my wife, Fran,
whose tireless and patient support
made this book possible

Table of Contents

Preface	1

Part I. Era of the Barnums

1 ♦ The First and Foremost Barnum: Bill Veeck in Milwaukee, Cleveland, St. Louis, and Chicago	4
2 ♦ Later Barnums Had a Ball Until the Blast: Charlie O. Finley, Bill Giles, Bob Hope, and Back to Veeck	22

Part II. Outrageous Promotions Courtesy of Baseball's Four Barnums

3 ♦ Veeck Wrecks Baseball's Traditions: The Eddie Gaedel Game and Grandstand Managers Night	42
4 ♦ Finley's Baseball Folly: The Beatles and Charlie-O the Mule	59
5 ♦ Giles' Genius Goes Awry: Farewell to Connie Mack Stadium and Kiteman	74
6 ♦ Turner and Hope Run Amok with Baseball's Dignity: Wedlock and Headlock Day and Wet T-Shirt Night	91
7 ♦ Veeck Breaks a Slew of Records: Disco Demolition Night	107

Part III. Other Outrageous Promotions

8 ♦ Askew Over Scrap Metal: Scrap Metal Day	124
9 ♦ A Stadium Full of Souvenirs: Washington Senators Last Game	138
10 ♦ A Surfeit of Beer: Ten-Cent Beer Night	152
11 ♦ A Shower of Baseballs: Souvenir Baseball Night	165

Epilogue: The Thrill Is Gone   179

Appendix I. If You Give It Away, They Will Come: Outrageous Giveaways   187

Appendix II. Show Me the Money: The Demise of the Reserve Clause   194

Chapter Notes   197

Bibliography   229

Index   239

Preface

Former Dodgers manager Tommy Lasorda, whom we'll meet in Chapter 11, once said, "In baseball and in business, there are three types of people. Those who make it happen, those who watch it happen, and those who wonder what happened."[1] Let me introduce two major league baseball owners—Bill Veeck, Jr., and Charlie O. Finley—and two executives—Bill Giles and Bob Hope—who made it happen in a big way. These four showmen, who recall the great circus impresario P.T. Barnum, ushered into baseball the Era of the Barnums, the period between 1946 and the early 1980s, when they raised to an art form the use of promotions as marketing tools to increase attendance in major league ballparks. These promotions ranged from the merely entertaining to the truly outrageous. While presenting the former, this book spotlights the latter—nine promotions, some of which were designed to be outrageous and others that were vastly ill-conceived or run-of-the-mill but went terribly wrong. As a bonus, this book presents four additional promotions not associated with the Barnums that were equally outrageous, largely due to their shocking conclusions.

This book contributes to the understanding of major league baseball history by bringing to light the Era of the Barnums and discussing in detail major league baseball's most outrageous promotions in one volume and in context. Our survey of these 13 promotions, some of which were years in the making, shows that they did not happen in a vacuum. In some cases, the context is readily understood to be baseball-related. For example, some promotions are presented within the framework of the franchise's history, others within the context of the owner's or a team executive's career, and one from the perspective of a manager's baseball career. Other promotions were part and parcel of nationwide developments that, like ocean currents, swept major league baseball teams, willingly or not, into their deep waters.

After a brief economic history of major league baseball from its beginnings to the early 1940s, when Veeck purchased the minor league baseball team where he first tried his promotional ideas, I will be your

1

guide as we visit various ballparks, some of which now exist only in memory, to view especially interesting and entertaining promotions sponsored by these showmen. We follow with an extended visit to nine outrageous promotions (eight in-game and one stand-alone) produced by Veeck and company. Our sojourn to each event includes a guided tour of what happened leading up to the promotion, the promotion itself, and its aftermath. What's more, at no extra charge, we take similar extended side trips to four other outrageous in-game promotions from the 1940s to the 1990s that rival those of the four showmen.

As we tour the 13 outrageous promotions, I suggest that you hold onto your handrails because you will witness astonishing events that are unimaginable within the normal context of a major league baseball game. These include a battle with weapons between baseball players and fans, children running willy-nilly on a baseball field, naked fans running the bases, drunken fans trashing baseball fields, fans dismantling a stadium during a game, a little person taking an official major league at-bat, fans managing a game from the stands, banners hurling insults at a team owner, a woman exposing herself, a father-son team mooning the bleachers, women parading in wet t-shirts, professional wrestling, mass marriages, fans throwing hundreds of souvenir baseballs onto the field, the Beatles playing to a nearly half-empty stadium, a mule mascot treated better than players, and an explosion on a baseball field large enough to create a crater as part of a promotion that possibly heralded the death of disco music.

Part I

◆ ◆ ◆

Era of the Barnums

◊ CHAPTER 1 ◊

The First and Foremost Barnum
Bill Veeck in Milwaukee, Cleveland, St. Louis, and Chicago

In the beginning, major league baseball was a promotional wasteland. The staid and stodgy powers-that-be saw the game as a solemn ritual, almost a holy calling,[1] staged for men who venerated the game. Owners believed that using in-game promotions to increase attendance, which at the time represented the lion's share of revenue, lacked appropriate respect for this hallowed institution. This ecclesiastical view of baseball lasted for 70 years, from the 1870s to the 1940s, when Bill Veeck, the brash owner of the minor league Milwaukee Brewers from 1941 to 1943, bought the Cleveland Indians (now the Guardians) in 1946. Veeck brought with him an innovative marketing strategy that breathed new life into the old game. With the Indians, Veeck achieved unparalleled success by aggressively using unheard-of promotions to fundamentally reorient baseball from a ritual staged for a few to entertainment for the many. Veeck eventually moved his sideshow to St. Louis, where, as owner of the Browns, he was unable to replicate his prior success but staged two of the most outrageous promotions in baseball history. Later in Chicago, he enjoyed greater success with the White Sox.

The Business History of Major League Baseball, Pre-Barnums

In 1871, baseball players—not wealthy owners—formed the National Association of Professional Base Ball Players, which was the first professional baseball league.[2] As described by John B. Lord in *Bill Giles & Baseball*, which serves as the source for much of the following discussion, "professional" may have been a misnomer, since the league, which was short-lived, experienced significant financial and organizational difficulties and was beleaguered by rowdiness on the part of players and fans.

Recognizing that this nascent league was not on a positive trajectory, a wealthy businessman named William Hulbert formed the National League in 1876. His intent was that this new league, which was composed of eight franchises, would operate on sound business principles and provide a fan-friendly experience for those who attended its games.[3] The National League, although on a firmer footing than its predecessor, had a problem that threatened its viability—players' salaries. Team owners couldn't hang onto players, who would bounce from team to team for better deals. This practice, known at the time as "revolving," resulted in the escalation of salaries as owners sought to outbid each other for the services of talented players.[4]

The owners came to an agreement that temporarily solved this problem.[5] To limit revolving, owners agreed that they would each reserve a certain number of players; these players would be bound to their teams and lose their opportunity to seek higher salaries elsewhere. Eventually, the owners expanded this practice to include all professional baseball players and thus put an end to revolving—that is, until a threat from a new league drove salaries up again.

In the 1890s, a struggling league of minor league teams, called the Western League, turned to a former Cincinnati newspaper reporter, Ban Johnson, for leadership. Over time, Johnson expanded the league to include franchises in such major cities as Chicago and Philadelphia and, in 1901, he announced that the Western League was now a major league. He called the new league, which at the time also had eight franchises, the American League.[6] In order to stock these teams with professional athletes, the American League franchises recruited several dozen National League players, including such stars as Nap Lajoie and Ed Delahanty, by offering them much more money than they earned with their present teams. This process caused salaries to rise precipitously once again, to the financial detriment of teams in both leagues.[7]

Soon thereafter, the owners in the National and American Leagues entered what is known as the National Agreement of 1903, which established two leagues of eight teams each and formed a three-man National Commission to govern the two leagues.[8] As part of this watershed agreement, the owners in both leagues agreed to adopt and abide by the "reserve clause," which tied a player to his current team in perpetuity. As such, it put a stop to owners' efforts to recruit players from other teams. With the reserve clause universally accepted, major league teams could once and for all suppress players' salaries. Once this agreement was in place, running a baseball franchise was straightforward. Each major league franchise saw as its primary business objective to "fill the stadiums and keep costs to a minimum [using the reserve clause], maximizing their profits."[9]

The Federal League was created in 1913 as a major league in competition with the two existing leagues, which now had to battle another threat to their solvency—unwanted expansion.[10] This league, which was composed of eight teams, lasted for two years before disbanding. The original two leagues put them out of business by enforcing the reserve clause with a pledge to blackball any player who dared jump to a team in the Federal League. This threat helped to minimize the number of players changing leagues. Unable to raid American and National League teams for players, the Federal League teams simply didn't have enough professional players to compete at a performance level commensurate with the original leagues.

However, the owners of Federal League teams did not give up before mounting a momentous legal battle. They filed suit against the two original leagues on antitrust grounds, but the case died in the federal courtroom of Judge Kenesaw Mountain Landis. To compensate the Federal League owners, the American and National League teams gave them cash payments and permitted certain Federal League owners, such as Charles Weeghman, who owned the Chicago Whales, to purchase National and American League franchises.[11] The owners of the Federal League Baltimore Terrapins were displeased with this arrangement and filed another antitrust suit against the American and National Leagues. In 1922, this case was decided in favor of the defendants when Supreme Court Chief Justice Oliver Wendell Holmes, in a momentous decision that lasts until this day, determined that major league baseball was exempt from antitrust rules because it did not operate in interstate commerce.[12] This ruling permitted major league teams to operate as a "legal monopoly," obviating the possibility of unwanted expansion.[13]

While these inter-league legal maneuverings were taking place, the United States entered World War I in April 1916 which, combined with the Spanish flu—first reported in the United States in 1918—once again threatened the financial viability of major league baseball. Attendance at major league baseball games decreased 20 percent from approximately 6.5 million in 1916 to 5.2 million in 1917. By 1918, major league attendance had plummeted to just over 3 million, a significant drop, even considering that teams played 20 percent fewer games that year.[14] Attendance took a favorable turn to about 6.5 million in 1919 and 9.1 million in 1920.[15] However, there were storm clouds on the horizon.

Late in the 1920 season, there was another threat to the solvency of the major leagues—the Black Sox scandal in which players on the White Sox were accused of conspiring with gamblers to throw the 1919 World

Series.[16] This scandal threatened to drive away fans, whose loyalty to teams depended on their understanding that the games were legitimate competitions. Major league owners decided to take forceful action in addressing this scandal. They scrapped the largely ineffective three-man commission that had been governing baseball and replaced it with a commissioner with broad powers to govern the leagues. For this Commissioner, they chose Judge Landis, who was instructed to take whatever action necessary to clean up the game and restore public confidence. As his first major act as commissioner, Landis sent an unequivocal message to all major league baseball by banning for life from baseball the eight players involved in the scandal, including star player "Shoeless" Joe Jackson. In reaction to the commissioner's decisive response to the scandal, the general public was willing to forgive and forget, seeing the scandal as an isolated incident (which it wasn't) that tarnished the game only temporarily.

After major league baseball increased in popularity during the 1920s, when baseball became America's sport, the 1930s saw a downturn in major league baseball's fortunes.[17] The stock market crash of 1929 signaled the beginning of the Great Depression, which lasted the entire decade. The United States labor market experienced 25 percent unemployment. Soup kitchens served those who might otherwise go without food. Families who lacked money for necessities didn't have disposable income for entertainment such as a baseball game. Attendance at major league baseball games sharply decreased. The resultant decline in revenue hurt the bottom line for many major league baseball teams, who were still nearly totally reliant on paid attendance for their income.

While the United States was still hurting from the Depression at the turn of the 1940s, major league baseball had rebounded. The attendance decreases of the Depression were erased.[18] When the Japanese attacked Pearl Harbor in 1941 and America entered World War II, President Franklin Roosevelt, with his famous "Green Light" letter, informed Commissioner Landis that, in his opinion, it would be best for the morale of the country if major league baseball continued during the fighting. While that was good news to the owners, so many players went into the armed forces, to be replaced by less talented athletes, that the teams experienced a significant decrease in the quality of play.[19] Major league teams experienced a concomitant decrease in attendance, which in 1939 represented nearly 80 percent of an average team's revenue. By 1943, the major leagues did not turn a profit.[20]

The end of World War II saw a revival of the U.S. economy. While major league baseball had rebounded once again, setting attendance records in 1945 and 1946,[21] the rapidly expanding economy gave owners an opportunity to further increase and expand their fan base.[22] But still, "baseball continued to earn the lion's share of its revenue through the live gate."[23] Other than ticket sales, major league teams raised small amounts of income from concessions, local radio deals, local sponsors, and ballpark signage. However, these teams had very few tools with which to market their teams and otherwise generate increased attendance. Baseball business executives depended largely on the local newspapers' sports pages to generate interest in the teams. Marketing by the teams consisted of radio advertising and scarce promotions.[24] What more could they do to expand attendance? Waiting in the wings, Bill Veeck, a wounded World War II veteran who owned the minor league Milwaukee Brewers, was eager for his opportunity to show them the way.

Rehearsal in Milwaukee (1941 to 1943)

Bill Veeck, who was born on February 19, 1914, in Hinsdale, Illinois,[25] spent his entire life in and around professional baseball. When he was a child, his father, William Veeck, Sr., was a sports reporter for the *Chicago Evening American*.[26] In 1918, the senior Veeck wrote a series of articles that were especially critical of Chicago Cubs management, both in the front office and on the field. In response, chewing gum (and baking soda) magnate William Wrigley, Jr., who owned a controlling interest in the Cubs, challenged the elder Veeck to take a management position with his team. The senior Veeck accepted the challenge and went on to be an integral part of Cubs baseball for 25 years.[27]

It is possible that Bill Veeck inherited his promotional wizardry from his father, who introduced advancements to baseball still prevalent today. In his book, *Veeck as in Wreck: The Autobiography of Bill Veeck*, Veeck describes his father as "far too dignified a man to pull any promotional stunts. He was a man of imagination though, and easily the greatest innovator of his

Bill Veeck was the first major league owner to make extensive use of promotions to increase attendance. As owner of the Cleveland Indians, St. Louis Browns, and Chicago White Sox (twice), he is best known for two outrageous promotions—the Eddie Gaedel Game and Grandstand Managers Night—and one disastrous one—Disco Demolition Night (National Baseball Hall of Fame and Museum).

time."[28] For example, under Veeck's father, the Chicago Cubs were the first team to broadcast games over the radio. Veeck Sr. introduced this innovation, which greatly expanded the fanbase for major league baseball, in the face of furious opposition from virtually all other team owners, who thought it would reduce attendance.[29] Possibly the elder Veeck's most significant contribution to professional baseball was to promote the game to families. He reintroduced Ladies' Days promotions, when women could gain entrance to the ballpark for free, and children under 12 could enter the ballpark for a reduced price.[30]

When the elder Veeck died on October 5, 1933, his son returned from Kenyon College to take a place in Cubs management. At the age of 22, Veeck was asked to take charge of an effort to beautify Wrigley Field in time for the 1937 World Series, which the Cubs hoped to be a part of.[31] (Alas, it was not to be, but the Cubs did compete in the 1938 World Series.) Among other things, Veeck added bleacher ticket booths, redesigned concession stands, and supervised the construction of a new scoreboard built above the bleachers that used lights and flags to let people passing by on the elevated train know whether the Cubs had won that day's game.[32] But arguably his greatest contribution to Wrigley Field was to plant "the world's best known horticultural display,"[33] that is, the famous ivy that still covers its outfield walls.[34]

Inspired by his father's success with the Chicago Cubs, Veeck set out to purchase a team of his own.[35] Without anywhere near the personal resources needed to do so, in the summer of 1941, Veeck put together a syndicate of Chicago and Milwaukee businessmen to purchase the moribund Milwaukee Brewers of the Double-A American Association, then the highest level in the minor leagues.[36] At the time of Veeck's purchase, the franchise was in dire financial straits; the league had taken over the franchise, which was teetering close to bankruptcy and facing imminent foreclosure.[37] Veeck described the team, which was 18½ games out of first place, as "absolutely the worst Double-A team he had ever seen."[38] On the night that Veeck took control of the team, the Brewers had a paid attendance of 22 fans.[39]

Veeck and his partners had their work cut out for them. Veeck pursued a four-pronged strategy for moving the Brewers into solvency. First, he tried to improve the woeful product on the field by seeking to bring onto the team men who could play the game of baseball. Indeed, according to Dickson, in *Bill Veeck: Baseball's Greatest Maverick*, Veeck "shuttled players in and out on an almost daily basis."[40] In fewer than three months, he "bought, sold, or exchanged a record fifty-one players."[41] Second, Veeck sought to create a personal rapport with the fans by greeting them as they entered and exited the ballpark, meeting with them

Veeck (right, in trench coat) is shown with members of the Milwaukee Brewers minor league team in 1943. As owner of the Brewers, Veeck experimented extensively with promotions before he introduced them to major league baseball (*Look Magazine* via National Baseball Hall of Fame and Museum).

person-to-person in the stands during games, and speaking to any group, regardless of size, that would have him. These exchanges were more than just meet-and-greet; Veeck was constantly looking for ideas on ways to improve the fan experience and sometimes put into practice the advice he received.[42]

Third, Veeck sought to improve the fan experience at Borchert Field, where the Brewers played their home games. At the time of the purchase, it was a dilapidated wooden stadium built in 1902, whose one claim to fame was that it was "the only [ballpark] in the world perhaps where no spectator, no matter where he sits, can see the entire field."[43] Not having the money for a new stadium, Veeck did what he could with the extant one[44]: He borrowed $50,000 to spruce up the stadium. He obtained zoning approval to move light stanchions that were blocking fans' views of the field, and he rebuilt the sagging bleachers that were likely unsafe.[45] Veeck hired 100 cleaning women to scrub the park down, and no surface was left untouched. Veeck brought in a crew of painters to brighten the stadium by repainting it light grey. A construction crew was brought in to install a new restroom for female patrons[46] and refurbish the men's restroom. He also built a new press box stocked with beer and cold meat for sportswriters.[47]

Finally, and most importantly given the topic of this book, Veeck sought to promote attendance by giving fans entertainment above and beyond the baseball game. According to Dan Vukelich, in his article "The Great White Sox Hope," "[Veeck] opened a whole trunkful of ideas, gimmicks, promotions, and fan grabbers designed to make a day at the ballpark a memorable experience."[48] At the time, promotional efforts were rare. Promotions such as those pondered by Veeck were nonexistent.[49] The baseball establishment at the time did not look kindly at any form of extra entertainment. But Veeck saw baseball as a business operating for a profit and, like any other business, the product needed to be packaged as attractively as possible and aggressively sold to the public.[50] Veeck believed that, by "adding a few moments of fairly simple pleasure," he could attract people, including women and families, to baseball games and make fans of them.[51]

Veeck had a penchant for entertainment that involved raffling off odd items. He believed that "it isn't enough for a promotion to be entertaining or even amusing. It must create conversation."[52] These lottery giveaways, staged during the 1941 and 1942 seasons, certainly did that. At one game, he awarded a patron a 50-pound block of ice that Veeck personally thrust into the fan's arms. He awarded a keg of nails to a second fan and a step ladder to a third.[53] Veeck followed up these promotions with fruit- and vegetable-themed nights during which lucky fans would be awarded a supply of seasonal produce.[54] During livestock nights, Veeck held lotteries to award fans with turkeys, geese, rabbits, pigeons, and pigs. These animals often escaped onto the field, followed by their owners who were expected to collect them.[55] Fans in the stands roared with laughter at seeing other patrons attempt to take possession of these often dubious and unruly prizes.[56] On another night, patrons entering the gates of Borchert Field were stunned to see a swayback horse, in full realization that one of them would likely be taking the horse home before the night was through.[57] According to Veeck, the Brewers once gave "six live squab to the most dignified man we could find in the ball park in order to answer the burning question of how a dignified man would hold onto six live squab while watching a ball game."[58] Veeck in his autobiography acknowledged that those who received gag gifts were always sent something more valuable than the prize they won at the ballpark.[59] Other non-lottery promotions included pig races, tightrope walkers,[60] swing bands, free lunches, and vaudeville acts,[61]

Unless the nature of the gag demanded it, Veeck never advertised these lottery and other promotions, so fans were always surprised to learn what the entertainment would be that night.[62] Veeck said, "What we want to do is to get the whole city in a frame of mind where they are asking, 'What is that screwball going to do next?'"[63] Whatever that is, potential customers should understand that, win or lose, when they come to the ballpark, they "are going to experience something enjoyable and, if we are lucky, memorable."[64]

No discussion of Veeck's promotions would be complete without mentioning the award he gave his own team for best Opening Day attendance in 1942. This promotion wasn't so much designed to entertain fans as to express his resentment with league officials for giving the award, which Veeck felt rightly belonged to the Brewers, to another team. A little background: the American Association gave an award to the team that had the best Opening Day attendance. The trophy in 1942 was awarded to Indianapolis, whose crowd numbered 11,546, even though Milwaukee's attendance was 15,599. Turns out that the award was given to the team with the best attendance *in relation to the city's population.*

Veeck was fighting mad.[65] In the next home game after the award of the trophy, Veeck awarded to himself, in a ceremony at home plate, a four-foot-tall trophy of his own design. The trophy, which was delivered to Borchert Stadium in an armored car complete with armed guards, cost $300. According to Dickson, the trophy was engraved:

> PRESENTED TO MILWAUKEE BY THE MILWAUKEE
> BASEBALL CLUB BECAUSE OF A TECHNICAL ERROR
> ON THE PART OF THE LEAGUE MANAGEMENT[66]

Veeck continued the presentation by awarding George Trautman, owner of the Columbus Blue Jays as well as President of the American Association, who had given the trophy to Indianapolis, with a striped cane and seeing-eye dog (in actuality, Veeck's own English Bulldog). While he was at it, Veeck decided to mock another group that seemed to infuriate him on almost a nightly basis. He topped off the ceremony by awarding the umpiring crew bouquets of vegetables, while the loudspeakers played "Three Blind Mice."[67]

In 1943, Veeck added a new wrinkle to his promotion schedule. He sought to increase attendance at Brewers games by holding them when fans were available to see them. During World Wat II, factories manufacturing war supplies worked around the clock. Those laborers working the late-afternoon or night shift were unable to attend regularly scheduled night games.[68] So Veeck created "breakfast baseball"[69]—games scheduled for 10:30 in the morning. Veeck had gone into the factories during the offseason to hear fans' concerns and came away with this idea.[70] Dickson quotes Veeck as saying, "Those who work from four to midnight will have plenty of sleep before game time, and those on the midnight to eight a.m.

shift can have their breakfasts, come out to the park, and then go home for their rest."[71]

The first of these games was scheduled for May 7, 1943.[72] The Brewers sold the tickets at factories near Borchert Field. When the fans arrived, they were treated to hot coffee and donuts, and they could purchase breakfast cereal such as Kellogg's Corn Flakes at a heavily discounted price.[73] Veeck himself was among those serving breakfast. A seven-piece swing band dressed in nightgowns and stocking caps entertained while the fans ate their breakfast.[74] As things turned out, the visiting team arrived late because the train bringing them was delayed, so the game didn't start until noon. Veeck agreed to refund the full price of 2,000 tickets. This was the first of Veeck's promotions to receive national publicity.[75]

Veeck in his autobiography tells of another morning game scheduled specially for women[76] The Brewers sponsored a "Rosie the Riveter" game starting at 9:00 a.m. Like the earlier breakfast baseball games, this morning start time was ideal for women who worked the night and early morning shifts. Women wearing their riveting masks or welding caps were admitted to the ballpark free of charge. They must have been amazed to see ushers in nightgowns and nightcaps serving them breakfasts of cereal and donuts, with milk and coffee.

Late in the 1943 season, on August 28, the Brewers held a promotion to honor the team's manager, Charlie Grimm, on his 45th birthday.[77] Veeck arranged for Grimm to receive several gifts in the presence of fans, including a $1,000 war bond (which Grimm later said was deducted from his next paycheck).[78] The highlight of the celebration was a 12-foot-wide birthday cake containing 12 dancing girls, each of whom popped out of the cake as it was presented to Grimm, to the delight of fans. But that wasn't all. These dancing girls escorted the real surprise; a left-handed pitcher named Julio Acosta, who also popped out of the cake looking rather sheepish.[79] Acosta was a star pitcher in the Piedmont League, where he had a 17–6 record for Richmond. Grimm, who was floored by the celebration, named Acosta as his starting pitcher for the game.[80] This promotion also garnered significant media attention, and Veeck achieved national celebrity status when popular magazines such as *Look*, *The Saturday Evening Post* and *Esquire* all published feature articles on his exploits.[81] The *Look* article, in particular, anointed Veeck as "Baseball's No. 1 Screwball" and contained a quote from his wife, who, before their marriage, had been an equestrienne in the Ringling Brothers Circus:[82] "When I got married, I thought I was all through with circuses. Apparently, I was wrong."[83]

By the end of the 1943 season, Veeck had achieved his goal of making the Milwaukee Brewers into a successful baseball franchise.[84] Veeck's wheeling and dealing of players had finally begun to pay off. The team, which had dramatically improved its quality of play,[85] finished the 1943 season with a 90–61 record. Attendance at Milwaukee Brewers home games increased from about 98,000 during the 1941 season to 332,597 in 1943, which set an American Association record.[86] Fans came to the ballpark not only to see inspired play on the field but also to enjoy the promotions and the improvements, such as they were, to Borchert Field. Veeck would move on to new challenges.

But first, Veeck strongly felt the need to perform his patriotic duty during World War II. In November 1943, while still owner of the Milwaukee Brewers, Veeck was sworn into the Marines,[87] and he asked to fight overseas.[88] In March 1944, after Veeck had completed basic training, he was sent to Camp Elliott in Southern California, where he trained as an antiaircraft gunner.[89] Veeck asked to serve as a Marine Raider, who "specialized in amphibious light infantry warfare." His request was denied,[90] and his battalion was shipped to Nouméa, New Caledonia, and then to Guadalcanal in the South Pacific.[91] There, Veeck asked that he be transferred to the Third Division, which he learned was about to invade Guam. His request was also denied, and, on April 27, 1944, Veeck's Third Defense Battalion was instead sent to Bougainville.[92]

In his biography of Veeck, Paul Dickson charitably refers to Bougainville as a "a tropical hellhole."[93] While there, Veeck made many visits to sick bay for the treatment of abscesses that covered his body, including "under his arms, on his hands, around his waist, and on his buttocks, legs, and face."[94] His health was further compromised by a "jungle rot" that threatened to dissolve the bones in his legs.[95] The worst injury happened when Veeck was working with an artillery piece that fired prematurely and recoiled into his right foot, creating a ragged gash that exposed bone and would become infected.[96] This injury would plague him for the rest of his life. Veeck's right leg was first amputated in November 1946 and required additional surgeries.[97] Veeck walked on an artificial or wooden leg almost his entire adult life. But Veeck made the best of it; he had a hole built into the wooden leg, where he would flick the ashes from his cigarettes.[98]

Veeck returned to the United States on August 19, 1945,[99] determined to purchase a major league baseball team. His ownership of the Milwaukee Brewers had served its purpose as a proving ground where Veeck "tried out all my ideas, the good and the bad, without the terrible pressure to succeed that comes with a major league franchise."[100] On October 27, 1945, Veeck sold his interest in the Milwaukee Brewers for a $270,000 profit[101] to Oscar Salenger, a Chicago attorney who was reputed to be a true baseball "fanatic."[102] Veeck wasn't going to permit his injuries, no matter how painful, to stop him from pursuing his dream of owning a major league team.

Veeck Wows in Cleveland (1946 to 1949)

Having severed his ties to the minor league Milwaukee Brewers, Veeck assembled the backing to purchase a major league team and monitored the comings and goings of big league owners like "a vulture in search of a dying club."[103] After dalliances with the two Chicago clubs,[104] Veeck set his sights on the Cleveland Indians, which he and a group of partners purchased for $1,750,000 in June 1946.[105] According to Veeck, "The team looked hopeless, so I bought it."[106] In 1948, after just two years under Veeck's marketing strategy, this so-called "hopeless" team won the World Series and attracted a record 2,620,627 fans.[107]

Cleveland Indians Won-Lost Record and Attendance (1946–1949)

Year	Won-Lost Record	Attendance
1946	68–86	1,057,289
1947	80–74	1,521,978
1948 (Won World Series)	97–58	2,620,627
1949	89–65	2,233,771

Source: Baseball Reference Online

As owner of the Indians, Veeck pursued an overall strategy similar to the one used in Milwaukee, including a multiplicity of promotions.[108] These included, among others, promotions to recognize certain groups of fans, such as bartenders and cabdrivers, from whom Veeck got his inside scoop on what fans thought of the Indians.[109] Veeck also sponsored several giveaways, including one promotion in which over 20,000 women received a coveted pair of nylon stockings which, at the time, were very scarce. (To this day, no one knows where he procured them.)[110] In addition, Veeck held promotions that introduced fireworks to ballgames; paid tribute to the Indians' long-time trainer, Max "Lefty" Weisman[111]; and raised $40,000 for Indians pitcher Don Black, who had been stricken with a brain aneurism.[112]

No discussion of Veeck's marketing efforts in Cleveland would be complete without a deep dive into one of his most inspired promotions— Good Old Joe Earley Night, held on September 28, 1948. Who was Joe Earley? He was a guard at a Chevrolet plant[113] who wrote a letter that was printed in the *Cleveland Press* complaining that there were too many special promotions to honor athletes. He asked, what about holding a special promotion to honor a fan who supports professional athletes and otherwise keeps the economy afloat?[114]

When Veeck read the letter, he was inspired to devise a promotion that *Life* magazine called "a night to end all nights."[115] Not only would the Indians honor Joe Earley (and, by extension, all Cleveland fans), but Veeck also arranged that, as a special thank you to women, the Indians would sponsor a Princess Aloha Orchid Night, with the first 20,000 women in attendance receiving an orchid. As if that wasn't enough, Veeck arranged for some fans to win gag gifts, just as he did in Milwaukee.

That night, a near-capacity crowd filled cavernous Municipal Stadium.[116] The first 20,000 women entering the ballpark each received an orchid personally handed to her by a team official. A woman dressed like a Hawaiian hula dancer was on hand to provide authenticity. Once the fans settled into their seats, Veeck appeared on the field, microphone in hand, to serve as the master of ceremony. First thing, fans were selected randomly to receive gag gifts, including "fifty-pound blocks of ice; live turkeys, guinea pigs, white rabbits, a sow with her piglets; and bushel baskets of apples, peaches, and tomatoes."

Then it was time for the main event. Joe Earley, looking like a Hollywood leading man walking the red carpet to a movie premier, was escorted onto the field with his wife.[117] Veeck announced that, as their first gift, the Earleys would receive a magnificent new house built "in early American architecture." No sooner had Veeck made the announcement than a flatbed truck appeared on the field carrying a ramshackle outhouse. Veeck announced that Joe and his wife would be presented with a brand-new car. Just then, a rickety Model T Ford rolled onto the field. This was no ordinary Model T Ford, but a tricked-up circus car filled with attractive young models who piled out. After a few additional gag gifts, it was time to bestow on Joe Earley and his wife some real gifts. These included household appliances, clothing, luggage, and books, not to mention a cocker spaniel. To top off the evening, the Indians gave Joe and his wife a 1949 Ford convertible, and Joe received a lifetime pass to any American League ballpark.[118]

Two other Veeck promotions in Cleveland bear special mention, both predicated on the realization that the Indians would not repeat as American League champs in 1949. On September 23, Veeck held a controversial mock funeral for the 1948 pennant flag, complete with a horse-drawn hearse, grave site, and eulogy.[119] The other promotion, on September 25, involved an intrepid fan named Charley Lupica, who committed himself to sit atop a flagpole for several months until the Indians won the pennant or were mathematically eliminated. While on the flagpole, Lupica had some comforts of home—"lights, a telephone, a portable radio, a television, and a public address system, most donated by admirers." Once Lupica announced that he would descend the flagpole, Veeck arranged for the pole to be placed on a hydraulic lift and driven to Municipal Stadium, where it was placed at home plate. Prior to a game, Lupica descended the flagpole into the waiting arms of his wife and four children, plus three nurses and an ambulance. Once he got his bearings, Lupica and his family were presented with, among other things, a bed, a bathtub, bicycles for the four children, a gas range, puppies, and a new automobile.[120]

Before the end of the 1949 season, rumors began to circulate that Veeck was ready to sell the Cleveland Indians. He needed money to finance his impending divorce.[121] In November 1949, Veeck sold the Indians to an insurance executive named Ellis W. Ryan, a transaction in which Veeck earned $500,000.[122]

Veeck's Flight of Fancy in St. Louis (1951 to 1953)

After two years away from baseball, Veeck led a syndicate that purchased the hapless St. Louis Browns on July 3, 1951, for $1.5 million. Veeck went into this venture realizing that he was buying a franchise with an entrenched history of consistently poor play and pitiful attendance.[123] What's more, Veeck knew that his challenge in St. Louis went beyond just turning around a franchise with a history of failure. His Browns had to compete for fans with the St. Louis Cardinals—a team with a history of winning championships and fielding players who were famous nationwide—in a city that Veeck suspected could support only one major league team. Veeck saw that his only course of action in this struggle for survival was to eliminate the competition by driving the Cardinals out of town.[124] Things did not work out as intended. During Veeck's tenure as owner, the team continued to be plagued by poor play on the field and attendance in the stands.

St. Louis Browns Won-Lost Record and Attendance (1951–1953)

Year	Won-Lost Record	Attendance
1951	52–102	293,790
1952	64–90	518,796
1953	54–100	297,238

Source: Baseball Reference Online

Clearly, Veeck knew he initially had to heavily promote the Browns to compete with the Cardinals. Soon after taking control of the Browns, Veeck gave fans a taste of the types of promotions he had in store for them.[125] He planned to surprise fans attending a doubleheader by giving them a party, including drinks on the house. He made sure that he had plenty of beer and soft drinks in reserve for the fans in attendance that day. After Veeck announced on the public address system, "As a tribute to the Browns' future success, let's all have a drink on the house,"[126] the vendors worked double-time to make sure everyone received their free drink. Veeck himself passed out two buckets of beers in the bleachers, telling everyone in earshot that he intended to turn the Browns into a winning franchise. According to Dickson, the Browns distributed 6,041 soft drinks and 7,596 bottles of beer. Veeck also arranged for a band to entertain the fans between games and fireworks to astound them after the games. Reporter Harry Mittauer, who worked for the *Globe-Democrat*, wrote, "Happy with it all was Veeck. He was as enthusiastic as a kid with a new toy."

By his own estimation, Veeck that first year accomplished the best promotion job of his life.[127] In addition to the beer and soft drink party, Veeck held a promotion during which the Browns gave away free orchids to female fans[128] and another which featured a miniature circus, in which fans watched "Millie the Queen of the Air" slide down a tightwire that extended from right field to third base.[129] While these promotions were no doubt entertaining, they cannot hold a candle to the two truly outrageous promotions staged by Bill Veeck during August 1951. In the first of these promotions, Veeck arranged for a three-foot, seven-inch performer, Eddie Gaedel, to take an official major league at-bat during the second game of a doubleheader. In the second, Veeck arranged for fans in the stands to manage the Browns during a major league baseball game. Certain fans were given placards saying "YES" on one side and "NO" on the other, that they would display in response to questions about in-game strategy. These promotions, which are addressed in detail in Part II of this book, were unique in the history of major league baseball in that each was a once-in-a-lifetime publicity stunt that was interwoven with the play of the game.

By 1953, despite Veeck's frenzied use of promotions, attendance continued to lag behind other major league teams, possibly because the Browns continued to play poorly on the field. While Veeck pondered new ways to turn the St. Louis Browns franchise around, St. Louis Cardinals owner Frank Saigh was found guilty of income tax evasion and sentenced to 15 months in prison. Saigh, who was told by Commissioner Ford Frick to sell the club before he began serving his sentence, initially received a bid that would have moved the Cardinals to Houston.[130] Veeck was thrilled that he got what he wanted—St. Louis all to himself. But before Veeck could uncork the champagne, the Houston bid fell through, and Saigh sold the club on February 20, 1953, to the St. Louis-based Anheuser-Busch

Brewery.[131] Realizing that he could not compete with the vast wealth of the brewery, Veeck decided that it was time for the Browns to skedaddle out of town.[132] Veeck set his sights on Baltimore, which had just built a new 51,000 seat stadium.[133]

But it was not to be. Angry with Veeck over a disagreement about television rights to ballgames, not to mention the Eddie Gaedel and Grandstand Managers games, which they believed were beneath the dignity of baseball, the other American League owners twice vetoed Veeck's attempt to move the Browns to Baltimore.[134] Upset that Veeck was planning to move the team, fans stayed away from Browns games in droves.[135] Nearly bankrupt, Veeck was forced to sell the team to a syndicate headed by Clarence Miles, who was permitted to move the club to Baltimore.[136] When Veeck sold the franchise in 1953, the franchise was just as hapless as when he bought it.[137]

Veeck Rekindles His Magic in Chicago (1959 to 1961)

Towards the end of 1958, Veeck set his sights on purchasing the Chicago White Sox from owner Dorothy Comiskey Rigney. Veeck moved quickly and, with a seven-member syndicate of backers, purchased Mrs. Rigney's stock in the White Sox for $2.7 million.[138] Veeck had his work cut out for him. Although the White Sox had winning records for some time, the team attracted only 797,451 fans in 1958.[139] Unlike in St. Louis, it seems that Veeck wasn't concerned that the White Sox competed for fans with the crosstown Cubs, since it was generally agreed that Chicago was large enough to support two teams. In Chicago, Veeck was able to recapture the magic that had eluded him in St. Louis; during his tenure, the White Sox won the American League pennant in 1959, and the next year, attendance peaked at 1,644,460.[140]

Chicago White Sox Won-Lost Record and Attendance (1959–1961)

Year	Won-Lost Record	Attendance
1959 (Won AL Pennant)	94–60	1,423,144
1960	87–67	1,644,460
1961	86–76–1	1,146,019

Source: Baseball Reference Online

Always mindful of the vendetta that prevented him from moving the Browns to Baltimore, it sometimes seemed that Veeck held promotions in Chicago just to get back at his critics. Veeck's detractors complained that he was turning baseball into a circus. Veeck doubled down on that idea by arranging for fans at a doubleheader to experience the Cristiani Bros. Circus.[141] Critics also complained that it was un-American to add outside entertainment to so hallowed an American institution as baseball. So Veeck doubled down on that idea too. Two weeks after the circus, Veeck arranged for an exhibition cricket match to be played between games of a doubleheader against Kansas City.[142] Veeck's faultfinders seemed most critical of any promotion that involved barnyard animals. His response was to hold a promotion celebrating National Dairy Week. The White Sox gave away all sorts of dairy products and held a milking contest between White Sox and visiting players.[143]

Otherwise, the White Sox sponsored several promotions during which lucky fans received regular giveaways, such as S&H green stamps[144] and miniature orchids,[145] and others won unusual prizes, such as 10,000 cupcakes.[146] The team held special nights for various members of the fan base, such as striking steel workers and teachers.[147] In what must have been the first promotion of its kind, Veeck held a tribute not to a star player, but to one—Al Smith—who was slumping and had fallen out of favor with the fans.[148] He also sponsored two promotions involving Eddie Gaedel and other little people. In one promotion, after hearing a complaint about roving vendors blocking fans' views of the games, Veeck arranged for several little people to serve as vendors who, because of their short stature, did not obstruct fans from seeing the field.[149]

On April 1, 1960, Veeck held a promotion that introduced a stadium innovation that would become a fan favorite in Chicago and one of Veeck's signature contributions to baseball—the exploding scoreboard.[150] The scoreboard would erupt whenever a White Sox player hit a home run. Veeck was concerned that the home run had become so commonplace that fans were becoming bored with them. He thought that an exploding scoreboard would put the "kick" back in the home run.[151] As described by Dickson, the scoreboard, which in time became known as "The Monster," featured

> a dazzling array of flashing strobe lights, fireworks and explosions. Loaded with ten mortars that fired Roman candles, it was a theatrical set piece lasting thirty-two seconds with sounds galore—foghorns, fire engine sirens, a calvary-charge bugle, crashing trains, a steam calliope, the *William Tell* overture, and a woman screaming, "Fireman, save my child."[152]

It also fired skyrockets and aerial bombs.[153] Fans would never grow bored with the scoreboard because they never knew precisely what sights and sounds it would produce.[154]

At about the same time the scoreboard was introduced, Veeck's health began to deteriorate. On June 25, 1960, Veeck entered the hospital because he was having issues with his seriously injured right leg, which doctors told him required further amputation.[155] Not fully recovered from the trauma to his leg, Veeck became plagued by coughing fits and frequent headaches. He would sometimes lose control of the right side of his body and experienced occasional blackouts. Recognizing that his health obviated his ability to run the White Sox, Veeck decided in 1961 to sell his controlling interest in the team to Arthur Allyn, Jr., the son of Arthur Allyn, who had provided financial backing when Veeck bought the St. Louis Browns.[156]

◊ **CHAPTER 2** ◊

Later Barnums Had a Ball Until the Blast

Charlie O. Finley, Bill Giles, Bob Hope, and Back to Veeck

With Bill Veeck on the sidelines, three new Barnums entered the fray—Charlie O. Finley, owner of the Kansas City (and later Oakland) Athletics; Bill Giles, front office executive for the Philadelphia Phillies; and Bob Hope, public relations director for the Atlanta Braves. From the 1960s to the early 1980s, they replicated and, in some instances, may have surpassed Veeck's promotional razzle-dazzle, with varied levels of success. Each of them, however, managed to stage some of the most outrageous promotions in baseball history. It all came crashing down when Veeck, nearly 30 years after starting this marketing bandwagon, reemerged as owner of the White Sox, where he inadvertently sponsored what is generally considered the most disastrous promotion in major league history.

Finley's Folly in Kansas City (1961 to 1967)

Baseball's second Barnum, Charlie O. Finley—a highly successful insurance executive and self-made millionaire—entered the stage in the early-1960s. He had made the acquaintance of Will Harridge, president of the American League, who suggested that Finley purchase a major league baseball franchise. Finley acted on the recommendation and, on December 6, 1960, after years of trying, led a syndicate that purchased the struggling Kansas City Athletics for $1,975,000.[1] Finley's efforts to revive the Kansas City franchise were undermined by poor decision-making and abysmal public relations.[2]

Kansas City Athletics Won-Lost Record and Attendance (1961–1967)

Year	Won-Lost Record	Attendance
1961	61–100	683,817
1962	72–90	635,675
1963	73–89	762,364
1964	57–105	642,478
1965	59–103	528,344
1966	74–86	773,929
1967	62–99	726,639

Source: Baseball Reference Online

Before the sale, Joe Inglehart, chairman of the Baltimore Orioles, was asked by other major league owners to conduct background research on Finley. Inglehart responded with this stark warning: "Under no condition should this person be allowed in our league."[3] Inglehart didn't have to peer far beneath the surface to see the blind ambition that powered Finley's rise to the top. Finley was a self-made man who, according to sportswriter Jim Murray, "worshipped his creator."[4] He sought to control everyone and everything around him. He could be "brash, profane, and overbearing," possessing the subtlety of a "wrecking ball."[5] When bullying didn't work, Finley fell back on ethical flexibility.[6]

As owner of the Kansas City (and later Oakland) Athletics, Charlie O. Finley pursued Bill Veeck's marketing strategy of using promotions to increase attendance. He is best known for bringing the Beatles to Kansas City and introducing Charlie-O the Mule as his team's mascot (National Baseball Hall of Fame and Museum).

True to form, Finley almost immediately set about developing a management plan for operating the Athletics that gathered virtually all decision-making and control to himself. Essentially, Finley ran the Athletics "the way 18th century British sea captains ran their vessels."[7] Finley only half-jokingly liked to tell people that the "O" in his name stood for owner, which in his parlance stood for total control.[8] If there was a snag in the Athletics' decision-making, whether in the baseball or business side of the shop, the buck stopped with Finley, who seemed to believe that he understood baseball better than anyone else.[9] Problem was, according to Hank Peters, the Athletics' minor league director, "Charlie Finley didn't know beans about baseball."[10]

No episode better demonstrates Finley's lack of savvy in baseball matters than his efforts to promote the pitching career of Lew Krausse, Jr., a pitching phenom from Media, Pennsylvania. Finley signed Krausse for $125,000—at the time one of the highest bonuses ever paid to someone entering professional baseball.[11] Anyone with baseball sense would have sent this prize catch to the minor leagues to permit him to grow into this talent and gradually refine his art until he was ready for the major leagues. But Finley thought he knew better. Over the objections of manager Joe Gordon, on June 16, 1961, Finley inserted Krausse, just two days out of high school, into the Athletics' rotation and treated the game as a promotion. He sold tickets to fans with the promise that they would see a phenom make his first pitching performance. Krausse did not disappoint. The approximately 26,000 fans in attendance watched Krausse pitch a complete-game, four-hit shutout. Naively believing that Krausse would continue mowing down major league hitters, Finley saw a tremendous gate attraction that would draw fans to the ballpark whenever he pitched.[12] But the reality of big leagues baseball intervened. Hitters adjusted to Krausse's pitching, and the long baseball season tired his arm. As a result, Krausse, who had a 12-year career in major league baseball, seemed to lose confidence and finished his rookie season with a 2–5 won-lost record[13]

Finley also had a lot to learn on the business side of baseball about public relations. For reasons that are unclear, Finley quickly became alienated in Kansas City. He exclaimed, "This is a horse shit town. No one will ever do any good here."[14] From 1961 to 1964, Finley "bitterly warred" with Kansas City officials and the local press,[15] especially during negotiations for a new lease.[16] He used "manipulation, connivance, and cajolery" to get what he wanted.[17] As early as 1961, Finley "stopped most customary promotional activities."[18] While claiming fealty to Kansas City, he continually threatened to move the team to Dallas (and other locales) if local officials didn't cave to his demands.[19] In the process, Finley managed to burn his bridges with fans, public officials, and the Kansas City press.[20]

In his no-holds-barred battle with Kansas City officials, Finley went so far as to use a promotion to antagonize a respected Kansas City sportswriter.[21] Ernie Mehl, a noted editor and sports columnist for the *Kansas City Star*, was told by a reliable source that Finley had secretly scouted Dallas as a possible new location for the Athletics.[22] Mehl, who had been tracking rumors about Finley's intent to move the team, began reporting on Finley's shenanigans. Mehl's reporting came to a head on August 17, 1961, with a front-page article that laid bare Finley's intentions. In this article, Mehl criticized Finley's management of the club, saying, "Had the ownership made a deliberate attempt to sabotage a baseball organization, it could not have succeeded as well."[23]

Finley responded by staging a promotion, sarcastically called Ernie Mehl Appreciation Day, to publicly humiliate Mehl for having dared to lay bare Finley's duplicity. No other promotion so clearly demonstrated that Finley was, to quote sportswriter Bill Slocum, "equal parts P.T. Barnum and Caligula."[24] The so-called promotion took place on August 20, 1961. Between games of a doubleheader with the White Sox,[25] a flatbed truck was driven around the field bearing large posters on each side with the caption: ERNIE MEHL APPRECIATION DAY—POISON PEN AWARD FOR 1961. The poster had a likeness of Mehl sitting at a desk dipping a quill pen into a bottle labelled POISON INK.[26] As the trucks circled the field, their loudspeakers blared the song, "Who's Afraid of the Big Bad Wolf." Finley held an on-field ceremony during which Mehl, in absentia, was given a Poison Pen Award.[27]

In 1964, Finley was compelled by other American League owners to sign a new, iron-clad, four-year lease for the Athletics to play at Municipal Stadium.[28] He apparently believed that all the unpleasantness would go away and fans would flock to Municipal Stadium if he did something spectacular to get back in their good graces. And what could be more spectacular than the greatest rock and roll band ever, making its first tour of the United States—the Beatles![29] The outrageous story of the Beatles' visit to Kansas City is told in Part II of this book.

Realizing that he was stuck in Kansas City for the time being, Finley began relying heavily on in-game promotions to bring fans to the ballpark. Like Veeck, Finley "figured that more people would come to see a badly played ball game that had stunts and promotions than would come to see only a badly played ballgame."[30] On Opening Day 1965, Finley introduced his most famous promotion—a mule named "Charlie-O," who would serve as a mascot for the Kansas City Athletics. Charlie-O, whom Finley reputedly treated better than his ballplayers, became a fixture at Athletics games both in Municipal Stadium and other big-league stadiums, and served as the basis for several promotions.[31] Finley's outrageous antics with Charlie-O are also discussed in Part II of this book.

Two other promotions during this period bear mention, both of which went awry in their own ways:

> AUTOMOBILE INDUSTRY NIGHT—The Athletics sponsored a promotion in which Finley gave away clunker cars that were dressed up with new coats of paint and accessories.[32] No doubt, patrons who won these cars were thrilled to be leaving the game in a car they had obtained for free. It was unclear whether they realized that the dressed-up cars were just run-down jalopies. At any rate, many of them grasped the true value of what they won when they couldn't drive out of the stadium parking lot before the car engine died.
>
> BERT CAMPANERIS NIGHT—In another promotion, held on September 28, 1965, Finley arranged for star shortstop Bert "Campy" Campaneris to play all nine positions.[33] All went well until Campaneris, playing catcher, tried to block the plate as the equivalent of a runaway train, in the person of Angels outfielder and catcher Ed Kirkpatrick, tried to score. Let's just say that Campaneris did not get the better of the hard collision. Nothing was broken, but Campaneris was knocked unconscious and missed the next five games.[34]

By 1967, the handwriting on the wall had become a mural. Once the lease ended, Finley sought to move the Athletics to what he believed were greener pastures in Oakland, California. To compensate Kansas City for the loss of the Athletics, major league baseball agreed to give the city a new franchise in 1969. On October 18, 1967, the American League owners voted to approve the move.[35] Before the ink was dry on the new lease in Oakland, U.S. Senator Stuart Symington III, who represented Missouri, took to the floor of the Senate, ostensibly to give a postmortem. Symington said that even though Kansas City would be without baseball for one year, "the loss is more than recompensed for by the pleasure resulting from getting rid of Mr. Finley." He concluded by saying, "Oakland is the luckiest city since Hiroshima."[36]

Finley Fares No Better in Oakland (1968 to 1980)

Finley had one massive advantage in promoting the Oakland version of the Athletics; they were extremely successful on the field.[37] How did Finley turn the proverbial pig's ear into a silk purse? By shrewdly drafting amateur talent. Finley, being somewhat self-centered, tended not to take advice from other people, particularly subordinates. But while still in Kansas City, he took some good advice from his minor league director, Hank Peters, that paid dividends after the team moved to Oakland. "Peters convinced Finley that the only way to turn the [Athletics] into winners was to spend money to sign players and develop them in a strong minor-league farm organization."[38] Finley, who had a reputation for being frugal, took this advice to heart and spent money to bring top talent, such as Jim "Catfish" Hunter and Reggie Jackson, into the Athletics organization. Yet despite this advantage, Finley still failed to attract the level of attendance one would expect.[39]

Oakland Athletics Won-Lost Record and Attendance (1968–1980)

Year	Won-Lost Record	Attendance
1968	82–80	837,466
1969	88–74	778,232
1970	89–73	778,355
1971 (in playoffs)	101–60	914,993
1972 (won World Series)	93–62	921,323
1973 (won World Series)	94–68	1,000,763
1974 (won World Series)	90–72	845,693
1975 (in playoffs)	98–64	1,075,518
1976	87–74	780,593
1977	63–98	495,599
1978	69–93	526,999
1979	54–108	306,763
1980	83–79	842,259

Source: Baseball Reference Online

As was the case in Kansas City, Finley had hoarded all decision-making authority for himself. If the Athletics' front office was making missteps, the fault surely rested with the boss.[40] Finley heavily promoted the team in Oakland.[41] Three promotions bear mentioning, two of which demonstrated faulty decision-making:

> CEREMONY HONORING VIDA BLUE—Finley decided to hold a mid-season promotion to honor his star pitcher, Vida Blue, during a Bat Day promotion scheduled for June 26, 1971. On this day, Finley presented Blue with a baby blue Cadillac El Dorado. Rather than be honored, Blue was displeased that Finley singled him out for a mid-season honor, which he saw as slighting his teammates. Blue was also less than enamored with the choice of a Cadillac

as his gift, which he saw as perpetuating a Black stereotype. Blue reportedly said under his breath, "You should have filled the trunk up with watermelons since you gave me that f**king Cadillac."[42]

HOT PANTS DAY—On June 27, 1971, the Athletics held Hot Pants Day during a doubleheader.[43] Women wearing hot pants (tight shorts) were admitted free of charge to the stadium. About 6,000 women took the opportunity to gain free entry. At some point during the afternoon, these women were given the opportunity to parade on the second deck from the right field corner to the left field corner, while no doubt being ogled by the men in attendance.

MUSTACHE DAY—In the next promotion, held on Father's Day, June 18, 1972, Finley sponsored Mustache Day, during which patrons with facial hair could enter the park for free.[44] He held this promotion to celebrate the audacity of Athletics players, who grew facial hair in contravention of major league baseball custom. Although this had all the earmarks of a successful promotion, Finley almost managed to grasp defeat from the jaws of victory. Finley ordered ticket takers to be strict in determining what nature of facial hair was sufficient for a patron to enter for free. After all, does a three-day stubble really constitute facial hair? Ticket takers, not wanting to turn fans away, ignored Finley's instructions and tended to be lenient in deciding who entered the park for free.[45]

Finley also made decisions which, counterintuitively, discouraged fans from attending games. First, fans were disheartened by the poor service at the ballpark. Finley's penny-pinching extended to staffing Athletics home games. At most games, fans had trouble: buying tickets since there were only two ticket sellers; entering and exiting the ballpark because Finley opened only one gate; and locating scarce ushers and vendors.[46] Second, Finley alienated fans by pursuing the tired strategy of playing cities against each other by exploring the possibility of moving the team to Toronto or Denver. He even had the audacity to go on national television during the 1974 World Series to complain that Oakland couldn't support a major league team.[47]

In the end, Finley's shortcomings as a baseball executive did not matter because players' salaries became too expensive even for someone of his wealth.[48] While Finley could be generous towards his players (unexpected gifts, personal loans, financial advice),[49] he was known to be cheap when it came to players' salaries and perks. Indeed, one player characterized Finley as "the cheapest son of a bitch in baseball."[50] But because of the reserve clause, Athletics players were hamstrung in their efforts to demand better treatment.

All that came to an end in December 1975, when a major league baseball management-labor grievance panel ruled that the reserve clause was invalid, meaning any player who played out his contract would be free to play for the team of their choosing.[51] (See Appendix II for a detailed discussion of the demise of the reserve clause.) It wasn't long before many players who served as the foundation of Oakland's pennant-winning teams escaped Finley for other teams via free agency.[52] Things went from bad to worse: In 1979, a pathetic 306,763 fans paid to get into Oakland-Alameda County Coliseum.[53] Finley had no choice but to sell the team, which he did in August 1980 for $12.7 million[54] to Walter H. Haas, Jr., chairman of the Levi Strauss clothing company.[55]

Giles Excels in Philadelphia (1969 to 1980)

In September 1969, Bob Carpenter, owner of the Philadelphia Phillies, asked Bill Giles—our third Barnum—to serve as his team's director of business operations. In this capacity, Giles, who like Veeck was a baseball lifer, would be responsible for sales, public relations, marketing, stadium operations, radio and television, and promotions.[56] As Giles learned, the Phillies were moving out of antiquated Connie Mack Stadium (formerly Shibe Park) and into a new facility—Veterans Stadium—in 18 months.[57] Giles' job initially was to boost sagging attendance at Connie Mack Stadium and generate interest in the Phillies that would carry over to the new stadium when it opened in April 1971.[58]

With the Phillies, Giles elevated the art form of promotions and was an unabashed success in promoting attendance.[59] Even when the Phillies had poor seasons on the field during Giles' tenure, they always enjoyed strong attendance.

Philadelphia Phillies Won-Lost Record and Attendance (1970–1980)

Year	Won-Lost Record	Attendance
1970 (Connie Mack Stadium)	73–88	708,247
1971 (Veterans Stadium)	67–95	1,511,223
1972	59–97	1,343,329
1973	71–91	1,475,934
1974	80–82	1,808,648
1975	86–76	1,909,233
1976 (in playoffs)	101–61	2,480,150
1977 (in playoffs)	101–61	2,700,070

Year	Won-Lost Record	Attendance
1978 (in playoffs)	90–72	2,583,389
1979	84–78	2,775,011
1980 (won World Series)	91–71	2,651,650

Source: Baseball Reference Online

Giles states in his baseball memoir, *Pouring Six Beers at a Time: Stories from a Lifetime in Baseball*, that he saw his job as converting "the Phillies stodgy, conservative, and tired marketing strategy into a new era of creativity and risk taking."[60] Like Veeck, Giles was a promoter who understood that baseball teams were in the entertainment business. He wanted fans to leave the ballpark with the idea that they had thoroughly enjoyed themselves, regardless of whether the Phillies won the ballgame.[61]

Giles ran several promotions at Connie Mack Stadium.[62] The most famous of these was the Farewell to Connie Mack Stadium. The Phillies gave all 31,822 fans in attendance a certificate verifying that they attended the final game at the ballpark. Knowing that the seats at the new Veterans Stadium would be made of plastic, Giles also decided to hand out to fans as a souvenir of the game 5,000 useless wooden seat slats that were sitting in storage.[63] Well, as it turns out, things got outrageously out of hand when fans started to dismantle the stadium, and the game was in danger of being called a forfeit.[64] See Part II to get the full story on what happened during the last game at Connie Mack Stadium.

Giles, who was raised in Cincinnati where Opening Day was treated as a holiday, decided that the Phillies needed to sponsor a big promotion for the opening of Veterans Stadium on April 10, 1971.[65] The Phillies' opponent at this first game was the Montreal Expos, who hailed from Canada. Giles arranged that,

Bill Giles, an executive with the Philadelphia Phillies, had a talent for devising promotions that were inventive and entertaining. Some of his best-known promotions, such as the Farewell to Connie Mack Stadium and the original Kiteman, went outrageously awry (National Baseball Hall of Fame and Museum).

prior to the opening game, Expos General Manager Jim Fanning would arrive at the stadium by dogsled, followed by very colorfully dressed Royal Canadian Mounted Police. Once at the stadium, Fanning transferred the ball to someone sitting in an Arco Go-Patrol helicopter, which flew 150 feet over the stadium just prior to the game and dropped the first ball to Phillies bullpen catcher "Irish" Mike Ryan,[66] who was awaiting it on the field.[67]

For Opening Day in 1972, Giles knew he had to sponsor a spectacular promotion to outdo the prior Opening Day promotion.[68] He had read in *Sports Illustrated* about a man, known to Giles as Kiteman, who jumped off cliffs with a kite on his back and sailed through the air, landing safely on the ground. Giles envisioned this Kiteman jumping off the roof of Veterans Stadium and sailing through the air until he reached the infield, where he would deliver the first ball. The promotion went outrageously wrong; maybe the best thing that can be said was that it didn't result in any serious bodily injury. See Part II to get the full story on the Kiteman promotion.

Under Giles, innovative Opening Day promotions became a tradition for the Phillies. In 1977, Giles arranged for Pat Mulhern, also known as Parachute Man, to jump from a plane just before the game and land on the pitching mound with the first ball.[69] On several occasions, Giles arranged for the U.S. Army Golden Knights and U.S. Navy Leap Frogs to present the first ball. These parachuting acts, which involved teams of five to eight individuals, including one parachutist carrying the American flag and another carrying the first ball, were both exciting and patriotic.[70] On a few occasions, Giles used an entertainer who went by the moniker "Benny the Bomb" to deliver the first ball. In his act, Benny would lie in a two-foot by six-foot box placed at second base. The box would explode, reducing itself to rubble and strewing shards all over the field. Benny, a bit dazed and shaken but none the worse for wear, would pop out with the first ball.[71]

Giles' promotional activities weren't limited to Opening Days. Giles sponsored arguably one of his greatest mid-year promotions on August 13, 1972, when he arranged for the great Karl Wallenda to walk a tightrope between games of a doubleheader with Montreal.[72] The tightrope was strung from the left-field foul pole to the right-field foul pole and 140 feet above the ground, without a safety net. The cable, which had to be stretched in a hurry, wasn't as taut as it should be.[73] Approximately 33,000 fans in attendance watched in rapt attention as Wallenda, carrying a balancing pole,[74] walked 15 feet onto the wire and, apparently deciding it wasn't safe, sat down. Wallenda instructed the ushers holding the guide wires along the way to pull on them, thus eliminating some of the slack. Wallenda then proceeded to stand up and walk to the middle of the wire, where he performed a handstand. Wallenda walked the remainder of the wire to the dulcet strains of the song, *You Will Never Walk Alone*, which could be heard throughout the stadium. Giles received very positive press on this promotion. Indeed, Bill Conlin of the *Philadelphia Daily News* wrote that Wallenda's sky walk across Veterans Stadium was "Giles' finest hour as baseball's P.T. Barnum forever enshrined."[75]

One of Giles' favorite promotions was the Cash Scramble.[76] Stadium employees would scrunch-up paper money in denominations ranging from $1 to $100 and distribute them across the infield. In theory, six fans would be selected at random to go down on the field and compete against each other in a mad scramble to see who could pick up the most money. Giles acknowledged that it would have been dangerous to select the contestants at random, perhaps because the people chosen might be too aggressive. So Giles instructed his staff to select two children, two elderly fans, and two attractive women. Yes, they actually scanned the stands with binoculars to find very attractive women, preferably in halter tops. Apparently, the fans enjoyed watching the six participants scramble after the money. In all the years that the Phillies sponsored this event, the most successful contestant was a nun who was able to use the large sleeves and pockets of her habit to collect the most cash.

Not all of Giles' promotions worked well. Giles wrote in his baseball memoir, "in all facets of baseball you must learn to expect the unexpected. You never know what's going to happen next, what's going to hit and what's going to miss, and when the law of unintended consequences is going to kick in."[77] Exhibit number one: Giles thought it would be a fun promotion to have an ostrich race around the stadium's warning track. He arranged for Phillies announcers Richie Ashburn and Harry Kalas to sit in sulky carts (the type used in harness racing), except the carts were pulled by grown ostriches rather than horses. Unfortunately, when the ostriches were given the signal to go, the fans watched as the ostriches, with the sulky carts in tow, ran crazily around the field. Ashburn and Kalas became frightened and jumped out of the carts. Before stadium personal were able to corral the two ostriches, one had jumped into the stands.[78]

The duck race didn't work out much better. Giles thought fans would enjoy watching ducks race each other.[79] He arranged for 16 ducks to be lined up between second and third base. Each duck had a number on its back. Paired with each duck was a member of the Phillies Hot Pants Patrol. The Hot Pants Patrol was composed of about 40 attractive women clad in hot pants who, among other things, served as distinctive usherettes during games. Each of these women also had a number on her back corresponding to the duck for which she was responsible. Their job was to entice their duck toward the finish line by feeding it breadcrumbs. Regrettably, just as the signal was given to start the race, a loud thunderclap frightened the ducks, causing them to run helter skelter in every direction, including into the third base dugout.[80]

On Easter Sunday, April 22, 1973. Giles decided to sponsor a special Easter-oriented, family-friendly promotion.[81] First, it included what was called the world's largest Easter egg hunt, with thousands of plastic Easter eggs taped below stadium seats. The second stage, called the Highest Jumping Bunny, involved arranging for someone in a bunny outfit to get into a hot air balloon tethered to the Veterans Stadium field. The hot air balloon, with the "bunny" in its basket, would take off for parts unknown. The Phillies would reward the person who found the balloon with $1,000 and Phillies season tickets for the whole family.

The big day came, and Paul Callahan, a Giles subordinate, dressed in a full-body Easter Bunny outfit, was about to be lofted in a hot air balloon.[82] However, every time the balloon rose ten feet in the air, it came crashing down to the ground. Apparently, the hot air balloon could not overcome the stadium downdrafts that thwarted its flight. On the third attempt to take flight, the balloon crashed onto the field and tipped over. Callahan, still in his bunny suit, felt the heat from the hot air balloon's open flame and, believing that he might be on fire, rolled around on the field to put out the flames.

While Callahan managed to escape injury in the Highest Jumping Bunny promotion, participants in this next promotion weren't as lucky.[83] Giles arranged a mattress stacking contest for one of the Phillies College Nights. Giles invited students from 15 universities and laid out 15 mattresses on the field. The competition involved the students from each university stacking themselves on their respective mattresses. The university that stacked the most students on its mattress would win the contest. Unfortunately, problems—big problems—ensued. Some of the students on the bottom of the pile were injured, three or four of them seriously, by the weight of those above them, and they sued for damages. Also, some students at the bottom of the piles lost control of their bodily functions. Remember, all this was done in front of tens of thousands of people. In case you are wondering, the engineering students at Lehigh University, who came with a student-stacking diagram, won the contest.

Giles continued to rise in the Phillies front office to become an executive vice president and, in 1981, president. He became chairman in 1997. In 1981, Giles also became part of an ownership group that purchased the Philadelphia Phillies. Around 2013, Giles sold his last shares in the Phillies. As of this writing, Giles serves as Chairman Emeritus of the team.[84]

Hope Springs Eternal in Atlanta (1976 to 1979)

When Ted Turner purchased the Atlanta Braves in December 1975, it was as if he bought a very pricey and highly sophisticated piece of equipment that came with no instruction manual. Lacking guidance, Turner brought his business acumen to bear on the team. He spared no expense in bringing talented baseball players to the Braves.[85] Like no owner before him, he built a relationship with his players through which he sought to motivate them and make them feel appreciated.[86] Turner wrote in his memoir, *Call Me Ted*, "I figured I'd simply go in there, fire up the team with enthusiasm, and we'd be tearing up the league in no time."[87] But no matter how hard he tried—and there is no doubt that Turner put a Herculean effort into making the Braves a success—the team failed miserably on the field for years.

While Turner sought to improve the product on the field, he figured that, in the meantime, the franchise had to find some other way to attract fans, and he turned to his public relations director, Bob Hope, and gave him *carte blanche* in marketing the Braves.[88] Turns out, Hope was a whiz

When Ted Turner owned the Atlanta Braves, his public relations director Bob Hope was responsible for numerous inventive promotions. Two of these—Wedlock and Headlock Day and Wet T-Shirt Night—number among the most outrageous in major league baseball history (National Baseball Hall of Fame and Museum).

at using promotions to increase attendance. During Hope's tenure with the Turner-led team, while the Braves were dismal on the field, his promotions, aided and abetted by the enthusiasm Turner generated for the team, significantly increased attendance. While attendance at Braves games did not reach one million fans during this period, it remained substantially above the 534,672 who saw the Braves in 1975, just prior to Turner's ownership.[89]

Atlanta Braves Won-Lost Record and Attendance (1976–1979)

Year	Won-Lost Record	Attendance
1976	70–92	818,179
1977	61–101	872,464
1978	69–93	904,494
1979	66–94	769,465

Source: Baseball Reference Online

Said Hope in his baseball memoir, *We Could've Finished Last Without You*, "We were intent on keeping the body kicking even if the team was dead."[90] He sought to accomplish that by sponsoring "as many promotions as humanly possible,"[91] with a goal of having some sort of promotional event at every home game.[92] It is beyond the scope of this book to recount every Hope promotion, so we will just focus on some highlights.

Hope's first foray into promoting Braves attendance included the participation of Ted Turner. Like the Giles promotion, on April 16, 1976, the Braves sponsored a Great Mattress Stacking Championship. After a game, 16 college fraternities and one sorority participated in a competition to determine which could stack the most students on a double bed mattress in one minute.[93] Hope arranged for a timekeeper and four officials in striped shirts to referee the contest and invited a representative from the *Guinness Book of World Records* to be on hand just in case one of the college groups broke the world record for this sort of activity.[94] Not only was Ted Turner aware of this promotion, but he also participated! He spontaneously joined the team from Emory University's Sigma Phi fraternity. According to Hope, "Ted jumped on the mattress on the bottom of the pile and turned red-faced as the others piled on top." After the conclusion of the event, which Turner's team lost, he was heard to ask Hope, "Why do you let me do these kinds of things? I've got to stop. I'll kill myself and I've never been to a World Series."[95]

Hope's next notable promotion was scheduled for April 18, Easter Sunday. The Braves perennially experienced trouble attracting fans on Easter, and Hope thought that he might use an Easter-related promotion to drum up attendance. What is better than an Easter egg hunt? After the game, Braves front office staff would spread foil-wrapped chocolate Easter eggs across the outfield and invite youngsters to find them.[96] The front office initially estimated that paid attendance would be about 10,000 fans. That was until they learned that Atlanta star pitcher Andy Messersmith would be making his first start of the year that Sunday. Suddenly, the front office increased its anticipated attendance to 40,000. Even with the increased attendance, those planning the promotion anticipated they would need to manage no more than 2,000 children.[97] How hard could that be?

After the game, Braves announcer Peter Van Wieren, standing at home plate, instructed the children over the public address system to walk down the steps leading to the six gates that led onto the field. The youngsters waited ... and waited ... and waited. Turns out that the staff who were supposed to distribute the eggs were locked out of the office where the eggs were stored. After what must have seemed like an eternity, the grounds crew showed up with the eggs and began distributing them across the field. As this was happening, Van Wieren instructed the youngsters to walk through the gates and line up on the field. Suddenly, as if a dam broke, thousands of children jumped the low fence separating the stands from the field and stampeded toward the staff still distributing the chocolates. Seeing the stampede of children, these individuals dropped their boxes and ran toward the outfield, where they jumped the wall and entered the stands.[98] Recognizing that they had distributed only half the Easter eggs, Hope and company tried once again to conduct an orderly hunt. But as it turned out, past was prologue, as the children once again swarmed the staff distributing Easter eggs, who ran for the lives, throwing chocolates behind them.[99]

After a cash scramble on May 15 and a Wallenda Skywalk on June 19, which was every bit as harrowing as the Phillies' promotion, on July 11, the Braves staged an outrageous promotion called Wedlock and Headlock Day.[100] Prior to the game, the Braves staged a marriage ceremony for 10 couples who sought to make their wedding special by somehow connecting it to major league baseball. After the game, the Braves staged several professional wrestling matches[101] during which, one would assume, participants got their rivals in numerous headlocks. These somewhat anomalous events took place on the same day due to a scheduling mix-up between Turner and Hope.[102] At any rate, this outrageous promotion is discussed in detail in Part II of this book.

In August 1976, in honor of the 1976 Olympics, which were ongoing in Montreal, Canada, the Braves staged the Baseball Nose Push promotion, in which two participants would compete by pushing a baseball with their nose from first and third base, respectively, to home plate. Rather than invite fans to participate in this event, Hope staged it as a competition between representatives of the two teams. The Braves were playing the Phillies, whose relief pitcher *extraordinaire* Tug McGraw volunteered to participate. Try as he might, Hope could not find a Braves player willing to test his egg-pushing mettle.[103] (Could it be that the Braves players knew something that was not apparent to the other contestant?) Recognizing that the show must go on, Ted Turner leapt into the fray and agreed to represent the Braves. At first, the contestants made negligible progress as they tried to inch the ball forward with just their noses. While McGraw was apparently satisfied with little progress, Turner "started jamming his forehead into the ball and shoving it into the direction of home plate." Turner won the match; as he emerged from his crouch to acknowledge the cheers of the crowd, everyone could see that his face was bloodied from scraping it against the dirt. As the crowd hailed their conquering hero, Turner raised the bloody baseball high in his hands.[104]

Other promotions included: a frog jumping contest; an ostrich race, which involved a grudge match between Turner and a newspaper reporter who had publicly insulted him; a promotion during which ham radio operators tried to contact alien spaceships[105]; and a "chilling leap into the world's largest dish of ice cream," which almost ended in tragedy. This latter promotion was sponsored by Baskin-Robbins, the purveyor of ice cream.[106] To set the scene, an Atlanta disc jockey named "Skinny" Bobby Harper was chosen to make the leap from a diving board into a giant-sized ice cream sundae. Prior to the game, a pickup truck with a diving board assembled on its back was driven onto the field. At about the same time, another truck pulling a flatbed trailer drove onto the field. The trailer contained a child's plastic swimming pool over-filled with ice cream (unsellable seconds donated by Baskin-Robbins for the event), topped with copious amounts of Cool Whip and fudge sauce and a red beachball representing the ubiquitous cherry.[107]

Harper mounted the diving board but looked hesitant to make the leap.[108] The crowd booed; Harper apparently overcame whatever second thoughts he was experiencing and jumped. He sank into the ice cream. Unable to swim or surface, he remained submerged for a couple of minutes before Phillies staff dove in after him to stage a rescue. Turns out, ice cream has the consistency of quicksand. Harper, who had turned blue from not breathing but was otherwise none the worse for wear, was helped from the ice cream and raised his arms to acknowledge the cheers of the crowd, who must have thought he was a goner. The field was a sticky mess that night, but so it goes in the promotion business.

Arguably the Braves' most outrageous promotion during this era was

Wet T-Shirt Night, which was held on May 20, 1977.[109] For this event, Hope was in partnership with Turner. Knowing full well that such a promotion, typically sponsored by dive bars during college Spring Break, was beneath the dignity of major league baseball, Braves officials allowed themselves to be led into sponsoring such a promotion. That night, 43 women volunteered to be doused with water and display themselves for the mostly male crowd. You can read more about how the Braves got themselves into this mess in Part II of this book.

Realizing that sex sells, the Braves also sponsored a promotion to select the 1,000 most beautiful women in Atlanta, a Farrah Fawcett Look-Alike Contest, and a Blind Date Night. The first two were successful; the latter promotion not so much, since many more men participated than women.[110]

In 1979, when he was passed up for a position as general manager of the Braves, Hope left Turner's employ and moved on to the Coca Cola Company, which turned out to be a steppingstone to a very successful career in public relations.[111]

Veeck's Last Hurrah in Chicago (1975 to 1980)

After regaining his health, Bill Veeck was itching to get back into major league baseball and went in search of a major league franchise. Veeck heard that the owner of the Chicago White Sox, would soon be interested in selling the team.[112] In October 1975, Veeck announced a complicated financial transaction through which he would lead a syndicate that would buy the White Sox.[113] After much wrangling with the American League owners, who weren't pleased to see Veeck rejoin their exclusive club, Veeck, on December 16, 1975, completed the deal to purchase the White Sox.[114] Despite the mediocre play of the White Sox, Veeck experienced some success with promotions in Chicago until the era of the Barnums ended, not with a whimper, but with a bang.

Chicago White Sox Won-Lost Record and Attendance (1975 to 1980)

Year	Won-Lost Record	Attendance
1975	75–86	750,802
1976	64–97	914,945
1977	90–72	1,657,135
1978	71–90	1,491,100
1979	73–87	1,280,702
1980	70–90–2	1,200,365

Source: Baseball Reference Online

While Veeck was trying to get his new franchise off the ground, there were changes taking place that would fundamentally alter major league baseball forever. While Veeck was trimming his Christmas tree, he learned (as did Finley) that the grievance panel had ruled against the validity of major league baseball's reserve clause.[115] He realized immediately that, because of this decision, which he had supported for many years, "it was going to take a miracle for him to survive."[116]

Veeck, along with his son Mike, whom he hired as a promotions manager, relied heavily on promotions to sell tickets to White Sox games. Among the most notable promotions: On Opening Day 1976, America's Bicentennial, Veeck and two other White Sox officials paraded across the infield mimicking the three battered Continental Army soldiers in Archibald McNeal Willard's famous painting, "The Spirit of '76."[117] On August 8, 1976, Veeck sponsored one of his more celebrated promotions, when the White Sox Donned Shorts. During the first game of a doubleheader against Kansas City, the White Sox players came out of the dugout to take the field in Bermuda-length navy blue shorts with white pullover shirts.[118] Before the end of the 1976 season, Veeck honored premiere White Sox baseball announcer Harry Caray by sponsoring Harry Caray Appreciation Night. Every fan who attended that promotion received a gift bag that contained a recording of Caray singing four variations of *Take Me Out to the Ballgame*.[119]

By the time the 1979 season rolled around, Veeck was having difficulty finding affordable, talented players. It had become crystal clear to Veeck that, given his limited means, "he would have to rely increasingly on gimmicks to keep the ballpark filled."[120] Maybe it was their desperation to attract fans that caused Bill and Mike Veeck to so completely misjudge the likelihood that Disco Demolition Night would be a success. As we will discuss in detail in Part II, Disco Demolition Night, held on July 12, 1979, was the most infamous promotion in the history of baseball. The promotion, during which a crate containing tens of thousands of vinyl records was exploded on the field between games of a doubleheader, caused a fan riot, which, in turn, caused the White Sox to forfeit the second game; it was also seen by many as insulting to those who supported disco—women and the African American and LGBTQ communities. While major league baseball teams continued to stage promotions, some of which were noteworthy, the Era of the Barnums had symbolically come to an end.

Unable to compete financially for top talent, Bill Veeck sold the White Sox in January 1981[121] to Jerry Reinsdorf, a real estate developer, for $20 million.[122] During his retirement, Veeck could often be seen hobnobbing with the bleacher fans at Wrigley Field.[123] Veeck died on January 2, 1986, and in 1991 was inducted into the Baseball Hall of Fame.[124]

PART II

◆ ◆ ◆

Outrageous Promotions Courtesy of Baseball's Four Barnums

◊ **CHAPTER 3** ◊

Veeck Wrecks Baseball's Traditions

The Eddie Gaedel Game and Grandstand Managers Night

Bill Veeck/St. Louis Browns

The Eddie Gaedel Game	Grandstand Managers Night
Detroit Tigers at St. Louis Browns	Philadelphia Athletics at St. Louis Browns
Sportsman's Park	
August 19, 1951	August 24, 1951

When Bill Veeck purchased the St. Louis Browns, little did he know that he was becoming owner of a cursed franchise. The curse has its origins in 1919, when the Browns owner drove away one of the greatest minds in major league baseball history—Branch Rickey—who moved to the team's in-town rival, the St. Louis Cardinals. Rickey went on to spin his magic with the Cardinals, setting the foundation for them to become one of the most successful teams in major league history. Except for the seasons during World War II, when everything in baseball was topsy-turvy, the Browns became the laughingstock of baseball. Whether he knew it or not, Veeck's job was somehow to lift this curse and restore some semblance of competence to the St. Louis Browns franchise. History will show that Veeck's efforts to promote the Browns were nothing short of brilliant. Among others, he sponsored two outrageous promotions—the Eddie Gaedel Game and Grandstand Managers Night—that brought national acclaim (and censure) to the St. Louis Browns. But in the end, promotions weren't enough. Veeck couldn't find in his bag of tricks a way to transform the Browns into a winning team.

The Curse of Branch Rickey

Although the St. Louis Browns franchise dates its existence back to 1902,[1] its downward spiral is often dated from the leadership of Phil Ball, the hard-drinking, tough-talking businessman who owned the Browns from 1916 to 1933. You've no doubt heard of the Curse of the Bambino that hovered over the Boston Red Sox like a black cloud for decades. But have you ever heard of the Curse of Branch Rickey that supposedly led to the Browns' demise? The story goes that Phil Ball could not abide the deeply religious Rickey, the great baseball innovator who was then in Ball's employ. The first time they met, Ball exclaimed, "So you're the God-damned prohibitionist!" Rickey, possibly objecting to Ball's bluster, jumped ship and took a position in 1919 with the St. Louis Cardinals.[2]

It took a while, but Rickey transformed the Cardinals into one of the juggernauts of the National League. Notably, Rickey had an idea to build a farm system of minor league teams that would feed quality ballplayers solely to the St. Louis Cardinals.[3] At this time, the minor leagues operated as separate entities that found, developed, and sold baseball talent to all major league teams.[4] When Rickey switched franchises, the Cardinals did not have the money to make this idea a reality.

Ball added insult to injury by unknowingly removing that obstacle too. The Cardinals played in Robison Field, which had fallen into severe disrepair. Not having the money to refurbish or replace it, Sam Breadon, president of the Cardinals, approached Ball, asking if his team could possibly share Sportsman's Park, for which the Cardinals would pay rent. At first, Ball outright rejected Breadon's proposal, saying he would never be party to a deal that would permit Branch Rickey to set foot in Sportsman's Park.[5] After several entreaties, however, Ball eventually agreed, not realizing that his decision would lead to the Cardinals' ascendency in St. Louis.[6] According to Dennis Pajot and Greg Erion, in their article "St. Louis Browns Team Ownership History," "With Ball's agreement to take on the Cardinals as tenants, Breadon was able to sell Robison Field for $275,000, clear outstanding debt and provide working capital for the future. One of the main initiatives Breadon—and Rickey—could now pursue was establishment of a minor league system *that generated competitive clubs for decades to come.*"[7] [Emphasis added.]

The Cardinals became a formidable team led by players who became household names not just in St. Louis, but among baseball fans throughout the United States.[8] In the 1920s, Rogers Hornsby, winner of the Triple Crown in 1922 and 1925, led the Cardinals to the World Series in 1926, an exciting seven-game Series that transfixed baseball fans everywhere. In the early 1930s, the Cardinals, led by Dizzy Dean and the infamous

Gashouse Gang, won the National League pennant in 1930, 1931, and 1934. Aided by a strong radio signal that broadcasted beyond the environs of St. Louis, the Cardinals became a regional team, followed by baseball fans in the south and west of the United States. With Johnny Mize, the Cardinals remained competitive throughout the late-1930s. In the 1940s and early 1950s, the team, led by the indomitable Stan "The Man" Musial, won three pennants from 1942 to 1946.

Meanwhile, the Browns floundered under a series of underfinanced owners. When Ball died in 1933, the St. Louis Browns were in such disrepair that no one wanted to buy the club.[9] The team struggled without clear ownership. By 1935, the Browns finished with a 65–87[10] record and attracted a minuscule 80,992 spectators to the ballpark. At one game that year, just 34 fans showed up.[11] It wasn't until 1936 that financier Donald Barnes, president of American Investment Company, and Bill DeWitt, who had worked for the Cardinals, led a syndicate that purchased the Browns.[12] In contrast to Ball, both Barnes and DeWitt were "wonderful fellows."[13] Unfortunately, they operated "hand to mouth"[14] and built a team composed of rejects and has-beens from other teams who were playing just for a paycheck and weren't too concerned about winning ballgames.[15] The fans responded to their lackluster performance by staying away from Sportsman's Park. In 1939, the Browns lost 111 games, finishing 64–1/2 games behind the first-place Yankees, and attracted 109,159 fans.[16]

In 1941, after five losing seasons, Barnes finally saw the handwriting on the wall: He realized that the Browns were doomed to perpetually play a distant second fiddle to the Cardinals in St. Louis.[17] In a masterstroke, Barnes arranged to have the team relocated to greener pastures in Los Angeles. But even this decision was doomed. After protracted negotiations with all parties involved, American League owners were set to give their final approval of the move on December 8, 1941.

However, on December 7, 1941, the imperial forces of Japan attacked the American naval base at Pearl Harbor. The meeting was held as scheduled the day after the attack, but those in attendance unanimously voted to reject the proposal to move the Browns to Los Angeles.[18] Even the Browns voted against their own proposal. The American League owners were concerned that, with a war on the horizon, the federal government would restrict air travel, so that team travel to the West Coast would become problematic. The Browns remained in St. Louis for a dozen more years.

Unable to move the team, Barnes decided to try once and for all to make a go of it in St. Louis. He convinced several "angels" to invest in the team and, with that money, brought some quality ballplayers to the Browns, including second baseman Don Gutteridge and shortstop Vern Stephens.[19] He also hired Luke Sewell as manager. Sewell, who was initially concerned about taking a job known as "the graveyard of managers,"[20] brought a winning attitude to the clubhouse.[21] This investment in talent and change of attitude paid almost instant dividends. In 1942, the Browns finished the season with a record of 82–69, the first winning record in 13 years.[22] Despite the winning record, the franchise attracted only 255,617 fans to Sportsman's Park; but team management never despaired, believing that, if the team continued its winning ways, fans would come.[23]

The World War II years offered a brief respite for long-suffering Browns fans. After a down year in 1943,[24] the unimaginable happened in 1944. The Browns had their best year in decades; the team finished the season with a record of 89–65,[25] won the American League pennant, and attracted 508,644 fans to Sportsman's Park.[26] Despite the hoopla that surrounded the successful season, it was apparent that the team didn't so much ascend to first place as tread water while the other teams sank. Put another way, Browns historian Bill Mead likened the 1944 Browns to "an ugly stump in a draining swamp."[27] Unlike other American League teams, the Browns had many otherwise healthy players who where not inducted into military service. Some of these men were already on the Brown's roster. DeWitt supplemented these players by shrewdly beating the bushes for additional baseball talent not taken by their draft boards. As a result, the Browns during the war years were able to field competitive teams,[28] while other teams saw their quality of play deteriorate because they lost star players who could not readily be replaced. For example, the Yankees lost Joe DiMaggio, Phil Rizzuto, Red Ruffing, and Bill Dickey to military service. The Red Sox lost Ted Williams, Johnny Pesky, and Dom DiMaggio.[29] When, on the last day of the season, the Browns won the pennant, Barnes was ecstatic.[30] In his euphoria, he said that winning "the pennant would purify the team's history and remove the curse of the Browns."[31] In that, he was wrong.

The following years were not very kind to the St. Louis Browns and their fans. Businessman Richard Muckerman purchased the Browns from Donald Barnes in 1945. Believing that the Browns were a viable franchise, he invested $750,000 in making improvements to Sportsman's Park, depleting his bank accounts. But his faith in the team proved unfounded. While the Browns had another winning record in 1945, major leaguers were leaving the military to rejoin their teams and, beginning in 1946, the Browns resumed their losing ways.[32] Attendance at Sportsman's Park plummeted to about 4,000 per game. With the banks threatening to foreclose,[33] Muckerman, in an act of desperation, started selling off his star players. After the 1947 season, he sold Vern Stephens and Jackie Kramer to the Boston Red Sox and, in return, received $310,000 and a host of nondescript journeymen. The very next day, Muckerman sold Ellis Kinder and

Billy Hitchcock to Boston for $65,000. In all, Muckerman sold about $1 million of talented ballplayers.[34]

With the team teetering on the edge of bankruptcy, Muckerman finally threw in the towel and, in December 1949, sold the team to his friends Bill and Charlie DeWitt.[35] Problem was that the new owners didn't have anywhere near the funds needed to pull the Browns out of the morass the franchise experienced in the late 1940s. The team, having lost its quality players in the Muckerman fire sale, was truly awful. The Browns won 59 games in 1947 and 1948, and 53 games in 1949.[36] The next two seasons were more of the same.[37] The few Browns fans that hadn't changed their allegiance to the Cardinals or lost interest in baseball altogether were so disillusioned that they stopped coming to see their team play.[38] It was time to sell, but who would buy a failing franchise that seemingly had no future?[39]

Like the cavalry charging over a hill to save the wagon train, Bill Veeck entered the scene in 1951 to buy the Browns from the beleaguered DeWitt brothers. One can only imagine that Veeck went into this purchase with *eyes open*. The St. Louis Browns were the worst franchise in baseball, bar none. From 1946 to 1950, the team "averaged 59 wins and 95 losses, and were last in attendance each season." As mentioned in Chapter 1, the Browns needed to compete for attendance with their intercity rival, the Cardinals, who, as we've seen, had "a history of success and drew over a million fans each season from 1946 to 1950."[40]

Like the team's former owners, Veeck didn't have a great deal of money to pump into the failing franchise. But he had a plan: Suspecting that St. Louis wasn't large enough to support two major league baseball teams, Veeck planned to drive the Cardinals out of town.[41] He would accomplish this by improving the team's play on the field,[42] using promotions to augment attendance at Browns games,[43] and publicly hectoring the Cardinals owner, Frank Saigh, until he would do anything to get his team out of town. This strategy, which seemed farfetched to begin with, crashed and burned once Saigh sold the Cardinals to the deep-pocketed Anheuser-Busch brewery,[44] but not before Veeck staged two truly outrageous promotions that have become part of baseball lore.

The Eddie Gaedel Game

It was still 1951, and Veeck was already desperate to increase attendance at Sportsman's Park.[45] One thing was perfectly clear: The team, left to its own resources, would drive Veeck to financial ruin, as it had done to virtually every owner before him. He knew he had to fall back on his old standby—promotions. Veeck, who knew he needed to do something more than run-of-the-mill promotions, decided to hold a stadium-wide birthday party for the American League, which was celebrating its golden jubilee in 1951. Even better, according to Veeck, he would tie into the festivities a birthday party for the Browns' radio sponsor, Falstaff Brewing Company. Including the brewery had the added benefit of "their distributors and dealers hustling tickets for us all over the state."[46] Veeck wasn't at all troubled that no one knew quite when the company was founded.

Veeck, of course, had to clear the promotion with his Falstaff Brewery counterparts.[47] He met with company executives and various department heads. According to Veeck, he told them, "In addition to the regular party, the acts and so on, I'll do something for you that I have never done before. Something so original and spectacular that it will get you national publicity." Understandably, the Falstaff officials pressed Veeck for specifics. But Veeck told them that his idea for the promotion was so explosive that he could not afford to take even the slightest chance of a leak. The real reason Veeck didn't inform the Falstaff officials was that he had no idea what he was going to do. But he knew it had to be spectacular. He had promised!

The answer came to him from the fans. When Veeck spoke with Browns fans about ways to improve the team, he often heard complaints that the Browns didn't have a leadoff hitter who could consistently get on base.[48] Veeck could have addressed this deficiency in any number of ways. He could *go for broke* and seek a trade for Richie Ashburn, arguably the best leadoff hitter in the 1950s, but it was unlikely that the Phillies would part with their star center fielder. As a lesser option, Veeck could have tried to find someone on the Browns who could hit leadoff or traded for someone other than Ashburn who might fit the bill. Instead, Veeck decided to be creative and, as the saying goes, *kill two birds with one stone*. He would obtain a new leadoff hitter, yet unknown to the baseball world, whose appearance in a Browns uniform would garner attention nationwide, and he would debut this new player at the birthday promotion, showering Fallstaff Brewing Company with nationwide publicity. Who was this player? Veeck didn't yet know his name but was almost certain of his physical characteristics: Veeck planned to use a little person in a major league baseball game!

It is unclear where Veeck obtained the inspiration for this planned tour de force.[49] At the time, both *The Sporting News* and *Toledo Blade* surmised that Veeck's inspiration came from a James Thurber story published in the April 5, 1941, issue of the *Saturday Evening Post*. Veeck, as it turns out, was extremely well-read and conceivably might have come across the Thurber story in his travels. In this story, fictional manager Squawks Magrew, with two outs and the bases loaded, instructs batter Pearl du Monville, a player of very short stature with a minuscule strike zone, to hold his bat on his shoulder and not to swing, no matter how tempting the pitch. Magrew knew that "there ain't a man in the world who can throw three strikes in there before he throws four balls."

While never denying that he read the Thurber story, Veeck propounded a different origin for his idea to send a little person up to bat in a major league game.[50] It turns out that John McGraw, the great manager of the New York Giants, was occasionally a guest at the Veeck household when Veeck was a child. Apparently, after dinner, when the grown-ups were enjoying cigars, McGraw would regale Veeck's father, who was a longtime executive with the Chicago Cubs,[51] with all sorts of stories drawn from McGraw's long experience in baseball. Bill Veeck would be permitted to hear these conversations (although likely not partake in the cigars). From time to time, McGraw would talk about a "hunchback/gnome," named Eddie Morrow,[52] that he kept around the Giants' clubhouse for good luck. McGraw would swear that, some day before he retired, he would send this individual up to bat in a major league game.

Veeck set out to find the ideal little person for the job. Working with talent agent Marty Caine, with whom Veeck had good experiences when he was in Cleveland,[53] Veeck sought to find a "perfectly proportioned" little person who would be certain to get a base on balls; in other words, someone with virtually no strike zone.[54] After interviewing several candidates he rejected for one reason or another, Veeck selected Eddie Gaedel, a performer from Chicago who, for several reasons, appeared to be ideal for the job. According to Browns executive Bob Fishel, "When we saw him, there was no question that Eddie was right. He was actually a very attractive guy."[55]

When he heard what Veeck had in mind, Gaedel was at first dubious.[56] Veeck needed to make a sales pitch to talk him into participating in the promotion. And he laid it on thick. He explained to Gaedel that he would become the only little person in the history of the game. Veeck added, "You'll be appearing before thousands of people. Your name will go into the record books for all time. You'll be famous.... You'll be immortal." Gaedel, who "had more than a little ham in him," fell for it hook, line and sinker. Veeck demonstrated how Gaedel, when he stepped up to the plate, should go into a crouch so low that his strike zone was no more than a few inches tall. When Gaedel, trying to replicate Veeck's batting stance, got into a crouch with a toy bat in hand, he took a lunging swing. Veeck emphasized that he didn't want Gaedel to swing. "You just stay in that crouch. All you have to do is stand there and take four balls. Then you'll trot down to first base and we'll send someone in to run for you." Veeck could see that Gaedel was crestfallen to realize he wouldn't get to swing the bat. Veeck emphasized his instruction by gently saying, "Eddie, I'm going to be up on the roof with a high-powered rifle watching every move you make. If you so much as look like you're going to swing, I'm going to shoot you dead."

Gaedel signed two contracts, both guaranteeing him $100 for one plate appearance. Veeck sent one contract to American League president Will Harridge, making sure that Harridge would not receive the document until after the event. Veeck had well-grounded fears that Harridge would find a way to void the contract if he got wind of what Veeck planned to do. Veeck gave the other copy to manager Zack Taylor in case an umpire should object to Gaedel taking his at-bat.[57] He also purchased a $1 million insurance policy on Gaedel to, according to Veeck, "protect us in case of sudden death, sudden growth or some other pernicious act of nature."[58]

Veeck scheduled the birthday promotion for Sunday, August 19, 1951, during a doubleheader against the Detroit Tigers.[59] He decided to pull out all the stops in preparation for this birthday celebration. There would be giveaways, some with tie-ins to Falstaff Brewery. Veeck also arranged numerous forms of entertainment, including circus acts, troubadours, and Max Patkin, who was known as the Clown Prince of Baseball. Patkin was a tall man with a rubber face who could contort his body into seemingly impossible positions.[60] Veeck also arranged that, during the ceremony, Browns manager Zack Taylor, as an integral part of the promotion, would also receive a special birthday gift.[61] Veeck apparently was also unfazed that Taylor was born on July 27.[62]

Although everyone involved was sworn to secrecy, Veeck had to find some way to make sure the promotion received widespread publicity.[63] The evening before the event, Veeck arranged to have a few late-night drinks with Bob Broeg of the *St. Louis Post-Dispatch*. At about midnight, when Veeck knew the last edition of the newspaper had been "put to bed," Veeck offhandedly told Broeg that he intended to have a little person take an official at-bat the next day when the Browns played the Detroit Tigers. Broeg replied that his newspaper didn't have many photographers working on Sunday. But Broeg arranged for one photographer to be there who took that iconic photo of Gaedel crouching at the plate.[64]

The day of the event, as this was after all a birthday celebration, the 18,369 fans (the largest crowd of the season) who streamed into Sportsman's Park received "a can of beer, a slice of birthday cake, and a box of ice cream."[65] Spectators also received salt and pepper shakers in the shape of Falstaff bottles. Once the promotion was completed, Veeck hoped that those in attendance would see the salt and pepper shakers as diminutive beer bottles, reflecting the little person who starred in the promotion. However, this subtlety appeared to elude everyone completely.

Those in attendance on a hot and muggy Sunday afternoon saw the

Tigers win the first game, 5–2.⁶⁶ Once the players had exited the field to their respective clubhouses, it was time for the between-game celebrations to commence. The crowd was first regaled by an assortment of acts. Several vintage automobiles paraded around the field. Two men and two women, dressed in Gay Nineties costumes, rode around the park on tandem bicycles. Troubadours entertained fans in the stands. The Browns' own band, featuring the team's celebrated pitcher Satchel Paige on the drums, performed several tunes. There was also a three-ring circus, including "a hand balancing act at first base, a trampoline act on second, and a team of jugglers at third." Max Patkin performed a jitterbug dance with a woman from the grandstand.⁶⁷

Meanwhile, under the stands, Bill Durney, who worked for the Browns, was preparing a reluctant Eddie Gaedel for a between-game ceremony during which he jumped out of a cake.⁶⁸ Gaedel became frightened when the crowd roared in response to Max Patkin's jitterbug dance. The sound of the roar probably reverberated under the stands because it was an enclosed space. Gaedel told Durney, "I don't feel so good. I don't think I'm going to do it." Durney, who was an imposing figure at six foot, four inches, 250 pounds, responded, "Listen Eddie, there are eighteen thousand people in this park and there's one I know I can lick. You. Dead or alive, you're going in there." With that, Durney lifted Gaedel and began to place him in the cake. Dangling over the cake, Gaedel continued his lament: "Bill, these [elf] shoes hurt my feet. I don't think I'll be able to go on." Ignoring Gaedel's plea, Durney placed him in the cake and covered the top.

After the pre-ceremony entertainment had concluded, a large papier mâché cake containing Gaedel was rolled onto the field.⁶⁹ The stadium public address system announced that, for his "birthday," manager Zack Taylor was going to receive a brand-new "Brownie." The cake was tapped by someone dressed like Sir John Falstaff, in honor of the Browns' sponsor, and out of the cake popped Eddie Gaedel, dressed in a Browns uniform with elf shoes. The fans, thinking that there would be no more escapades that day, applauded approvingly and settled in for the second game of the doubleheader.

The Falstaff Brewery officials seated in Veeck's box were quite displeased.⁷⁰ They were promised a memorable event that would gain national publicity for their brewery; a little person popping out of a cake didn't quite measure up to their expectations. One Falstaff official lamented, "Holy Smokes, this is what your big thing is? A [little person] jumps out of a cake and he's wearing a baseball uniform and he's a bat boy or something?" Another complained, "Aw, this is lousy, Bill. Even the cake gimmick, you've used that before in Milwaukee and Cleveland. You haven't given us anything new at all." Veeck, looking appropriately apologetic, didn't let on what was to come.

Other than Veeck, his wife, Mary Frances,[71] and a few loyal assistants, no one in the ballpark that afternoon expected anything more than the second game of a doubleheader.[72] The top of the first inning happened without incident. In the bottom of the first, fans who were expecting reserve rookie outfielder Frank Saucier to lead off for the Browns against Tigers pitcher Bob Cain heard the public address announcer say those immortal words: "For the Browns, number one-eighth, Eddie Gaedel, batting for Saucier." Up to the batter's box strode three-foot, seven-inch Eddie Gaedel, brandishing a toy bat and wearing a Browns uniform with the number 1/8 on his back. The uniform originally belonged to Bill DeWitt, the nine-year-old son of the Browns' vice president.[73] The fans gave him a standing ovation.[74] He stood in the batter's box and crouched so low that his strike zone was about 1.5 inches tall.[75]

Home plate umpire Ed Hurley took one look at Gaedel and exclaimed, "What the hell?"[76] The umpires immediately tried to stop Gaedel from batting, but Browns manager Zack Taylor showed the umpires that the Browns had a bona fide contract for Gaedel's services. The umpires deliberated for about 15 minutes and, who knows, may have made a call to American League headquarters in Chicago on the off chance that someone was there. Home plate umpire Ed Hurley, realizing that Gaedel's at-bat was perfectly legal despite being bizarre, announced "Play ball." To compensate for Gaedel's short stature, catcher Bob Swift readied himself on his knees to receive the ball. The pitcher, realizing that he had no chance of throwing a strike to Gaedel, walked him. Gaedel was fortunate that Bob Cain was pitching; Cain's teammate pitcher Dizzy Trout said that, if he had been pitching, he would have drilled Gaedel. At any rate, after hearing ball four, Gaedel trotted down to first base, where he was replaced by pinch-runner Jim Delsing. Gaedel waved to the crowd roaring their appreciation and disappeared into the Browns' dugout. The Browns ultimately lost the game, 6–2.

As Veeck expected, the promotion (and by extension Falstaff Brewery) received nationwide attention.[77] A photograph of Gaedel awaiting a pitch at home plate appeared in newspapers across the country. Gaedel became a household name, and he milked it for all it was worth. Rather than put the promotion in the rearview mirror, Gaedel said that he looked forward to additional major league at-bats. He told reporters that he would next like to bat against Bob Feller and Dizzy Trout. In the weeks that followed, Gaedel basked in the media attention. He earned $17,000 by appearing on the Ed Sullivan and Bing Crosby television shows. He also "worked as a Buster Brown shoe man, appeared in the Ringling Brothers Circus, and worked in promotions for Mercury automobiles."

The response from the press was mixed.[78] Vincent X. Flaherty, legendary sportswriter for the *Los Angeles Examiner*,[79] wrote, "I do not advocate baseball burlesque. Such practices do not redound to the better interests of the game—but I claim that [the Eddie Gaedel Game] was the funniest thing that has happened to baseball in years." Others were less charitable. Their views on the Eddie Gaedel Game were summed up in an article written by Joe Williams of the *New York World-Telegram*, which said, "It didn't matter that this made a mockery of the sport or that it exploited a freak of biology in a shameful disgraceful way.... What [Veeck] calls showmanship can more often be accurately identified as vulgarity." Similar articles often made good use of the words "cheap," "tawdry," "travesty," and "mockery" to describe Eddie Gaedel's at-bat in a major league game. Positive or negative, everyone likely agreed with Bob Broeg, who wrote: "The austere American League, celebrating its fiftieth anniversary this year, will reach the ripe old age 100 before anyone other than Phineas T. Veeck, the Barnum of baseball, tops the colorful substitute for winning ball the sports-shirted showman offered yesterday at Sportsman's Park."[80]

The response from major league baseball headquarters was predictable. In the absence of a major league commissioner, American League president Will Harridge immediately voided Gaedel's contract with the Browns and banned little people from playing in the major leagues. A rule was also passed requiring that all player contracts be filed with *and approved* by the president.[81] Unofficially, individual players' response to the Eddie Gaedel Game was mixed. In his autobiography, the great Ted Williams believed the promotion increased interest in baseball. Larry Doby, whom Veeck signed in Cleveland as the first Black baseball player in the American League and a great Veeck supporter, was of a different opinion. He said in an interview many years later that there were very few promotions that, in his opinion, hadn't worked for Veeck. "The only thing I could think of that worked against him was the [little person]."[82]

Veeck took the opportunity presented by Harridge's action to have some fun with major league baseball. He responded, "I am puzzled, baffled and grieved by Mr. Harridge's ruling. Why, we're paying a lot of guys on the Browns' roster good money to get on base and even though they don't do it, nobody sympathizes with us. But when this little guy goes up to the plate and draws a walk on his only time at bat, they call it 'conduct detrimental to baseball.'"[83] He also demanded a ruling on whether Yankees star shortstop Phil Rizzuto, who stood five foot, six inches in height, was a short ballplayer or a tall little person. Veeck also sought a ruling on whether the Boston Red Sox Walt Dropo, who stood six foot, five inches in height, was too tall to play major league baseball. As to whether Eddie Gaedel gave the Browns an unfair advantage, Veeck said, "I might humbly suggest that Ted Williams provides unfair competition as far as St. Louis is concerned."[84]

Harridge even went so far as to decree that Gaedel's at-bat be removed from the official records of major league baseball.[85] This action presented a dilemma for Veeck, who had promised Gaedel that his at-bat would appear for all time in the official major league record books. Veeck went so far as to say that his appearance in the record books would grant Gaedel a sort of immortality. Arguably, not the same immortality that Babe Ruth enjoyed, but immortality, nonetheless. Veeck told Harridge that he was overreacting to one at-bat. He pointed out that Gaedel had a legal contract with the Browns to play in the August 19, 1951, game. Gaedel also participated in a game presided over by major league umpires, who permitted him to play. Veeck also pointed out that, if Harridge voided Gaedel's at bat, he would also somehow need to make commensurate changes to Cain's pitching and Swift's catching. It would also mean that Delsing entered the game to pinch-run for ... no one! Harridge got the message and chose to keep the official records of major league baseball sacrosanct.

Gaedel was of two minds about major league baseball's reaction to his day in the sun. On the one hand, Gaedel, who was somewhat combative, wasn't going to take the ban lying down. He said, "Where does Harridge get that stuff? What did I do? I didn't talk to no gamblers. There ain't nothing in the rules about my size." On the other hand, in the final analysis, Gaedel was pleased that Harridge didn't expunge his at-bat from the record books. He told the Associated Press, "I am happy—I've got a clipping of a box score that shows: Gaedel—walked for Saucier in [first]."[86] Of course, Gaedel is far more important to baseball than one notation in a box score. Look in the record book for the shortest man ever to play in major league baseball. The answer isn't Pee Wee Reese, Wee Willie Keeler, or even Phil "Scooter" Rizzuto. The major league record for the shortest person ever to appear in a baseball game is held by none other than Eddie Gaedel. And, unlikely as it may seem, while someone may break Cal Ripken, Jr.'s, consecutive game streak, Cy Young's record for career wins, or even Hack Wilson's record for runs batted in in a season, it is very unlikely that anyone one shorter than Eddie Gaedel will ever play in a major league baseball game.

According to Paul Dickson in *Bill Veeck: Baseball's Greatest Maverick*, the greatest impact of the Eddie Gaedel Game may have been to expand the audience for major league baseball by showing that it was suitable for the new medium of television.[87] Major league baseball owners were concerned in the early 1950s that showing baseball on television would greatly reduce the number of fans going to the ballparks. Veeck's promotion with Eddie Gaedel, which was extremely visual, helped the owners see that baseball on television might expand the fanbase for the game, which could increase the number of fans attending games.

Postscript: Eddie Gaedel's at-bat lasted but a few minutes but reverberated throughout the history of baseball. When we look back on the Browns' 1951 season, it's as if the other 153 games and all the effort made day-in and day-out by the other players never happened. Ned Garver, who pitched for the Browns that season, said, "I won 20 games that year for a team that lost 102. I batted .305, sometimes sixth in the order. But all anybody ever wants me to talk about is that damn [Gaedel]."[88] On a much larger scale, Veeck also believed that, in some ways, all his accomplishments in his decades-long baseball career were eclipsed by Eddie Gaedel. According to Veeck in *Veeck as in Wreck: The Autobiography of Bill Veeck*:

> I have done a few other things in baseball, you know.... I have operated five clubs—three in the major leagues and two in the minors [including a team in Miami]—and in three of the towns I won pennants and broke attendance records.... But no one has to tell me that, if I returned to baseball tomorrow, won ten straight pennants and left all the old attendance records moldering in the dust, I would still be remembered, in the end, as the man who sent a [little person] up to bat.[89]

Eddie Gaedel died on June 18, 1961, after a fight outside a bowling alley that left him "battered, bleeding, and suffering internal injuries."[90] With Bill Veeck at the Mayo Clinic, the only representative of major league baseball at the funeral was pitcher Bob Cain. Until his death in 1997, Cain sent out Christmas cards which featured a picture of Eddie Gaedel taking his one major league at-bat. The inscription inside the card read, "Hope your target in the future is better than mine in 1951."

Decades later, Veeck remained unapologetic about the Eddie Gaedel Game. He said, "Were it in my power to turn back the clock, I'd never send a [little person] to bat. No, I'd use nine of the little fellows, including the designated hitter."[91]

Veeck's plaque in the Baseball Hall of Fame lists his many accomplishments as a major league owner and ends with the statement, "A champion of the little guy."[92]

Grandstand Managers Night

Consistent with Veeck's willingness to speak before any group interested in hearing him talk about the Browns, on August 10, 1951, Veeck went down into a coal mine, where he spoke with about 200 coal miners. The coal miners listened politely as Veeck, as expected, discussed his plans for improving the Browns the following season. But they were startled to hear what came next: In two weeks, Veeck planned to permit the fans to manage the Browns in a game against the Philadelphia Athletics while manager Zack Taylor took the day off.[93] Veeck came by this idea honestly; he spent most games sitting in the bleacher seats hobnobbing with fans, whom he found to be knowledgeable. Veeck particularly liked speaking with fans in the bleacher section of the ballpark since he had "discovered in 20 years of moving around a ballpark that the knowledge of the game is usually in inverse proportion to the price of the seats."[94]

With this promotion, Veeck, something of a baseball philosopher, sought to raise fans' experience of the game to a level unheard-of in the annals of major league baseball.[95] Veeck explained to *Sports Illustrated* that "the fan comes away from the ballpark with nothing more to show for it than what's in his mind, an ephemeral feeling of having been entertained. You've got to heighten and preserve that illusion. You have to give him more vivid pictures to carry around in his head." It is reasonable to surmise that fans who are literally in control of a baseball game would pay closer attention to what is happening on the field and thus have a deeper experience of the game. Their memories of the game would be more vivid since they, in some way, participated, rather than only watched. Of course, while beneficial to the fans' experience of the game, Veeck knew that having fans manage the game on an ongoing basis was not practical. Yet what a wonderful gift to give to those fans who participated!

Word of Veeck's intentions spread like wildfire throughout major league baseball.[96] About half a dozen other owners lambasted Veeck for contemplating such a promotion. Teams in the lowest rungs of the minor leagues and barnstorming teams had, in the past, staged such events, but to do so in the major leagues was out of the question. Arthur Ehlers, general manager of the Athletics, denounced Veeck for "making a joke out of the game." Veeck surmised that Ehlers was just concerned that his grandstand managers might "outsmart" his professional coaches.[97] The press became equally unhinged at the prospect of fans managing a game. C.M. Gibbs, who wrote for the *Baltimore Sun*, called Veeck's plan "an irresponsible idea, indicating that the foresight of the eminent Veeck is limited to the length of his nose."[98]

Undaunted, Veeck set about preparing for a promotion he would call Grandstand Managers Night,[99] scheduled for August 24, 1951. The first task was to select the fans who were to manage the game. In his autobiography, Veeck explained that, unlike other promotions, the nature of this activity required that it be advertised ahead of time. To select the chosen few, on August 15, the Browns placed in the *St. Louis Globe-Democrat* newspaper the following notice:

> If you would like to be a Grandstand Manager of the Browns on the night of Aug. 24 in their game against the Athletics, fill in your name, address, zone number and city or town below ... [I]f you would like to be one of the coaches append a brief letter stating your reasons. The shorter the better. Your membership card, entitling you to admission to park upon payment of tax, will be mailed to you.[100]

The notice also asked the respondents to choose the starting eight (minus the pitcher) for that night's game.[101] The notice ran in only one edition of the newspaper before it was removed by one of the more conservative editors.[102]

In response, the newspaper received about 4,000 completed ballots, at least one coming from as far away as Anchorage, Alaska.[103] The responses led to two changes to the Browns' usual lineup. They replaced Taylor's choice of catcher, Matt Batts, with Sherm Lollar and placed Hank Arft over Ben Taylor[104] at first base. These changes were fortuitous as Lollar and Arft played major roles in the game for St. Louis.[105] The Browns mailed to each reader submitting a ballot a special pass for the game, which would entitle them to sit together in the Grandstand Managers section of Sportsman's Park behind the Browns' dugout. The Browns selected two respondents who sent in letters—Clark Mitze and Charles E. Hughes—to serve as coaches. Mitze, a former B-26 bomber pilot in World War II, specialized in the work of composer Aaron Copland as a music professor at Washington University in St. Louis.[106] (Similar information is not available on Hughes.)

The night of the event, only 3,295 people entered the ballpark—very disappointing attendance given the promotional build-up of the game. According to Paul Dickson, of these, some 1,115 "grandstand managers" came to the park that night.[107] As they walked through the turnstiles, they were given placards: On one side was written the word "YES" in large green lettering, and on the other side was written the word "NO" in red lettering. When they made their way to the special section set aside for these fans, some noticed that they were among baseball royalty. Also seated in this section was Veeck, his wife Mary Frances, and the legendary, now-retired owner/manager of the Philadelphia Athletics, Connie Mack. Veeck explained that Mack, who was 89 years old, still travelled with the Athletics. Although he was fairly spry for his age, his mind had begun to wander. Whenever he came to Sportsman's Park, there was a schedule posted in the office to make sure that someone always sat with him during the games.[108]

While manager Zack Taylor, wearing civilian clothes, sat in a rocking chair placed on the field, smoking a curved stem pipe and reading a newspaper,[109] the grandstand managers took control of the game. According to Norm King, in his article "August 24, 1951: St. Louis Browns Fans Manage to Get It Right in Veeck Promotion," here is how it worked:[110] Whenever

Mitze or Hughes, who weren't allowed onto the field due to a contract issue, thought that an in-game strategy decision was needed, they contacted Browns executive Bob Fishel by walkie-talkie. Fishel, who stood in front of the special section of grandstand managers, had large cards printed up with every conceivable baseball situation that needed a manager's decision. The cards asked such questions as SHALL WE JERK THE BUM?[111] Whenever asked, Fishel would hold up the appropriate card asking the grandstand managers to render a yes-or-no decision on the in-game strategy. The grandstand managers would hold up their cards showing their decisions. A circuit judge standing next to Fishel would tabulate the result and, using a walkie-talkie, relay the majority decision to Johnnie Bernadino in the Browns' dugout, who would inform the players.[112]

There were some technical issues to address before the game could get started.[113] Given Ehler's opinion of the promotion, it should come as no surprise that, before the game even got started, Jimmy Dykes, manager of the Athletics, informed the umpires that he was ready to protest the game if the vote tabulating caused a delay. To make sure that everyone in the stands knew that he was upset, Dykes kicked dirt on home plate and sneered at the grandstand managers who, according to Veeck, sneered back. Then there was the issue regarding the placement of Taylor's rocking chair. Umpire Bill Summers informed the Browns that they had to move Taylor from his position on the field because he wasn't in uniform. The Browns moved him to a spot just beside the Browns' dugout, which satisfied the umpires.

Now was the time for the grandstand managers to show their stuff.[114] Browns outfielder Frank Saucier remembered having his doubts; he said that, when he looked at the grandstand managers during batting practice and noticed that a surprising number of them were women, he thought, "This is absolutely insane."[115] But the fans proved him wrong; as for the in-game strategy, the grandstand managers were almost perfect. The Browns' pitcher, Ned Garver, who at that point in the season had a 14–8 and a solid 3.89 ERA,[116] was hit hard in the first inning. With one out, Ferris Fain and Elmer Valo both singled, and Gus Zernial hit a three-run homer to give the Athletics a 3–0 lead. Hank Majeski reached first base on an error and Dave Philley singled, moving Majeski to third.[117]

With three runs in and runners at first and third, Fishel held up a sign asking the grandstand managers, SHALL WE WARM UP PITCHER?[118] The grandstand managers voted to keep Garver in the game, according to Veeck, "presumably on the theory that Garver's feelings might get hurt." While Veeck and Mack voted to warm up a new pitcher, Veeck's wife voted against it. Mary Frances and most of the grandstand managers who voted with her turned out to be right since Garver pitched a shutout the rest of the way. Fishel held aloft a sign that read INFIELD BACK? While, by most accounts, the grandstand managers voted in favor of this suggestion, Garver remembers it differently. He recalls that the fans voted to keep the infield in. Since neither he nor catcher Lollar agreed with that call, they stalled until the people managing the grandstand managers got the message to ask again. Finally, on the third try, the fans voted to keep the infield back, which again turned out to be the right move; the Athletics' next batter, Pete Suder, obligingly hit into an inning-ending double play.

The Browns tied the score in the bottom of the first inning. With one out, Jim Delsing doubled to center field and Lollar hit a single to drive Delsing home with the Browns' first run. With a 3–2 count on Chris Mapes, the grandstand managers were asked whether Lollar at first should be off with the pitch. The grandstand managers voted for him to stay on base, which was wise because Mapes struck out. Ken Wood then hit a double, sending Lollar to third base. Arft singled to drive in both runs and tied the score at 3–3. The fans were then asked whether Arft should steal second base. The grandstand managers voted for Arft to steal, but the Athletics catcher, made aware of this decision by the public nature of the decision-making process, threw him out by two feet.[119] At that point, it seems the grandstand managers were given a respite for the remainder of the game. Lollar hit a solo home run in the third inning to give the Browns the lead, and in the eighth inning, he scored from second on a single.[120] With Garver pitching a complete game, the Browns won, 5–3, improving their record to 38–81,[121] in a game that remarkably took only about two hours to complete.[122]

After the game, there was a show of fireworks that spelled out, "THANKS G.S. MANAGERS FOR A SWELL JOB. ZACK MANAGES TOMORROW."[123] According to one source, Veeck gave a trophy to Mitze which was inscribed, "One of the Best Coaches Ever Banned from the Coaching Lines."[124] I imagine Hughes received a similar trophy. Veeck later wrote that he "retired all [his] amateur managers with honors, went back to [his] professionals, and lost five of the next six games."[125]

The reviews of the game were surprisingly mostly positive. There was a big spread about the game in *The Sporting News*.[126]

Postscript: Imitation being the highest form of flattery, Bill Veeck's son Mike complimented his father by staging grandstand managers nights of his own with minor league teams.[127] In 2004, the Brockton Rox held a grandstand managers night, and in 2013, the Saint Paul Saints sponsored a promotion that was a variation on the theme. In this game, Little Leaguers umpired from the sidelines.

◊ **CHAPTER 4** ◊

Finley's Baseball Folly
The Beatles and Charlie-O the Mule

Charlie O. Finley/Kansas City and Oakland Athletics

The Beatles	Opening Day 1965/ Charlie-O the Mule
Stand Alone Concert	Detroit Tigers at Kansas City Athletics
Municipal Stadium	
September 17, 1964	April 12, 1965

Raised in a poor working-class family, Charlie O. Finley used his preternatural ability as a salesman and shrewd business acumen to become a top executive in the insurance business, making a fortune in the process. In December 1960, he purchased the woeful Kansas City Athletics, no doubt expecting a continuation of his success story. Instead, unable to turn the franchise around, a frustrated Finley secretly looked to move the team elsewhere. When his scheme was exposed, Finley embarked on a years-long campaign in which he lambasted Kansas City, lashed out at his critics, and redoubled his efforts to move the franchise, in the process alienating fans, city officials, and members of the press. Compelled by other American League owners in February 1964 to sign an iron-clad, four-year lease keeping the Athletics in Kansas City. Finley sought to save his franchise by making amends. So he brought to Kansas City in September 1964 the greatest show on earth—the Beatles! Remarkably, that outrageous gesture didn't work, as many Kansas City music aficionados boycotted the concert. Next, Finley obtained a mule named Charlie-O which, on Opening Day 1965, he introduced to the Kansas City fans as the team's mascot. It appears that he hoped that the fans' goodwill towards Charlie-O might reflect positively on Finley and generate attendance at Athletics games. The mule gambit didn't work either, but Finley and Charlie-O had outrageous escapades as they traveled around the American League together.

Finley Makes a Fortune

Finley's life reads like a Horatio Alger story. He was born on February 2, 1918, into a poor working-class family[1] in Ensley (near Birmingham), Alabama,[2] where his father and grandfather both worked in the steel and iron mill industry.[3] When Finley was in his teens, his father moved to Gary, Indiana, for work, taking his family with him. After graduating high school in 1936, the 18-year-old Finley, like his father and grandfather before him, became a steelworker.[4]

When the United States entered World War II, Finley took a position in the defense industry and worked for Kingsbury Ordnance Plant, near La Porte, Indiana.[5] While working in the ordnance plant, Finley started selling insurance on the side for Travelers Insurance Company. When Finley left the Kingsbury Ordnance Plant in 1946, he was firmly ensconced in the insurance business and making a good living.

Unfortunately, Finley's career as an insurance salesman was derailed when he was diagnosed with pneumonic tuberculosis[6] in December 1946, and had to remain indefinitely in the Parramore Sanitorium, a county institution at Crown Point, Indiana.[7] While laid up at the sanitorium, Finley began talking to doctors about their plans for maintaining their lifestyle should they be unable to work due to disability. Lo and behold, they had none.[8] Finley had a brainstorm: Once recovered and released from the sanatorium, Finley began selling group disability insurance to doctors.[9]

By the time Finley finally left Parramore for good in March 1949, he was ready to execute his plan. Working at first with insurance companies, Finley sold policies to medical groups representing 92 percent of doctors in the Chicago area, and eventually he went nationwide. By 1952, Finley went into business for himself, forming Charlie O. Finley & Associates, located in Chicago.[10] The business thrived: At its height, Finley's group policies covered over 50 medical associations and 70,000 doctors; they generated $20 million in business annually.[11] Finley had become a millionaire many times over.

It just so happened that Finley's business and the American League offices were headquartered in the same building. There, Finley made the acquaintance of Will Harridge, the president of the American League.[12] Finley and Harridge, who were both self-made men,[13] bonded on their mutual interest in baseball.[14] Harridge, recognizing Finley as a man with both leadership skills and wealth, encouraged Finley to purchase a major league franchise.[15] Beginning in 1954, Finley sought to purchase one major league team after another.[16]

Finley Strikes Out in Kansas City

Having learned that Arnold Johnson, the owner of the Kansas City Athletics, had died and the franchise was up for sale, Finley, in December 1960, submitted the winning bid of $1,975,000 to purchase 52 percent of the team,[17] making him the majority owner. Finley, at the relatively young age of 42, was in the rarefied air of a select group of men who owned major league baseball franchises.

Finley initially said and did all the right things. He made hundreds of presentations to groups in Kansas City, talking up his new team and inviting everyone to his ballpark. At each stop, he swore that he would keep the team in Kansas City and transform it into a winning franchise.[18] The lease Finley had signed contained a clause allowing him to move the team if attendance at games did not reach 850,000 per season. In February 1961, Finley burned what looked to be the lease in public, ostensibly to demonstrate that he would never use the attendance clause for reasons of moving the team. However, Finley's seemingly magnanimous act was just for show. Little did anyone know that Finley that day burned a meaningless piece of paper. The attendance clause remained in effect.[19]

Finley also made a public display of his promise to improve the play of the Kansas City Athletics. Under Johnson's leadership, the Athletics were a perennially losing team. This should come as no surprise since Johnson had a penchant for trading Kansas City's upcoming stars, such as Roger Maris, to the New York Yankees in exchange for their has-beens. Indeed, under the leadership of Johnson, the Athletics had basically served as a Yankees farm team.[20] In February 1961, Finley made a show of publicly burning a school bus to demonstrate that the Athletics would no longer be shipping their up-and-coming stars to New York.[21]

Finley also embarked on a major renovation of Municipal Stadium, where the Athletics played their home games, costing him, according to his own estimation, about $580,000.[22] Finley added much-needed lighting to the outside of the stadium, as well as new concession stands and restrooms. He arranged for radio broadcasts of the game to be piped into restrooms. Finley repainted the seats bright yellow, turquoise, and orange. He added new scoreboards, and a small zoo[23] and a picnic area were constructed behind left field with maple trees for shade and carriage lights for night games. Finley also lowered, lengthened, and lighted the dugouts so fans had a better view of players who were not at bat or on the field.[24]

Finley sure knew how to use innovative gadgets to grab the attention of the public. For example, rather than have a batboy run from the dugout to the umpire to replenish his supply of baseballs, Finley installed a mechanical rabbit named Harvey[25] that popped up out of the ground behind home plate with a supply of new balls for the umpire.[26] To save the umpire from needing to dust off home plate, Finley installed a compressed air device with a spout in the middle of the plate, named Little Blowhard,[27] that blew off the dirt.[28]

So far, so good.

Meanwhile, behind the scenes, Finley was taking total control of the franchise. Not wanting any interference in managing what was "his" franchise, Finley bought out all the minority owners in February 1961.[29] Finley distrusted those who had been running the business side of the Athletics, so he arranged to accumulate all decision-making on business matters for himself.[30] His management style often involved berating and firing front office personnel.[31] According to baseball announcer Bob Elson, "[Finley] just doesn't treat people like human beings."[32] On the baseball side of the franchise, Finley initially thought he might need some help. He kept Joe Gordon as the Athletics manager but sacked the popular general manager, Parke Carroll,[33] and replaced him with the very experienced Frank "Trader" Lane.

By 1962, both Gordon and Lane were gone, replaced by more pliable subordinates.[34] It is entirely possible that, by the time they were fired, both Gordon and Lane were fed up with working for Finley. The new Athletics owner was well known for not showing respect for his baseball players[35] and interfering with his staff, including manager and general manager.[36] Among his many transgressions, Finley kept telling Gordon who should play. As one example, he reportedly told Gordon to start relief pitcher Jack Aker. Gordon lamented that "it was tough to manage when you weren't permitted to manage."[37]

Despite (or possibly because of) Finley efforts, the team continued to play poorly, and the franchise's poor attendance remained stagnant. Finley, in total control of the franchise, began to question whether Kansas City's small market could support a major league team. He wanted out. While publicly claiming fealty to Kansas City, Finley behind the scenes initiated a years-long process of looking for someplace to move the team.[38] He sought approval for a move from American League owners on several occasions, but he was rebuffed time and time again.

Once his duplicity was exposed by Mehl, sports reporter for *Kansas City Star*, rather than own up to his own actions, Finley thought he could fast talk his way out of this mess. His tactic of choice, which was to discredit Mehl, likely didn't endear him to the people of Kansas City. Mehl was a highly respected journalist known for his integrity. Finley alleged that Mehl would stoop so low as to badmouth Finley because he refused to pay travel expenses for reporters from the *Kansas City Star* and *Times* (the other major newspaper in Kansas City). Finley added that Mehl had inappropriately accepted $1,000 to edit the Athletics' yearbook for the prior owner. Mehl stood by his reporting and fought back against Finley's accusations by stating that he never sought travel expenses from the Athletics and explaining that he edited the yearbook on his vacation.[39]

As discussed in Chapter 2, an enraged Finley used a so-called promotion, called Ernie Mehl Appreciation Day, to lash out at Mehl and publicly humiliate him.[40] In response, Ford Frick, the Commissioner of Baseball, called Mehl to personally apologize for Finley's tantrum, and he issued a statement that read, "Such things do not belong in baseball and I called Mehl this morning to apologize to him personally and in the name of baseball." Finley, adding insult to injury, pushed back against Frick's legitimate concerns. He met with Tom Gavin, the mayor pro-tem of Kansas City, and several councilmen and convinced them to send a message to Frick, which read in part, "If any apologies are due to anyone, they are due to Mr. Finley and no one else. It is our feeling that baseball should be praising rather than criticizing Mr. Finley for his courage, his sacrifices, and his faith in Kansas City." Finley exacerbated his maltreatment of the Kansas City press by, among other things, ordering his staff to discontinue sending team information or press releases to the *Star* or the *Times*, instructing the team's traveling secretary to stop making travel arrangements for their reporters for road games, and excluding the Kansas City press from an important press conference.[41]

While steadfastly believing that the press deserved total blame for his predicament, Finley wasn't blind to the fact that baseball fans in Kansas City had turned on him.[42] He recognized that he needed to win them back by making some public gesture that would lead fans to believe that the Athletics franchise was in Kansas City to stay. So, on August 26, 1961, still bitter about his treatment by the press, Finley signed an amendment to the original lease, deleting the attendance clause.[43]

At the same time, growing discouraged about his own ability to generate attendance for a losing team, Finley quietly discontinued "most customary promotional activities and player appearances."[44] He focused his promotional efforts solely on direct mail within the Kansas City metro area, ignoring fans in the outer suburbs and neighboring towns and counties. Finley also discontinued the Athletics' efforts to develop future fans by "disbanding several popular youth programs during the season," including a booster club organization operating in Missouri and four neighboring states that offered discounted tickets to high school fans.

In 1962, with the franchise languishing, Finley tried a new tactic; he asked that city leaders construct a new 50,000-seat ballpark for the Athletics, to be paid for by general obligation bonds.[45] To Finley's way of thinking, Municipal Stadium had no redeeming features. According to Finley, a new stadium was all that was needed to turn Kansas City into a premiere baseball town.[46] With these discussions ongoing, Finley was meeting with officials in Seattle and San Diego to move the Athletics to one of these cities and negotiating with officials in Oakland to play in the new stadium there.[47] Finley also became publicly infuriated by those civic leaders who suggested that the Athletics should receive a new stadium only when the team started winning and attracting more fans.[48] By the fall of 1962, Finley's grand scheme to replace Municipal Stadium was all but dead.[49]

In 1963, while negotiating a new lease for Municipal Stadium, which was scheduled to expire at the end of that calendar year, Finley pursued a strategy of threatening to move the franchise elsewhere if his demands weren't met and the old lease was permitted to expire.[50] Throughout the negotiations, Finley gave credence to his threats by visiting other cities to determine their suitability for the Athletics franchise. Regarding his efforts to increase attendance by improving the product on the field, rather than overhaul the roster,[51] Finley changed the team's uniform, which was transformed from their traditional blue and white to Kelly green, Fort Knox gold, and Wedding Gown white, with the name Athletics in script emblazoned on the front of the jersey.

When the lease expired at the end of 1963, Finley had to move his staff out of its offices in Municipal Stadium. The mayor, apparently fed up with Finley's negotiating tactics, stopped the team's front office staff from moving into space made available by Civic Plaza National Bank. So Finley moved his business staff out of Municipal Stadium and into the garage of team scout Joe Bowman. He didn't even bother to arrange for a telephone to be installed; anyone needing to make a call needed to go into Joe Bowman's kitchen.[52] On January 16, Finley's fellow American League owners met in New York and instructed Finley to put an end to these shenanigans. In accordance with a vote of American League owners, who pronounced the lease being offered by Kansas City to be fair and reasonable, Finley on February 23, 1964, signed an iron-clad, four-year lease.[53]

Finley had become *persona non grata* in Kansas City, although, despite everything that had transpired, it is doubtful that he understood why. According to Bill Libby in *Charlie O. and the Angry A's*, Mehl, trying to understand Finley, said, "Somehow men like Finley do not consider themselves responsible for their own actions. They blame everyone but themselves for what goes wrong."[54] His mismanagement of the Athletics and continued efforts to scout new destinations for his franchise, had succeeded in accomplishing one thing: He had burned his bridges with Kansas City civic leaders and baseball fans. Someone perusing the January 11, 1964, edition of *The Sporting News* would have seen a picture of a lawn jockey painted in Athletics colors sporting a sign that said, "FINLEY GO

HOME." The situation got so bad that Kansas City citizens began displaying "dummies dressed like Finley hanging from their houses."[55]

Money Can't Buy Me Love

Stuck in Kansas City, Finley wanted to make the unpleasantness of the last four years go away. He seemed to believe that he needed to do something spectacular (dare I say outrageous) to get back in the good graces of Kansas City baseball fans. What could be more spectacular than the greatest rock and roll band ever, making its first tour of the United States—the Beatles! Having learned that the Fab Four did not intend to give a concert in Kansas City, Finley met with their manager, Brian Epstein, and offered $50,000 for the Beatles to give a concert in Municipal Stadium. Finley ended up paying the unheard-of sum of $150,000—at the time the most ever paid for a music concert[56]—for the Beatles to perform at Municipal Stadium on September 17, 1964. Proceeds from the concert were to

Charlie O. Finley staged a Beatles concert in Kansas City in hopes that it would lead to greater attendance at Athletics games. It didn't. In this photograph, the Beatles (from left, John Lennon, Paul McCartney, George Harrison and Ringo Starr) wave to fans after disembarking a plane at Kennedy Airport (United Press International, photographer unknown, public domain, via Wikimedia Commons).

benefit Children's Mercy Hospital.[57] The Beatles had planned to take the day off but couldn't pass up $150,000, which was double what they usually received for a concert at the time.[58]

Although this promotion wasn't connected to a particular baseball game, it counts as a major league baseball promotion since it was clearly designed to promote attendance at Athletics games. Finley's motto for the event was, "Today's Beatle fans are tomorrow's baseball fans."[59] Finley made sure that those going to the concert knew who it was that brought the Beatles to Kansas City. Tickets to the concert read, CHARLES O. FINLEY IS PLEASED TO PRESENT FOR THE ENJOYMENT OF THE BEATLES FANS IN MID-AMERICA THE BEATLES IN PERSON.[60] On the back of each ticket was a photo of Finley wearing a Beatles wig.[61]

According to one article, when Finley realized, after the contract had been signed, that the Beatles intended to give only a 30-minute performance, especially considering how much he paid for the concert, he tried to convince them to extend their play list.[62] Rather than make his entreaties to Brian Epstein, he somehow spoke directly with John Lennon. Finley met with Lennon in the alcove of a parlor at Kansas City's historic Muehlenbach Hotel, which was visited by every president from Theodore Roosevelt to Ronald Reagan. He pressed Lennon to play a few additional songs. Lennon disliked Finley, whom he saw as a member of the monied establishment, and refused to extend the concert. Even when Finley offered additional money, Lennon reportedly responded, "Not enough [money] man. We won't do it." After Finley pressed the issue, Lennon reportedly ended the discussion by saying, "No f**king way."

You would think the youth in Kansas City would be in a tizzy about the Beatles' appearance in their city. But the long shadow of the Mehl affair and the bad taste of rancorous negotiations still hung over Finley. The *Kansas City Star* and other media sources urged the good people of Kansas City to boycott the concert "as a way of showing displeasure with Finley." The boycott was effective; whereas Municipal Stadium had a seating capacity of 34,165, only 20,280 concertgoers attended the Beatles' performance. (Finley had to sell 28,000 tickets to break even.)[63] The Kansas City concert was the only concert on the Beatles' tour of the United States that year not to sell out.[64]

Prior to the concert, the Beatles were to participate in a morning press conference to which all the high school journalists in the Kansas City area were invited.[65] Problem was the Beatles were very tired, having arrived in Kansas City at 2:00 a.m. Jim Schaaf, the Athletics' promotion manager, couldn't wake John, Paul, George, or Ringo in time for them to participate in the press conference. He said, "I felt a heck of a lot of pressure because they wouldn't wake up!" Schaaf knew that this event was important to

Finley. His only option was to delay the press conference until noon; by this time, the "Fab Four" had awakened and participated in the press conference, which turned out well.

The concert, which lasted 31 minutes, consisted of 12 songs.[66] Those in attendance were boisterous. Despite the presence of 350 officers to manage the crowd, Beatles fans stormed the stage just before the concert was to begin; they didn't retreat until told that the event might be cancelled.[67] The Beatles, doing something a little extra for the hometown crowd, began the concert with the song, "Kansas City/Hey-Hey-Hey-Hey," which they would record a month later for their *Beatles for Sale* album.[68] The youth in attendance were thrilled to hear the Beatles play some of their biggest hits: "Ticket to Ride," "Can't Buy Me Love," and "A Hard Day's Night." Some adults in the audience had a different take on the Beatles' performance, saying that the music as it came out of the sound system was just noise, and they couldn't understand the lyrics.

Once again demonstrating that no good deed goes unpunished, Finley lost money on the concert. (And to be clear, no one else ever lost money staging a Beatles concert.) Uncharacteristically performing before a nearly half-empty stadium, the Beatles may have been trying to send Finley a message when they sang "Can't Buy Me Love."[69] To add insult to injury, Finley, who had promised to donate all profits from the concert to Children's Mercy Hospital, felt obligated to make a $25,000 donation to the hospital out of his own pocket.[70] In an attempt to put a positive spin on a losing proposition, Finley stated, "I don't consider it any loss at all. The Beatles were brought here for the enjoyment of the children in this area and watching them last night they had complete enjoyment. I'm happy about that. Mercy Hospital benefitted by $25,000. The hospital gained and I had a great gain by seeing the children and the hospital gain."[71]

As things turned out, the concert wasn't a financial loss for all involved.[72] Two enterprising people obtained the bedsheets (16 sheets and eight pillowcases) from the hotel rooms where the Beatles stayed. They cut them into small pieces and sold them as souvenirs. They reportedly paid $750 for the intact bedsheets and earned $159,000 from the souvenirs.

The Finest Mule in All Missouri

By the 1965 season, Finley began relying heavily on promotions to bring fans to the ballpark. The team certainly wasn't doing anything on the field to generate fan interest. According to his biographers, G. Michael Green and Roger D. Launius, in *Charlie Finley: The Outrageous Story of Baseball's Super Showman,* Finley took a page from Bill Veeck's playbook

Charlie O. Finley was so proud of his team's mascot, Charlie-O the Mule, that he insisted on bringing it along with the team when the Athletics visited other cities. On these sojourns, Finley would house the mule in hotels and hold press conferences in its honor (National Baseball Hall of Fame and Museum).

and began staging promotions, hoping to increase attendance.[73] As an aside, one would think that Veeck would be flattered that another owner was following in his footsteps. But no. Veeck, who was reportedly peeved that Finley was relying on promotions, said of Finley, "I don't mean to say that he's slow with ideas. It's just that he, uh, copies."[74] He added, "If I ever run out of ideas Charlie Finley would be out of business."[75]

As part of this new strategy, Finley became convinced that the Athletics could increase interest if only they would jettison the elephant mascot and logo that the franchise had used since it was in Philadelphia and obtain a new Missouri-focused mascot that would be an attraction at the ballpark.[76] Very late one night, Finley excitedly called Jim Schaaf with an idea for the perfect mascot. He read in the *Chicago Tribune* about how Missouri mules aided the American military in World War I. Apparently, while the enemy was having trouble bringing armaments and supplies through the mud and snow of France to the front lines, the Americans were successfully relying on strong, sure-footed Missouri mules to do so.

Finley told Schaaf, "We need to get a mule, and we need to get the finest mule in the state of Missouri.... That's the job and I want you to do it."[77]

Not sure where to find the finest mule in Missouri,[78] Schaaf called Howard Benjamin, who owned a horse farm on the outskirts of Kansas City that housed the Kansas City Chiefs' horse, named War Paint, that galloped all around the field every time the Chiefs scored a touchdown. Schaaf asked Benjamin to find him a mule, but not just any mule; this had to be the best mule in the state of Missouri. Using his connections in the equine industry, Benjamin located just the right mule. The mule stood 16.2 hands high and weighed 1,400 pounds; its lineage was unclear, except it was certain that, as is the case for all mules, its mother was a horse and its father a donkey.[79] Benjamin called Schaaf, and they arranged for Finley to see the mule. It was love at first sight. Finley named the mule after himself, "Charlie-O," and arranged for the governor of Missouri, Warren Hearnes, to donate the mule to the Athletics franchise. Finley was confident the mule would attract people to Municipal Stadium.[80]

On Opening Day (April 12) 1965, prior to a game against the Detroit Tigers, Finley introduced Charlie-O to the Athletics fans.[81] The Missouri governor was on hand to formally present the mule to the Kansas City Athletics. In accepting the gift, Finley announced that Charlie-O resulted from the greatest mule search in history. Proud of the team's new mascot, Finley exclaimed, "Everybody's got to see this mule." Finley, clearly in his element, mounted the mule and rode it around the stadium to the cheers of laughing fans.

It soon became apparent that Finley had every intention to pamper Charlie-O.[82] Indeed, several players privately complained that Finley treated Charlie-O better than he treated them. Finley arranged for the mule to be transported to home games in an air-conditioned trailer equipped with a music system that played "mule music," such as "Mule Train," which goes, "Mule train!/Clippety cloppin' over hill and plain." The trailer was pulled by a custom green and gold station wagon.[83] While at home games, Charlie-O stayed in a pen in the stadium's zoo, where fans could visit and pet him, and otherwise show affection for the team's new mascot. The mule even got his own uniform, which consisted of "a green and gold blanket, bridle, and Athletics cap." While not at home games, Charlie-O served as a roving ambassador for the Athletics. For instance, Charlie-O was on hand when a high school in Lawson, Kansas, unveiled a new scoreboard for its athletic field.[84]

It wasn't enough that Athletics fans had the opportunity to get to know Charlie-O; Finley was so proud of his team's new mascot that he wanted to share him with the rest of baseball.[85] According to Finley, "[Charlie-O] is something different. This is unique. Nobody has a mascot like this.... I want to take him all over the American League." Finley arranged to take the mule on a promotional tour during the 1965 and 1966 seasons. At many stops on the promotional tour, Charlie-O stayed at the same hotel that housed the Athletics players. Finley also arranged for the mule to parade down each town's thoroughfares as players and ball girls passed out souvenirs, such as bats, balls, pens, and caps, all emblazoned with the Athletics' colors of green and gold.

Charlie-O's debut in New York City in 1965 was certainly a highlight of the tour.[86] When they arrived, Finley arranged to parade the mule from Central Park down Seventh Avenue with a full police escort stopping traffic along the way. The parade made its way to the Americana Hotel, where Athletics players stood outside passing out souvenirs and signing autographs. Finley made a show of bringing the mule into the hotel and registering him there. The hotel had set up a space by the parking area of the hotel to house Charlie-O. Not wanting the mule to realize he was staying in a garage, Finley arranged to build for the mule an actual room complete with homey touches, such as furniture and pictures of Finley and Charlie-O on the wall.

Apparently thinking that Charlie-O's visit was one of the biggest events to hit the Big Apple in quite some time, Finley arranged for a press conference.[87] Charlie-O being a mule of few words, one would assume that Finley or Schaaf did most of the talking. According to Schaaf, "Everybody in New York was at that press conference," including sports reporting legends Howard Cosell and Frank Gifford. He added, "Every news outlet in New York ... sent someone to cover the press conference." The meeting was held in one of the large exhibition rooms at the hotel, which was packed with people coming to see Charlie-O, whose picture was in every New York newspaper the following day. Indeed, the *New York Daily News* devoted its whole back page to a picture of the mule. Finley must have been thrilled; Charlie-O was a sensation.

Next for Charlie-O was his debut at one of the Athletics-Yankees Games.[88] Finley thought the best way to introduce the mule to Yankees fans was for a player from the Athletics to ride him around the stadium. Ken "Hawk" Harrelson volunteered for riding duty; he apparently had ridden mules at his grandfather's farm when growing up. Problem was that Harrelson had always used a saddle when riding mules as a youngster, but Charlie-O had no saddle. Undaunted, they put a blanket on the mule's back, and Harrelson started riding him around the stadium. All went well until Charlie-O began to trot, and Harrelson started to lose his grip on the animal and slide off. Those watching in the stands and in the dugout found Harrelson's predicament hilarious and started laughing. The mule began to buck, possibly spooked by the boisterous crowd, and threw Harrelson off his back and onto the ground. Riderless, Charlie-O meandered into the outfield, while Harrelson, apparently unscathed, picked himself up, dusted himself off, and headed to the dugout. Finley laughed so hard that he almost cried as he watched Harrelson try to ride the mule. Of course, pictures of Harrelson hanging onto the mule for dear life appeared in all the New York newspapers the next day.

Charlie-O's visit to the Chicago White Sox was also a highlight of the tour, but for different reasons.[89] Green and Launius, in their biography of Finley,[90] and Bill Libby, in *Charlie O. and the Angry A's*,[91] give detailed accounts of Finley's shenanigans in Chicago. On this trip, Finley was able to arrange a luncheon for Charlie-O and the Athletics players at the Sheraton Hotel, where local reporters took the opportunity to make the acquaintance of the mule. But Arthur Allyn, Jr., who owned the White Sox, banned Charlie-O from Comiskey Park. Said team general manager Ed Short, "If I let Finley ride that mule around the park, I won't be able to tell which one is the jackass."[92] To Finley, those were fighting words. He instructed Jim Schaap to rent a vacant lot across from Comiskey Park, where he placed Charlie-O. Schaap also arranged for a six-piece[93] band located in the lot to play mule songs, amplified by a truck with a powerful sound system. In case that wasn't enough to aggravate Allyn, Schaap hired attractive young women whose job it was to picket directly outside the stadium, carrying signs that announced WHITE SOX UNFAIR TO MISSOURI MULE.[94]

Finley was bound and determined to bring a mule into Comiskey Park.[95] Realizing that he could not sneak an animal as large as Charlie-O into the stadium, Finley hatched an alternate plan. With Schaaf as an accomplice, Finley arranged for a crate containing a smaller mule to be delivered to the visitors' clubhouse at Comiskey Park. He rationalized that only Charlie-O was barred from the ballpark, not the smaller mule.[96] Schaaf told White Sox officials that the crate contained baseball and training equipment. Finley himself supervised delivery of the crate to the visitors' clubhouse. Harrelson, who was not in the starting lineup that day, just happened to be in the clubhouse as the crate was delivered. Finley asked him to help the delivery men, who were having difficulty getting the crate through the door.[97]

After the crate was delivered, Finley opened it, and Harrelson was amazed to see a mule jump out.[98] This mule wasn't as large as Charlie-O but was a smaller version that looked just like the Athletics' mascot. Finley asked Harrelson to help him bring the mule onto the field. Harrelson balked at Finley's suggestion, saying, "You can't take him on the field, Charlie. It's right in the middle of the ballgame." Finley snapped back, "I don't give a damn when it is. I got this mule this far and we're going to get him the rest of the way. Now, come on. Are you going to help me or not?" An incredulous Harrison helped Finley coax the mule up the tunnel leading to the dugout, with Finley up front pulling on a rope around the mule's neck and Harrelson pushing from behind.[99]

The Athletics broke into laughter as they saw the mule emerge from the tunnel into the dugout.[100] Just as Finley readied himself to push the mule onto the field, Schaap contacted the sound truck by walkie-talkie and instructed them to play "Mule Train" and crank up the sound so loud it could be heard throughout the stadium. At this point in the game, the White Sox had men on base and were threatening to score against Jack Aker.[101] Finley asked Harrelson to "help me push [the mule] up the steps to the field so the customers can see him." Harrelson said, "We can't do this.," to which Finley responded, "The hell we can't." With that, Finley and Harrelson shoved the animal onto the field outside the dugout.

Baseball games had been invaded before by animals, such as swarms of insects, birds, and even cats, but never by a mule.[102] The crowd laughed hysterically as the mule galloped around the field. The umpires, clearly perturbed by this distraction, ordered Finley and Harrelson to remove the animal from the field. They threatened, "Get that mule off the field or every player in the dugout is gonna be out of the game."[103] After gamboling on the field for a while, the mule reentered the dugout of its own accord, stepping on Harrelson's foot, causing him to miss the next three games.[104] Finley, Harrelson, and some of the players removed the mule in due course. Whitey Herzog, an Athletics coach in 1965 who was in the bullpen at Comiskey Park that day, said, "This is nothing more than a damned side show. Winning over here is a joke."[105] Nonetheless, Finley was quite proud of what he did. While the mule was on the field, Finley pointed at Allyn sitting in his box seat, laughing so hard that tears rolled down his cheeks.[106] Said Schaaf, "Getting the mule into the stadium was what Charlie wanted.... That was his deal because he was in Chicago. Chicago was his town. He wanted to do something spectacular. They said he couldn't do it; he said he's going to do it." Advantage Finley.[107]

As shown in the chart in Chapter 2, Charlie-O may have been a sensation across the American League, but as a gate attraction, the mule was an abject failure.[108] The Athletics attracted only 528,344 fans to Municipal Stadium in 1965, worst in the league and lower than the year before.

When Finley moved the Athletics to Oakland, Charlie-O went along for the ride.[109] There, the mule made an appearance before every Athletics weekend home game. He and his trainer would walk around the warning track, at the conclusion of which Charlie-O would bow to the crowd. Fans in Oakland might arrive at the park a little early to have their picture taken with Charlie-O or possibly have a child sit on its back.[110] There was a story going around baseball that Charlie-O once startled future Hall of Fame catcher Carlton Fisk when the mule was led into a hotel coffee shop where Fisk was a patron.[111]

POSTSCRIPT: Charlie-O died of deterioration of the liver in December 1976.[112] When Finley sold the Athletics to Walter Haas five years later, the new owner discontinued using Charlie-O as its mascot and, once again, adopted the elephant logo originally used by the Athletics during their incarnation in Philadelphia.[113]

◊ CHAPTER 5 ◊

Giles' Genius Goes Awry
Farewell to Connie Mack Stadium and Kiteman

Bill Giles/Philadelphia Phillies

Farewell to Connie Mack Stadium	Kiteman
Montreal Expos at Philadelphia Phillies	St. Louis Cardinals at Philadelphia Phillies
Connie Mack Stadium	Veterans Stadium
October 1, 1970	April 17, 1972

Like Bill Veeck, Bill Giles was a baseball lifer. During his youth and much of his adolescence, his father was president of the Cincinnati Reds. The young Giles had the opportunity to work in various junior positions for the Reds and, later, served as business manager for the minor league Nashville Volunteers, travelling secretary for the Reds, and promotions manager for the Houston Astros. Giles learned from his work experience that, in all aspects of baseball, one should expect the unexpected. When Giles became an executive with the Philadelphia Phillies, the unexpected became the hallmark of his promotions. With the Phillies, Giles was responsible for promoting the final game at the venerable Connie Mack Stadium, which had a long and illustrious history dating back to 1909. Little did he know that, during the final game promotion, riotous fans would seek to disassemble the stadium and invade the playing field, almost causing the Phillies to forfeit the game. Giles was inclined to stage spectacular Opening Day promotions. He had no expectation that, at the second Opening Day at Veterans Stadium, a well-hyped stunt performer known as Kiteman, who was supposed to soar into the air and deliver the first ball to the infield, would crash land in the stands, causing those in attendance to boo vociferously.

An Apprenticeship in Baseball

When Giles was born on September 7, 1934, his father was President of the minor league Rochester Red Wings, the top affiliate of the St. Louis Cardinals.[1] In 1937, Giles' father became president of the Cincinnati Reds and, from 1951 to 1969, served as President of the National League. Having spent his teenage and young adult years working a whole range of tasks for the Cincinnati Reds and later the Houston Astros, Giles knew baseball from the ground up. This discussion of Giles' experiences with the Reds and Astros is largely drawn from his baseball memoir, *Pouring Six Beers at a Time: Stories from a Lifetime in Baseball*. When Giles was just 14 years old, he did sound effects for the radio announcement of a few Cincinnati Reds games. These games were reenacted on radio using ticker-tape, which reported the details of the game as they happened.[2] In 1949, he worked as an assistant to Hank Zureick, the Reds' publicity director, where he mostly did grunt work, like folding and mailing news releases.[3] In 1950, Giles worked in the Reds' ticket office; there, his job was to respond to out-of-town requests for tickets.[4]

In 1954, Giles worked as an assistant to the Reds' farm director, where he organized and filed scouting reports. Giles sometimes read these scouting reports and learned early in life that scouting baseball talent was a very inexact science. He remembered a scouting report on a flamethrowing future Hall of Famer Sandy Koufax that read, "Too wild to make the big leagues as a pitcher, but he can hit and may make it as a first baseman." He also read a scouting report on the indomitable Pete Rose that read, "Not much power, fair speed, heavy legs, big butt—will only make it as a catcher."[5] Later in life, Giles would add to this collection of misleading scouting reports when he was asked to look at a promising third baseman in Corpus Christi, Texas. After watching the prospect play ball, Giles wrote that he "was good enough to hit in the big leagues but would never be able to field his position." The subject of that scouting report was Brooks Robinson,[6] arguably the greatest fielding third baseman of all time.

Gabe Paul, who became General Manager of the Reds in 1951,[7] gave Giles his first substantive assignment.[8] In 1954, Paul asked Giles to briefly run the Reds' minor league team in Morristown, Tennessee, in the Class D Mountain States League. It was in Morristown that Giles learned just how demeaning the low minor leagues could be. Soon after arriving, Giles met the owner, who was an alcoholic, and learned that the team was in dire financial straits. His living and working space consisted of a small room in a dilapidated hotel, which he shared with a player who couldn't find a place to live. The only relief from the oppressive heat was an overhead fan that did little more than circulate the hot air. Ten days after Giles gave a speech about saving baseball in Morristown, the entire league folded, and Giles was on his way back to Cincinnati.

In the fall of 1959, after Giles graduated from college and served three years as a navigator in the Strategic Air Command, Gabe Paul gave Giles his first real opportunity to work as a baseball executive.[9] He was asked to serve as business manager for the Nashville Volunteers, Cincinnati's minor league affiliate in the Southern Association. Given the typical skeletal staffing of minor league teams, Giles was responsible for public relations, promotions, advertising, ticket sales, and concessions.[10] While light years better than his prior position in Morristown, Giles' position with the Volunteers had its own issues. In particular, the ballpark, known as Sulphur Dell, was located next to, and too often downwind from, a waste management site. It was also located near the Cumberland River, which sometimes overflowed its banks and flooded the park. Also, the playing field was peculiar in that the outfield had 45-degree slopes that extended 20-40 feet from the outfield walls. While business manager of the Volunteers, Giles learned that "[y]ou had to be on your toes, hustling, and always selling to keep a minor league team in the black."[11] That lesson would serve him well when he worked in the big leagues.

Giles was in Nashville only one season when Paul asked him to serve as travelling secretary for the Reds for the 1961 season.[12] Paul, who himself had served as a travelling secretary, thought that the experience would be invaluable for Giles, who someday hoped to be a general manager of a big league club.[13] Although Giles had apparently made the acquaintance of several big leaguers in his youth, there were some aspects of their lives that were kept from the young Giles. (However, three players once took the underage Giles to a burlesque house without telling his father.)[14] Serving as travelling secretary would help Giles to get to know the current players better and see how they acted. As Giles interacted with the players over the course of his duties, he found them entertaining and more than once was shocked by their behavior.

When Paul moved to the new Houston franchise in 1962, he asked Giles to come along.[15] After a while, Giles settled into the position of publicity director.[16] When the Astrodome opened in April 1965, Giles was given the additional responsibility of using promotions to attract fans to the ballpark. Not that the new Houston Astros needed to rely heavily on promotions. The Astrodome—the first multipurpose domed stadium in major league baseball—was an attraction in and of itself. Nonetheless, Giles was very creative and aggressive in his promotions. Possibly one of the most popular promotions featured someone known as Rocket Man, an entertainer who would dress up like a spaceman and, using a jet pack attached to his back, fly as high as 150 feet around the Astrodome. He was invited back several times.[17]

In this position, Giles got his first inkling that not all promotions work out as planned[18]—a precursor of things to come. For example, on Flag Day, Giles invited the local Shriners to give a presentation on each of the flags (13 in all) that had flown over the United States. What Giles didn't realize is that they would play the national anthem after presenting each flag. As a result, the approximately 40,000 fans in attendance needed to stand for the "Star Spangled Banner" during each of 13 presentations. Another promotion that misfired featured a golfing trick-shot expert who could hit golf balls from different positions. Problem was that, in so doing, he broke expensive lights on the Astrodome's scoreboard.

Giles made a name for himself while with the Astros and in September 1969, Bob Carpenter, owner of the Philadelphia Phillies, asked him to serve as director of business operations. In this capacity, Giles was responsible for sales, public relations, marketing, stadium operations, radio and television, and promotions.[19] As Giles learned, the Phillies were moving out of antiquated Connie Mack Stadium (formerly Shibe Park) and into a new facility—Veterans Stadium—in 18 months. Over the past five years, attendance at Phillies games had suffered a precipitous decline from about 1.5 million in 1964 to about 519,000 in 1969.[20] As we saw in Chapter 2, Carpenter wanted Giles to improve attendance at Connie Mack Stadium during its last year of use, with the expectation that there would be a carryover when the Phillies opened Veterans Stadium in April 1971.[21]

The Grande Dame of Baseball Stadiums

Shibe Park was built in 1909 for the very popular Philadelphia Athletics.[22] Benjamin Franklin Shibe, who owned the franchise (and after whom the stadium was named) picked a site on Lehigh Avenue, between 20th and 21st Streets, in Philadelphia, "some three miles north of downtown on the fringes of the countryside,"[23] because the land was cheap and was close to public transportation. The land could be purchased inexpensively because it was just one block away from the Philadelphia Hospital for Contagious Diseases, which people avoided for obvious reasons. Shibe had inside information that the hospital was to be torn down, and he purchased the property in parcels and sometimes through associates. He had to buy all the land before the hospital's demise became public information and the price for the land increased.[24]

Shibe Park represented a giant leap forward in the architecture of

At the time of its construction, Shibe Park (later to be renamed Connie Mack Stadium) was the grande dame of major league baseball stadiums. It came to an ignoble end when fans rioted during the last game played on its field (National Baseball Hall of Fame and Museum).

major league baseball stadiums.[25] Up until then, major league baseball ballparks tended to be architecturally unimpressive structures made of wood.[26] In contrast, Shibe Park had a French Renaissance-inspired exterior that was nothing short of opulent for its time. The structure was constructed of 500 tons of steel and several thousand cubic yards of reinforced concrete, using the latest construction technology. As such, Shibe Park was the first of only three baseball stadiums that represent seminal turning points in the history of ballpark design and construction, with the other two being the domed/multipurpose Houston Astrodome and the retro Oriole Park at Camden Yards. All three stadiums changed the landscape for stadiums for decades to come.[27]

As described by James Lincoln Ray, in his article "Connie Mack Stadium (Philadelphia)":

> The exterior of the stadium was more French palace than ballpark. Outside the grandstand, an ornate brick façade had huge arched windows separated by Ionic pilasters, decorative friezes with baseball motifs, and gabled dormer windows on the upper deck's copper-trimmed green-slate mansard roof. Figurative sculptures in terra cotta of Shibe and co-owner/manager Connie Mack peered out over the main entrances.[28]

On the corner of 21st Street and Lehigh Avenue stood a domed tower which housed offices for Shibe's sons, who served as the team's business managers, topped by a domed cupola, which housed Connie Mack's Oval Office. It was, according to the *Philadelphia Public Ledger*, "A palace for fans, the most beautiful and capacious baseball structure in the world."[29]

The first Opening Day at Shibe Park, on April 12, 1909 (which the Athletics won over the Red Sox, 8–1),[30] was not without incident.[31] Apparently, thousands of fans lined up the day of the game to purchase tickets to see the Athletics play their first game at Shibe Park. Fans waiting to purchase their tickets became impatient with the slow movement of the line, which snaked around the stadium. When they started to get rowdy, apprehensive ushers thought it would be safest to close the entrance gates. As things turned out, it wasn't. The line of fans waiting to buy tickets became a howling mob that surged forward into the entrance gates, one of which gave way, permitting hundreds of fans into the ballpark without paying. The 20,000-seat stadium[32] was bursting at its seams to contain that Opening Day crowd. So many fans attended that 7,000 of them, standing seven deep, watched the game from the outfield, held back by a rope. Another 6,000 fans watched the game from the rooftops of buildings that had a view of the stadium.

In addition to the riot, an on-the-field injury resulted in the death of an Athletics ballplayer.[33] Athletics catcher Doc Powers, who joined the team in 1901, inadvertently ran into a concrete wall while chasing a pop up. (Note that other stadiums were made of wood so that their walls may have had more give.) After the game, Powers fell ill with intestinal pains. He died two weeks later, having lost a battle with an illness doctors described as "gangrene of the bowels." Some attributed this illness to a sandwich that Powers consumed prior to the game. But others felt just as strongly that his collision with a concrete wall fatally disrupted his digestive tract, leading to his death.

Powers' death notwithstanding, those first few years after the opening of Shibe Park must have been nirvana for Athletics fans.[34] They got to watch one of the best teams in baseball play their home games at arguably the most beautiful baseball stadium in the major leagues. In what is known as Connie Mack's first dynasty, the Athletics won the World Series in 1910, 1911, and 1913, and won the American League pennant in 1914. However, beginning with the 1914 season, storm clouds began to gather. Despite the success of the team on the field, attendance and, with it, revenue began to decline precipitously. Further, the nascent Federal League, which began operations in 1914, sought to induce players from the American and National Leagues to jump to the new league. Despite the threat to blackball players who jumped leagues, two star pitchers for the

Athletics—Albert "Chief" Bender and Eddie Plank—signed with the Federal League in December 1914. Given the franchise's need to generate revenue, Mack decided that it would be better to sell his remaining stars rather than lose them for nothing to the rival league. In short order, Mack dismantled his multi-championship team by selling, among others, future Hall of Famers Eddie Collins, Frank "Home Run" Baker, and Herb Pennock. It didn't take long for the Athletics to run out of gas. In 1915, the team lost 109 games and, in 1916, they finished with a 36–117 record.[35]

After 15 years in the doldrums, Mack, who in 1922 became the majority owner of the Athletics with the passing of Shibe,[36] assembled one of the greatest teams in baseball history.[37] Known as Connie Mack's Second Dynasty, this team contained such future Hall of Famers as Mickey Cochrane, Jimmie Foxx, Lefty Grove, and Al Simmons. With these players leading the way, the Athletics won the World Series in 1929 and 1930 and the American League pennant in 1931. Athletics fans looked forward to a promising future, but it was not to be. The team's financial viability was upended once again, this time by the Great Depression, which started to affect team finances in 1932. From 1933 to 1936, the Athletics attracted fewer than 300,000 fans during three of those seasons; the low point came in 1935, when the team drew only 233,173 fans. The resultant financial pressures left Mack no choice but to, once again, sell off his star players. From 1935 to 1943, the Athletics finished last or next to last in the American League. Indeed, after the 1932 dismantling, the team never again played in the post-season until the Oakland incarnation of the Athletics did so nearly 40 years later from 1971 to 1975.

In 1938, the Philadelphia Phillies, who predate the Athletics as a franchise, moved into Shibe Park, leaving the Baker Bowl, where they previously played their home games.[38] The change in scenery became necessary because the Baker Bowl could no longer meet the needs of a major league team. Due to lack of maintenance and upkeep by the penurious Phillies owners, the ballpark had become dilapidated. It had also experienced two disasters, where portions of the ballpark collapsed, killing 12 and injuring over 200 patrons. The Phillies may not have felt welcome at a stadium that flew several championship pennants for the Athletics and none for the Phillies but, as they say, *any port in a storm*. From 1938 to 1950, both occupants of Shibe Park had unremarkable seasons, although the Athletics were in a crowded pennant race in 1948, ultimately finishing in fourth place. In 1950, the Phillies captured the National League pennant in dramatic come-from-behind fashion over the Brooklyn Dodgers.

After the 1950 season, the redoubtable 87-year-old Mack, who had managed the Athletics for 50 years, decided to retire from baseball.[39] Mack's 50 years at the helm of the Athletics is a major league record; his closest competitor is John McGraw, who managed the New York Giants for 31 years. With the elder Mack's retirement, his sons—Earle and Roy—were left in charge.[40] Hoping to profit from their father's fame, Mack's children renamed Shibe Park to Connie Mack Stadium just before the 1953 season. Despite the changed moniker, only 362,113 fans visited the newly named stadium to see a team that finished the season with a 59–95 record. The situation worsened in 1954, when the Phillies' attendance more than doubled the 304,666 fans that came to the ballpark to see the Athletics. When the team fell heavily into debt, the brothers began feuding with each other and other family members.[41] The handwriting was on the wall; Philadelphia could no longer support two major league baseball teams, and it looked like the Athletics were the odd man out. In August 1954, the owners of the Athletics, heavily in debt to banks, sold the team to industrialist Arnold Johnson, who moved the franchise out west to Kansas City, Missouri, for the 1955 season.[42]

From the 1955 to 1970 seasons, the Phillies were the sole occupants of Connie Mack Stadium.[43] Although changes had been made since its opening, Connie Mack Stadium was still a great place to watch a baseball game.[44] But there were issues. Bob Carpenter, owner of the Phillies, who had purchased Connie Mack Stadium before the 1955 season, learned quickly that upkeep and maintenance costs for the old facility were astronomical. Further, the neighborhood around Connie Mack Stadium had deteriorated dramatically over the years, causing the crime rate to increase; and there was very little parking and poor access to public transportation.[45] Consequently, the stadium was sold and resold several times. Attendance at the stadium was never impressive but tended to reflect the quality of play on the field; when the Phillies had winning records, they tended to draw upwards of 1,000,000 fans, but Phillies teams with losing records drew substantially fewer fans. Carpenter became alarmed when Phillies attendance dropped to only 519,404 in 1969.[46]

The Phillies were slated to move into Veterans Stadium, a new, state-of-the-art ballpark located on the southside of Philadelphia, beginning with the 1971 season. But Bob Carpenter didn't want to wait until then to correct declining attendance. He knew something had to be done before the move, so he called in Giles to work some magic.[47] Giles states in his baseball memoir that he wanted to bring the Phillies' very conservative marketing strategy into a new era where the team's promotions were creative and, when appropriate, involved taking calculated risks.[48] Giles more than met the expectations he met for himself on both fronts. Like Bill Veeck, Giles was a promoter who understood that baseball teams were in the entertainment business. Giles wanted fans leaving the ballpark with the idea that they had thoroughly enjoyed themselves, whether or not the

Phillies won the ballgame.[49] According to Rich Wescott, in his book *Veterans Stadium: Field of Memories*, Giles hoped fans would say, upon leaving the ballpark after a loss, "Gee, it's too bad the Phillies didn't win the game, but we had a good time."[50]

Reckless Abandonment

Giles wanted the last game at Connie Mack Stadium, slated for October 1, 1970, to be well attended. After all, at one time, Connie Mack Stadium was one of the most majestic ballparks in the major leagues and, over its 62 seasons, had been the locale for several memorable major league baseball events.[51] Just to name a few, the Athletics and Phillies had won eight pennants while in residence at Connie Mack Stadium. The stadium was the site for the 1943 and 1952 All-Star Games. In addition, Lou Gehrig on June 3, 1932, hit four home runs and narrowly missed a fifth when Al Simmons made a great running catch at the wall in center field. Ted Williams secured a .406 batting average when he played in a doubleheader at Shibe Park on the last day of the 1941 season. And, in 1964, Sandy Koufax threw a no-hitter, narrowly missing a perfect game when he walked Richie Allen on a full count in the fourth inning.

The stadium's notoriety wasn't limited to major league baseball events.[52] Shibe Park hosted its first Negro League game in 1919 and served as the neutral site for the 1945 Negro League championship series between the Homestead Grays and Cleveland Buckeyes. The Negro League Philadelphia Stars played their home games at Shibe Park in the 1940s, often attracting crowds of more than 10,000 fans. The Philadelphia Eagles played in Shibe Park/Connie Mack Stadium from 1940 through the 1957 season, winning National Football League championships in 1948 and 1949. The stadium was also the locale for several speeches by national politicians, the Ringling Brothers Circus, a presentation by televangelist Billy Graham, and something you don't see very often in Philadelphia—a rodeo.

Giles suspected that, absent some promotion, the last game at Connie Mack Stadium, which pitted the hapless Phillies against the last-place Montreal Expos, on its own wasn't going to bring in the fans.[53] Given attendance at the first two games of the Phillies-Montreal series, Giles was probably right. On September 29, the first game of the series, which the Phillies lost by a 10–3 margin, was attended by a minuscule 1,055 fans. Attendance at the next game on September 30, a 5–4 loss to Montreal, was slightly better; there were 1,186 fans in attendance. This game dropped the Phillies into last place; the only way they would not finish the season in the National League cellar was to win the final game.

The more Giles thought about it, the more he was assured that he was correct in his plans to maximize attendance by pulling out all the stops for what was called Farewell to Connie Mack Stadium.[54] He recounted all the acts he had lined up: Giles had invited all-star baseball players, as well as some of the greatest old-timers to attend. There would also be marching bands and fireworks, and all fans entering the ballpark would receive a certificate verifying that they had attended the Farewell to Connie Mack Stadium. In addition, 5,000 fans would receive complimentary 18-inch wooden seat slats; these were intended for use in repairing seats at Connie Mack Stadium but now served no purpose. The new stadium had plastic seats.[55] After the game, there would be a raffle for stadium memorabilia, including signed jerseys[56] and a new Ford Mustang. What's more, to top everything off, at the conclusion of the event, Councilman Paul D'Ortona would land on the field in the ARCO Go-Patrol helicopter, collect home plate from Connie Mack Stadium, and fly off to Veterans Stadium, where the home plate would be installed, signaling a new era in Phillies baseball.[57]

Event planners generally accept it as a bad omen when members of the medical profession become involved with their event at the outset.[58] That is what happened on Farewell to Connie Mack Stadium night. A fan named Joseph Sohesky of Exton, Pennsylvania, was stabbed in the back while at the box office purchasing a ticket. He was taken to Temple University Hospital, where they addressed his injury and got him back to the ballgame before the first pitch. Further, Joan Rosney, a nurse who also worked at the stadium, begged the planners not to hand out the wooden slats. Over the years, she could see how much trouble rowdy Philadelphia fans got into on their own; she was very concerned what might happen if they were handed what amounted to weapons.

Giles was amazed to see that 31,822 fans showed up for the promotion.[59] As they bought their snacks and drinks prior to the game, fans in attendance were pleased to see that, as part of the promotion, employees manning the promotion were dressed in 1909 garb (when the stadium opened) and they were selling certain items for 1909 prices. Beer and hot dogs were regular price, but other items, such as Crackerjacks and peanuts, were discounted. The regular price for the beer apparently didn't discourage patrons from imbibing. Fans that night consumed about 20,000 cans of beer during the game. (Compare that with the 60,000 cups of beer consumed by a smaller crowd on Ten-Cent Beer Night, discussed in Part III of this book.) That doesn't count the beer they drank before the game at home or at Charlie Quinn's Deep Right Field Café, located just across the street from the stadium. The point of all this is that many of the fans that night ranged from having a beer buzz to being outright drunk.

The fans, now loaded up with hotdogs, Crackerjacks, and beer, found their seats and were ready to enjoy the game and entertainment.[60] Prior to the game, among other acts, they listened to music from the Cardinal Dougherty High School Band, who must have been awed to play before more than 30,000 people, and watched acrobats doing stunts and tricks on old-fashioned bicycles. Just before the game was to start, a 1933 Rolls Royce was driven onto the field with three dignitaries on board. Up until then, the fans behaved like fans in any ballpark around the country. When the dignitaries arrived, the Philadelphia fans booed. (Philadelphia football fans once booed Santa Claus.)[61] The fans then cheered as Claude Passeau, the first Phillies pitcher to notch a win at Connie Mack Stadium, threw the ceremonial first ball.

Giles could see from the outset that the situation in the ballpark that night was becoming dicey.[62] He had anticipated that a large crowd might present problems, so the team hired 200 off-duty police officers to keep the peace. However, the guards were instructed to tread lightly with misbehaving fans who, after all, weren't committing crimes but were just a little overexcited. The police officers apparently took this advice to heart and weren't as strict as they probably should have been when dealing with unruly behavior.

The situation quickly got out of hand.[63] Even before the game started, fans threw the seat slats they received as mementos of the game and other items at the players in the bullpen and outfield. While shagging fly balls before the game, Jackie Donnelly was hit in the head by a bolt that was removed from a seat. Phillies pitcher Chris Short complained that he was hit in the foot by beer cans on two occasions, both thrown by the same guy. Throughout the game, fans in the stands managed to elude security and run onto the field, forcing umpires to stop the game until the miscreants could be removed. In the eighth inning, five fans ran onto the field, ostensibly in search of souvenirs.

When parts of stadium seats started flying onto the field, it became apparent that the fans were literally removing the seats and possibly dismantling other stadium fixtures.[64] Some fans came prepared to remove seats, which they apparently saw as the ultimate souvenir. They brought hammers, pliers, screwdrivers, wrenches,[65] and other tools into the ballpark for that purpose. Other fans simply used makeshift tools, such as the slats, to hammer out the seats. Others just rocked the stadium seats back and forth until they became loosened from their moorings. The mob also dislodged pipes, wooden signs, and concession equipment.[66] Some fans, who were apparently nostalgic regarding the stadium's restrooms, stole urinals and a toilet.[67] The offices[68] and locker rooms,[69] which were guarded by police, were the only two areas the vandals were unable to get into. Still, according to Giles, those working in the press box could feel the stadium shaking; they and stadium employees were "scared to death."[70] To the players, it likely sounded like workmen had jumped the gun and were dismantling the stadium while they were playing the game.

According to Jack McCafferty, in his article, "All of 50 years later, Bowa and Vankowski can't forget Phillies' last hours at Connie Mack Stadium," the umpires met in the eighth inning with Philadelphia manager Frank Lucchesi and Montreal manager Gene Mauch, who was familiar with Connie Mack Stadium, having once managed the Phillies.[71] The Phillies led, 1–0. Given that the crowd was out of control, the umpires suggested forfeiting the game to the visiting Expos. Mauch, who was aware of the volatility of Phillies fans, advised against such a move, fearing that it would cause a riot. Instead, they decided to call the game at the end of the 10th inning if no team won by then.[72]

According to David White, in his article "The Graveyard of Baseball: October 1, 1970 was a day that will live in infamy," an instance of fan interference in the ninth inning caused the umpiring crew to request that an announcement be made over the public address system.[73] With a man on base, Expos catcher John Bateman hit a deep, routine fly ball; Phillies left fielder Ron Stone readied himself on the warning track to catch the ball. But before he could secure the ball in his glove, a youngster grabbed his arm, yelling, "Great game, great game!" causing him to misplay the ball. What should have been a routine out became a game-tying RBI double, as a baserunner made it home and Bateman scampered around to second base.[74] The umpires had seen enough. They instructed the stadium announcer, Art Wolfe, to announce over the public address system that the Phillies would forfeit the game if there was any more fan interference.[75]

The public address announcement worked ... for a while.[76] For the next inning and a half, the fans did not disturb the game, possibly because they did not want to cause a forfeit. In the bottom of the 10th inning, with the score tied at 1–1, Phillies right fielder Oscar Gamble hit a single up the middle, scoring catcher Tim McCarver from second. The hit was momentous; not only did the Phillies win the game, but the win lifted the team out of last place and into fifth place. The Phillies started to leave the dugout *en masse* to congratulate Gamble for his walk-off hit and otherwise celebrate a positive ending to what was a long season.

Their celebration was not to be.[77] Thousands of fans, apparently also elated by the Phillies' win, poured onto the field. The guards, who had trouble keeping individuals and small groups of fans off the field during the game, were overwhelmed by the mass exodus of fans from their seats onto the playing field. They managed to form a cordon around home plate, where Bill Giles, realizing that stadium authorities had lost control, pleaded with the mob to leave the field so post-game festivities could commence. Oscar Gamble saw the massive wave of fans pouring onto the field; after touching first, he made a beeline for the Phillies' dugout, grabbing manager Franck Lucchesi along the way. He reportedly told Lucchesi, "Run, man, run like hell. We'll be happy later." Tim McCarver, the other Phillies player on the field, likewise saw the mob and started running for the dugout and the safety of the clubhouse. He later said, "I've never been afraid to admit that I am a coward in a mob." Phillies coach Billy DeMars was hit in the back by a karate chop. When a fan tried to grab Phillies pitcher Bill Wilson's hat, scratching him in the process, he responded by knocking the miscreant down and punching him a few times.

With Giles looking on, the fans on the field completely looted and trashed the ballpark.[78] With this riot, Connie Mack Stadium, which you will remember experienced a riot on its opening day, came full circle. The guards hired for the occasion were powerless to stop the mob, which ransacked the dugouts and bullpens, stealing helmets, bats, and anything else that the players and coaches left behind in their haste to exit the field. The rioters rolled out the infield tarpaulin and ripped it up into small pieces, convenient to take home as souvenirs. They ripped boards from the outfield wall. Rapacious fans even dug up sod from the outfield and dirt from the infield, and they stole the bases and the pitching rubber. Throughout this rampage, the guards maintained their cordon around home plate, ensuring its safety.

Once they had finished trashing the field and stealing everything that wasn't too hot or too heavy to carry, the fans in the field turned their weapons, particularly the slats, on each other.[79] In what amounted to a full-blown riot, countless fans were injured, 25 of whom needed assistance in the infirmary. Nurse Rosney, who predicted this carnage, characterized the evening's events as "Unreal, horrible." She added, "I thought this might happen. Especially with those planks. They're worse than beer cans. Heads were slashed open.... It was truly horrible." Eventually, the riot spun itself out, and many of the fans took their ill-gotten booty and left the stadium. At that point, it was safe for guards to usher the remaining people out. There was no widespread reporting of arrests. However, in the aftermath of the riot, Temple University Hospital treated the nine most severe injury cases. These unfortunates were joined by a 65-year-old gentleman who was swept into the melee and suffered a stroke.

Giles had no choice but to cancel the post-game festivities; instead, he pondered the need for a post-game clean-up.[80] The ARCO Go-Patrol helicopter arrived as planned but was waved off. Cleared of the rioters, Giles looked onto a baseball field that had been totally trashed. In addition to what had been ripped up or ripped off, the field was covered with divots where fans had dug up dirt or sod. It was littered with cups, bottles, wrappers, and whatever other garbage the rioters had left behind. The stands were marred by seats that had been removed from their moorings and often left elsewhere by fans who realized they had no way to take them home. As it turns out, the Phillies, who had discontinued their insurance coverage for the last few games of the season as a money-saving measure, were responsible for paying for the cleanup. As a final gesture to underserving fans, Giles decided to go ahead with the raffle of the Ford Mustang, which was won by John O. Hoover of Glenside, Pennsylvania.

In the days following the final game, the newspapers predicably expressed dismay and bewilderment at the events that night.[81] The *Philadelphia Daily News* expressed the views of other newspapers by exclaiming that the fans had "raped" the stadium and characterizing the riot as a "homicide." John Dell of the *Philadelphia Inquirer* confused ancient history a bit when he wrote, "It was the greatest day for vandals since the Huns played Rome." One letter writer tried to put the melee in perspective by arguing that the destruction was just payback for many years of mediocre baseball.

POSTSCRIPT: In 1971, Connie Mack Stadium, the *grande dame* of major league stadiums, experienced a fire that left it a hulking mass of concrete and twisted metal spires.[82] Under a court order, the stadium was demolished in 1976, to be replaced by Deliverance Evangelistic Church.[83] Several of the seats unaffected by vandalism and fire were removed and sent to minor league baseball facilities in Greensboro, North Carolina, and Spartanburg, South Carolina, where, as of this writing, they are still in use.[84]

Kiteman's Fall from Grace

Giles was raised in Cincinnati, where Opening Day was treated as a holiday.[85] According to Giles, "Schools were closed; they had a big parade downtown; there were bands and banners; and politicians spoke. The game was sold out. Opening Day was almost as big a deal in Cincinnati as Christmas." When Giles arrived in Philadelphia, he researched Opening Day attendance at Connie Mack Stadium and found it to be poorly attended. He asked around about whether the Phillies did anything special for Opening Day; those in the know responded, "Well, we have the Salvation Army Band and salute the American flag. Some city council guy throws out the first ball."

After a very successful first Opening Day at Veterans Stadium (discussed in Chapter 2), Giles pondered what to do for the second Opening

Day in 1972.[86] It had to be something splashy to bring the fans in. It had to be something memorable. As Giles was pondering this Opening Day conundrum, he happened to read an article in *Sports Illustrated* about a stunt man, using the moniker of Kiteman, who jumped off mountains with a giant kite on his back, sailed majestically through the air, and landed safely on the ground. Giles envisioned Kiteman jumping off the roof of Veterans Stadium and gliding down to the infield, where he would deliver the first ball. Giles obtained Kiteman's contact information and called him, asking him to fly (by plane, of course) from his home in Seattle to Philadelphia. Giles had a proposition. Better yet, Giles hoped to make Kiteman the kind of offer he couldn't refuse.

With Kiteman in Philadelphia, Giles explained what he had in mind for Opening Day 1972.[87] Kiteman was intrigued, and he agreed to perform the flight if Giles would build an 80-foot ramp on top of the seats in right field. The idea was that Kiteman would slide on water skis down the ramp and, in the process, get sufficient draft under his kite to airlift him for his flight down to the infield. Giles and Kiteman came to an agreement. A month before Opening Day, Giles arranged for a ramp to be built over the seats in right field at a cost of about $5,000. The ramp stood at the ready. Unfortunately, major league baseball players went on strike that year, delaying Opening Day by a week. When Giles contacted Kiteman to tell him of the delay, Kiteman responded that he was unavailable on the rescheduled Opening Day because he had a prior commitment to teach the president of Mexico how to waterski.

Well, as Hardy would say to Laurel, "Here's another fine mess you've gotten me into." Giles knew that the show must go on.[88] The Phillies had heavily advertised that Kiteman would perform on Opening Day. But where to find another Kiteman who, as one would imagine, was one of a kind? Giles, in *Serving Six Beers at a Time: Stories from a Lifetime in Baseball*, wrote that he scoured the Philadelphia Yellow Pages, but there was no Kiteman to be found. Then, out of the blue, Giles got a phone call from a man who owned a hardware store in Paoli (a Main Line suburb of Philadelphia) who knew someone who might fill in for the original Kiteman. He recommended that Giles contact his friend, Richard Johnson, who flew while attached to kites for a show in Cypress Gardens, Florida.

Giles, who at this point was short on time and desperate, got right on it.[89] He contacted Johnson in Florida, who was amenable to flying (once again, by plane) to Philadelphia to discuss what Giles had in mind. When Johnson visited Veterans Stadium, Giles explained the stunt, for which Johnson would receive $1,000, and showed him the ramp. Johnson was wary of sliding down the ramp but had another suggestion. He proffered the idea that a car could pull him while he was wearing roller skates outside of Veterans Stadium. While being pulled, he would get enough draft under his kite to sail up and over the roof of the stadium, and glide down to deliver the first ball. Giles liked the idea enough to run it by Philadelphia police chief Frank Rizzo, who rejected the plan because it would disrupt traffic. Giles was once again at square one.

Painfully aware that Philadelphia fans might react poorly if the promised Kiteman didn't materialize, Giles approached Johnson again, but this time upped the renumeration to $1,500.[90] No one knows whether it was the increased pay or Giles' look of desperation that swayed Johnson, but he agreed to slide down the ramp on Opening Day. Giles, who was relieved to have a Kiteman, asked him if he would like to take some practice runs. Johnson declined, saying, "Mr. Giles, if I am going to kill myself, I want someone other than just you watching me."

Then came the big day: Opening Day, April 17, 1972, Phillies versus the St. Louis Cardinals.[91] About 38,000 people came through the turnstiles at Veterans Stadium on a cool and windy night. Giles was all ready for Kiteman's big event; he hoped Kiteman was also ready. Giles sent one of his sales agents, Paul Callahan (remember the man in the bunny suit for the Highest Jumping Bunny promotion?) to accompany Kiteman to his ramp in the upper deck of the stadium, while Giles went into the public announcer's booth, where he would orchestrate the Kiteman show. As luck would have it, Dan Baker, the Phillies' public address announcer, had worked in the daredevil circuit in New England, announcing Evel Knievel and other stuntmen, so he knew how to introduce the Kiteman's jump in a way that got the crowd excited with anticipation.

According to Giles' baseball memoir, *Pouring Six Beers at a Time: Stories from a Lifetime in Baseball*,[92] the event transpired as follows:

> "Never before seen in a major league stadium," Baker said, his voice booming out across the Vet, "the world-renowned Kiteman will fly high above the stadium to deliver the first ball of the 1972 season." He had worked out a 30-second introduction that built to a crescendo—a peak of emotion to get the fans revved up—closing with: "Here's the Kiteman!"
>
> The organist did a drum roll.
> The fans stared anxiously at the ramp in right field.
> The Kiteman did not move.
> I turned to Baker and said, "He must not be able to hear us. Introduce him again."
> Baker said, "Ladies and gentlemen, the Kiteman is summoning up the courage to take on this death-defying stunt." He went through yet another intro that built to yet another peak, then finally said, "Here's the Kiteman!"
> The organist did yet another drumroll.
> The Kiteman still did not move.

You have to understand Phillies fans. They are not the most patient people in the world. They were already booing.

I got on the walkie-talkie with Callahan and asked, "Does he hear the PA?"

"Yes, he hears it."

"Well, then what's the problem?"

"The problem? The problem is that he's scared to death. He's frozen."

In a touching display of sensitivity and sympathy, I told Callahan, "Give him a little push."

But Callahan couldn't give him a push because he was down in the front row of the upper deck in the 500 Level, having been given explicit orders by Kiteman to catch him if he wasn't airborne by then. Little did Kiteman know that Callahan had already figured out that if you grab someone skiing down a ramp before he goes over an upper deck railing, you're going over with him. Kiteman had only 48 rows of seats to get airborne or he'd be falling into the lower level—Callahan or no Callahan.

Kiteman finally started down the ramp on his water skis. Halfway down the 600 level, a gust of wind knocked him sideways off the ramp. He crashed through row after row of seats and into the railing of the upper deck.

I thought he was dead.

The fans were booing lustily.

Callahan, having figured that Kiteman had at least two broken legs and possibly a broken back, rushed over to him. Someone had to throw out the first ball, you understand, and it was taped to the kite.

"Give me the ball," Callahan said.

"That's my job," Kiteman replied.

Miraculously, Kiteman got to his feet and heaved the ball—as if he thought it would sail to the pitcher's mound from the 500 Level. It ended up in the Phillies bullpen behind the outfield fence.

The fans booed even louder.

As for me, I was just relieved that he was alive. Generally speaking, a dead body is not a good omen for the start of a baseball season.

POSTSCRIPT: Undeterred by the unfortunate fate of Kiteman in 1972, Giles reprised the promotion on several occasions.[93] In 1973, Kiteman II's attempt to deliver the ball to home plate ended in a crash landing in the stands in left-center field. In 1980, Kiteman III made it to center field. In 1990, a Kiteman named Pete Bonifay was the first to make it all the way to the pitcher's mound. Bonifay also successfully delivered the first ball in 1995, 1999, and 2003. Turns out that a successful Kiteman promotion was not necessarily an omen of a successful season. The Phillies had losing records in 1990, 1995, and 1999. The team did complete the 2003 season with a winning record of 86–76.[94]

◊ CHAPTER 6 ◊

Turner and Hope Run Amok with Baseball's Dignity
Wedlock and Headlock Day and Wet T-Shirt Night

Ted Turner and Bob Hope/Atlanta Braves

Wedlock and Headlock Day	Wet T-Shirt Night
New York Mets at Atlanta Braves	Chicago Cubs at Atlanta Braves
Atlanta-Fulton County Stadium	
July 11, 1976	May 20, 1977

When he purchased the Atlanta Braves franchise in January 1976, Ted Turner acknowledged that he knew little about baseball, but his lack of knowledge did not trouble him. Turner had a track record of turning businesses he owned into a rousing success, even when he was new to the industry. He anticipated that, despite his lack of experience in baseball, he could work his magic with the Braves. However, he soon found owning a major league franchise to be a far greater challenge than he counted on. Despite his infectious enthusiasm, motivating skills, and eagerness to spend money on talent, the team floundered. The more superstitious observers may point out that, soon after his purchase, the Braves were publicly cursed by someone believing herself to be a witch. More likely, the challenge resulted from Turner's difficulty maneuvering in the idiosyncratic world of professional baseball, which constrained his management style. Recognizing that, for the time being, the Braves themselves weren't going to attract enough fans to keep the franchise in the black, Turner unleashed his director of public relations, Bob Hope, to drum up attendance by using in-game promotions to market the team. Among the many noteworthy promotions sponsored by the Braves from 1976 to 1979, when Hope left the team, Turner and Hope conspired to sponsor two outrageous promotions—Wedlock and Headlock Day and Wet T-Shirt Night—the latter of which may be the most tasteless promotion ever held by a major league franchise.

The Business Whiz from Cincinnati

Robert Edward "Ted" Turner III was born on November 19, 1938, in Cincinnati, Ohio, to what would become an affluent family.[1] Sometime prior to 1947, Turner's father purchased a billboard advertising company[2] that turned out to be quite profitable. Despite the family's comfortable lifestyle,[3] Turner's childhood was troubled. His father was domineering and ran the family as his personal fiefdom. He was an alcoholic and heavy smoker who, despite his drinking, managed to run a mid-sized business.[4] Ted Turner's autobiography, *Call Me Ted*, serves as the source for much of the following discussion of his pre-baseball life and career.

Turner's father sent him away throughout his childhood and adolescence to several boarding schools, where he was often lonely and bullied, and developed a mischievous streak. When Turner was only four years old, his father joined the military and sent Turner to a boarding school in Cincinnati, where he was extremely unhappy.[5] His unhappiness must have been apparent to his family, who then sent him to live with his fraternal grandparents in Mississippi.[6] The following year, Turner's father returned from the military and reunited his family in Cincinnati, where Turner attended a public school for kindergarten and, for first grade, a private school, called Lotspeich.[7] At this private school, Turner started to get a reputation for mischief-making, nothing serious but enough for school administrators to ask that Turner not return for the following school year.[8] From there, Turner attended a local public school, Avondale, where he continued his antics but managed to stay, largely because it was harder to get expelled from a public school.[9]

Turner attended school at Avondale until early in fifth grade, when, in October 1947, his parents moved from Cincinnati to Savannah, Georgia. Rather than take him with them, Turner's father sent him away to the Georgia Military Academy to complete fifth grade. There, the largely Southern student population seemed to go out of their way to make a Yankee miserable.[10] Apparently recognizing that the military academy was not a good fit for their son, his parents permitted him to come home once again and attend sixth grade at a public school in Savannah.[11] But that was short-lived; for seventh grade, Turner's father sent him to the McCallie Military Academy in Chattanooga, Tennessee. There, he honed his troublemaking skills to a fine art. All in good fun, he and his partners in crime would leave containers of water on the top of an open door so that, when someone passed through, the water would fall on their head; throw paper sacks full of water down from upper floors onto unsuspecting victims; and once let a pack of squirrels loose in a building.[12] After three-plus years of poor behavior, bad grades, and demerits, Turner made a complete turnaround at McCallie and, thereon in, became a model student.[13]

Despite graduating McCallie with a "C" average,[14] Turner managed to get accepted to Brown University. While his family lived in Savannah, Turner became adept at sailing. At Brown, he joined the sailing team and honed his seaman skills.[15] However, after being a model student for a while, he fell in with the heaviest drinking crowd in the school and at full throttle managed to get in all sorts of trouble. Unlike the Georgia and McCallie military academies, Brown did not have strict institutional rules that might keep Turner in line.[16] One night, Turner and his pals visited nearby Wheaton College (then a women's school) where, inebriated, they threw chairs out of dormitory windows. Brown University suspended Turner for his part in this activity, so he joined the Coast Guard as a reservist for six months.[17] After completing his responsibility to the Coast Guard, Turner returned to Brown. However, after he informed his father of his intention to major in classics, the elder Turner refused to continue paying for his college education.[18] Turner returned to his wanton ways (even getting suspended again for having a girl in his room) and eventually ran out of money.[19]

Turner left Brown without obtaining a degree and joined his father's billboard business. He enjoyed working for his father, who gave him significant responsibility despite his being only 21 years old.[20] This time, however, proved to be the calm before the storm. In 1962, the elder Turner participated in a major acquisition of a rival billboard company that made him owner of the largest such company in the South.[21] It was a shrewd business move, but Turner's father started to become unnerved by the size of the transaction. Although nothing was amiss, he seemed to fear that he wouldn't be able to repay loans his company took out to make the purchase, and he would lose everything. The father's behavior became more erratic than usual. About six months after the acquisition,[22] the strain apparently became more than the elder Turner could bear, and he took his own life.[23]

Turner found himself owner of a major billboard company, doing business throughout the United States. Despite his relative youth, Turner masterfully grew the company and stabilized its finances.[24] But Turner started to perceive turbulent waters ahead for the billboard industry. Lady Bird Johnson, the President's wife, saw billboards as an eyesore and sought to eradicate them from highways. Although the eventual law passed by

Congress—the Highway Beautification Act—was significantly watered down, permitting billboards in commercial and industrial areas along highways, Turner saw the handwriting on the wall. It was time to diversify with new ways to advertise. At first, Turner purchased several radio stations, but he wanted something more.[25] The wave of the future in advertising was television, and Turner was intrigued by its potential.[26]

By the mid-1960s, the interest in sailing that he nurtured while an adolescent in Savannah became an all-consuming passion.[27] Said Turner, "my passion for sailing grew to be nearly as intense as my drive to succeed in business." At the time, Turner owned a Flying Dutchman, basically a small, two-man boat. While he experienced success sailing a small boat, Turner felt his skills were more suited to the ocean racing done in large boats. Later, he chartered a Block Island 40 which, at 40 feet in length, was much bigger than anything he had sailed before. Turner raced in the Southern Ocean Racing Conference (SORC), where his boat at first performed poorly but did manage to win a few trophies for second- and third-place finishes. Consumed by the sport, Turner decided to buy his own boat—a Cal 40 39-foot sloop made of fiberglass. With this boat, everything came together, and Turner won the overall SORC championship.

Turner's billboard company purchased a local UHF (Ultra High Frequency) television station, WJRJ, and changed the call letters to WTCG, which stood for Turner Communications Group.[28] About six months after buying WTCG, Turner used his own money to purchase another station, which he renamed WRET, which happened to be his initials.[29] He was able to afford these stations because UHF television utilized a new broadcasting technology whose signal could only be captured by homes with special antennas. A station that used the more common VHF (Very High Frequency) signal available to virtually all homes was out of Turner's price range.[30] Nevertheless, UHF proved to be a sound investment since its use in the United States was on the rise.[31]

This was a brand-new industry to Turner, but he attacked it with gusto, determined to be a success.[32] While he understood the advertising aspects of the business, he was a neophyte when it came to all-important programming.[33] Turner remedied that deficiency and, over the years, obtained the rights to broadcast popular shows, movies, and sporting events over his stations.[34] One of his biggest coups was to obtain the right to broadcast 60 Atlanta Braves games per season. By 1973, Turner's stations were moving into profitability.[35]

According to Turner in his autobiography, *Call Me Ted*, he never intended to buy the Atlanta Braves; the sale was just thrust upon him.[36] Late in the 1975 season, Turner was concerned that the Braves were doing poorly both in games and at the gate. When he asked Dan Donahue, the team president, whether he had any plans for improving the team for the next season, Donahue stunned Turner by responding that he planned to sell the team. When Turner asked whether he had a buyer, Donahue responded that he planned to sell the team to Turner. This was the first Turner had heard about the possibility that he might own the Braves. After giving it some thought, Turner agreed to purchase the Braves prior to the 1976 season for $10 million, with $1 million down and the remainder to be paid over nine years.

Turner's Wizardry Fizzles with the Braves

Turner, who in his young life had achieved success in billboard advertising, broadcasting, and yacht racing, anticipated that he would also be a successful owner of the Braves. When he applied his "dedication, motivation, smarts and plain old hard work," he could accomplish anything he put his mind to.[37] Turner knew perfectly well that he had purchased a team with a losing record. The 1975 team, which finished 67–94, suffered from a "[l]ack of effort, lack of speed, [and] lack of leadership."[38] Confident in his leadership abilities, at his first press conference after buying the Braves, Turner told those in attendance that his goal was to bring a championship to Atlanta in five years.[39] Turner "assumed baseball would be no different [from my prior endeavors]."

Just in case enthusiasm alone didn't make for a winning team in the major leagues, Turner figured that he would augment the team's talent. He sought the advice of baseball insiders on how to improve the Braves. Many of these sages told Turner that strong pitching would play a key role in improving the Braves' fortunes on the field. Turner looked around for available pitching and set his sights on free agent Andy Messersmith, who at the time was considered to be one of the finest pitchers in the major leagues.[40] Many other owners would have nothing to do with Messersmith because he was one of the players that successfully brought down the reserve system that tied players to their teams.[41] Turner didn't care about all that; he was willing to forgive and forget if it would improve the Braves. After Messersmith rejected a perfectly good contract offer from the Yankees because, among other things, it contained a clause requiring that he keep his hair short and remain clean-shaven, Turner, who after all had a mustache himself, signed Messersmith for the tidy sum of $1 million over three years.[42]

Under Turner, the Braves also sought to strengthen their everyday players. The Braves obtained for the 1976 season infielder Darrel Chaney of the National League champion Cincinnati Reds. They added from the

Dodgers outfielder Lee Lacey, outfielder and first baseman Tom Paciorek, infielder Jerry Royster, and outfielder Jimmy "the Toy Cannon" Wynn; and from the White Sox, they signed all-star outfielder Ken Henderson. In June 1976, the Braves obtained Willie Montanez from the Giants.[43] That season, the Braves finished with a 70–92 record. They initially enjoyed an 8–6 record, but then then went on a 13-game losing streak that all but cemented their cellar-dweller status. The Braves lost every game from April 27 to May 10, and they continued to play poorly for the remainder of the season.[44] And they continued to post losing records through 1981.[45]

According to Hope, in his book *We Could Have Finished Last Without You*, "[o]n paper, the Braves couldn't lose. On the field, it was the first season in last place. And they continued in last place for the next four seasons."[46] Why this discrepancy between the talent of the Braves players and their record as a team? Some commentators suggested that the reasons are within the realm of the supernatural. Others argued, more prosaically, that Turner was constrained from running his team by the rules governing the activities of major league owners. Could it be that both are true?

The Whammy on Turner's New Team

One must ask: Why, despite Turner's apparently well-reasoned efforts to turn the Braves around, did the team flounder on the field for the first five years of his ownership? One possible answer: the team was cursed.

Turner, on April 24, 1976, fired Donald Davidson, a longtime Braves front office official. His wife, who just happened to dabble in the occult, cursed the Braves.[47] Donald Davidson had been with the Braves in various capacities for 38 years, since they were the Boston Braves. Over the course of his career, he served in many roles, including bat boy, traveling secretary, public relations director, and vice president. Over the years, Davidson had done a lot of favors for others associated with the team, who were no doubt beholden to him.[48] Davidson didn't approve of Turner from the moment he became aware of him as owner. Davidson was "old school," a traditionalist who didn't appreciate Turner's "show biz" approach to his role as a major league owner. Davidson was particularly opposed to the use of promotions to market the team. Davidson, who saw baseball as a sacrosanct institution, believed that baseball could sell itself, as it had done for generations. Promotions were superfluous at best and, at worst, sullied the sanctity of the game.[49]

Apparently believing that his long tenure with the team ensured his continued employment, Davidson seemed to go out of his way to antagonize Turner. Once, he approached Turner and pronounced, "Don't expect me to be a yes man around here."[50] Then there was the issue of transportation and lodging. Davidson, who made all the Braves' travel arrangements, insisted on using limousines, flying first class, and residing at VIP suites at hotels where players stayed in lesser rooms.[51] Davidson felt his use of the suites was justified for public relations reasons.[52] Hope suggests that such transportation and lodging were sometimes given by travel companies to Davidson free of charge as a thank you for using their services to transport and lodge the team.[53] After several discussions about this practice, Turner, who expected his front office employees to be restrained when spending money on transportation and lodging, made clear that he disapproved of Davidson's use of first-class travel arrangements and prohibited him from this style of travel, even if it was provided free of charge. Yet Davidson persisted in doing so. After a confrontation in the lobby of a Philadelphia hotel, Turner summarily fired Davidson. He called Davidson at his suite and said, "It's over, Davidson. Get your bags packed and get out of town."[54] Davidson was the only team employee Turner ever fired.[55]

Almost immediately, the press came to the defense of Davidson, who had worked with members of the fourth estate for decades. Melvin Durslag wrote in the *Los Angeles Herald Examiner*, "Turner gives Andy Messersmith upward of a million dollars—and he would reduce the living standard of Donald Davidson. Why Messersmith deserved a massive bonus and doubling of his salary ... will never be known. But he got it from Mr. Turner, who begrudged a suite and breakfast on a tray in a style to which [Davidson] had become accustomed."[56] Perhaps the article that perturbed Turner the most was penned by Frank Hyland, one of Davidson's closest friends, in the *Atlanta Journal-Constitution*. He wrote about the Davidson affair, "Ted Turner has money. Ted Turner has a lot of money. Ted Turner has enthusiasm. Ted Turner has his own baseball team. Ted Turner belongs to some of the world's most prestigious clubs. But *Ted Turner has no class.*"[57] [Emphasis added.]

While the frigid reception Turner's firing of Davidson received from the press caused the bloom to fall off the rose, Davidson's wife apparently sought to kill the whole plant. Some of those who knew her suggested that Patti Davidson dabbled in the occult. She was apparently so upset with Turner's treatment of her husband that she put a hex on the team.[58] Even those of you who don't believe in hexes could concede that the curse placed on the Braves may have affected the team's play on the field. Baseball players tend to be a superstitious lot who may subconsciously be influenced by the supernatural. Remember, it was soon after Davidson was fired that the Braves lost 13 games in a row.

Turner's Management Style: You Can't Do That

For those of us who don't believe in hexes, there may be a more matter-of-fact reason why the Braves played so poorly during Turner's initial years. The powers that be in major league baseball at the time disapproved of Turner's effervescent ownership style, and they often thwarted Turner from doing what he felt he needed to do to motivate and better understand his team.

First, there was the incident involving the Braves' first home run of the 1976 season. While most owners watch their team from glass-enclosed skyboxes, Turner argued that doing so was akin to kissing someone through a window. Instead, for the first game of the season, Turner took a seat close to the field, right next to the Braves' dugout.[59] Remember, this was Turner's first in-season game as owner, and he might have been a little excited to begin with. In the bottom of the second inning against the Cincinnati Reds, Braves outfielder Ken Henderson came up to bat. The Braves had acquired the talented Henderson in the offseason, and a buzz of anticipation encircled the stadium as he took his practice swings. All eyes were on Henderson as he hit the Braves' first home run of the season.[60] As he rounded the bases, the fans cheered, whooped, and hollered. As Henderson approached home plate, he saw a tall, mustachioed man not in a baseball uniform standing at home plate. Turner had become so excited at the site of the ball flying over the field and landing in the stands that he jumped the railing and stood at home plate waiting to shake Henderson's hand.[61] Spurred on by unbridled enthusiasm, Turner apparently just wanted to congratulate Henderson on his home run and, in so doing, motivate him (as well as his teammates) to hit more of them. Could that be so wrong?

Other major league owners, who may have felt that it was unseemly to show unbridled enthusiasm for their teams, didn't take kindly to the handshake.[62] When the Braves visited the Reds at Riverfront Stadium, Reds management gave Turner a seat near the field adjacent to the Braves' dugout, as he requested. However, for the duration of the game, a member of the security team stood guard facing Turner with his back to the field. According to Turner, the Reds placed him there with specific orders to keep Turner off the field, and they notified the Brave's promotion department that, should Turner have the audacity to enter the field of play, he would be arrested. One must wonder if the Reds' security guard would have really restrained Turner, a major league owner, and had him carted him off to jail as if he were some common trespasser. I guess we'll never know because Turner never reprised his congratulatory escapade.

Second, there was the incident involving Turner's efforts to bring

6 • Turner and Hope Run Amok with Baseball's Dignity

Gary Matthews from the San Francisco Giants to the Braves for the 1977 season. Turner had just hired John Alevizos from the Boston Red Sox to serve as the Braves' general manager. Turner was impressed by Alevizos' in-depth knowledge of the game, but the new general manager, out of the chute, may have been too aggressive in trying to improve the Braves. Alevizos had spoken with San Francisco left fielder Gary Matthews about becoming a Brave, but before he was a free agent. Commissioner of Baseball Bowie Kuhn flagged Alevizos' encounter with Matthews as a violation of baseball's tampering policy and fined the team $10,000.[63] Turner, in his enthusiasm to improve his team, made a bad situation worse. At a cocktail party held in conjunction with the 1976 World Series, Turner was chatting with Bob Lurie, owner of the Giants. He told Lurie that, no matter what the Giants offered Matthews for the 1977 season and beyond, the Braves would offer more. Turner was talking loudly enough for others to overhear the conversation.[64]

Lurie filed a complaint with Commissioner Kuhn, who called Turner into his headquarters in New York to, shall we say, call him on the carpet. Kuhn told Turner that, because of repeat offenses (Turner had surreptitiously tried to advertise one of his television stations on the uniform of Andy Messersmith.),[65] Kuhn was going to suspend him for a year and take away the Braves' first draft choice.[66] Turner wasn't concerned about the year suspension. He had planned to devote the entire baseball season to racing his yacht in the America's Cup competition, and the suspension gave him an excuse not to be with the team. But Turner was upset about the team losing its first draft choice.[67] The Braves continued to play woeful baseball, and that draft choice gave it the opportunity to bring onboard a potential star player. So Turner litigated the matter.[68]

While Turner waited for the judge's decision, he became embroiled in the third incident. The Braves lost 16 straight games, and Turner was at his wits end trying to understand why a team of talented players should fare so poorly. Turner was the first to admit that he had a lot to learn about baseball at the major league level. What better way to get firsthand experience about the players on your team, their talents and deficiencies, than to manage a few games? Turner's first and last experience managing the Braves happened on May 11, 1977, in a game against the Pittsburgh Pirates. Turner thought of firing the manager, Dave Bristol, but decided just to give him a few weeks off, tell everyone that he was on a "scouting" trip, and serve as skipper.[69] Other than Bristol, Turner told no one of his plans.[70] Turner probably didn't know any more than the average fan regarding the nuts and bolts of in-game management, so he relied on third base coach Vern Benson and bullpen coach Chris Cannizzaro, who both spent time in the dugout that evening, to explain things to him.[71] Turner was clueless about how to communicate with the team in the field, so he informed one of the coaches about in-game maneuvers, and the coach would signal the players in the field. Since Phil Niekro, the pitcher that evening, threw a complete game, Turner didn't have to leave the dugout to replace the pitcher. All in all, a pretty easy night. Unfortunately, the Braves lost the game, 2–1.[72]

Once again, the baseball establishment took a dim view of Turner's effort to manage his team. The morning after his managing stint, Turner received a telegram from National League president Chub Feeney instructing Turner to cease and desist all in-game management activities.[73] Feeney, who was supported in this decision by Kuhn, informed Turner that anyone who owns stock in a team is prohibited from managing it.[74] It is hard to tell how much Turner would have learned about his players had he continued managing games. But there is no doubt that he would have learned something that improved his ability to run the Braves franchise, even if he only learned just how complicated in-game management was in the major leagues. At any rate, soon after this third incident, the judges made a ruling regarding Turner's tampering situation. They decided that the suspension would stand, but the Braves would not lose their first draft pick in 1978.[75] The decision worked for Turner, who was able to keep his draft pick and spend the next year sailing without anyone being the wiser.

In amongst the hexes and baseball establishment efforts to undermine Turner's efforts to better understand and improve his ball club, Bob Hope was busy coming up with promotions to attract fans to the ballpark. As we have seen in Chapter 2, many of Hope's promotions were innovative and entertaining. But he collaborated with his boss on two that were outrageous—Wedlock and Headlock Day and Wet T-Shirt Night. Regarding the former, I ask you, is it not outrageous to combine into one promotion a sacred rite such as matrimony and a coarse spectacle such as a professional wrestling match? About the latter, is it not beneath the dignity of professional baseball to stage a contest in which young women make a spectacle of themselves in wet t-shirts?

Wedlock and Headlock Day

The Braves had a promotional scheduling conflict for July 11, 1976, when the team was playing the New York Mets. On the one hand, Hope planned a home plate wedding for that day.[76] Initially, it wasn't clear that the promotion would happen, since Hope hadn't found a couple willing to get hitched in a pre-game ceremony at Atlanta-Fulton County Stadium. Hope instructed his assistant, Kris Krebs, to search high and low for such a couple. He also arranged for messages soliciting such a couple to be broadcast on the radio during Braves games and appear on the stadium message board. After a while, Krebs located a couple willing to be married at a pre-game ceremony. Soon thereafter, they were deluged with such couples; 34 had volunteered. Rather than choose one couple from among the volunteers, Hope decided to marry all of them in a grand ceremony.

According to Robert Ashley Fields in *Take Me Out to the Crowd: Ted Turner and the Atlanta Braves*, upon closer inspection, Hope and company had to winnow down the number of participating couples.[77] Hope interviewed each couple and found that many were not appropriate for the ceremony. For example, several of the couples were underage. That would never do. After this process, it was decided that "eleven pairs of lovebirds would join in holy matrimony." One pair changed their minds, so that 10 remained to be married en masse.

Next, Hope had to locate a minister willing to preside over this ceremony.[78] Krebs contacted every church in the Atlanta metropolitan area, including several different denominations, in his search for such a minister. Finally, he found a justice of the peace who operated a chapel on the side to preside over the wedding. The promotion was ready to go.

But there was a scheduling dilemma. Turner had promised his friend, Jim Barnett, who owned Georgia Championship Wrestling, that the Braves would stage a series of wrestling matches as a promotion on July 11. Turner agreed to have a championship wrestling ring constructed in the ballpark and to televise the wrestling matches as part of the broadcast of the Braves game.[79] Barnett had arranged for "a complete lineup of fearsome wrestlers" who would participate in matches emceed by Freddie Miller, a well-known wrestling broadcaster.[80]

Presented with the double-booking, the Braves' brain trust had to decide which promotion to either cancel or postpone. Doing so was no easy matter. It would be very difficult to tell one bride, much less numerous brides, that they must change their wedding day.[81] After all, the couples may have already invited friends and family to the ballpark for the ceremony and may have arranged for, among other things, limousines to carry them to and from the stadium, flowers, and photography. It was impossible to reschedule the wrestling matches because July 11 was the only open day on the wrestling schedule. After deliberating on the matter for some time, Turner, Hope, and company decided, incredibly, that there was nothing incompatible between a wedding ceremony and wrestling matches. They would go ahead with both promotions, the weddings before the game and wrestling afterward.[82] One would imagine that Turner, who by this point in his life was married twice,[83] was comfortable with this decision.

July 11 turned out to be a beautiful day for a wedding. The brides all wore white dresses; one even had a train of Braves pennants sown together.

The bridesmaids all wore fancy frocks. According to Hope, all the grooms and groomsmen wore tuxedos with tails.[84] When the stadium organist started playing the wedding march, players from both teams stood in two lines and held bats aloft and crossed, creating a tunnel of sorts from the pitcher's mound to home plate for the brides, grooms, and their retinues to proceed through.[85] Jesse Outlar, a noted Atlanta sportswriter, said, "When the grooms slipped the rings on during ceremonies at home plate, Turner became the first owner to have 10 diamonds in action at the same time."[86] (Actually, engagement rings have diamonds. Wedding rings are usually just gold bands.) Afterward, the Braves held a reception for the couples, wedding party participants, and, possibly, family and friends.[87]

After the game, which the Braves won, 9–8, a wrestling ring was set up in the first base picnic area.[88] Television cameras were positioned to broadcast the action, and ballplayers and fans alike settled in to watch professional wrestling.[89] Fans who remained after the game were treated to four bouts of wrestling action. The headline contest featured a no holds barred bout between Mr. Wrestling II and Abdullah the Butcher, also known as the "Madman from the Sudan."[90] Other wrestlers, including Stan Stasiak, Tully Blanchard, Wayne Cowan, and Ted Oates, also entertained the fans by grappling in the ring.[91] There were no reports of any of the married couples hanging around for the wrestling match. They were, no doubt, already traveling to their respective honeymoons.

Wet T-Shirt Night

According to Hope, he and Ted Turner never planned Wet T-Shirt Night; it just happened.[92] The Braves used a committee of students to help plan promotions for the team's College Nights throughout the season. Turner had just completed his one and only night of managing the team, which turned out to be the team's 17th loss in a row. Attendance had hit rock bottom. Hope and company were desperate to come up with anything that would bring fans to the games. Figuring any port in a storm, one of the students—what makes me think it was a guy?—suggested a wet t-shirt contest, like they have on Spring Break in Florida. Hope immediately dismissed the idea, which he saw as inappropriate and in poor taste for a major league baseball team.

After the meeting, Hope was discussing some of the ideas that were brainstormed with the college students; none of the ideas seemed to spark an interest in his colleagues. Then he mentioned that one of the students had mentioned a wet t-shirt contest. Suddenly, the Braves' front office was abuzz with the idea that the team would sponsor just such a contest.[93]

Someone who worked for the Braves must have mentioned the contest to the press because, next day, Hope received a call from sportswriter Lewis Grizzard, who said that he understood that the Braves planned to hold a wet t-shirt contest. Hope said that under no circumstances would the Braves hold such a promotion, but he was willing to "explore the possibility" with someone who had shown interest in the team. Remember, the Braves were playing very poorly; after days with the phone not ringing, Hope must have been thrilled that someone showed interest in the team, regardless of the reason.[94]

One thing led to another, and Grizzard suggested that he write a column asking fans whether they would support the Braves holding a wet t-shirt contest. (Are you beginning to see a slippery slope here?) Grizzard argued that such a column would give Braves fans the opportunity to decide whether such a contest would be appropriate. Hope decided to go along with the scheme and let fans decide the correct course of action. After all, as he wrote, "It wasn't [his] responsibility to set the moral standards for big league baseball."[95] Reader response to the column was inconclusive, so Grizzard wrote another article, this time specifying a date that the Braves were considering for the wet t-shirt contest. This time, he struck a nerve; suddenly, the Braves (who otherwise couldn't give away a ticket) were selling loads of tickets for a promotion that they hadn't even scheduled.[96]

The Braves were in a bind. They found themselves in a situation where the fans were clamoring for a promotion that many would see as tasteless. According to Hope, Braves officials at this point were saying that they "hadn't made up our minds" regarding the promotion. One would imagine that Braves officials were of two minds. One train of thought suggested that a wet t-shirt contest was one way to generate interest in a team that, for all intents and purposes, had fallen off the face of the earth as far as Atlanta sports fans were concerned. When desperation sets in, proposals to generate interest in the team that would otherwise have been rejected out of hand become reasonable.[97] Another train of thought suggested that, regardless of the box office situation, the team could not sink so low as to hold an event that objectified women. As discussed, the Oakland Athletics had held a Hot Pants promotions during which women in tight shorts paraded around the stadium[98] but, somehow, this was worse.

The Braves' front office decided that it needed some cover regardless of the final decision on whether to proceed with Wet T-Shirt Night. So, Turner and Hope, and possibly other Braves officials, met with the Atlanta Christian Council to obtain its view on the promotion. They figured, if the Council approved of the promotion, then, if some outfit like the National

Organization for Women complained, the Braves could say that so highly regarded an organization as the Atlanta Christian Council condoned the event.[99] If the Council disapproved the event, the Braves could point to its decision as conclusive evidence that a wet t-shirt promotion was inconsistent with the moral standards of Atlanta society.[100] Surprisingly, the Council approved the wet t-shirt contest if: (1) the event was held after the game so that anyone who wanted to leave could do so; and (2) someone associated with the Council could serve as one of the judges![101] As they left, according to one source, Turner turned to Hope and said, "Looks like we're having a wet t-shirt night."[102] One can only imagine that they were surprised at this unlikely turn of events.

Confident that the event would not break any of the Ten Commandments, the Braves were losing reasons for not going forward with the wet t-shirt contest.[103] The promotion, without any boost from the Braves, had picked up a head of steam and seemed to be moving forward on its own. Disc jockeys in the Atlanta metropolitan area played up the contest, and the Braves were receiving messages from a who's who of Atlanta luminaries offering their services as judges. Of course, Turner volunteered to serve as one of the judges. With the support of the community, the Braves felt they had no choice but to confirm that the team would stage a Wet T-Shirt Night promotion on May 20, 1977, after a game against the Chicago Cubs.

Despite the pouring rain that evening, 11,451 intrepid fans came through the turnstiles of Atlanta-Fulton County Stadium to see a baseball game and what many assumed would be a once in a lifetime event—a wet t-shirt contest sponsored by a major league baseball team.[104] It rained for so long that game officials considered postponing the game. But if there was no game, then there was no contest. Let's face it, those in attendance that night were probably not there to a see a team with a 13–24 record play baseball. Without the contest, all those who came to witness, judge, and (yes) participate in the event would go home disappointed. That would never do, so they waited two-and-a-half hours to start the game. Amazingly, it was reported that no one left the stadium.[105]

Throughout the first six innings of the game, Braves officials were on pins and needles. They had not preregistered the contestants, so they had no way of knowing if any of the women in the stands that night would participate.[106] At the end of the seventh inning, the public address announcer asked that women participating in the contest report to the first base picnic area, which was in public view. For what seemed like forever, but was in truth only a few minutes, no one could be seen walking to the picnic area. Possibly, nobody wanted to be the first to volunteer. But then, Hope could see one young lady walk down the aisle and toward the picnic area, and soon, she was followed by 42 other women. The crowd gave them a standing ovation. By this point, the Cubs were winning, 11–0, and it seemed that everyone had mentally left the game behind and was anticipating the contest.[107]

Bobby Murcer, right fielder for the Chicago Cubs, was also engrossed with what was happening in the picnic area.[108] He stood in right field with his glove tucked under his arm, watching the women as they registered for the event. A Braves batter hit a fly ball to the right fielder, but Murcer never bothered to catch the ball, which landed at his feet and rolled to the outfield wall. Reminded by the hit that a game was in play, Murcer pulled on his glove and ran after the ball, which he threw into the infield. Murcer then took his position in right field, re-tucked his glove under his arm and, once again, turned his attention to the women registering for the contest.

Apparently indicating that they were anxious for the contest to start, the crowd stood and applauded for the final two innings. The game, which the Cubs won, 13–4,[109] mercifully came to an end after midnight, and the contest commenced at about 1:00 in the morning. The 43 participants stood along the third base line. Their every move was watched closely by the Cubs players, who sat just outside their dugout.[110] The grounds crew had previously held an Olympics-style event to determine which of them would have the honor of hosing down the young ladies. Another member of the grounds crew was selected to use a Windex bottle, possibly to "touch up" any areas that were missed by the hose.[111]

The women paraded before the judges. It is unclear what criteria were used by the judges to make their determination of the winner, but you can use your imagination. At any rate, after careful consideration, the contest was won by a Methodist minister's daughter.[112] No surprise, her father was unaware that his daughter had entered the contest. You know what they say, though, that everything comes out in the wash. The minister learned of his daughter's victory two weeks later from a stranger. The young lady had asked the Braves if she could sing the national anthem before a game. Apparently, she sang well enough for the team to agree. As her proud father sat in the stands listening to her rendition of the anthem, someone sitting behind him mentioned loud enough for him to hear that the singer had won the Braves' wet t-shirt contest.[113]

Braves officials took 300 photos of the contest.[114] (Don't bother to look, this book does not contain any.) Word got out, so that whenever a new team came to town, the players beat a path to Hope's door, wanting to see the photos. Hope tells the story that he heard from Ruly Carpenter, owner of the Philadelphia Phillies and a power in major league baseball, asking for a set of the photos. Hope was concerned that Carpenter planned to pass them onto Commissioner Kuhn, who might become upset at a major league team holding a wet t-shirt contest. Hope wondered whether he and Turner might be facing a suspension. But, not to worry, it seems Carpenter just wanted a set of photos to show his friends.[115]

◊ CHAPTER 7 ◊

Veeck Breaks a Slew of Records
Disco Demolition Night

Veeck/Chicago White Sox

Disco Demolition Night
Detroit Tigers at Chicago White Sox
Comiskey Park
July 12, 1979

What can we make of Disco Demolition Night, symbolically the last promotion of the Era of the Barnums? After 40 years, it remains the most infamous promotion in major league baseball history.[1] On Disco Demolition Night, tens of thousands of disco and apparently other records stored in a bin behind second base were blown up between games of a doubleheader, after which upwards of 7,000 attendees descended onto the playing field, creating mayhem and causing the second game of a doubleheader to be forfeited. This fiasco, incomprehensible in pure baseball terms, can only be understood within the context of the disco movement in America. Within that context, this chapter looks at the following questions: First, what caused seasoned baseball executives to agree to such an unorthodox promotion that negatively reflected on millions of Americans? Did their desire to increase attendance overwhelm their business acumen and common sense? Second, what motivated the anti-disco contingent in Comiskey Park that night to participate in the Disco Demolition Night promotion? Were they just kids showing their disdain for a musical genre they disliked or, more to the point, did they seek to stamp out disco because it was associated with women and with racial and sexual minorities? Third, what impact did Disco Demolition Night have on disco music in America? Did this promotion end the disco craze, as some have suggested, or, to quote Shakespeare's *Macbeth*, was it "sound and fury, signifying nothing?"

Bill Veeck (right), who had just repurchased the Chicago White Sox, confers with Hank Greenberg (left) and John Rigney. At the time, little did he know that the White Sox under his ownership would stage what is considered the most disastrous promotion in baseball history—Disco Demolition Night (National Baseball Hall of Fame and Museum).

Dahl Versus Disco

The series of events that led to Disco Demolition Night was set in motion when Steve Dahl, a 24-year-old disc jockey who played what is now called classic rock, lost his job at Chicago station WDAI on Christmas Eve in 1978[2] because the station changed to the commercially dominant[3] disco format.[4] Disco, which gained popularity in the 1970s, is a form of popular music intended mainly for dancing; it tends to be heavily soul-influenced and melodic, with a predominant bass beat.

Dahl quickly found work at a rival rock-and roll station, WLUP, known as "The Loop,"[5] but apparently never got over being fired. At WLUP, Dahl, along with his on-air partner, Greg Meier, took every opportunity to mock disco.[6] He would briefly play a disco record and then scratch the needle across the record or pretend that he was destroying the record by playing sounds of an explosion.[7] He would mock WDAI's "Disco DAI" slogan by rebranding it as Disco DIE.[8] Sometimes Dahl may have taken the routine too far: When disco star Van McCoy died unexpectedly of a heart attack in July 1979, Dahl appeared to celebrate by destroying one of McCoy's most popular records on the air.[9]

Dahl formed a rock band called Teenage Radiation,[10] which recorded the anti-disco song, "Do You Think I'm Disco," a parody of "Do Ya Think I'm Sexy," which was a hit for Rod Stewart, a rock star who had the audacity to record a disco song.[11] The lyrics to Dahl's song present a superficial disco fan who, realizing that his only goal in life is to look hip, wonders whether it is too late to get into rock and roll.

Dahl formed his most rabid listeners into a disco-hating organization called the Insane Coho Lips, who "were dedicated to the eradication of the of the dreaded musical disease known as disco." Dahl and his followers held "Death to Disco" rallies at nightclubs and staged other anti-disco events, several of which became unruly.[12] When Dahl staged an event to support a former discotheque (i.e., dance club) in Linwood, Illinois, that changed its format to rock and roll in June 1979, 5,000 of his most ardent followers showed up.[13] Fifty police officers were needed to intervene when several thousand of them became disorderly.[14] Towards the end of June 1979, Dahl urged his followers to throw marshmallows at a WDAI van promoting disco music at a shopping mall. They chased the van and cornered it in a local park.[15] By the end of June 1979, the Insane Coho Lips had reportedly grown to 10,000 strong. WLUP had to hire two people to handle the mail.[16]

While Dahl may have been among the best-known crusaders against disco, he certainly wasn't alone. He was part of a larger, though disjointed, national backlash against the spread of disco music. The evangelical community sought to counter the spread of disco into mainstream America. Religious conservatives saw disco as "the continuation of sixties hedonism and all-around depravity."[17] Anita Bryant, a former Miss America and spokeswoman for Florida's citrus industry, took it upon herself to crusade against homosexuality and warned that gay individuals were "producing [disco] records with double meanings ... then having 'straight' children buy them."[18] Jerry Falwell, a prominent evangelical preacher and founder of Liberty University, in a speech before 8,000 supporters, denounced "President Carter, homosexuality, pornography, television comedies, abortion, *discos*, divorce, and sex education."[19] (Emphasis added.)

At the opposite end of the spectrum, progressives saw disco as "the final nail in the coffin of the sixties."[20] They saw disco not as a rival to rock and roll but as the death of rock and roll, and they sought the elimination of this musical genre. Disco had, in effect, transformed popular music from the voice of counterculture rebellion[21] that called upon listeners to seek sexual and other forms of liberation and fight oppression, to a musical genre that exhorted listeners to simply dress up and dance. Unlike rock and roll, which progressives saw as an art form despite its commercialization, disco was innocuous and conventional, a mass-produced opium with a danceable beat that caused its aficionados to detach from society, lose themselves in the music, and move their bodies.[22] In their eyes, people who bought into disco music "were merely vapid followers of fashion, superficial losers who didn't appreciate 'real' music."[23]

Some suggested that there was an intimidation factor at play. Proponents of disco maintained that disco could be intimidating to many rock and roll fans, whose dress code required nothing more than jeans and t-shirt, and whose movements at a concert consisted of little more than jumping up and down. In her book, *Hot Stuff: Disco and the Remaking of American Culture,* Alice Echols suggests that "progressive rock and roll fans were intimidated by the highly sexed and, one might add, female-centered quality of disco and by the physical and sartorial demands of glitterball culture." Rock and roll aficionados resisted disco's seeming requirement that men have sculpted bodies, be fashion-conscious and well-groomed, and know how to dance.[24] Said Dahl, "The disco culture represents the surreal, insidious, weird oppression because you have to look good, you know, tuck your shirt in, perfect this, perfect that."[25]

Progressives found their voice in rock and roll disc jockeys, who simply saw their meal ticket disappearing from the onslaught of disco music and organized most effectively against it.[26] In addition to Dahl, three such disc jockeys are worth noting. Possibly the first deejay to make "discophobia" part of his schtick was Dennis Erectus of KOMR in San Jose, California. According to the *Village Voice,* Erectus' routine was somewhat like Dahl's. He would "play a couple of bars of a [disco] record, then crank the turntable up to 78 rpm ... grind the needle into the vinyl, play sound effects of toilets flushing or people throwing up, and follow it up with the searing guitar chords of rock groups Van Halen or AC/DC." Two deejays at Detroit's WWWW radio station formed a disco hate group. When they moved to station WRIF, these disc jockeys formed another group called the Detroit Rockers Engaged in the Abolition of Disco (DREAD), whose intelligence arm reported to them the names of disco aficionados. These people were symbolically electrocuted on air.

Discomania

The problem was that all their anti-disco speeches and antics didn't seem to touch this music genre, which was spreading like wildfire across America. By 1979, disco became a nationwide mainstream movement and a certified cash cow for both record labels and club owners. Disco entered mainstream America by virtue of two happenings widely reported by the media. April 1977 saw the opening of the luxe disco palace Studio 54 in New York City, frequented by celebrities and those rich or attractive enough to gain entrance. This disco cathedral, located at 54th Street near 8th Avenue (a decidedly untrendy section of New York City) had a 5,400-square-foot dance floor and state of the art sound and lighting systems.[27] Noted author Truman Capote characterized Studio 54 as "the nightclub of the future." He added, "It's very democratic. Boys with boys, girls with girls, girls with boys, blacks with whites, capitalists and Marxists, Chinese and everything else—all one big mix!"[28]

The disco music genre exploded with the December 1977 release of "Saturday Night Fever," starring John Travolta, and the related album soundtrack, awarded the Grammy for Album of the Year.[29] If Studio 54 was the fire starter, "Saturday Night Fever" was the match. This movie succeeded in presenting a more heterosexual image of disco. In essence, this film "took disco out of the closet"[30] and institutionalized this music genre in mainstream America.[31]

Discos were opening all over metropolitan New York and across the country. One year after the release of "Saturday Night Fever," there were 1,000 discos blaring dance music throughout New York City and the surrounding area.[32] By the end of 1978, there were between 15-20,000 such establishments operating in America, leaving fewer and fewer venues for rock musicians.[33] Club owners found it easier to hire deejays instead of live bands, which came replete with demanding managers and entire road crews.[34] There was also plenty of disco music to play. Record company executives found it more cost effective to produce disco music, which could be made quickly compared with locking up a rock band in a studio for six months.[35] According to Echols, "All across America, supermarkets were converted into discos and bars and clubs that had featured rock bands were being made over into discos." And why not? The business magazine, *Forbes*, reported that, if managed properly, discos yielded very hefty profits.[36] For example, one Washington, D.C., club, called Tramps Discotheque, boasted an average annual gross income of just under $1,000,000, of which $400,000 was profit.[37]

Like Dahl's WDAI, radio stations that formerly played rock and roll were converting to a disco format. No longer did disco afficionados need to listen to R&B stations to hear the spare disco song.[38] While radio stations were initially reluctant to play music whose popularity stemmed from club play, that soon changed when they realized they could expand their audiences by playing disco. For example, WKTU in New York City, a mellow rock station with unimpressive ratings, switched to a disco format in the summer of 1978. Within nine months, WKTU was the most popular station in the city. This turnabout didn't go unnoticed by other stations. Soon thereafter, KIIS-FM in Los Angeles changed to a disco format. Boston's WBOS and Detroit's WLBS followed suit.[39] By 1979, there were 200 radio stations nationwide playing all disco music. Even the Voice of America, a radio station operated by the federal government that broadcasts worldwide, reported that its Saturday-night disco program was unexpectedly popular.[40]

Increasingly, disco was overwhelming rock and roll on the airwaves and relegating it to the fringes of American music.[41] In 1978, disco singles commandeered the number one position on the charts for 37 out of 52 weeks. In the first half of 1979, 13 of the 16 singles that made the top of the charts were disco tracks.[42] At the 21st annual Grammy Awards Ceremony that same month, disco performers, with the Bee Gees in the lead, won eight of the 14 awards.[43] By the summer of 1979, disco records represented 40 percent of all chart activity.[44] Popular mainstream rock and roll acts, such as Blondie, Kiss, Queen, Rod Stewart, and the Rolling Stones,[45] were putting out disco records. Other recording artists, such as Broadway star Ethel Merman, folk singers Joan Baez and Janice Ian, and the mellow Percy Faith Orchestra all recorded disco songs.[46] Rod Stewart had the biggest hit of his career with "Do Ya Think I'm Sexy?"[47] Barry Manilow had a huge summer hit with the disco-inspired "Copacabana."[48]

The American press noted the decline of rock and roll by publishing article after article on the ascendancy of disco. For example, *Fortune* magazine ran a feature on disco. A leading socialist newspaper, *In These Times,* published the results of a forum on the meaning of disco.[49] Even *Rolling Stone* magazine, which was never enamored with disco, published a remarkably even-handed issue that focused on disco. *Newsweek's* cover story, "The Disco Takeover," seemed to sum up the consensus regarding the prevalence of this music genre.[50]

Disco Demolition Night: The Plan

In the summer of 1979, the Chicago White Sox staged a promotion that unwittingly entangled the team in the controversy surrounding disco. The White Sox presented Dahl with an opportunity to do something big and splashy that could incite his followers and disco-haters everywhere. Dahl initially intended to blow up a crate of records live on the air at a shopping mall.[51] But the potential impact of his plans was exponentially amplified when he connected with Mike Veeck, son of Bill Veeck who, in addition to serving as Promotions Manager for the Chicago White Sox,[52] worked as a sports broadcaster at WLUP.⁵³ He needed to come up with some event to attract teenagers to Comiskey Park on what was being billed as Teen Night, scheduled for a twilight-night doubleheader⁵⁴ on July 12, 1979.⁵⁵

As far as I could discern, it went down like this: Early in the 1979 season, WLUP Sales Manager Jeff Schwartz told Mike Veeck of Dahl's plan to blow up a crate of disco records live at a shopping mall. In a later meeting, Schwartz, WLUP Promotions Director Dave Logan, and Mike Veeck discussed the idea of an anti-disco night promotion at Comiskey Park.⁵⁶ Veeck apparently convinced the WLUP officials that the ballpark (and not a shopping mall) would be the perfect place to destroy disco records. During a meeting at WLUP, Dahl was asked whether he would be interested in blowing up records at Comiskey Park on July 12.⁵⁷ The records would be brought to the park by fans who, for their contribution, would pay a discounted fee of 98 cents to enter the ballpark.⁵⁸ (This admissions price coincided with WLUP's radio frequency of 97.9).⁵⁹ They called it Disco Demolition Night!⁶⁰ Dahl was initially reluctant to go along with the proposal because he was concerned that only about 10,000 people would show up, making the stadium, which had a capacity of 44,492 people,⁶¹ look empty. He eventually agreed and promoted the event heavily on the air.⁶²

Before he could go forward with the event, Mike Veeck had to sell it to his father. Disco Demolition Night wasn't your run-of-the-mill baseball promotion, like giving out T-shirts with the likeness of a popular player. But Mike knew that his father was a showman who liked to entertain the crowd.⁶³ He was also a maverick who took chances. Important to the history of baseball, Bill Veeck in 1948 signed Larry Doby, the first Black player in the American League and, a year later, hired African American pitcher Satchel Paige.⁶⁴ He was the only Major League Baseball owner to testify in favor of Curt Flood in this lawsuit to end the reserve clause and to vote against the 1976 spring training lockout.⁶⁵

Veeck reluctantly agreed to the Disco Demolition Night promotion. However, White Sox management took the added precaution of increasing ballpark security to manage a crowd as large as 35,000,⁶⁶ many more than had been attending White Sox games. Altogether, the security detail for the game numbered about 50.⁶⁷ Even after increasing security, Bill Veeck apparently had misgivings about the promotion. Fearing that the planned promotion could result in something catastrophic, the night before the doubleheader, he checked himself out of the hospital where he was taking medical tests, so he could be at the ballpark.⁶⁸ No one knows what concerns he had while lying in his hospital bed, but they were likely no match for the mayhem that really happened.

Disco Demolition Night: The Event

Disco Demolition Night was envisioned by White Sox management as two baseball games that would serve as the main attraction with a promotional event—the destruction of disco records—as an interlude between the games. One might imagine that they expected to attract baseball fans who also had some interest in the clash between the aficionados of rock & roll and disco music. No doubt, some people in attendance were legitimate baseball fans, some of whom took the opportunity presented by the discounted entrance price to bring their entire families to a wholesome evening at the ballpark.[69] As things turned out, however, the games themselves weren't compelling enough to attract many baseball fans. Neither team was having an impressive season. Both teams were in fifth place in their respective divisions, although the White Sox were on a four-game win streak and had won seven of eight games. Leading up to this game, the Tigers had lost four of five games.[70] The stands, instead, were jammed with those who came to see the metaphorical destruction of disco music.

Seen purely in terms of attendance, Disco Demolition Night could not have been more of a success. On a muggy Thursday night,[71] with the mediocre White Sox playing the mediocre Detroit Tigers,[72] attendance at the stadium was officially reported at 47,795.[73] Looking at the crowd, Bill Veeck surmised that there were an estimated 50,000 to 55,000 fans in Comiskey Park.[74] Dan Epstein, in his book about baseball in the 1970s, *Big Hair and Plastic Grass,* estimates that, altogether, there were 90,000 people inside and outside the ballpark that night. There were tens of thousands of potential patrons, unable to pay their way into Comiskey Park, who were laying siege to the ballpark entrances. In fact, the throng of fans brought the nearby Dan Ryan Expressway to a standstill.[75] Apparently, many of these people entered the ballpark by bulldozing through the entrance gates[76] or bypassing them altogether, climbing fences, and squirming through open windows.[77] Whatever the estimate, do a little math and you arrive at the undeniable realization that thousands of attendees did not have seats. Having been informed that ticket takers at the entrances were in fear that they would be overtaken by rowdy disappointed fans, Mike Veeck sent 15 security guards to secure the ballpark entrances.[78]

Before the first game, Lorelei Shark, known as the "Loop Rock Girl,"[79] who was featured in several WLUP advertisements,[80] threw out the ceremonial first pitch.[81] The pitching match-up featured Fred Howard, with a record of 1–3, pitching for the White Sox, versus Pat Underwood, with a record of 3–0, for the Tigers. The Tigers scored two unearned runs in the first two innings. For their part, the White Sox scored one run in the second inning, on an RBI double by Greg Pryor, which cut Detroit's lead to

7 ✦ Veeck Breaks a Slew of Records 115

As part of Disco Demolition Night, staged in July 1979, a bin full of thousands of disco and other vinyl records was exploded, causing shards of records to fly all over the field and a crater to form behind second base. This promotion not only led to the forfeit of a game but was seen as being insulting to those segments of American society that supported disco music (Alamy.com).

2–1. In the third inning, Jerry Morales hit an RBI single which increased the Tigers lead to 3–1. The Tigers increased their advantage in the sixth inning with an RBI single by Lance Parrish. The final score of the game was 4–1.[82]

During the first game, it became painfully clear that too many of the people in the ballpark had come to see the explosion rather than the baseball games.[83] By the time these attendees found their seats, they were clearly in party mode, drinking alcohol and smoking marijuana.[84] Indeed, Durwood Merrill, one of the umpires officiating at the doubleheader, recalled that he "could smell marijuana the moment I walked onto the field."[85] The umpiring crew chief that evening, Dave Phillips, described the ballpark that night as looking like "a small Woodstock drug fest."[86] Attendees displayed anti-disco banners and chanted epithets, most notably "Disco Sucks!"[87]

Further, not expecting so large a crowd, the team management didn't place enough bins at the ballpark entrances to hold all the albums contributed by the fans. Unable to place their records in the filled-up bins, those entering the ballpark later that night held onto their records and took them to their seats. Attendees started to throw these hard disks from their seats like frisbees onto the field. They also threw firecrackers, empty liquor bottles, and lighters onto the field.[88] The first game had to be stopped several times to clear the field of debris.[89] Reporters for a suburban Chicago newspaper, the *Daily Herald*, wrote that all this commotion created an atmosphere that was "ripe for trouble."[90]

Ballplayers, some of whom donned batting helmets in the field for protection,[91] just missed getting hit, and possibly injured, by these spinning records and other projectiles from the stands. The *Chicago Tribune* reported that players for both teams "were forced ... to play the first game under a constant bombardment of records and firecrackers."[92] Detroit catcher Ed Putman said that he had to leave the bullpen because of the cherry bombs being thrown there. Putnam later told a reporter that a "cherry bomb landed so close to the back of my head that I could feel the explosion." Rusty Torres, White Sox outfielder, reported that he was the target for a constant barrage of lighters and empty liquor bottles. He joked that, the way things were going, he had wished that the bottle of Puerto Rican rum that was thrown his way still had some of the contents. Apparently, he could have used a drink.[93]

Somehow, while dodging records and trying not to breathe in the marijuana smoke, the teams completed the first game at 8:16 p.m.[94] and exited the field for their clubhouses so the promotion for that evening could proceed. A large bin full of tens of thousands of records was carted onto center field behind second base. This bin not only contained the records but enough explosives to splinter the discs and send them flying.[95] At 8:40 p.m.,[96] Dahl, in full military regalia, including a combat helmet, was driven onto the field in a military-style Jeep[97] through a door in the center field wall.[98] According to Mike Veeck, "when Steve [Dahl] rode in on his Jeep, the electricity picked up several volts."[99] Dahl was accompanied by his disc jockey partner, Meier, and Shark. The Jeep came to a stop in center field, where Dahl dismounted, grabbed a microphone, and addressed the crowd.[100]

It was obvious to many that he did not plan to make a speech and, as a result, he had no idea what to say to a throng of people who largely paid their 98 cents to see him. Said Dahl, "I had no prepared remarks. So, I just yelled stuff."[101] If Dahl had sensed the agitation in the crowd, he might have given a calming speech to help them stay in control. In the videos available, it appears that Shark, who saw this whole event as nothing more than a public relations stunt,[102] sensed hostility in the crowd and was somewhat unnerved to be there. She admits being "absolutely frightened."[103] Dahl gave a rambling presentation filled with anti-disco invective[104] that, if nothing else, further enraged the crowd against disco music. Among the more incendiary lines: "And we're never going to let them forget it! They're never going to shove [disco] down our throats. We rock & rollers will resist, and we will triumph."[105] After his brief presentation, he led all attendees in a rousing chorus of "Disco Sucks," which was repeated over and over.[106]

Then came the moment those in attendance were waiting for. In a blaze of fireworks, the bin full of records was exploded, flattening the bin and sending thousands of records in pieces about 25-30 feet in the air.[107] The resulting smoke settled on the field, giving it a surreal aspect.[108] Unexpectedly, the explosion also created a large crater in center field.[109] (One can only imagine how the grounds crew felt when they saw that crater on their meticulously maintained field.) Dahl made a valiant attempt to lead those in attendance in the singing of what he called his "anthem," the aforementioned "Do You Think I'm Disco?"[110]

At this point, Dahl and his entourage exited to the cheers and applause of the crowd. The Jeep, with Dahl standing in the back, took a victory lap around the field[111] and was driven out of the stadium and through the streets surrounding Comiskey Park, much to the delight of the Dahl followers who could not gain entrance to the stadium. The occupants of the Jeep were eventually taken to the front of the stadium, where they were whisked into Comiskey Park through the entrance and taken up to the press room.[112]

Once Dahl left the field, all hell broke loose.[113] At first, it was just a few members of the crowd who climbed out of the stands and onto the field.[114] However, once it became apparent that security inside the ballpark could not stop them (recall, some were guarding the entrance to the stadium), thousands more poured onto the field in celebration. It is estimated that, at the height of the riot, there were 5,000 to 7,000 anti-disco revelers on the baseball field.[115]

Finding that they had, at least temporarily, occupied the playing field with little to no resistance, they milled about, looking for something to do. While many just walked around surprised that they found themselves on the Comiskey Park playing field,[116] others got into mayhem. They set about to start a bonfire with the records scattered across the center field grass, some of the banners they brought to the ballpark,[117] and picnic table seats from a picnic area near left field.[118] For reasons that are unclear, they took possession of and destroyed the batting cage.[119] They pantomimed baseball players batting, pitching, and sliding,[120] climbed the foul pole, and pulled up and took the bases.[121] Those on the field also tried to break down the clubhouse doors, but to no avail.[122] The Detroit Tigers announcers—Hall of Famers George Kell and Al Kaline—reported on what they were witnessing as if it was the Hindenburg disaster or, possibly, the apocalypse.[123] In *Disco Demolition: The Night Disco Died*, Dahl with his co-writers, Dave Hoekstra and Phil Natkin, acknowledge that "it was lunacy defined."[124]

Bill Veeck and Harry Caray, Frick Award–winning announcer for the Chicago White Sox, took turns using the public address system to reason with the rioters and urge them to leave the playing field and take their seats in the stands. The scoreboard flashed "PLEASE RETURN TO YOUR SEATS."[125] (Given that the ballpark was overcrowded, there is some question whether those on the field even had seats in the stands to return to.) Caray and Veeck even went so far as to serenade the crowd with a rendition of "Take Me Out to the Ball Game"[126] in hopes that singing the baseball anthem would remind those on the field why they came to the ballpark. Dahl asked for the opportunity to address his followers in hope that he might be able to persuade them to leave the field. Bill Veeck thought it best to deny Dahl this opportunity.[127]

At 9:08 p.m., Chicago police arrived on horseback and in full riot gear[128] to clear the field,[129] which they did with remarkable effectiveness in 37 minutes.[130] Chicago Police Lieutenant Robert Reilly, who was head of the park detail, remarked that Disco Demolition Night was "as bad as the night the Beatles were here."[131] In all, 39 people were arrested for disorderly conduct,[132] which was a new major league baseball record.[133] There was one major injury: a vendor's broken hip.[134] Altogether, six people were taken to local hospitals.[135]

After the field was cleared, a meeting was convened to determine the next course of action. In attendance were: Nestor Chylak, a supervisor of umpires, who happened to be at Comiskey Park that night; the umpiring crew for the game, headed by crew chief Dave Phillips; Bill Veeck; Detroit manager Sparky Anderson; and Detroit commentator Al Kaline. The participants were concerned that, given the condition of the field, a player might become injured playing the second game of the doubleheader. Also, it was noted that home plate had been uprooted and not replaced properly. Phillips called American League president Lee MacPhail, who decided that the second game should be postponed until the following Sunday. Anderson, not satisfied with this decision, insisted that the second game should be forfeited because the White Sox were derelict in their responsibility to ensure that the field be playable. The next day, Lee MacPhail called Bill Veeck to tell him that Anderson was correct in his interpretation of the rules.[136] According to baseball rules, a game can only be postponed due to an act of God. The game would be forfeited to the Tigers.[137]

On the radio the next morning, Dahl tried to downplay the events of the night before. He said, "I think for the most part that everything was wonderful. Some maniac Cohos got wild and went down on the field. Which you shouldn't have done. Bad little Cohos."[138]

In contrast to Dahl's comments the reviews the next day in the newspapers were brutal.[139] Bill Gleason of the *Chicago Sun*-Times characterized Disco Demolition Night as "the most disgraceful night in the long history of major league baseball." The blame for the disaster was initially laid at the feet of Bill Veeck. The *Chicago Tribune* contained an editorial that held Veeck personally responsible for the "hucksterism that disgraced the game of baseball." The editorial added that Veeck had created an environment that included drunken fans and flying records, which endangered fans and players. One reporter described Disco Demolition Night as "a night when Veeck's circus atmosphere came crashing down around him." An editorial in the *Daily Herald* said that Veeck—characterized as the "king of promoters" and the "master showman"—was "lucky that the worst that happened is the team forfeited a game as a result."

Bill Veeck valiantly tried to deflect the blame for the riot away from his son. He said, "I didn't investigate as carefully as I obviously should have."[140] The mastermind behind Disco Demolition Night, Mike Veeck,[141] nevertheless suffered repercussions.[142] The younger Veeck was on the field when the records were exploded. As he watched the pyrotechnics, he said some 40 years later, "I was just standing there thinking about what my next job would be, because I knew that my life as I knew it right then was over."[143] He had clearly misread the situation. Said Mike Veeck, "I'm into music and this was my kind of concept." He added, "But the mistake I can't get over is that I didn't read it right."[144] Mike Veeck resigned from the White Sox in late-1980 and, claiming he was blackballed,[145] was unable to find work in major league baseball for nearly a decade after Disco Demolition Night. In 1981, Bill Veeck sold the White Sox[146] to ownership with deeper pockets, apparently realizing that it would take more than promotions to keep a baseball team afloat in the age of free agency.

But the criticism went beyond just the riot. There was a steady drumbeat of commentators who suggested that the event appeared to have drilled down into "a potent stream of racism, sexism, and homophobia."[147] They saw the behavior of the crowd at Disco Demolition Night as an example of racist and homophobic impulses that drove the late–70s backlash against disco music.[148] "Fear of disco was partly the fear that American identity was no longer synonymous with whiteness."[149] Famously, Dave Marsh of *Rolling Stone* magazine, who attended the event, characterized Disco Demolition Night as "Your most paranoid fantasy about where the ethnic cleansing of the rock radio could ultimately lead."[150] He added, "there was something distinctly ugly about the vast crowd of white men publicly destroying music predominantly made by Black artists, dominated by female stars with a core audience that was, at least initially, largely gay."[151] National Public Radio indicated that this event had come "to be seen as a not-so-subtle attack against disco's early adopters: Blacks, Latinos, and gay people."[152] Others compared the destruction of records to book burnings.[153]

In their book, Dahl with his co-authors wrote that they saw nothing wrong with the behavior of his followers that evening. "The event was not racist, not anti-gay."[154] They "were just kids pissing on a musical genre."[155] This genre apparently was offensive to their sensibilities.[156] They added, "We were choosing to remain faithful to the [rock and roll] bands that provided the backdrop to our lives."[157] Sometime after the event, Dahl argued that we were seeing an event in 1979 through lenses shaded with current values: "[A]nnexing this event to today's advocacy is lazy academically and inappropriate geographically."[158]

Vince Lawrence, a teenage usher at Comiskey Park who worked Disco Demolition Night and was one of the few Black individuals at the ballpark that night, focused on the racism he saw in the event. Lawrence pointed out that, even though he was wearing a t-shirt endorsing WLUP, many of those in attendance confronted him about his affiliation with disco.[159] Ushers at the ballpark that night also pointed out that many of those entering the ballpark did not bring disco records with them to the game that evening; rather, they took records by Black artists in other genres of music, such as funk and rhythm & blues.[160] Such artists included Otis Clay, Tyrone Davis, Curtis Mayfield,[161] Marvin Gaye, and Stevie Wonder[162]— performers who clearly weren't disco artists. This was seen as evidence that many at the ballpark on Disco Demolition Night were not protesting disco as much as they were protesting all music associated with the Black community in the United States. Said Vince Lawrence, "How many other times in American history has some ... racist thing happened when they say it wasn't really racism, that [it] was something else?"[163] Vince Lawrence adds, "If Steve Dahl says he wasn't calling these people out ... funny how they came."[164] He concludes that Dahl's protests that Disco Demolition Night focused solely on disco music are either "naive or dishonest."[165]

The Decline of Disco

Dahl titled his book about Disco Demolition Night *Disco Demolition: The Night Disco Died*. This begs the question: did Disco Demolition Night have such a far-reaching effect as to end the disco craze in the United States? There are those who would say yes. For example, a source no less authoritative than History.com stated:

> [D]isco didn't quite die a natural death by collapsing under its own weight. Instead, it was killed by a public backlash that reached its peak on July 12, 1979 with the infamous "Disco Demolition Night" at Chicago's Comiskey Park. That incident ... is widely credited—or, depending on your perspective, blamed—with dealing disco its death blow.[166]

While it would not be possible to show a causal relationship, there is little doubt that Disco Demolition Night was a harbinger of doom for disco music.

Apparently, there was rot in the foundation under the glittery surface of disco. In hindsight, it appears that disco had run its course by 1979. Erstwhile fans saw this goose as laying golden eggs that sounded plastic, innocuous, and conventional.[167] According to Echols, "Evidence suggests that listeners were beginning to sour on disco even before Disco Demolition [Night]."[168] It had lost its trendiness.[169] The Arbitron ratings of American radio stations indicated a leveling of consumer interest in disco.[170]

It seems that recording industry executives were also beginning to have their concerns about disco music. Even though record companies were profiting from this music, sales of disco records were trending downward. Even in good times, disco fared poorly in selling the traditionally more lucrative long-playing albums. What's more, there was also a growing sentiment that "disco was superficial, boring, repetitive, and short on 'balls.'"[171] One Salsoul executive admitted that the label "ended up releasing inferior garbage."[172] All of a sudden, "disco" became a bad word in the music industry. Warner Records renamed its disco department the dance music department. Other record companies followed suit.[173] As a result, a disco band like Chic, which had a string of hits for Warner/Electra/Asylum, could not get any further traction with their record company.[174]

Broadcast companies, always looking for the next musical trend, saw the backlash against disco as an indication that the music genre was losing momentum. Eerily, the day after Disco Demolition Night, a dedicated disco station in Chicago played Donna Summer's "Last Dance" for 24 hours straight and then announced it was changing formats to Top 40 rock songs.[175] By 1980, Billboard reported that American radio had adopted a "virtual ban" on disco as a format. In 1980, the 21st Grammy Awards established a special category for disco music to prevent it from running away with most of the awards as happened the prior year. Within a year of virtually owning the Top 10, disco seemed to have disappeared.[176]

In reality, disco didn't die; it retreated underground to its original audience,[177] where it re-emerged as hip-hop, house, and other types of music.[178] Vince Lawrence, the Disco Demolition Night usher, went on to become one of the leading innovators of the early house music scene[179] and, in 1984, co-wrote the first house single, "On and On."[180] Interestingly, according to Alice Echols, the music that followed in disco's footsteps tended to be more sexually explicit and queerer than traditional disco, and its influence on mainstream music was much more widespread. This new-wave music gave opportunity to popular performers who were more flamboyantly androgenous in their self-presentation. Gender bending and sexual ambiguity became commonplace, not only among male performers, such as Phillip Oakley of Human League and Martin Gore of Depeche Mode, but also of female performers, such as Madonna and Grace Jones, who displayed a certain amount of masculinity in their music performances.[181]

Part III

♦ ♦ ♦

Other Outrageous Promotions

◊ **Chapter 8** ◊

Askew Over Scrap Metal

Scrap Metal Day

Scrap Metal Day
Boston Braves at New York Giants
Polo Grounds
September 26, 1942

When, on Sunday, December 7, 1941, the imperial forces of Japan attacked the U.S. naval base at Pearl Harbor, and soon thereafter Germany and Italy declared war on the United States, the U.S. government mobilized the country to fight the Axis powers. The Armed Forces trained hundreds of thousands of men, including thousands of professional baseball players, to fight at battle fronts overseas. On the home front, the federal War Production Board encouraged Americans to support the war effort by collecting strategic items for the manufacture of armaments and munitions, and other items needed to ensure victory. On September 26, 1942, the New York Giants sponsored a promotion that sought to contribute to the war effort. The Giants permitted children who donated scrap metal to enter the game free of charge. While only 2,916 fans paid to enter the stadium, they brought in tow over 11,000 youngsters who were doing their patriotic duty. Although this well-conceived promotion had a laudable purpose, the afternoon went horribly wrong when the youngsters stormed the field, and the Giants were forced to forfeit the second game of a doubleheader.

Breakfast with Warren Spahn

I would imagine that, when future Hall of Fame pitcher Warren Spahn woke up in his New York hotel room on September 26, 1942, he might have been a bit anxious. Like many, he probably read the newspaper while eating his breakfast and drinking a cup of coffee. He turned to the sports page first and read the article on yesterday's game. The Brooklyn Dodgers had defeated his Braves, 6–5[1]; Spahn may have just scanned the article, not particularly wanting to relive a loss. He took a gander at the standings. Beneath the standings, he perused the starting pitchers for that day's games and saw, as he expected, that he would be pitching the second game of a doubleheader versus the New York Giants. Although the Giants had just been mathematically eliminated from the pennant race, they had a good team that year, and Spahn knew he couldn't take them lightly.

At that point in his career—a rookie who was starting only his second game in the big leagues—Spahn had no way of knowing that he would finish his Hall of Fame career as arguably one of the 10 best pitchers in the history of baseball.[2] Over parts of 21 seasons, from 1942 to 1965, Spahn won a total of 363 games, more than any left-hander in baseball history, with a winning percentage of .597 and an ERA of 3.09. Spahn would hold or share modern major league records for 20-win seasons, most years leading the league in games won, and career innings by a left-hander. He would be named to 14 All Star teams and win the Cy Young Award in 1957. He would win eight games over three World Series (1948, 1957, and 1958) and pitch to a postseason ERA of 3.05.

After perusing the sports page, Spahn may have turned to the front page of the newspaper, where he would likely see numerous articles on a world at war. The headline may have dealt with the Battle of Guadalcanal, which was raging in the South Pacific. Ever since the Japanese invasion of Pearl Harbor, the United States was totally focused on victory over the Axis powers. It wasn't just soldiers fighting the war. Spahn may have read an article about regular people on the home front doing what they could to support the men in uniform, like collecting scrap metal and rubber items to be made into munitions and other combat-related materials. Women were even donating their stockings! Major league baseball wasn't spared the war's impact. Another article might have dealt with baseball players who were being inducted into the armed forces; Spahn may have contemplated enlisting himself. He possibly read that baseball teams were having special promotions to sell war bonds and collect money for causes that supported the war effort. In fact, he may have heard somewhere that the Giants were letting kids into the ballpark for free that day if they donated some scrap metal. If nothing else, with thousands of youngsters in the stands, today's doubleheader would certainly be loud.

World War II on the Homefront

When the United States entered World War II, the economy was placed on a war footing. Factories that once made consumer goods overhauled their manufacturing processes to produce items needed for the war effort. One very significant problem soon became apparent. The United States lacked certain materials, such as scrap metal, rubber, paper, nylon, and silk in sufficient quantities to produce the items needed by our war fighters overseas.[3] Some of these materials were in short supply because the United States obtained them from Japan. Also, Japan had invaded and captured countries that had once supplied these goods to the United States.[4] In addition, prior to the war, the United States had unadvisedly sold tons of scrap metal to Japan.[5] The U.S. government instituted a program for the rationing of needed items, but it soon became apparent that more needed to be done.

In January 1942, President Franklin D. Roosevelt established the War Production Board (WPB) to ensure that the military had sufficient materials to defeat the Axis powers.[6] Among other things, the WPB initiated programs called scrap drives, whereby American citizens could collect and donate needed items for military use.[7] These WPB scrap collection drives were publicized nationally but mobilized locally.[8] They would use celebrities, both real and fanciful, such as Bing Crosby and Mickey Mouse, to encourage Americans at home to "Salvage for Victory" and "Get in the Scrap."[9] Even movie star Rita Hayworth, a favorite among American servicemen, got into the act by publicly donating the metal fenders off her car; then gave the boys in uniform a cheesecake pose for them to remember her by.[10] Millions of Americans, ranging from children to high-ranking elected officials, answered the call.[11] They were all anxious to make a meaningful contribution to the war effort[12] and do their part to help loved ones and others fighting overseas.[13] These scrap drives not only served to collect essential materials for the war effort but improved the morale of the citizenry by helping them feel they were a crucial part of the war effort.[14]

SCRAP METAL. On January 10, 1942, just one month after the Japanese attack on Pearl Harbor, the U.S. government launched the Salvage for Victory program, which aimed at collecting scrap metal, including aluminum, steel, and iron, for use by the U.S. military.[15] These scrap metals were used to produce a plethora of military equipment, such as warships, warplanes, tanks, and ammunition.[16] Apparently, scrap steel was used in the process of turning iron ore into steel.[17] The amounts of scrap metal collected from each contributor may have been small, but they accumulated nationwide into tons of scrap metal. In 1942 alone, the government collected 24 million tons of scrap metal.[18]

Federal agencies collected scrap metal from local governments, industry, agriculture, stores, civilian homes, and other groups that sought to do their patriotic duty, such as the Girl and Boy[19] Scouts of America. Local jurisdictions and states would participate in competitions to see who could collect the most scrap metal for the war effort, with the winners boasting about their collection prowess.[20] In support of these competitions, shopkeepers made a practice of requiring customers to return empty tin containers of toothpaste and shaving cream for them to purchase new such items. Households donated items such as pots and pans, metal toys, tools and other equipment that they could spare. Youth groups across the country would collect cleaned crushed cans from households and sell them for scrap to raise funds.[21] In 1942, Roosevelt ordered federal and state entities to "scrap monuments and other ornamental metal not absolutely indispensable to the public well-being."[22] Towns and cities across the United States donated metal monuments, historic cannons, wrought iron fences and fountains that graced their parks, cemeteries, and the lawns outside city halls. Notably, the U.S. Military Academy at West Point donated a dozen cannons.[23]

American organizations often came up with innovative ways to contribute to the scrap metal effort.[24] Movie theaters held matinees at which patrons could pay their way into the theater by donating a few pounds of scrap metal. Traffic courts in San Francisco agreed to permit violators to pay their fines by donating their car bumpers in lieu of cash. Others donated irreplaceable items of historical significance. These included: an autogiro employed by Admiral Byrd on his expedition to Antarctica in 1936; a massive typesetting machine, called a Paige Compositor, once owned by Mark Twain; and horseshoes once worn by a horse ridden by General Robert E. Lee during the Civil War. Arguably the largest item of historical significance donated to the war effort as part of the scrap metal drive was the battleship *Oregon*, which at the time was anchored in Portland, Oregon. It was taken despite vocal protest by local historical and veterans associations. (Note: In the end, rather than scrap the *Oregon*, the Navy used it as a munitions barge during the Battle of Guam.)[25]

RUBBER. The government also had a particular need for rubber to prosecute the war.[26] Rubber was used for, among other things, boots, tires, gas masks, life rafts, and pontoon bridges. Unfortunately, when the Japanese occupied what was then called Malaya and the Dutch East Indies, they cut the United States off from its supplies of natural rubber. How important were imports of natural rubber to the war effort? The head of the Army and Navy Munitions Board said that, unless they had a good replacement, the United States would have no option but to "call the entire thing [World War II] off."[27] To meet this need, the U.S. government moved in three directions. First, since most rubber was used domestically for car tires, the government rationed them by requiring households to sell back any tires they held in excess of five (the four tires on their one car plus a spare). The government also sought to lengthen the useful life of tires in use by rationing gasoline and reducing the speed limit.[28]

Second, from June 15–30, 1942, the government held a nationwide rubber drive through which citizens received one cent per pound for used and surplus rubber items donated, such as rubber hoses, hot water bottles, and rubber bands.[29] Even children were asked to contribute their rubber duckies. Although this rubber was not useful in the war effort, it was used to retread tires and for other civilian purposes, thus saving better quality rubber for use by warfighters overseas.[30] Third, the U.S. government sought to enhance manufacturing capacity for synthetic rubber by paying to construct and open 51 synthetic rubber factories. The government entered contracts with the four largest rubber companies (B.F. Goodrich, Firestone, Goodyear, and Jersey Standard) to manufacture 400,000 tons of synthetic rubber per year. This effort was so successful that, by 1944, the government was able to discontinue collection of reclaimed rubber.[31]

PAPER. Despite government limits on publishers' use of paper in the production of reading material, paper for use in the war effort was in short supply.[32] The military needed paper to produce several hundred thousand products needed to fight the war. Paper was used to produce draft cards, letters home, record keeping forms, orders, discharge papers, paper training targets, and wallboard for the construction of barracks. Paper was also used to package ammunition, field rations, and parachute flares.[33] The shortage resulted, in large part, because the civilian sector had increased its demand for paper to package consumer items that used to be packaged in cans. In addition, there were fewer lumberjacks to take down the trees used to make wood pulp necessary for the manufacture of paper. Lumberjacks were leaving the profession to take better-paying jobs in the defense industry.[34] The U.S. government urged households to save scrap paper and donate (or sell) it to collectors, who would forward the paper to the military. In addition, youth groups and schools got into the act by organizing paper drives whereby they would collect paper from residences.[35] A paper drive in 1942 was so successful that paper mills were inundated. But the surplus was gone by 1944, when an acute shortage of paper existed.[36]

NYLON AND SILK STOCKINGS. The government also collected women's stockings, whether nylon or silk, for the war effort.[37] The United States had previously imported all its silk from Japan, which ended shipments before the attack on Pearl Harbor.[38] The military needed silk to produce gunpowder bags for large caliber guns, such as those on warships. Other materials could be used but, unlike silk, every time a gun was fired, they left a residue that needed to be cleaned before the gun could be used again. The military needed nylon for war materials such as parachutes. One parachute contained the nylon equivalent of 2,300 stockings.[39] Various groups, including the Girl Scouts of America, collected stockings for use in the war effort. From November 1942 to March 1943, they and other organizations collected 88,000 pounds of stockings for use by the military.[40]

Baseball During Wartime

At the outset of World War II, major league owners were unsure whether they should prepare their teams to commence the 1942 season. Just 24 years earlier, when the United States embarked on World War I, the U.S. military had issued a "work or fight" order, which required men in nonessential occupations, including baseball players, to either be drafted into the military or support the war effort by obtaining a war-related job. Despite pleas from baseball owners, the 1918 season ended prematurely on September 2. Legendary ballplayers such as Grover Cleveland Alexander, "Rabbit" Maranville, and Christy Mathewson were inducted into the armed forces.[41] At the outset of World War II, owners pressured Commissioner Landis to seek guidance from President Roosevelt regarding the propriety of initiating the 1942 season during the current conflict.

Landis sent a handwritten letter to President Roosevelt, stating in part, "The time is approaching when, in ordinary conditions, our teams would be heading for spring training camps. However, inasmuch as these are not ordinary times, I venture to ask what you have in mind as to whether professional baseball should continue to operate."[42] Roosevelt was a well-known baseball fan who almost lost his job as a young attorney in New York City by leaving his post to watch Giants games at the Polo Grounds.[43] In his response, known as the "Green Light" letter, Roosevelt stated his personal unofficial opinion that "it would be best for the country to keep baseball going." He added, "There will be fewer people unemployed, and everybody will work longer hours and harder than ever before. And that means that they ought to have a chance for recreation and for taking their minds off their work than ever before."[44] While giving his opinion, the President said that he was leaving the official decision regarding whether to proceed with the baseball season up to Commissioner Landis and the club owners.[45] They decided to proceed with the season.

The President also made clear that, even though major league baseball teams may be playing games, the federal government was not exempting players eligible to serve in the armed forces from military service. Anticipating that America might need to enter the war, on September 16,

1940, the President had signed into law the Selective Training and Service Act, which required every American male (including professional baseball players) between the ages of 21 and 36 to register for 12 months of military service. The first major league player to be drafted under this law, on March 8, 1941, was Hugh "Losing Pitcher" Mulcahy, a 27-year-old pitcher who had the distinction of losing 76 games between 1937 and 1940 for the perennial cellar-dwelling Philadelphia Phillies. The first legendary major leaguer to be drafted was future Hall of Famer first baseman Hank Greenberg, who received his notice on May 7, 1941.[46] Recognizing that the military draft would eventually cause baseball to lose many of its stars, the President voiced his opinion that, "[e]ven if the quality of the teams is lowered by greater use of older players, this will not dampen the popularity of the sport."[47]

Subsequently, numerous major (and minor league) baseball players played a role in fighting the war. In total, the military inducted over 500 major league baseball players,[48] representing 90 percent of the rosters of major league teams.[49] In addition, 2,000 minor league baseball players (and, as far as we know, one minor league owner) were inducted into the armed forces.[50] This loss of players had a devastating effect on minor league teams, which reduced from 310 clubs in 44 leagues in 1940 to 66 clubs in nine leagues by 1943.[51] Major league baseball players who served during World War II included such stars as Yogi Berra, Bob Feller, Joe DiMaggio, Stan Musial, Phil Rizzuto, Warren Spahn, and Ted Williams.[52] Some, like Bob Feller, the future Hall of Fame fireballer for the Cleveland Indians, volunteered for duty. Feller was eligible for a deferment because he was the sole support of his family; his father, a farmer in Iowa, was dying of cancer. Nevertheless, when he heard of the Japanese attack on Pearl Harbor, he drove to a naval recruiting station and signed up for duty as a sailor.[53]

Many ballplayers saw no action whatsoever. The military, recognizing that they now had under their command some truly exceptional athletes capable of leading outstanding teams,[54] assigned many major leaguers to noncombat duty in which they continued to play baseball on military teams.[55] Some of these players sought to be transferred to combat units. Joe DiMaggio, once realizing that his superiors intended him to spend the war playing baseball in one form or another, requested to be transferred to a combat unit. He said that he "didn't enlist to play baseball." But his entreaties fell on deaf ears. Others did not seek combat. Either way, these former ballplayers found themselves wearing baseball uniforms as often as they wore Army fatigues. Rather than participate in the drills and other activities normally performed by servicemen readying themselves for combat, these former ballplayers were asked to compete in practices and games. The services often used these players when they staged interservice and intraservice games, and games against major leaguers staged to sell war bonds or otherwise generate funds for military causes.[56]

Some baseball players saw action during their enlistment.[57] Notably:

> BOB FELLER, who was spending his time in the service in Hawaii playing baseball and otherwise relaxing, requested that he be transferred to combat duty. Feller's superiors granted his request and assigned him to the battleship *Alabama* as a gun captain, where he participated in numerous battles in both Europe and the Pacific.[58]
>
> WARREN SPAHN initially played baseball stateside after his enlistment. But on November 9, 1944, he was sent to Europe as part of 276th Engineer Combat Battalion, 9th Armored Division. This group was charged with repairing roads and bridges in anticipation of the arrival of much larger groups of Allied troops.[59] Spahn and other members of the 276th were ordered to make the Bridge at Remagen, which straddled the Rhine River, safe for Allied troops to cross. Retreating German soldiers had riddled the bridge with explosives but, for some reason, never detonated them. As German V-2 rockets rained down, Spahn worked furiously to maintain the girders of the bridge as Allied troops crossed over it. Later, Spahn was hit by shrapnel in his left foot; the shrapnel was removed.[60] In all, Spahn won a Bronze Star, Purple Heart, a Presidential citation, and a battlefield promotion to lieutenant, making him the most decorated major league ballplayer in World War II.[61]

Numerous professional baseball players who did see combat were physically injured during hostilities, many of them seriously enough to affect their baseball careers.[62] For example:

> CECIL TRAVIS, a Washington Senator shortstop, who batted .314 as a major leaguer before the war, suffered frostbite during the Battle of the Bulge. In the three years spent in the majors after his return, the highest batting average he could achieve was .252 in 1946.[63]
>
> CHARLIE WAGNER AND HUGH MULCAHY, pitchers for the Boston Red Sox and Philadelphia Phillies, respectively, both of whom were successful prior to being inducted, contracted dysentery in the Pacific and, as a result, suffered substantial weight loss. Neither was able to pitch in the major leagues after their return from service.[64]

Other professional ballplayers suffered from the mental strain of being in combat, causing them to behave erratically when they returned from service.[65]

Still others who participated in combat made the ultimate sacrifice. Over 50 minor league ballplayers and two with major league experience lost their lives in World War II.[66] The two with major league experience, though they were not with major league teams at the time of their induction, were:

> HARRY O'NEILL, a catcher who played briefly for the Philadelphia Athletics, was killed by a sniper during the Battle of Iwo Jima[67]; and
> ELMER GEDEON, a one time outfielder for the Washington Senators, lost his life when his plane was shot down over France.[68]

Regardless of how they were used, serving in the military had a "devastating and irreversible" effect on the careers of many professional ballplayers.[69] Case in point: Hank Greenberg. Although he did not see combat, Greenberg feared that all the training and drilling he did while in service added "bulk to his already hefty frame," causing him to lose the agility that was so crucial to his superior ability as a baseball player. Once he returned from service, Greenberg lasted only two and a half years in the major leagues and showed only flashes of his former brilliance as a ballplayer. For a chosen few who played the game at the pinnacle of competitiveness, their time in the service may have robbed them of noteworthy achievements in baseball history. For example, while predicting lifetime statistics if a player had not gone into the military is a very inexact science, it is speculated that: Greenberg and DiMaggio would both have exceeded 500 home runs and 2,000 RBIs, Feller would have achieved 300 wins and broken Walter Johnson's 3,509 strikeout record, and Ted Williams would have broken Babe Ruth's record of 714 career home runs.

In the meantime, while many major league baseball players were in the military, major league baseball teams had to make do with an assortment of replacement players, many of whom would otherwise have no chance of playing major league baseball.[70] One of the more extraordinary replacement players was Pete Gray, an outfielder for the St. Louis Browns who lost his right arm in an accident. He would bat one-handed and, after making a catch in the outfield, he would return the ball to the infield using "a remarkable method of flipping and rolling the ball."[71] Also, Bert Shepherd, who lost his right leg when his fighter plane was gunned down over Germany, pitched in one game for the Washington Senators in 1945.[72] While the shortage of major league-caliber players did not cause team owners to reach out to African American players or, for that matter, women, the Negro Leagues and at least one professional women's baseball league (made famous in the movie *A League of Their Own*) continued to play during the war years side-by-side (though not necessarily in competition) with the major leagues.[73]

Major league baseball also supported the war effort by sending current baseball stars on tours of military installations overseas to help boost morale.[74] Early in 1943, *The Sporting News*, the veritable bible of baseball, suggested that the powers that be in major league baseball give serious consideration to staging baseball games overseas during the summer. Some months later, it reiterated this suggestion by stating that such a tour would represent "a tremendous opportunity to assist vitally in the war effort" by entertaining American warfighters who so loved the game as civilians.[75] Major league baseball considered the idea but was unable to send entire teams overseas because of scheduling conflicts. Instead, they did the next-best thing.

The major leagues sent baseball stars to Europe in 1943 to hobnob with the troops and occasionally display their baseball talents in exhibitions. These patriotic players included Hank Borowy, Frankie Frisch, Vernon "Lefty" Gomez, Dan Litwhiler, Stan Musial, and Fred "Dixie" Walker. In 1944, an almost identical group of ballplayers reprised their visit to servicemen.[76] For GI's who were lucky enough to participate in these events, it often meant "the fulfillment of a ... dream" to meet with their sports heroes and see them in action. Indeed, in January 1944, the military newspaper *Stars and Stripes* reported that "alarming news" was arriving from the European tour of major league ballplayers. Apparently, most of the soldiers "would rather [have] talk[ed] with big leaguers than with Betty Grable or any other dish."[77]

Major league teams also sought to support the war effort financially and materially.[78] Teams staged games against military squads made up of former major league ballplayers to promote the sale of war bonds or generate funds from gate receipts that they would donate to causes that supported the war effort. For example:

> WASHINGTON SENATORS VS. NORFOLK SAILORS. In June 1943, a crowd of 29,221 baseball fans watched the Washington Senators slip past the Norfolk Sailors military team by a score of 4–3. The Sailors team boasted such major league players as Dom DiMaggio, Phil Rizzuto, and Benny McCoy. In attendance were such well-known personages as Bing Crosby, Babe Ruth, and Kate Smith. Those in attendance purchased over $2 million in war bonds.
>
> NEW YORK ALL STAR TEAM VS. CAMP CUMBERLAND ARMY TEAM. A few months later, fans filed into the Polo Grounds to see a team comprised of players for the three major league New York teams defeat the Cumberland Army team, 5–2. The Cumberland team was stacked with baseball talent, including Hank Greenberg,

Birdie Tebbetts, and Enos Slaughter. The game was a financial success in raising money for the war effort.

AMERICAN LEAGUE ALL STARS VS. MILITARY TEAM COMPOSED MOSTLY OF FORMER BIG LEAGUERS. In July 1942, fans had the opportunity to watch a game that matched the American League All-Star team (winner of the major league All-Star Game) against a military team composed of former big-league ballplayers. This game generated about $193,000 for the Army and Navy Funds and resulted in the sale of $62,000 in Victory Stamps.

Major league baseball also supported military efforts to make sure that servicemen had the equipment needed to play baseball both in the United States and overseas.[79] Given that the American military devoted virtually all its funds to meet the enormous cost of defeating the enemy on two fronts, military leaders were able to set aside precious few funds to purchase baseball equipment for the troops. Major league baseball, with nearly every team participating, over the course of the war donated about $1 million for this cause. For example, the Pittsburgh Pirates donated the $35,844 from a game to a military equipment fund that benefited military athletics. In addition to its financial support, major league teams donated equipment directly to servicemen. For example, beginning in April 1942, the New York Giants asked fans to return balls hit into the Polo Grounds stands for donation to service teams needing equipment. By June 1942, big league ball clubs had donated over 80,000 pieces of baseball equipment to military teams at home and abroad.

Scrap Metal Day at the Polo Grounds

The New York Giants wanted to do their part to support our troops overseas. On September 26, 1942, they held Scrap Metal Day on an afternoon when they would play a doubleheader against the Boston Braves. Children bringing scrap metal to the ballpark, presumably with the aid of their parents,[80] would be admitted to the game for free.[81] This promotion was a win-win effort for the New York Giants; not only would they be helping the war effort, but they would be introducing Giants baseball to women and children who otherwise rarely attended baseball games.[82] They would also presumably increase attendance at an otherwise "unappealing" game between two teams that were out of the pennant race. Only 2,916 patrons paid their way into the Polo Grounds that day, but they had in tow 11,205 youngsters who brought scrap metal to the ballpark. Assuming the attendance figures are correct, every adult who purchased a ticket escorted on average about four children.[83]

Just three days earlier, on September 23, 1942, the Giants' cross-town rival, the Brooklyn Dodgers, held a Scrap Metal Day that was a success from a patriotic and baseball perspective.[84] The Dodgers offered free admission to anyone bringing at least 10 pounds of scrap metal to a ballgame against the Philadelphia Phillies. The 8,476 fans who went through the turnstiles free of charge donated 150 tons of scrap metal, stacked outside Ebbets Field.[85] This was a must-win game for the Dodgers, who were in a tight pennant race with the St. Louis Cardinals. Dodgers pitcher Larry French was certainly up to the challenge. He pitched a complete game one-hitter, and the Dodgers won, 6–0, to keep his team's pennant hopes alive. What's more, the one hit was a bad-hop single by Phillies first baseman Nick Etten. The *Brooklyn Daily Eagle* described the hit as follows: "Etten of the Phils hit a medium grounder just to the left of second base. Pee Wee Reese tore after the ball. He bent low and reached for the ball.... As his glove went down, the ball took a funny little hop, and skipped out to short center without touching the leather at all." Etten was later put out in a double play, so that French pitched to the minimum 27 batters. Soon after the season, French enlisted in the U.S. Navy.

When Warren Spahn entered the Polo Grounds that afternoon, he may have noticed the 56 tons of scrap metal (including the hollowed-out shell of a car) that was collected outside the stadium.[86] As Spahn watched the first game, he may have thought back on his career thus far as a professional pitcher. At the time, he was in a very different place in his career from Larry French. In 1941, with the minor league Evansville Braves, Spahn finished the season with 19 wins and a very impressive 1.83 earned run average. He pitched briefly for the big-league team in 1942 but was optioned to the Hartford Chiefs, where he compiled a 17–12 record with a sparkling 1.96 earned run average.[87]

Boston Braves manager Casey Stengel seemed to have great faith in Spahn; Stengel said of the young Spahn, "He's only twenty years old and needs work. But mark my words, if nothing happens to the kid, he can be a great one." Stengel added, "Someday, he's going to be one of the best left-handers in the league." But at this stage in his career, Spahn was just a rookie who struggled with his command. Truth be told, Spahn later admitted that, during his first few games with the Braves, "I didn't have anything resembling self-confidence," adding, "I was tight as a drum and worried about every pitch."[88] We can only assume that he tried to pick up a few pointers watching Carl Hubbell pitch the first game of the doubleheader, which the Giants won, 6–4, behind Hubbell's complete game and Mel Ott's 30th home run.[89]

Spahn took the mound for the second game.[90] He struggled with his command early and gave up a couple of walks in the first inning, which he knew from experience would likely come back to haunt him. And they did. Johnny Mize hit a sacrifice fly to account for the first run, and Babe Young drove in the second run with a single. The Braves fought back in the third inning. Spahn led off the inning with a single, moved to third on Skippy Roberge's double, and scampered home on a Paul Waner groundout. In the top of the fourth inning, the Giants, playing small ball, extended their lead on an infield hit, a walk, and Dick Bartell's single, which scored the Giants' third run. In the seventh inning, Spahn gave up two runs on an RBI triple by Babe Berna. Meanwhile, Spahn's mound opponent, Bob Carpenter, going for his 12th win of the season, effectively shut down the Braves through eight innings, giving up just two runs on six hits.

As the Braves recorded their last out in the top of the eighth inning and went to take the field with the Giants leading, 5–2, all hell broke loose.[91] The youngsters in the stands, who had sat quietly through several hours of baseball, became restless and, as if of one mind, "casting aside all adult restraint ... came tumbling out of the stands, engulfing all before them." They streamed onto the field, "first in a trickle, then in a tidal wave."[92] Finding themselves inundated with children, Spahn and his Braves teammates found it difficult to take the field, while the Giants had to fight against the tidal wave of children exiting the stands in their efforts to reach their dugout.[93] The *New York Times* later characterized the youngsters as "a hopeless, tangled, confused mass."[94] Unlike the mobs that inundated ballfields during the Farewell to Connie Mack Stadium and Disco Demolition Night promotions (as well as the Ten Cent Beer Night and the Washington Senators' Last Game promotions, which you will read about later), the youngsters didn't seek to remove items as souvenirs or otherwise damage the ballfields. After hours of sitting still, watching a game that many of them probably didn't fully understand, they apparently just enjoyed being free to run around.

Umpires Ziggy Sears and Tommy Dunn waded through the mass of children to the Giants' dugout, where they called upstairs and ordered that a public address announcement be made to clear the field. The public address announcer ordered the children to take their seats, but to no avail. No one could hear the public address announcement over the racket being made by the swirling mass of children.[95] It probably wouldn't have made any difference anyway. City police, security guards, and members of the grounds crew tried to corral the youngsters and lead them back to their seats but found it impossible.[96]

Under the circumstances, the umpires had no choice but to forfeit the games to the Braves. Giants president Horace Stoneham acceded to the decision, saying, "It was an unfortunate ending but there was no alternative under the circumstances." Still, he supported the Giants' effort to gather scrap metal for the military but said the team would learn from this occurrence. He said, "We will continue to admit children bearing war scraps, but we will try to marshal them into restricted sections tomorrow for our final season-ending doubleheader."[97] No one knows whether this alternative would have worked since the doubleheader was called on account of rain.[98]

Under forfeiture rules then in place, Spahn was given credit for pitching a complete game, but neither pitcher received a decision.[99] In 1963, forfeiture rules were revised so that pitchers of record would be granted a win or a loss "if the leading team after five or more innings had been played won via forfeit."[100]

That fall, Spahn enlisted in the armed forces where, as we've seen, he fought in Europe.[101]

◊ CHAPTER 9 ◊

A Stadium Full of Souvenirs
Washington Senators Last Game

Washington Senators Last Game
New York Yankees at Washington Senators
Robert F. Kennedy Memorial Stadium
September 30, 1971

Imagine attending the last performance of a Broadway play and, rather than going to a nearby shop for souvenirs, the audience rushes the stage before the conclusion of the play and steals the props. Ludicrous, you say. That is a fair representation of what happened at the Washington Senators' last-ever baseball game on September 30, 1971, in front of 14,460 fans (and about 30,000 empty seats)[1] at Robert F. Kennedy (RFK) Memorial Stadium.[2] It was their last game as a franchise. At one moment, the fans were watching a baseball game. With the Senators winning, 7–5, Yankees second baseman Horace Clarke was coming up to bat with two outs in the top of the ninth inning. But before he saw a pitch, the game abruptly ended as hundreds of fans rushed the field, many in search of souvenirs as a remembrance of their soon-to-be-departed Senators. When the dust settled, the souvenir hunters had removed everything that wasn't nailed down or too hot or too heavy to haul away, including the bases and scoreboard lights (at least those that had cooled). The Senators were forced to forfeit the game. It was one of the most chaotic nights in baseball history, a circus ending to a once-proud franchise.

The Bitter Legacy of Bob Short

Thursday, September 30, 1971, started as a dismal, rainy day in the nation's capital. Ron Menchine, play-by-play announcer for the Washington Senators, remembers waking up in the morning hoping that the rain would continue, and that night's game would be cancelled. For him, it was a sad day[3] to see Washington, D.C., lose major league baseball after 71 years.[4] But as they say: If you don't like the weather in Washington, D.C., just wait a few minutes and it will change. By evening, the rain had stopped,[5] leaving a hot, humid, and windy evening for baseball.[6] The Senators did not advertise such a melancholy day as a promotion, preferring to keep their departure from Washington, D.C., as low-key as possible. Nevertheless, for many Senators fans, it was still a special game where they would express their animosity towards the team's owner, Bob Short, whom they surmised had stolen the franchise right out from under them. It was as if, by word of mouth, the fans advertised a We Hate Bob Short promotion.

Ron Menchine's feelings reflected the collective angst of Senators fans everywhere, who were about to lose their second team in just over a decade.[7] Even though the Senators weren't a very successful franchise, especially compared to their American League rivals up Interstate 95—the Baltimore Orioles, New York Yankees, and Boston Red Sox—the team had a loyal and longstanding, if dwindling, fanbase.[8] When the American League was founded in 1901, Washington, D.C., was given a franchise. The Senators enjoyed some success in the early 1900s, culminating in a World Series win in 1924, powered by Hall of Famers Walter Johnson and Bucky Harris. However, with some exceptions, their performance over the 71 years was generally lackluster, causing famed sportswriter Charley Dryden to dub the city "First in war, first in peace, and last in the American League."[9]

Washington, D.C., lost the original Senators franchise in 1960, when they became the Minnesota Twins.[10] Major league baseball immediately replaced the original Senators by granting Washington, D.C., a new expansion team to begin play in 1961. Bob Short purchased the expansion Senators on January 28, 1969, for $9.4 million[11] in borrowed money. Short was a trucking and real estate magnate who had previously owned the Los Angeles Lakers basketball team. He also served as national coordinator of Hubert Humphrey's 1964 campaign for Vice President, national treasurer of the Democratic Party, and chief fundraiser for the 1968 Democratic campaign.[12] According to Shelby Whitfield in *Kiss It Goodbye*, Short borrowed $2 million from the First National Bank in St. Paul, Minnesota (the only secured loan); $4 million from the American Security & Trust Company in Washington, D.C.; and $3 million from the Johnston-Lemon Estate.[13] Upon purchasing the team, Short held a press conference and said all the right things: "I did not buy the Washington team to move it. I chose Washington for a baseball franchise—I could have invested in several other cities—but I invested in the nation's capital because I sincerely believe it can support a team."[14]

Short knowingly purchased a team with a history of losing records and poor attendance. During the eight seasons from 1961 to 1968, the expansion Senators just scuffled along. The team did not have a winning record, losing at least 100 games in four of those seasons. Attendance at Senators home games ranged from 535,604 in 1963 to 770,868 in 1967, low by major league baseball standards.

Table 1. Washington Senators Won-Lost Record and Attendance (1961–1968)

Year	Won-Lost Record	Attendance
1961	61–100	597,287
1962	60–101–1	729,775
1963	56–106	535,604
1964	62–100	600,106
1965	70–92	560,083
1966	71–88	576,260
1967	76–85	770,868
1968	65–96	546,661

Source: Baseball Reference Online

After Short purchased the Senators, the team enjoyed some initial success in 1969, when the Ted Williams-managed team won 86 games and attendance shot up to over 900,000, but the team reverted to its losing ways in 1970 and 1971, with attendance precipitously declining to 655,156 in 1971.

Table 2. Washington Senators Won-Lost Record and Attendance (1969–1971)

Year	Won-Lost Record	Attendance
1969	86–76	918,106
1970	70–92	824,789
1971	63–96	655,156

Source: Baseball Reference Online

If there was a theme song for Bob Short's ownership of the Senators, it would be "Hello, I Must be Going,"[15] from the classic 1930 Marx Brothers film *Animal Crackers*. The first verse of the song is "Hello, I must be going / I cannot stay. I came to say I must be going / I'm glad I came but just the same I must be going." In hindsight, it appears that Bob Short was only halfhearted about owning a team in Washington, D.C., and, over time, the handwriting on the wall made clear that Short intended to move the franchise to greener pastures. Whether purposeful or not, Short's often counterproductive decisions as owner of the Senators franchise placed the team in a position where it was charging the highest ticket prices in baseball to watch one of its worst performing teams. Hardly a recipe for success.

Bob Short made clear from the outset that he was *shocked ... shocked* at the poor attendance, and he reportedly lamented, "Look at last year's attendance. I can round up a girls' team and draw 500,000."[16] Yet, despite Short's concern about attendance, which admittedly was anemic, he increased ticket prices! As soon as he took ownership of the team in 1969, Short raised the prices of all seats and converted much of the regular grandstand seats into higher-priced reserved seats.[17] The team was a relative success on the field in 1969, winning 86 games, so that, despite the increased ticket prices, over 900,000 fans came to see the Senators play. This represented the second-highest attendance in the 71-year history of the Washington Senators.[18] You would think Short would be pleased. But he wasn't. Rather, Short was laser focused on the fact that the franchise lost about $600,000 that year.[19] He cried poverty to anyone who would listen: "If you can't excite a million people in your club, then you had better start looking around."[20]

There were some, including front-office personnel, who didn't understand how the team could have lost money while attracting over 900,000 fans to the stadium.[21] There were rumors that Short was skimming some of the Senators' income to his other businesses, but nothing was ever proven. Short never opened his books to the public, so it is impossible to know for sure.

In 1970, Short apparently sought to turn around his so-called failing enterprise by raising ticket prices again, effectively raising the cost of attendance overall between 50-100 percent.[22] The increased cost of attendance gave the Washington Senators the distinction of having the most expensive seats in major league baseball. Unfortunately, the Senators reverted to a losing record, and attendance decreased by about 94,000 fans; maybe more importantly to Short, the franchise lost even more money— about $1 million.

For the 1971 season, Short did not raise ticket prices further; instead, he made some questionable trades. He acted as the team's general manager, insisting on making all trades himself.[23] Short thought he could increase attendance by bringing players he believed to be stars onto the team. This strategy was doomed to fail; instead of bringing talent to the Senators, each move seemed to have the opposite effect of giving it away. Short reportedly declined trades that would have brought legitimate big leaguers to Washington.[24] Instead, he tried to attract to the Senators Curt

Flood, the former St. Louis Cardinals star outfielder who had fought in court to end the reserve clause.[25] Flood had not stayed in shape during his time away from baseball. Although he was in the starting lineup on Opening Day in 1971, Flood started the season with a .150 batting average. Two weeks into the season, he was benched and thereafter was used sparingly. Flood abruptly left the Senators on April 26, 1971, effectively ending his career in baseball.[26]

During the 1970 World Series, Short made one of the most disastrous trades in baseball history when he sent slick-fielding shortstop Ed Brinkman (.262 BA/1 HR/40 RBI in 1970), third baseman Aurelio Rodriguez (.247 BA/19 HRs/76 RBI in 1970), and pitchers Joe Coleman (8–12 record/3.58 ERA in 1970) and Jim Hannan (9–11/4.01 ERA in 1970) to the Detroit Tigers for a washed-up Denny McLain (3–5/4.65 ERA in 1970) and three other players. Short claimed that, even though McLain's skills had precipitously deteriorated since winning 31 games in 1968, having a megastar on the team would attract fans to the stadium.[27] In his first and only season with the Senators in 1971, Denny McLain won 10 games and lost 22.[28] In the meantime, Coleman won 62 games in his first three seasons in Detroit and, along with Brinkman and Rodriguez, became key contributors to the Tigers winning the American League East championship in 1972.[29] With this farcical trade, fans began to see the handwriting on the wall. According to Shelby Whitfield, "some of these same outraged fans began to think that Short had to skuttle the team a little in order to create the Finleyesque disgust that would make it easier for Short to pull out."[30]

By Spring Training 1971, the Senators had undergone a 50 percent roster turnover.[31] But Short wasn't finished. In May 1971, he traded star closer Darold Knowles (27 saves/2.04 ERA in 1970) and slugging first baseman Mike Epstein (.256 BA/20 HRs/56 RBI in 1970) to Oakland for Don Mincher (.246 BA/27 HRs/74 RBI in 1970), Paul Lindblad (8–2/2.70 ERA in 1970) and catcher Frank Fernandez.[32] While this was not as egregious as the Denny McLain trade, many fans were left scratching their heads over the loss of a star closer and slugger. Many fans apparently showed their resentment at these trades by not going to the ballpark.[33] In 1971, the Senators would win only 63 games and attract a paltry 655,156 fans to RFK Memorial Stadium.

To deflect attention from his high price/poor play decision-making, Short soon began blaming poor attendance on his perceived lack of safety in Washington, D.C.—in his estimation, a problem without a solution. Short complained, "No place in Washington was safe at night, and [President] Nixon can't do anything about it."[34] It wasn't long before Short started acting as if the team and its fans were under siege. For example, he demanded that fences be built around the outer parking lots.[35] There was some truth in what he was saying. According to Dan Epstein's history of baseball in the 1970s, *Big Hair and Plastic Grass*, the nation's capital had been scarred by the 1968 riots following the assassination of civil rights leader Dr. Martin Luther King, Jr. Increasing numbers of middle-class residents moved to the relative safety of the suburbs.[36] Obviously, there is no way of knowing whether these fans would have travelled back to the District of Columbia to root for a winning team.

Behind the scenes, Short's decisions appeared to be made by someone who was intent on the franchise leaving Washington, D.C. From the outset, he made certain that he was under no contractual obligation to keep the team in the nation's capital. During his entire tenure with the Senators, Short made no effort to modernize RFK Memorial stadium.[37] Despite protestations from Ted Williams, Short also never invested in developing a scouting operation in South America. Williams was heard to say, "Damn, I wish Short had the money to hire scouts we need to be competitive. We need scouts in South America…. That alone can be the difference in being a winner and a loser in the league." But Short refused, pleading that he didn't have the necessary funding, and the scouting system never improved.[38] Short, who paid for Ted Williams' lodging,[39] refused to move him from an apartment in the Shoreham West Hotel to a house, and dissuaded one of his better players—Del Unser—from purchasing a home in the Washington, D.C., area.[40] He reportedly told Unser, "[W]e may be somewhere else next season."[41] Short also declined to sign a radio and television contract with WWDC for 1971 because the station wanted an option for 1972, and he countered a three-year contract offer from WTOP-TV with an offer containing a clause rendering the contract null and void if he moved the team out of Washington, D.C.[42]

In the meantime, Short seemed to be going out of his way to alienate fans, business partners, and his own employees.[43] Let's just say that he didn't understand the fan optics when he refused to give free or discounted tickets to underprivileged children, saying that members of the business community should pay their way; stopped donating box seats to wounded veterans, making them climb to the top of RFK Memorial Stadium to watch games from the highest bleacher seats; and refused to televise the Presidential Opening Game, even though it was a sellout every year.

According to Shelby Whitfield in *Kiss It Goodbye*, Short "was as full of lawsuit threats as a scorpion is full of poison." For example, he sued WTOP-TV and WWDC over minor policy disagreements. Short sued Pompano Beach, Florida, for better training facilities and, absent improvements, threatened to leave Pompano Beach for training facilities in Arizona. He sued the Armory Board (RFK Memorial Stadium's landlord) and sued the Washington Redskins (now Commanders) football team for playing on wet turf and churning up the field.[44] Short also alienated people working for the franchise. After contentious contract negotiations, he fired Marjie Smith, a valuable employee who was instrumental in managing the farm system. She just wanted a long-overdue raise.[45] When Short refused to give them raises, the team trainer and groundskeeper also left for other major league teams.[46]

All the while Short was crying poverty, he neglected to pay the franchise's creditors. Short told the Armory Board he wanted a rent deal for RFK Memorial Stadium like Milwaukee's, under which the team would pay under $1 a year until the team reached one million in attendance,[47] which hadn't happened in Washington, D.C., since 1946. He often did not pay for items that had been purchased for premium giveaways for fans. C&P Telephone Company threatened to discontinue telephone service for the Senators' front office if Short did not pay the bill.[48] This behavior was associated with a steady drumbeat of threats to move the team elsewhere. Said Short, "Everybody keeps saying baseball must have a team in Washington. I don't happen to agree."[49] Yet Short managed to find the money (reportedly $400 per hour) to pay for a private Lear jet with a pilot and copilot to fly him all over the country.[50]

In July 1971, the Armory Board threatened to turn off RFK Stadium's lights and lock the stadium gates unless Short or his representative arranged a rent payment schedule.[51] Short owed the Armory Board $136,847.93 in unpaid rent over the last two seasons.[52] Other creditors followed suit.[53] Some would say Short's gambit had worked. According to Whitfield, Short now had his creditors where he wanted them. In the face of these threats, he concluded that "this town doesn't want me. You can't make me go broke in Washington. Nobody wants to buy [the Washington, D.C. franchise]. Let me go to Texas where they will appreciate me."[54] When the Washington press started lambasting Short for his poor management of the team and seemingly complete unwillingness to pay his bills, Short continued to double-down on his insistence that he was beleaguered from all sides, that no one wanted him in Washington, D.C., and his only option was to move the franchise.[55] When City Council Chairman Gilbert Hahn filed suit against Bob Short for failure to pay back rent, Short responded by saying, "Look, even the head of the city council is suing me in that damn town. How can I operate there?"[56]

As the situation evolved, the Armory Board was coming under pressure to give Short some slack and work with him to keep the franchise in Washington, D.C. After much internal deliberation, the Armory Board decided that it did not want to be blamed for losing the Senators franchise. They bent over backwards to meet Short's demands and, in the end, gave him the sweetheart deal that he was demanding.⁵⁷ According to Whitfield,

> The Armory Board would give him his free rent on the stadium for the first one million admissions; Short would have the right to name the concessionaire; he could operate the concessions during football and baseball seasons; and he would receive revenue from billboard and other stadium advertising during the baseball season.⁵⁸

Maybe it should have come as no surprise to Senators fans that, after years of losing ballgames and money, and pleading poverty due to, in his estimation, an "intractable safety problem," Short would refuse the offer, and decide to move their beloved Senators to greener pastures—namely Arlington, Texas, whose only claim to fame was that it was equidistant from the two major cities of Dallas and Ft. Worth, Texas.⁵⁹ Said Short, "I'll go anywhere before I am forced into bankruptcy."⁶⁰

There was some hope that Short would sell the team to someone who would keep it in Washington, D.C., but the sale was never culminated. Short wanted $12.4 million for the team—roughly the $9.4 million purchase price plus the $600,000 lost in 1969, the $1 million lost in 1970, and what he had lost so far in 1971.⁶¹ Short received offers from Washington, D.C., grocery store magnate Joe Danzansky, former major league baseball club owner Bill Veeck, Hall of Famer Hank Greenberg, and former St. Louis Cardinals owner Fred Saigh. Danzansky's offer appeared to be the most serious.⁶² The financing offered by Danzansky was stronger than that of any of the last three Senators owners. He thought that the other owners would force Short into selling the team to him to avoid the scandal of removing the nation's pastime from the Nation's Capital.⁶³ Apparently, none of these offers were impressive enough to entice the owners to keep baseball in Washington, D.C. At the last minute, another potential buyer, World Airways, Inc. chief Ed Daly, was contacted about his possible interest in purchasing the Senators, but he could not decide in time to stop the team's move to Texas.⁶⁴

Interestingly, leadership of major league baseball was against the move. After all, both Bowie Kuhn, Commissioner of Baseball, and Joe Cronin, President of the American League, had ties to the Senators. Kuhn was a Washington, D.C., area native who once operated the manual scoreboard in old Griffith Stadium.⁶⁵ Cronin had been player-manager of the Senators' last pennant-winning team in 1933.⁶⁶ Kuhn did everything he could to save the franchise, but it was to no avail. In the end, on September 21, 1971, after meeting for 13 hours,⁶⁷ American League owners approved by a vote⁶⁸ of 10 to 2 to move the Senators to Texas.⁶⁹ Bowie Kuhn, who attended that meeting, said that, despite his misgivings, he "couldn't make an argument against it."⁷⁰ Although Tom Hanks famously said in the movie, *A League of Their Own*, that there is no crying in baseball, Bowie Kuhn said that it was the only time he cried as Commissioner of Baseball.⁷¹

On September 23, 1971, the grandmaster of Washington, D.C., sports writers, Shirley Povich, writing in the *Washington Post*, nicely summed up the "self-imposed" dilemma of Senators owner Bob Short:

> [The owners] paid scant heed to the fact that Short foolishly overborrowed to buy the team and then pleaded poverty, and to the stubborn refusal of this novice club owner to hire a general manager, and his record of wrecking the club with absurd deals.... [T]he impoverished Senators were the only team in the league billed for the owner's private jet with co-pilots. The owners had ears only for his complaint that he couldn't operate profitably in Washington.... They showed utterly no concern for the Washington fans, who were asked to support last place teams by paying the highest prices in the league, a little matter Short arranged by trading away his infield and boosting the ticket prices far beyond those of the Baltimore Orioles, who were playing the best baseball in the league only forty miles away.⁷²

Short-Tempered Fans Invade Playing Field

As fans filed into the stadium to see the last game of their beloved franchise, bought their snacks and drinks, and took their seats, one could sense an undercurrent of anger and frustration. Attendance that night was nearly double the average home crowd that season.⁷³ Not pleased that they had lost the original franchise, Senators fans were downright enraged that they lost the new expansion franchise, especially after such a short, 11-year existence.⁷⁴ In the crowd was 74-year-old Bucky Harris who, as player-manager, had led the Senators to a World Series title about half a century earlier. He captured the sentiment of the crowd when he said, "I still can't believe it's happening, and I never thought I'd see the day when they would leave Washington without a franchise."⁷⁵ The focus of all this angst was Short. Phil Hochberg, who worked as the Senators' public address announcer, but was attending the game as a spectator, characterized Short as "forever a villain."⁷⁶

The Senators players could also sense the dark emotions of the crowd, which, in some ways, reflected how they felt about the move.⁷⁷ According to Dick Bosman, starting pitcher for the game that evening, when the players heard that the owners had approved the move, the mood in the clubhouse was grim. He said, "It was like the whole team had been traded." Bosman said, "Personally, I was resentful, and I was angry."

The fans' ire was visible for all to hear and see. Said Dick Bosman, "It wasn't your typical crowd because they were there to protest us leaving."⁷⁸

The baseball game was peppered with chants of "We want Short."[79] One woman reportedly wore a black mourning armband over her raincoat sleeve. A 14-year-old boy wept as he lugged around a Styrofoam likeness of Short around the stands with him.[80] On display that night of the last game were large signs that declared "SHORT STINKS,"[81] "SHORT SUCKS," and other epitaphs that are frankly too crude to repeat.[82] Several banners simply displayed Bob Short's initials.[83] One of the largest banners, hung by two students from Northern Virginia Community College, said "HOW DARE YOU SELL US SHORT." Another said, "WE'VE BEEN SHORT CHANGED."[84] (Puns clearly intended.) When stadium security confiscated a sign unfurled in the third inning that said, "SHORT STINKS," it was replaced to loud cheers by another sign that said, "SHORT STILL STINKS."[85]

Knowing that he would be the target of the wrath of the fans, Short did not attend the final game. It was decided, with good reason, that it would be too dangerous for him to be at the ballpark that night. The fans didn't see the Yankees as their nemesis that night, as might be the case in a regular game. Their anger and antipathy were directed at Short, who sat home in Minnesota listening to the game on the radio.[86] You would think that, unlike the enraged fans, Short would have listened to that last game with the satisfaction of knowing that he had gotten what he wanted. Instead, he was combative until the end. Short called the radio station to complain about the broadcast when, in the fifth inning, Menchine said on the air that "[m]ajor league baseball shouldn't run [the Senators] out of town ... the American League club owners took the cowards' way out." When informed about Short's complaint, a defiant Menchine responded, "What is he going to do, fire me?"[87]

Up until the eighth inning, the game proceeded without incident. Over the first six innings, the Yankees took a 5–1 lead behind the pitching of starter Mike Kekich.[88] Bosman gave up an RBI single to Yankee John Ellis in the top of the first inning; soon thereafter, he gave up a two-run home run by Bobby Murcer, and solo home runs by Yankees outfielders Roy White and Rusty Torres, who also happened to be at the Disco Demolition Night and Ten-Cent Beer Night forfeits.[89] (See Chapters 7 and 10.) The Senators scored their one run on an error by Yankees shortstop Frank Baker, who misplayed Senators second baseman Tom Ragland's grounder, permitting third baseman Dave Nelson to score.[90] Up until this point, despite the chants, the signs, and the ripped-up programs that rained down from the bleacher seats,[91] the crowd was reasonably well-behaved.

In the bottom of the sixth inning, Senators fan favorite Frank "Hondo" Howard (known as the "Capital Punisher") slugged his 26th[92] home run of the season[93] to the back of the bullpen wall, making the score

5–2. Howard desperately wanted to give the home crowd something positive to cheer about on this otherwise dismal evening.[94] Apparently, Mike Kekich was thinking along the. same lines. According to the *Washington Post*, when Frank Howard crossed home plate after his home run, he thanked Yankees catcher Thurman Munson for the "gift," recognizing that Kekich had given him an easy pitch to hit. Kekich all but acknowledged as much later, when he said, "Let's just say I tried to throw him a straight pitch."[95]

After the homer, the crowd came to life. Howard emerged twice from the dugout to acknowledge the wildly cheering crowd and, in a gesture that might have presaged what happened subsequently, threw his batting helmet into the crowd to give one lucky fan a very special souvenir.[96] In the words of Menchine, as he called the game:

> He comes out again.... Hondo threw his helmet into the stands, a souvenir of the big guy's finest hour in Washington.... The crowd screaming for Howard to come out again ... and here he comes again! ... A tremendous display of the enthusiasm of Washington fans for Frank Howard.... Hondo loves Washington as much as the fans love him.[97]

Frank Howard's homer appeared to awaken the Senators' bats.[98] Catcher Rick Billings and left fielder Jeff Burroughs followed Howard with back-to-back singles. At this point, Kekich was replaced by Jack Aker. Nelson bunted up the first base line and beat Aker's throw to first, which was offline and got past first baseman Ellis, allowing Billings to score, making the score 5–3, and Burroughs to take third. Senators right fielder Del Unser grounded back to the pitcher, whose only play was to first, allowing Burroughs to score, making the score 5–4. After Aker struck out Thomas Ragland, he intentionally walked Don Mincher and gave up a double to Elliott Maddox, scoring Nelson, tying the score at 5–5. The inning ended when Mincher was thrown out trying to score behind Nelson.[99]

In the seventh inning, when Howard fouled out to the catcher, he returned to the dugout to a standing ovation and the raucous cheers of the fans in the stands, some of whom took the opportunity to chant, "We want Short."[100]

It was in the bottom of the eighth inning that the fans' animosity towards Short began to spill out onto the field. The Senators managed to take a 7–5 lead thanks to an RBI bloop single by Tommy McGraw and a sacrifice fly by Elliot Maddox. The game was delayed by groups of fans running onto the field. However, order was restored in due course, and the game resumed. During this disruption, stadium management announced that the Senators would forfeit the game unless the field was cleared of fans.[101] While the fans returned to their seats, it was clear that their mood had darkened. They no longer pretended to behave like fans watching a baseball game and rooting for the home team. As if by telepathy, fans experiencing an undercurrent of frustration transformed into an angry mob itching to demonstrate their anger at Short and all of baseball. Shirley Povich characterized their "We want Bob Short" chants as "the baying-fury sound of a lynch mob."[102] This was not going to end well.

In the top of the ninth inning, Senators relief pitcher Joe Grzenda was brought in from the bullpen to get the final three outs. Once again, play was disrupted by fans running on the field, but order was restored with an announcement that the Senators would forfeit the game unless the field was cleared of fans.[103] Grzenda was determined to keep the Yankees from winning, to "salvage a small satisfaction from the most heart-rending day" of his career.[104] Grzenda got Felipe Alou and Bobby Murcer to ground out.[105] During the Murcer at-bat, a few fans trickled onto the field, but they were driven back to their seats by police.[106] Horace Clarke, the next batter, proceeded from the on-deck circle to the batter's box. Grzenda, a fast worker, remembers that he shouted to Clarke to get into the batter's box. "C'mon, let's go!"[107]

Grzenda never had the opportunity to throw another pitch.[108] Before Horace Clarke could assume his batting stance,[109] fans invaded the field from the first base side of the infield and left field. The police were able to move them back to the stands. Another announcement was made that any additional fans encroaching onto the playing field would cause the Senators to forfeit the game,[110] but to no avail. A fan raced out to shake hands with the players, possibly as a parting gesture of friendship. He rounded the bases and, after passing second, dove into the dirt, scrambled up, and headed for the outfielders before security guards could catch him.[111] (Shirley Povich[112] reported that this initial fan who took the field stole first base, while David Nemec and Eric Miklich[113] in their book, *Forfeits and Successfully Protested Games in Major League Baseball: A Complete record, 1871–2013*, reported that he only began removing it.) Recognizing the potential for disruption, the Senators called time to allow players in both bullpens to move safely to their respective dugouts.[114] According to Senators second baseman Tim Cullen, "That final strategic move ignited an already hostile crowd and started the rampage."[115]

All hell broke loose.[116] Hundreds, maybe as much as a couple of thousand[117] heartsick[118] fans swarmed the field, rendering the police, security guards, and umpires helpless.[119] Even with extra police on duty, security was unable to stem the tide of fans[120] who jumped the barriers all around the stadium and stormed onto the field. The players on the field were at first concerned for their safety, but it soon became apparent that these fans were not after the players. Rather, they were taking their revenge by defacing the baseball field.[121] Tony Roberts, Menchine's radio broadcast partner, said on the air, "It's like an army of ants out there going through the jungle."[122] While the fans in their seats looked on, those on the field stole whatever they could carry. They lifted the bases (though not home plate)[123] and disassembled the scoreboard.[124] Shirley Povich described what happened:

> One young rebel from the stands set off again. He grabbed first base and ran off with it. Some unbelievers, undaunted by the warning of forfeit, cheered, and from out of the stands poured hundreds, maybe a couple of thousands of fans. They took over the infield, the outfield, grabbed off every base as a souvenir, tried to get the numbers and lights from the scoreboard or anything else removable, and by their numbers left police and four umpires helpless to intervene.[125]

To those in the stands, the field became a "kaleidoscope of chaos" as players made broken field runs for the dugouts and the fans ran every which way.[126] All this time, Menchine was trying to describe the utter chaos to his listeners. Let's hear his call of the dying gasp of the Senators franchise:

> So we certainly hope that the ballgame can be concluded. The players now are clearing the field ... as pandemonium has broken loose ... and the field is filled with many souvenir hunters.... The Senators lead, 7 to 5, with two outs.... Police are trying to restore order, but the crowd continues to mill all around the field.... Some fans are scooping up dirt ... more and more now are converging on the field.[127]

Menchine finally lamented, "It's a shame that they couldn't have waited for one more out."[128]

Police started herding the crowd back into the stands. For what it was worth, the souvenir seekers for the most part left the field without incident, although three men were arrested for disorderly conduct.[129]

When he saw the destruction of the playing field, umpire-in-chief Jim Honochick had no choice but to forfeit the game to the Yankees,[130] the first in the majors since 1954.[131] With that decision, the Senators ended the 1971 season—their last season in Washington—with a lackluster record of 63 wins and 96 losses, their worst in seven years.[132]

The Aftermath

Several commentators performed postmortems regarding the game and the final season. Said Menchine, "Well, it was a strange way to lose a ballgame." He added, "It's a strange way to wind-up major league baseball in the nation's capital."[133] The *Washington Evening Star* proclaimed the game "the wildest funeral ever." The newspaper said that "the evening was a bitter wake, a joyous circus, a shouting match with an absentee offender named Bob Short."[134]

This Shakespearian tragedy was not lost on one of the Washington Senators' biggest fans, President Richard Nixon, who said that it was "heartbreaking" that Washington had lost its major league baseball franchise. Like his brethren fans, Nixon was not fond of Short who, as stated earlier, just happened to be affiliated with the Democratic Party. He characterized Short as a "jerk" and said that he could hear him "moaning and bitching" when he sat in earshot at Senators games.[135] According to a report in the *Washington Post*: "A couple of weeks after the last game [Nixon] strategized ... with Washington Mayor-Commissioner Walter E. Washington to identify teams that could take the Senators' place, including the Indians and White Sox."[136] Nixon predicted that baseball would return to Washington, D.C., by the time of the bicentennial celebration in 1976. Actually, it took 34 years for baseball to return to Washington, D.C., with the creation of the Washington Nationals.[137]

POSTSCRIPT: In 2005, Joe Gzenda attended the first game of the new Washington Nationals.[138] For 34 years, Grzenda had held onto the ball that was in play when the fans stormed the field during the Washington Senators last game. He presented the ball to President George W. Bush. It is unclear whether the President used that ball to make the ceremonial first pitch. Grzenda, through his actions, apparently sought to create a direct link between the defunct Senators franchise and the new Nationals franchise, as if the more than three decades that Washington, D.C., was without a baseball team didn't happen.

◊ **Chapter 10** ◊

A Surfeit of Beer

Ten-Cent Beer Night

Ten-Cent Beer Night
Texas Rangers at Cleveland Indians
Municipal Stadium
June 4, 1974

No doubt, a confluence—or more appropriately a perfect storm[1]—of events contributed to the fan riot that took place at the June 4, 1974, baseball game between the Cleveland Indians and Texas Rangers on Ten-Cent Beer Night. But one factor stands out among the rest. Some say that fans were swayed by the full moon that rose over Cleveland that evening. Indeed, many fans at that game did behave erratically, but it strains credulity to think that phases of the moon could alone cause such outlandish behavior on the part of so many people. Others blame Texas Rangers manager Billy Martin for inciting the Cleveland crowd, especially since there was bad blood between the teams. But then, we must consider that Billy Martin had a reputation for provoking opposition fans wherever he went, and riots didn't typically occur. In the final analysis, the most prominent factor was identified by American League President Lee MacPhail, who said, in what may be the greatest understatement in baseball history, "There was no question that beer played a part in the riot."[2]

The Mission to Save Baseball in Cleveland

By 1974, Indians management was on a mission to save baseball in Cleveland.[3] Attendance hadn't reached 1,000,000 fans in any season since 1959, when the Indians won 89 games and landed in second place, just five games behind the pennant-winning Chicago White Sox. In 1973, the Cleveland Indians attracted just 615,107 fans, an average of 7,594 per home game.[4] Attendance that year was the second-worst in major league baseball, behind only the San Diego Padres.[5] The low attendance manifested in the balance sheet as a loss of $1.4 million.[6] Cleveland's Municipal Stadium, which was the largest in major league baseball, seated about 74,400.[7] Consequently, with the average crowd in attendance, the cavernous stadium was 90 percent empty. Cleveland Indians players did not viscerally feel the support of the fans; rather, they were heartened by a rumor that fans were in attendance.

The Cleveland Indians franchise, which dates to 1901,[8] was losing its fan base due, in part, to deteriorating economic conditions in Cleveland. The once-proud industrial city was in decline. Its factories were often hampered by outmoded equipment and manufacturing processes, and they were finding it increasingly difficult to comply with ever more stringent labor, environmental, and other regulatory requirements. The environmental situation in Cleveland was particularly desperate; the Cuyahoga River, which runs through the city, was so polluted from decades of industrial waste that it caught fire in 1969.[9] These factors in combination caused Cleveland manufacturers to lose sales to increasing competition from overseas and other domestic manufacturers. In the decade preceding 1974, numerous factories and heavy industrial operations disappeared from the city's landscape, many of which moved out of state or overseas, or permanently closed.[10] As a consequence, Cleveland was losing its population as residents left the city in pursuit of better livelihoods. Since 1950, when Cleveland had enjoyed its largest population of approximately 914,000, the city's population dropped to about 750,000 by 1970.[11]

The Cleveland Indians' poor to mediocre play throughout the 1960s and early 1970s also contributed to consistently low attendance. In the 14 seasons from 1960 to 1973, the Indians had two winning seasons. Even in those seasons, they were out of the pennant race. In 1965, Cleveland finished in fifth place with a record of 87–75, 15 games behind the Minnesota Twins. In 1968, Cleveland finished in third place with a record of 86–75, 16½ games behind the Detroit Tigers. Every year from 1969 to 1973, the Indians finished last or next-to-last in the newly created American League East Division. During this period, the Indians also finished every year in the bottom half of the American League in attendance.[12]

To demonstrate just how desperate they were to attract fans, Cleveland management in 1970 committed the mortal sin of rushing a sure thing pitching project to the majors just to put people in the seats.[13] Cleveland used the second overall pick in the 1970 draft to select Steve Dunning, who was a pitching prodigy out of Stanford University. Dunning was paid a $50,000 signing bonus. Rather than send him to the minors to learn his craft and gain confidence, the Indians immediately threw him in the major league fray, hoping to win some games, but maybe more importantly, bring some fans into the ballpark. Just 11 days after signing with Cleveland, Dunning started a game against the Milwaukee Brewers. Over 25,000 fans, more than three times the usual attendance, packed into Municipal Stadium to see the wunderkind pitch. Dunning pitched the Indians to a 9—2 victory. But after that, it was mostly downhill for Dunning, who finished the 1970 season with a 4–9 record and a bloated 4.96 ERA.

Considering these troubling trends and past mistakes, in 1974, Indians management was grasping at straws as they sought ways to attract fans to the ballpark.[14] They could not rely on the team to win enough games to attract fans. Although an improvement on the 1969–73 squads,[15] the team in 1974 was mediocre at best, with no superstar to generate fan interest. Cleveland did not have any natural rivalries, like the decades-old New York Yankees-Boston Red Sox rivalry, to bring fans to the ballpark.[16] Nor could they rely on their stadium to draw fans. First opened in 1932, Municipal Stadium, which sacrificed fan comfort for quantity of fans,[17] had all the ambiance of an "open air mausoleum"[18] and was aptly nicknamed "the Mistake by the Lake."

After years of losing teams and poor attendance, Indians management ultimately decided to rely heavily on promotions to bring fans to the ballpark. Several baseball franchises were relying increasingly on promotions to improve attendance. One very successful promotion involved providing fans with reduced-price beer. The Milwaukee Brewers originated this promotion in June 1971, to great success. Fans showed up from across Wisconsin and even neighboring states for cheap beer.[19] A team employee suggested that Cleveland give this promotion a try. The Indians apparently had had success with a combined giveaway Helmet and Nickel Beer Day in 1971, during Independence Day weekend.[20] Some in Indians management were somewhat leery about whether this would work in Cleveland, but no one stepped in to stop the promotion. According to Dan Epstein, in *Big Hair and Plastic Grass*, "[I]t's hard to believe that no one in the Cleveland Indians' front office recognized the folly of offering Indians fans an endless supply of cold brew at a dime a cup."[21] However, desperate times called for desperate measures, and Cleveland ultimately planned to hold four cheap beer nights during the 1974 season, the first of which was scheduled for June 4, with Cleveland playing the Texas Rangers.[22]

Fracas at Arlington Stadium

At the time of this decision, Cleveland Indians management had no way of knowing that there would be bad blood between the Indians and

Rangers teams owing to a brawl that took place just six days prior to the June 4 promotion. Baseball had become more physical,[23] with rougher play and fights between teams breaking out far more often. To some degree, the fighting resulted from the American League's introduction of the designated hitter rule in 1973. Because of this rule, a designated position player batted for the pitcher. Because pitchers didn't come up to bat, they no longer feared that an opposing pitcher would retaliate against them if they hit a batter with a pitch. This led to pitchers increasingly throwing at batters, with batters getting their revenge by storming the mound.

On May 29, 1973, in a game at Arlington Stadium between Cleveland and the Texas Rangers, the teams fought in a dugout-clearing fracas over a close pitch thrown in retaliation for some rough play a few innings earlier.[24] Interestingly, this fracas occurred on cheap beer night at Arlington Stadium, during which fans were treated to Pearl and Lone Star beer at a discounted price.[25] Tom Grieve led off the bottom of the fourth inning for the Rangers with a walk. The next batter, Lenny Randle, hit a single, moving Grieve to second base. With Randle on first, Jim Fregosi hit a ground ball to John Lowenstein at third base. Grieve was out at third, and Lowenstein threw to second baseman Jack Brohamer. Randle slid hard into Brohamer, attempting to break up the potential double play.[26] The Indians took offense.

In the bottom of the eighth inning, Indians pitcher Milt Wilcox threw a pitch to Randle that came very close to hitting him.[27] Randle looked at the Cleveland catcher, Dave Duncan, and asked, "What's going on?" Duncan responded, "The pitch just slipped, I guess."[28] Randle took his stance in the batter's box and waited for the next pitch. Randle eventually bunted along the first base line, some say intentionally. Wilcox left the pitcher's mound to scoop up the ball. At about the same time, Randle left the baseline, ran toward Wilcox, and body slammed him to the ground. When Randle reached first base, "he tried to butt first baseman John Ellis square in the nuts."[29] Ellis, who earned money in the offseason working as a bounty hunter for a bail bondsman,[30] didn't take kindly to Randle's affront. He hit Randle in the face and knocked him to the ground. Both the Indians and Rangers charged out of their respective dugouts and began to brawl. This was no typical baseball brawl, in which the players hug and give each other dirty looks; the players threw real punches at one another.[31]

As if taking their cue from the players, the Texas crowd became hostile. The relatively few fans in attendance screamed and cursed at the Indians, throwing beer at them.[32] Indians manager Ken Aspromonte was drenched with beer.[33] Indians catcher Dave Duncan wanted to climb into the stands to confront the unruly fans who had just poured beer on his head, but was held back by his teammates.[34] To add insult to injury, the

Indians lost the game, 3–0.[35] Asked if he was concerned about playing in Cleveland in just six days, Texas manager Billy Martin quipped, "Naw. They don't have enough fans there to worry about."[36] The stage was set for the next meeting of these teams on June 4.

With little else to talk about in the interim between the games, Cleveland sports show host Pete Franklin used his popular Sportsline program on AM station WWWE[37] to "[whip] Cleveland fans into a frenzy."[38] He continually reminded fans that the upcoming series with Texas was an opportunity for payback.[39] Said Dan Coughlin, a former sports writer for the *Cleveland Plain Dealer*, "All week before the game, Pete Franklin kept up a steady drumbeat with listeners about how we need to get even with the Rangers for the brawl the previous week." He added, "He was priming the pump for an incident like the one that took place."[40] Joe Tait, a popular announcer for Cleveland Indians games, also talked up the need to get revenge against Texas.[41] Even the *Cleveland Plain Dealer* got into the act. One edition featured a picture of the Indians' logo, Chief Wahoo, in boxing gloves, with the caption, "Be ready for anything."[42]

The Riot on Ten-Cent Beer Night

The Indians couldn't have asked for better beer-drinking weather. Ten-Cent Beer Night was held on a hot and humid evening.[43] A full moon illuminated the sky.[44] Attendance records show that 25,134 fans passed through the turnstiles[45] with, as one scribe put it, "hate in their hearts and dimes in their pockets."[46] The fans were younger than usual, mostly in their early 20s.[47] The event coincided with the conclusion of the school year at many colleges.[48] These fans were expecting to see a major league baseball game between two mediocre teams. They also expected to drink a lot of beer.

The rules for beer purchases were a recipe for disaster. Those in attendance could purchase as many as six 12-ounce cups of Stroh's beer at one time for 10 cents a cup, a significant discount from the regular price of 60 cents per cup.[49] (Dan Coughlin, who was in attendance, says that the Indians' concession stands were selling Genesee brand beer. Maybe it was both.)[50] At any rate, what's important to remember is that there was no limit on how often fans could make a purchase.[51] Underage fans were not carded.[52] One fan there that night commented, "I was surprised at how many underage kids were there drinking."[53] Tim Russert, the future host of NBC's "Meet the Press," who was enrolled at Cleveland-Marshall College of Law, was in attendance that evening. He said, "I went with two dollars in my pocket. You do the math."[54]

10 ◆ A Surfeit of Beer

Recognizing the potential for mayhem, Cleveland Indians management doubled the security at the ballpark to 48 uniformed officers.[55] It became readily apparent very early that they would be overwhelmed. Ticket takers at the gates permitted fans, many of whom were already drunk (or stoned on marijuana) as they entered the ballpark, to bring in their own alcohol and marijuana, not to mention firecrackers and other explosive devises.[56] One fan apparently was able to bring in a gallon jug of Thunderbird wine, which he eventually flung in the vicinity of Texas Rangers first baseman Mike Hargrove.[57] Security had their hands full from the first pitch; firecrackers and smoke bombs could be heard exploding throughout the stadium, which was engulfed in smoke from the explosives, marijuana, and cigarettes.[58] Cleveland outfielder Jeff Burroughs commented that, because of the marijuana smoke, he "was higher than the fans."[59] In addition, according to one fan, "Beer started getting thrown around early. There's nothing worse than having beer thrown on you when it's a hot night. I remember feeling increasingly anxious to get out of there as the night went on."[60]

And that was just the beginning. Alcohol, mixed with testosterone and adrenaline, makes a very combustible compound.[61] Billy Martin was booed energetically as he brought the lineup card to the umpires to start the game. Typical Billy, he tipped his hat to the fans, who proceeded to curse him vociferously. Indeed, it soon became apparent that every Texas Rangers batter would be booed as his name was announced to take his turn at bat.[62] Other than the explosions and smoke, the game proceeded without incident until the second inning. Rangers designated hitter Tom Grieve hit a bases-empty home run off Fritz Peterson to start the scoring. That blast seemed to have served as a signal to the crowd to up the ante. A few pitches later,[63] a middle-aged woman scrambled onto the field, sprinted toward the batter's box, lifted her blouse, and exposed her breasts to the crowd.[64] She attempted to kiss Nestor Chylak, the home plate umpire. Chylak would have nothing to do with the woman,[65] who was escorted off the field by security.[66]

Soon thereafter, a young male fan stripped naked and streaked across the playing field. A security guard ran after him but struggled to keep up. According to Carl Fazio, Cleveland's director of sales and marketing, "The policemen were overweight, elderly guys who've got belts on with billy clubs, and walkie-talkies, and guns. They [had] to put their hands on their side to hold all this stuff so they can run after these kids, and here are these 19-year-old kids cutting on a dime and these older guys with all this equipment trying to keep up with them…. That was a bad sign right there."[67] The fan streaking across the playing field threw his clothes into the seats and made his way over the fence before the security officer could grab him.[68]

In the third inning, during which the Rangers took a 2–0 lead on consecutive one-out doubles by Jim Sundberg and Cesar Tovar,[69] another male streaker ran onto the field. As he was running alongside the fence, he did not know that security—coordinating their movements by radio—were following him on the opposite side of the wall in the stands. When the streaker climbed into the stands, security surprised him by throwing a large black plastic bag on top of him.[70] By their reaction, fans seemed to be enjoying this spectacle much more than the game.[71]

The inappropriate behavior continued in the fourth inning, which had its share of fan hijinks. In the top half, Tom Grieve hit his second home run of the game, increasing the Texas lead to 3–0. He rounded the bases as one might expect. However, before he could reach third base, a naked fan, continuing with the theme that night of exhibitionism, slid into second base, no doubt "getting dirt in places unsuitable for speculation."[72] In the bottom of that inning,[73] Ferguson Jenkins, the Rangers pitcher (and ultimately a Hall of Famer) was pitching to Leron Lee, left fielder for the Indians, who hit a line drive that smashed into Jenkins' midsection. As Jenkins writhed in pain, the fans in the upper deck, their common decency no doubt overwhelmed by a thirst for vengeance coupled with inebriation, could be heard chanting, "Hit him again. Hit him again. Harder. Harder."[74] Jenkins remained in the game but gave up singles to the next two batters, Charlie Spikes and Oscar Gamble, scoring Lee with the Indians' first run.[75]

The fifth inning did not provide a respite from outlandish fan behavior.[76] Apparently believing that the Cleveland fans had not yet exposed sufficient body parts, a father-son tandem ran out on the field, dropped their trousers, and mooned the outfield and bleachers.[77] They were soon taken into custody by security.[78] After this latest assault on public decency, "the stadium people had [Indians radio] announcer Herb Score implore the fans not to run on the field,"[79] but to no avail.

In the top of the sixth inning, the Rangers expanded their lead.[80] Grieve singled and Jim Fregosi doubled, sending Grieve to third. Toby Harrah tripled to drive in both base runners, to make the score 5–1. In the bottom of that frame, the Indians scored two runs. Jack Brohamer led off with a double and hustled all the way home when Rangers first baseman Mike Hargrove made an error on a hit by Lee. On the play, Lee advanced to second. Charlie Spikes and Oscar Gamble did not reach base, but Lee was called safe at third on a play resulting from Gamble's groundout.

Texas manager Martin dared to venture out of the dugout to question the close play at third base. The fans vociferously booed Martin and pelted him with empty cups, as well as cups full of beer. Martin responded by blowing kisses to the crowd as he returned to the dugout, which had the same effect as waving a red cape in front of a raging bull.[81] The public address announcer asked fans to refrain from throwing objects onto the field, which served no purpose as fans continued to throw onto the field anything they could get their hands on.[82] Jenkins, who was injured on the play at third, was replaced by Steve Foucault, who gave up a single to George Hendrick, scoring the second run of the inning for the Indians,[83] making the score 5–3 in favor of Texas.

From there on, it felt as if all semblance of restraint on the part of the fans disappeared. Indians manager Ken Aspromonte lamented, "I never saw anything like it. Every inning there was something. It never slowed down. Not for nine innings, it never slowed down. This is one we'll remember for a long time."[84] Security, ushers, and grounds crew were completely at the mercy of the now drunken fans.[85] Objects, including beer, rocks, golf balls, batteries, hot dogs—anything that fans could throw—rained onto the field.[86] Fans were entering the field in groups with seeming impunity.[87] They danced and did somersaults and cartwheels. One of their favorite things to do to shake hands with Rangers outfielder Jeff Burroughs,[88] who would later be voted the American League's Most Valuable Player for the 1974 season.[89] Another woman ran onto the field with unclear purpose. She waved to the fans, who loudly urged her to expose herself as the other woman had done earlier. When security knocked her to the ground in their attempt to usher her off the field, the fans booed security and screamed, "police brutality."[90]

Having won the right to wander over the playing field, the fans opened additional fronts in their onslaught of the baseball game. Fans climbed onto the roof of the Rangers' dugout, where they jumped up and down and peppered the players with taunts and expletives. Rangers batters, fearing hurled debris, avoided coming out to the on-deck circle to take their practice swings before each at-bat. Billy Martin banged a bat on the ceiling of the dugout,[91] although it was unclear what he was attempting to accomplish, other than aggravate the already out-of-control fans. Other fans climbed on top of the outfield wall. When security guards approached, they momentarily descended from the wall. As soon as the security officers left, however, the fans were back on the wall and continued to make mayhem.[92] Seeking reinforcements, these fans encouraged nearby spectators to join them. Soon, most of the fans in the bleachers had vacated their seats and made their way to the outfield wall.[93] In the seventh inning, fans began throwing garbage, tennis balls, batteries, rocks, and firecrackers at Rangers pitchers in the bullpen.[94] Home plate umpire Nestor Chylak, fearing for everyone's safety, emptied both bullpens.[95]

Amid all this mayhem, the stadium concession stands ran out of beer.[96] By then, 65,000 cups of beer had been consumed by the 25,134 fans in attendance.⁹⁷ Given that security was steadily losing control of the increasingly disruptive fans, did Cleveland Indians management take this opportunity to stop beer sales? Of course not. They simply instructed fans to obtain their beer directly from the Stroh's vehicle behind the outfield wall.⁹⁸ In order to maintain some semblance of control, tables were set up to separate the fans from the stadium employees dispensing the beer. At this point, fans had dispensed with the 12-ounce cups and instructed those dispensing the beer to fill mugs, pitchers, and even thermoses with beer. Fans became agitated as long lines formed at the beer truck. When some fans became angry and overturned the tables, the stadium employees fled for their safety. Security guards saw this and chose not to intervene. Losing all civility, some fans dispensed with drinking containers and began drinking beer directly from the truck spigots.⁹⁹

Despite the incessant interruptions (Dan Coughlin, in his memoir *Crazy with the Papers to Prove It,* estimated that, altogether, there were 19 streakers alone).¹⁰⁰ the game continued. In the bottom of the ninth inning, Cleveland tied the score. George Hendrick started the rally with a one-out double off Steve Foucault. Three consecutive pinch-hitters—Ed Crosby, Rusty Torres, and Alan Ashby—hit singles, with Hendrick scoring on the first of them. John Lowenstein hit a sacrifice fly that scored another run, tying the score at 5–5. The Indians had the potential winning run at second base, with two outs.¹⁰¹

That's when all hell broke loose.¹⁰² Terry Yerkic, a 19-year-old fan,¹⁰³ decided that he would like to obtain a game-used souvenir without having to pay. Like so many other spectators that night, he ran onto the field but, rather than simply make a spectacle of himself, he snatched the baseball cap from Jeff Burrough's head and ran like hell back into the stands, dropping the hat as he ran.¹⁰⁴ It is unclear what happened next,¹⁰⁵ but Burroughs made some attempt to intercept the young man and fell to the ground. Martin watched this transpire from the visitors' dugout.¹⁰⁶ However, from that vantage point, Martin was able to see little more than the players' feet.¹⁰⁷ He only saw Jeff Burroughs fall to the ground. Thinking that his player was under attack, he yelled, "Let's get 'em, boys." He rallied the players in the dugout, some carrying bats as weapons, to run to the outfield in defense of Burroughs.¹⁰⁸ This is when the fans rushed the field. The security force hired by the Indians to maintain control could not stem the onslaught of fans.¹⁰⁹

When Martin and his crew arrived in the outfield, they found Burroughs to be "flustered but unharmed."¹¹⁰ However, these baseball players also found themselves surrounded by about 200 unruly drunken fans who had climbed over the walls onto the playing field, seeking revenge. Many of these fans had weapons, including knives, chains, clubs, and bludgeons fashioned from stadium seats that had been pulled apart.[111] Photographer Ron Kuntz said, "The Rangers started going after [Terry Yerkic] and, before you knew it, there were thousands of fans all over the field. I was scared. The only thing I can compare it to was when I was covering riots in Venezuela and there were guys with Uzis running around."[112]

The Rangers initially retreated from the drunken mob but, after being taunted, regrouped and approached the fans with more determination.[113] Burroughs later admitted to feeling "like Custer at the Little Big Horn."[114] However, unlike at the Little Big Horn, the cavalry came to the aid of the Texas players. Ken Aspromonte, manager of the Indians, seeing what was transpiring on the field, rallied the players in his dugout, some with bats in hand, to reinforce the Texas players in their showdown against the fans.[115] According to Epstein, in *Big Hair and Plastic Grass*, "Mortal enemies just six days earlier, the two teams now suddenly united in battle against at least 50 drunken Clevelanders with hundreds more pouring onto the field against them."[116] (Not surprisingly, there was some confusion over the number of fans involved in the melee with players.) At this point, we had a full-blown riot. The drunken fans were no match for the armed baseball players, who stood their ground and fought numerous skirmishes.[117] Photographer Paul Tepley of the *Cleveland Press*, who was taking pictures on the field during the melee between the players and the fans, witnessed the following confrontation:

> I neared the pitcher's mound and it seemed that [the fighting] was all over. Suddenly, [Rangers catcher] Duke Sims wrestled a young fan to the ground. Through the viewfinder, I saw a number of Sims' teammates join in. I shuddered as I saw one of the Rangers throw blow after blow at the man. I thought he would be killed. If there is a more frightening or bewildering feeling than standing in the middle of a riot, I don't know what it is.[118]

Indeed, baseball players trying to defend themselves "pummeled, kicked, and punched" attendees who dared to do battle.[119]

Let's listen in as Indians announcers Joe Tait and Herb Score described what was happening[120]:

> TAIT: Tom Hilgendorf has been hit on the head. Hilgy is in definite pain. He's bent over, holding his head.... Aw, this is an absolute tragedy. Absolute tragedy.... I've been in this business for over 20 years, and I have never seen anything as disgusting as this.
> SCORE: I don't think this game will continue, Joe.... The unbelievable thing is people keep jumping out of the stands after they see what is going on!
> TAIT: The security people here are just totally incapable of handling the crowd. They just—well, short of the National Guard, I'm not sure what would handle this crowd right now. It's unbelievable. Just unbelievable.

According to Dan Coughlin, in *Crazy with the Papers to Prove It*, back in Texas, Mike Hargrove's young wife, Sharon Hargrove, was listening to the game on her car radio.[121] She commented that the goings-on did not so much sound like a baseball game but, rather, a war zone. She was terrified for her husband. She had never been to Cleveland. Listening to the game, which made the city sound more like a battleground, she figured that she never would visit.

At some point during this riot, the stadium organist played "Take Me Out to the Ballgame," possibly to remind everyone that they were attending a baseball game.[122] The drunken fans began to retreat, more likely due to the beating they were taking than to the rendering of the baseball anthem. The ballplayers took this opportunity to make their way to their respective dugouts and the safety of their clubhouses. Eventually, both teams made it to their clubhouses,[123] but not without some casualties. As Tait commented above, Indians relief pitcher Tom Hilgendorf was hit in the head by a flying chair and had to be helped off the field.[124] Also, Burroughs apparently jammed his thumb, and Rangers pitcher Steve Foucault received a black eye.[125]

The fans chose not to follow the retreating players but instead saw the opportunity to snatch souvenirs from the field of play. They stole first, second, and third base, and anything else that wasn't nailed down, or too hot or heavy to carry.[126] At this point, umpire-in-chief Nestor Chylak, who was hit by a rock and a chair,[127] and narrowly missed getting hit by a hurled hunting knife,[128] had no choice but to forfeit the game to the Rangers.[129]

Some commentators argued that Cleveland should have won the forfeited game because Martin effectively ended the game when he led his players into the outfield in defense of Burroughs.[130] Ted Bonda, Indians vice president said, "At some point Billy Martin started throwing gravel and shooting our fans the finger and when he led his men out of the dugout, that was when matters got out of hand."[131] Carl Fazio, Cleveland Indians director of sales and marketing, echoed the thoughts of his colleague, "Billy Martin wanted the forfeit. That's my personal opinion. He knew what he was doing. We were coming back. We had the winning run on second. He wasn't going to wait for that to happen. He led the team out of the dugout."[132]

However, one supposes that, in Chylak's way of thinking, the antics of the Cleveland fans and their nonstop incursions on the field, not to mention their stealing the bases, brought the game to an end.

The fans looted and damaged the field for another 20 minutes[133] until the police in riot gear finally arrived to quell the riot.[134] They used tear gas and batons to remove the fans from the field and send them home.[135] The police took 12 fans into custody, most of whom were charged with disorderly conduct.[136] Seven fans were hurt seriously enough to be taken to the hospital.[137] The baseball field, which required significant restoration, suffered the greatest injury.[138] Frank Ferrone, the chief of Cleveland stadium security, said, "We would have needed 25,000 cops to handle this crowd."[139]

The Rangers left the stadium under police escort.[140] According to Hargrove, "[W]e all left as a group, boarded the buses under police protection. They drove us up to the old Hollenden House, where we stayed, and we were told not to come down out of our rooms until noon the next day. I was told the police were stationed in the lobby all night."[141] Apparently, one Rangers player made it down to the lounge that evening. In his book about the Texas Rangers, *Seasons in Hell*, Mike Shropshire relates that, when he returned to the Hollenden House Hotel, he struck up a conversation with Jeff Burroughs in the hotel lounge. As he tells it: "Burroughs pulled me aside. 'Hey,' he wondered, 'Do the stats count in a forfeit? I hope not. I went 0-for-4.'"[142]

The Aftermath

The Cleveland Indians' front office tried to deflect blame from themselves. Cleveland general manager Phil Seghi blamed the umpires for losing control of the game.[143] Carl Fazio tried to make it appear that the Indians' management was blindsided by circumstances they could not envision. He said, "I don't look at it as a black eye at all. It was just one of those crazy things that happened because of a crazy set of circumstances that all came together and happened that night."[144] Team president Ted Bonda held a press conference the next day. After being pelted with questions by reporters about the Ten-Cent Beer Night promotion and how it was handled by the Indians' management, Bonda threw his hands up in the air and exclaimed, "You're giving beer a bad name."[145]

The reviews of the game otherwise were devastating. *Newsweek* characterized the game and resulting melee as "one of the ugliest incidents in the 105-year history of [baseball]." Joe Tait characterized the game as an "absolute tragedy."[146] He added, "I've been in this business for over twenty years and I have never seen anything as disgusting as this."[147] Umpire Joe Brinkman likened the game to a "battle zone."[148] Indians pitcher Dick Bosman, who was also present at the Senators' forfeit, described the situation as "mean, ugly, and frightening."[149] Martin said, "This is the closest you're ever going to be to seeing someone killed in this game of baseball. Burroughs seemed to be surrounded. Maybe it was silly for us to go out there, but we weren't about to leave a man on the field unprotected. It seemed that he might be destroyed."[150] He also expressed appreciation for the Indians coming to the rescue of his players: "I am very proud of the Cleveland players. They saved our lives."[151] Ken Aspromonte blamed society in general for the breakdown in law and order: "It's not just baseball. It's the society we live in. Nobody seems to care about anything. We complained about the people in Arlington last week when they threw beer on us and taunted us to fight. But look at our people—they were worse. I don't know what it was, and I don't know who to blame, but I'm scared."[152]

A bloodied Nestor Chylak, possibly most irate, stated, "We could have gotten killed out there very easily."[153] He described the fans as "uncontrollable beasts"[154] and "f**king animals,[155] that's what all these f**king people are."[156] He added, "I've never seen anything like it, except in a zoo."[157] He continued, "You just can't pull back a pack of animals. When uncontrollable beasts are out there, you got to do something. I saw two guys with knives, and I got hit with a chair. If the f**king war is coming on tomorrow, I'm going to join the other side to get a shot at them."[158]

None of what transpired on June 4, 1974, stopped Cleveland Indians management from following through with the three additional Ten-Cent beer Nights in 1974.[159] After the debacle, Cleveland Indians promotions director Jackie York attended a management meeting in the office of team president Ted Bonda. He expected to be fired. Instead, he was instructed to go to Milwaukee to learn how they ran their beer nights.[160] Based on what was learned in Milwaukee and lessons learned from the initial event, Cleveland management changed the rules to limit beer consumption and increased security from 50 to 150 police, sheriff's deputies, and private stadium force.[161] These events took place without incident.[162]

The camaraderie and adrenaline rush from the battle royal with the fans seemed to have a salutatory impact on the Cleveland Indians players.[163] They rebounded from playing mediocre ball to enjoying one of the best stretches of winning baseball the team had experienced in over a decade. They won 21 of the next 30 games to ascend to the top of the American League East. Cleveland remained within reach of first place until the team experienced a collapse beginning on September 11. All this winning baseball had a positive impact on attendance, which increased to over one million for the first time in 15 years. So we can say something positive about Ten-Cent Beer Night—it seems to have indirectly helped Cleveland to reach the one million mark in attendance.

◊ **CHAPTER 11** ◊

A Shower of Baseballs

Souvenir Baseball Night

Souvenir Baseball Night
St. Louis Cardinals at Los Angeles Dodgers
Dodger Stadium
August 10, 1995

There were four ingredients in the potion that caused the Los Angeles Dodgers to forfeit the game on August 10, 1995. First and foremost, the Dodgers handed out 15,000 souvenir baseballs to fans that evening even though recent history with such giveaways indicated that fans no longer felt restrained from flinging them onto the field. Second, home plate umpire Jim Quick had, shall we say, a fluid strike zone and a propensity for ejecting players, the combination of which resulted in some Dodgers being ejected for arguing balls and strikes. Third, Dodgers manager Tommy Lasorda's affable nature was coupled with a fiery competitive streak that caused him to get into raucous arguments with umpires when he felt that his players were being disrespected. Fourth, the Dodgers fans were on the same wavelength as Tommy Lasorda, who they did not see simply as the manager of the team, but as their personal representative on the field. When Lasorda approached Quick to raise concerns about his players being ejected, waving his arms as was his custom, his behavior served as a catalyst, causing this witches' brew to explode with hundreds of souvenir balls raining onto the field, inadvertently leading to the forfeit.

Patriarch of the Dodger Family

Tommy Lasorda was born on September 22, 1927, in Norristown, Pennsylvania, the son of Italian immigrants.[1] His father worked, at various times, on the railroad, in a meatpacking plant, and as a truck driver at

Tommy Lasorda was more than just the manager of the Los Angeles Dodgers. He was seen as the team's primary fan, so that, when he vociferously argued with the home plate umpire on Souvenir Baseball Night, fans felt compelled to support him by flinging their balls onto the field (National Baseball Hall of Fame and Museum).

a quarry owned by Bethlehem Steel.[2] While his four brothers went into the restaurant business,[3] Lasorda heard the siren call of baseball. As a child, he loved playing baseball and, as he grew into manhood, he developed into a noteworthy left-handed pitcher.[4]

After Lasorda graduated from high school, he got his first taste of professional baseball when he was signed in 1945 at the age of 18 by the Philadelphia Phillies,[5] who assigned him to the Concord Weavers of the North Carolina State League.[6] This was the start of a nearly 28-year journey as a professional baseball player, scout, and manager, mostly with the Dodgers' organization, before finally joining the major leagues for good. Lasorda's first year in professional ball was challenging. As a pitcher, he finished the season with a 3–12 record and a 4.09 ERA in 121 innings.[7] He spent 1945 to 1947 in the U.S. Army and, when discharged, joined the Phillies' Schenectady Blue Jays affiliate in 1948. There, on May 31, 1948, Lasorda enjoyed his best performance as a professional pitcher: He set a league record by striking out 25 batters in a 15-inning game in which he also drove in the winning run.[8]

The Brooklyn Dodgers acquired Lasorda from the Phillies' farm system[9] in 1949, and from 1950 to 1954, he pitched for the Dodgers' Montreal Royals minor league affiliate.[10] As shown in the following table, Lasorda experienced success during this period.

Table 1: Tommy Lasorda Minor League Pitching Record with Montreal Royals

Year	Team	Record	Earned Run Average
1950	Montreal	9–4	3.70
1951	Montreal	12–8	3.49
1952	Montreal	14–5	3.66
1953	Montreal	17–8	2.81
1954	Montreal	14–5	3.51

Source: Baseball Reference Online

Lasorda made his major league debut on August 5, 1954, pitching three innings against the St. Louis Cardinals at Ebbets Field.[11] He yielded six hits and three runs.[12] He also tore his knee down to the bone on a play at the plate resulting from a wild pitch.[13] Altogether, Lasorda didn't enjoy great success at the major league level with the Dodgers.[14] In four appearances in 1954, Lasorda posted a 5.00 ERA in nine innings of work with no wins or losses. In four appearances in 1955, Lasorda posted a 13.50 ERA in just four innings pitched with no wins or losses.[15] That same year, Lasorda learned that he was being sent back to the minor leagues so the Dodgers could keep a diamond-in-the-rough fireballer named Sandy Koufax,[16] who went on to become one of the greatest left-handed pitchers in major league history. Not having impressed at the major league level, Lasorda was traded to the Kansas City Athletics for the 1956 season.[17]

Lasorda received his largest major league workload with the Athletics. In 1956, Lasorda appeared in 18 games,[18] starting five and compiling a 0–4 record with a 6.15 ERA for an Athletics team that finished the season with a 52–102 record.[19] This was Lasorda's last season in the major leagues.[20] In July 1956, the Athletics traded Lasorda to the New York Yankees, where he was assigned to the Triple A Denver Bears. There he met Ralph Houk, who himself would become a very successful manager in the major leagues. Houk managed the Yankees to two world championships in 1961 and 1962. Houk is said to have had a profound impact on Lasorda that shaped his managerial style throughout his career. He taught Lasorda a great deal about managing and apparently impressed upon the young Lasorda that he should always treat players like human beings, not commodities.[21] Houk promised that, if he followed this rule, his players would perform like supermen.²² In 1957, the Dodgers once again obtained Lasorda from the Yankees. Lasorda spent three more years in the Dodgers' organization at the minor leagues²³ and, in 1960, he retired as a baseball player.²⁴

Once his playing days were over, Lasorda scouted for the Dodgers for four years. In 1966, he got his first managerial job in the Dodgers' organization with the Pocatello Chiefs of the rookie league.²⁵ From 1965 to 1972, he rose through the managerial ranks.²⁶ As a manager, Lasorda brought excitement to the game of baseball. The same passion and enthusiasm for baseball that carried him through his career as a player was more than evident in his career as a manager.²⁷ As a minor league manager, he was a highly positive motivating force, and it showed in the success of the players and his teams. In the minors, Lasorda's teams won five pennants in seven seasons, and 75 players he managed were promoted to the major leagues.²⁸

One story told about Lasorda as a minor league manager is indicative of his management style: Lasorda once managed a highly competitive Albuquerque team that experienced a losing streak. According to Colin Gunderson, in *Tommy Lasorda: My Way*, Lasorda sought to turn things around by building his team's confidence:

> "I don't want you hanging your heads," Tommy told them. "Yeah, you lost five in a row, but they were close tough games. Did you know that just a few weeks ago, the sportswriters took a poll on who was the greatest team in the history of baseball? They chose the 1927 Yankees. That team had Lou Gehrig, Tony Lazzeri, and the Babe. Well, the '27 Yankees lost seven in a row, and you guys only lost five, so don't worry about it. Let's go out and win tonight." They won that night and went on to win ten in a row. [When asked sometime later] if the 1927 Yankees really lost seven games in a row, [Lasorda] said "How the heck do I know? That was the year I was born..."²⁹

In 1973, Lasorda was invited to the big leagues to become the third base coach for the Los Angeles Dodgers.³⁰ While a third base coach, Lasorda rejected several offers to serve as manager for other teams.³¹ He succeeded Dodgers Hall of Fame manager Walter Alston when, with four games remaining in the 1976 season, Alston retired.³² Lasorda knew he had big shoes to fill; Alston had managed the Brooklyn and Los Angeles Dodgers for 23 years,³³ during which time the Dodgers won the National League pennant on seven occasions and four World Series championships.³⁴ Lasorda would not only fill those shoes but, like his buddy Frank Sinatra sang, Lasorda did it *his way*. Lasorda told the *New York Times* that he brought "a whole new philosophy of managing."³⁵ Whereas Alston was a colorless³⁶ manager, Lasorda was larger than life—outgoing, effusive, effervescent, and, seemingly in perpetual motion.³⁷ Lasorda also had a fiery aspect to his personality, which was in full display whenever he disagreed with an umpire's decision.[38]

Lasorda had a remarkably successful career as manager of the Dodgers. In the 20 seasons between 1977 and 1996, Lasorda's Dodgers made the playoffs on eight occasions, won four National League pennants, and won two World Series. As a manager, Lasorda compiled a 1,599–1,439 record, with a winning percentage of .526 in regular season games and a winning percentage of .508 in 61 post-season games.[39] During his first two full seasons leading the Dodgers, the team won the National League pennant, losing in the World Series to the New York Yankees on both occasions.[40] With those two pennants, Lasorda became the first National League manager to win pennants in his first two seasons.[41] Lasorda's Dodgers won the National League pennant again in 1981 and 1988, both times winning the World Series.[42] In the 1981 series, the Yankees won the first two games, but the Dodgers swept the next four games, winning the franchise's fifth championship since 1955.[43] In the second World Series, the Dodgers beat the Oakland Athletics four games to one.[44] Lasorda was named Manager of the Year in the National League in 1983 and 1988.[45] Only three men managed the same team for longer than Lasorda: Connie Mack, who managed the Philadelphia Athletics for 50 seasons; John McGraw, who led the New York Giants for all or part of 31 seasons; and Walter Alston,[46] who had managed the Dodgers for 23 seasons.[47] Lasorda was elected to the Hall of Fame in March 1997 by the Veterans Committee. The Dodgers later retired his No. 2 uniform.[48]

It wasn't just what Lasorda accomplished, but how he accomplished it, that defines his time as a major league manager. While not considered to be a great strategist,[49] Lasorda was a great motivator, a leader of men who, through praise, support, and the occasional kick-in-the-pants,[50] inspired his players to play up to their abilities, often exceed their abilities, and sometimes achieve greatness in a very demanding sport where failure lurks at every turn. According to Colin Gunderson, believing that he never had the opportunity he deserved to pitch in the major leagues, "[Lasorda] would go out of his way to give every player an opportunity, especially if he sensed a burning determination within them."[51]

Lasorda motivated his players with both words and actions, preaching teamwork and exhorting them not to get into tugs of war with each other, but to always pull from the same side of the rope.[52] He challenged them to be their best.[53] When they pleased him, Lasorda wasn't afraid to give them giant hugs.[54] He treated them almost like family, remembering the names of their wives and children.[55] Said Ned Colletti, a former Dodgers general manager, "He could make you laugh. He could motivate you. He could bring you confidence. He could question something to get you to think differently. And he could love you. And he could do all of that in about five minutes."[56] Lasorda even expanded the manager's office used by Walter Alston so that it could hold a television, couches, and a postgame buffet. He invited players to join him at the buffet and chat.[57]

Many of the players he managed in both the minor and major leagues praised his ability to prepare players to compete in the game of baseball. According to third baseman Ron Cey, "[Lasorda] was so outwardly passionate about things."[58] First baseman Steve Garvey said, "[Lasorda] would always be real positive. This positivity and his work ethic rubbed off on [his players]."[59] According to first baseman Eric Karros, "Tommy was a master at generating enthusiasm, especially among young players."[60] Pitcher Burt Hooton said, "Tommy was real good at making each one of his players feel special as a ball player and as a person." Hooton added, "Tommy was always really good at keeping you positive … and moving forward. [He] was always there for you when times were going bad… [Lasorda] was really good at getting you refocused on competing to the best of your ability."[61] According to pitcher Orel Hershiser, "[Lasorda] understands and teaches guys to embrace the big moment."[62] Several players attested that to play for Lasorda was to emulate his competitiveness and drive to win.[63] According to Terry Forster, "[Lasorda] taught us to dedicate ourselves to the Dodgers." Forster personally found Lasorda's love for Dodgers blue infectious.[64]

Possibly the most famous instance of a Dodger managed by Lasorda embracing the big moment happened in the 1988 World Series against the Oakland Athletics. With two outs in the bottom of the ninth of the first game, with a runner on base and the Dodgers losing, 4–3, Lasorda called upon Kirk Gibson to pinch-hit. Gibson, a star player in his own right, was on the bench with an injury.[65] The fans watched him hobble from the dugout to the batter's box, wondering how this obviously injured player could help the cause. It seemed apparent that, if Gibson hit a single to the outfield, the outfielder may have enough time to throw him out at first before he limped down the line to first base. Gibson had to hit a double or better to even reach first base. As things turned out, Gibson hit a slider from future Hall of Fame closer Dennis Eckersley for a home run, scoring two runs and winning the game.[66]

As a manager, Tommy Lasorda's colorful persona hid a fiery[67] competitive streak.[68] Lasorda had a voracious appetite for winning,[69] and this competitiveness sometimes caused him to get into heated, expletive-filled arguments with umpires who, in his opinion, made a bad call or somehow disrespected his players.[70] Lasorda was ejected from major league games on 48 occasions.[71] He would also at times argue vociferously with his own players who were not performing up to his expectations, and he wasn't averse to using expletives when talking to the press. Mike Scioscia, a catcher for Lasorda who went on be a manager himself, said about Lasorda: "He's the most competitive person I've met in my life, whether he's pitching horseshoes or shooting baskets or pitching baseballs."[72]

In Game Four of the 1977 World Series, Lasorda agreed to wear a microphone to enhance television coverage. After the New York Yankees got three straight hits off Dodgers pitcher Doug Rau, Lasorda called time out and visited the mound, where he and Rau verbally went at each other in an expletive-filled, knock-down, drag-out fight. Of course, that conversation never made it onto the air, but it later became a popular Internet sound bite.[73] In July 1982, Lasorda was accused of ordering his pitcher, Tom Niedenfuer, to throw at Joe Lefebvre of the San Diego Padres. When asked about the incident by the press, Lasorda denied doing so, in the process saying, "I certainly wouldn't make [Niedenfuer] throw at a f**king .130 hitter like Lefebvre who couldn't hit water if he fell out of a f**king boat."[74] During spring training in 2008 (long after his managerial career was over), when Dodgers manager Joe Torre took a portion of the team to play exhibition games in China, Lasorda was asked to manage a split squad game during spring training. When the Dodgers' James Loney was tagged out trying to bunt, Lasorda argued strenuously with the umpire, insisting that the ball had gone foul before the tag was applied. Said Loney, "But that's Tommy though. You've got to win, even though the game was meaningless."[75]

Tommy Lasorda had a unique and rather intense relationship with the fans, in which he was both the leader of the franchise and its most notable and important fan. According to pitcher Jerry Reuss, "So many fans have told me that they started loving the Dodgers [when Lasorda arrived] in the 1970s." He added, "It was all about the Dodgers … and the reason was the passion and excitement and enthusiasm that Tom brought to the table. He became the face of the Dodgers."[76] Unlike other managers who stayed in the clubhouse and let their players deal with the fans, Lasorda was out in front relating to the fans. In his encounters with fans both in person and through the media, Lasorda gave the impression that he didn't just work for the Dodgers in the same way that virtually all baseball managers simply work for a ballclub. Rather, he acted as if he were born into the franchise and, when he became manager of the big league club, it wasn't just a job that he might hold for a few years. Lasorda, for all intents and purposes, saw himself as the Italian patriarch of the proud and very large Dodgers family. And, like a charismatic populist leader, he not only made himself available to the fans but gave the impression that he was one of them. Ensconced in these roles of manager, patriarch and fan, over the years Lasorda became the leading light of the fanbase; he shared the fans' love for the Dodgers and, sharing this intimacy, the fans knew that, when it came to the Dodgers, they had his back.

A Pitchers' Duel

A sellout crowd[77] of 53,361 crammed into Dodger Stadium on Souvenir Baseball Night, hoping to watch the incomparable rookie, Hideo Nomo, pitch yet another brilliant game[78] and vanquish the visiting St. Louis Cardinals.[79] As an added inducement to attend—as if any were needed—the Dodgers handed out to fans entering the park that night 15,000[80] souvenir baseballs commemorating the 14 Dodgers[81] who, prior to 1995, had been named Rookie of the Year.[82]

This game was being played at the height of "Nomomania."[83] Hideo Nomo was a rookie sensation. When he joined the Dodgers on February 13, 1995, Nomo was the first Japanese ballplayer to appear in major league games since Masanori Murakami, who pitched 54 games for the San Francisco Giants in 1964–1965.[84] Nomo's first month in the major leagues was uneven, but even then, he showed promise. Once he hit his stride in early June, he was dominant. Over a span of 13 starts from June 2 to August 10 (the Souvenir Baseball game), "Nomo averaged nearly eight innings per outing, posted a 1.31 ERA, allowed a .419 opponent OPS, and struck out nearly 30 percent of hitters he faced."[85] During this period, Nomo also started the All-Star Game for the National League, striking out three of the six hitters he faced—Kenny Lofton, Edgar Martinez, and Albert Belle.[86] Everywhere he went, a retinue of reporters followed in his wake. By season's end, "Nomo would lead the [National League] in strikeouts, shutouts, and fewest hits allowed per nine innings, and finishing second, only behind [Greg] Maddux in ERA. He placed fourth in Cy Young voting and won the [National League] Rookie of the Year award over future Hall of Famer Chipper Jones."[87]

The Dodgers saw no harm with this baseball giveaway. Major league baseball teams had been giving away souvenir balls to fans attending ballgames for decades. According to Dodgers General Manager Fred Claire, "We had giveaway nights, ball nights, many times in the past, over the years." He added, "So it wasn't as if this was something new or different from what had been done."[88] However, had Dodgers management taken the time to study recent history with this type of giveaway, it might have given them reason to reconsider. In 1990, a game in San Diego was twice delayed by fans chucking souvenir balls onto the field to celebrate home runs. Padres future Hall of Famer Tony Gwynn said, "That was one of the dumbest things I have ever seen. I don't think we'll see that promotion again." A day later, fans at a San Francisco Giants game involving brawls, ejections, and big innings against Giants pitchers, threw their souvenir baseballs onto the field. That same year, Angels fans responded the same way to a game with brawls and ejections, littering the field with red and blue giveaway baseballs.[89] None of these games involved a forfeit, but it was just a matter of time.

The first six innings were uneventful with regard to fan disturbances. Hideo Nomo didn't disappoint; he gave up only two runs. In the second inning, Nomo gave up a solo home run to Cardinals center fielder Brian Jordan. Nomo threw another home run ball to rookie first baseman Mark Sweeney in the fourth inning. In the seventh, with the score 2–0 in favor of the Cardinals, a disturbance occurred. Several unruly fans, for reasons that are unclear (although they might be attributed to inebriation) threw souvenir balls onto the field.[90]

In the bottom of the eighth inning, home plate umpire Jim Quick began to expand his strike zone. The Dodgers cut the Cardinals' lead when José Offerman drove in Dave Hansen with a two-out single. With the score 2–1, future Hall of Fame catcher Mike Piazza hit an infield single, moving Offerman to second base.[91] When the next batter, former Rookie of the Year Eric Karros, took the plate with men on first and second and two out, tensions began to rise. Working with a one-ball, two-strikes count, Karros checked his swing as a fastball from Cardinals reliever T.J. Matthews whizzed by. He (and every Dodgers fan in the stadium that night) thought the pitch was outside the strike zone. However, the one person who counted most saw it differently. Quick called the pitch a strike, ending Karros' at-bat and killing a Dodgers rally in a close game. An exasperated Karros turned and argued the call. Apparently, Karros was too vehement or possibly his language was too colorful, because Quick threw him out of the game.[92] For the first time, fans began throwing souvenir balls onto the field in protest.[93]

After an uneventful top of the ninth inning, the Dodgers had their last chance to tie or win the game. John Mabry, who was playing right field, remembers that, at the start of the inning, a fan threw a ball onto the field near him. He picked it up and, after pretending to throw it back into the stands, he threw it into the bullpen, at which time another ball came out of the stands near center fielder Brian Jordan.[94] Neither outfielder knew that these balls foreshadowed what was to come.

Dodgers star Raul Mondesi led off for the Dodgers. Working with a three-ball, no-strike count,[95] Mondesi took a pitch from Cardinals relief pitcher Tom Henke that he believed was ball four. Henke admitted that he "lived on the edges [of the plate]. That's how I made my living, especially toward the end of my career.... I couldn't live in the middle of the plate, or those guys would have killed me."[96] Mondesi, thinking he had earned a walk, dropped his bat and headed for first base,[97] only to be stunned when he heard the home plate umpire call the pitch a strike. Mondesi returned to the plate. Henke threw him a pitch that looked well outside the strike zone, which Quick called a strike. Working now with a full count, Mondesi swung and missed at a pitch almost identical to the second called strike that was clearly outside.[98] Mondesi later stated that, although the last pitch was outside the strike zone, he felt he had to swing because it had previously been called a strike. Mondesi also argued with Quick and, despite being thrown out of the game, continued to argue.[99]

Lasorda quickly came out of the dugout to support Mondesi and protest having two stars thrown out of the game. Lasorda got right into Quick's face, shouting and waving his arms.[100] And he was ejected as well.[101] With that, all hell broke loose. A torrent of baseballs was unleashed from the stands in protest. John Mabry recalls that, in addition to the souvenir balls, a bottle of Southern Comfort[102] was thrown in his direction.[103] The Cardinals were instructed to leave the field for their safety.[104] The grounds crew filled 15 to 20 buckets with the souvenir balls and, within five minutes, the Cardinals returned to their positions.[105]

At that point, just as play was about to resume, David Nemec and Eric Miklich report in *Forfeits and Successfully Protested Games in Major League Baseball: A Complete Record, 1871–2013*, that a "hailstorm of balls" fell onto the field came from the stands. No sooner did the balls land on the field than umpire-in-chief Quick decided that the playing field wasn't safe and forfeited the game to the visiting Cardinals.[106] First base umpire Bob Davidson explained the thinking of the umpiring crew, "Obviously, it was an unsafe situation." He added, "We stopped the game on the third time and the fans kept throwing baseballs on the field, for our safety and the St. Louis Cardinals' safety, we forfeited the game."[107] It was the only game the Cardinals won on a nine-game road trip.[108] This was the first forfeit in the National League in 41 years and the last in either league since 1979.[109]

The first forfeit in major league baseball in 16 years was no small matter. In fact, it was so important that the umpiring crew called Leonard Coleman, the National League president, at three in the morning to give him the news. According to Anthony Castrovince, in his article, "The crazy story behind MLB's last forfeit," the conversation went like this[110]:

> Once Coleman answered the call, Jim Quick says, "Mr. Coleman, it's Jim Quick, and Bob Davidson's on the line too."
> "What's the matter?" asked Coleman.
> The umpires responded, "Well, we had to forfeit a game at Dodger Stadium."
> Coleman exclaimed, "You WHAT!"

Just two days later, the "baseball gods might have evened the cosmic scales for [Los Angeles]." In the bottom of the 11th inning, in a game against the Pittsburgh Pirates, the Dodgers won when opposing catcher

Angelo Encarnaciòn was called for catcher's interference when he picked up a pitch in the dirt with his mask.[111]

The Aftermath

The umpires defended their decision to forfeit the game to the Cardinals. Said umpire Bob Davidson, "As an umpire you hate to [forfeit a game]. Games are nine innings and that is what they are supposed to be, but this was a dangerous situation."[112]

It appears that Dodgers players were just stunned.[113]

Cardinals players agreed with the umpires' decision to forfeit the game. Some players were simply concerned about the baseballs raining down on the field. Said Cardinals center fielder Brian Jordan, "I'm not going to stand out there and get busted in the head with a ball. The umpires made a good decision."[114] Other Cardinals were concerned that objects other than baseballs were being thrown at them. John Mabry said to Bob Nightingale of *The Sporting News*, "I wasn't too worried until a bottle of Southern Comfort flew out of the stands and hit me."[115]

These players were giving voice to the concern of many major league baseball players. According to Sam Miller, in "25 years ago tonight, MLB had its last forfeit," playing baseball surrounded by as many as 50,000 fans can be scary.[116] This is particularly true for visiting teams; the people in the stands are, for all intents and purposes, held together by their animus toward the visiting team. "Scary like the ocean, scary like the edge of an enormous cliff, scary like a thunderclap—a crowd is just an incredible overwhelming gathering of potential energy."[117] J.J. Hardy, shortstop for the Baltimore Orioles from 2011 to 2017, said that he became alarmed when the hometown crowd of about 45,000 erupted in a thunderous response to Delmon Young's clutch bases-clearing double that gave the Orioles the lead in Game Two of the 2014 American League Division Series. We saw that potential become real on Ten Cent Beer Night (Chapter 10), when hundreds of fans entered the field to violently confront players from both teams. Baseball players make their living before a crowd that often outnumbers them 2,000- to 3,000-to-1. In a situation like that which took place at the Souvenir Baseball promotion, with balls and other heavy objects raining down from the stands to the field, all that potential energy became real.

Fred Claire also complained that no public address announcement was made to warn fans that their unruly behavior could cause the Dodgers to forfeit the game.[118] Lasorda felt the same way.[119] However, based on prior experience at Ten Cent Beer Night, Disco Demolition Night, and the Senators' last game, history does not indicate that public address announcements (or, for that matter, renditions of "Take Me Out to the Ballgame") would have made any difference. When the fans are riled enough to interrupt the game, they tend to throw caution to the wind. Interestingly, according to one report of the game, first base umpire Bob Davidson and Cardinals players John Mabry and Tom Henke (who was pitching the bottom of the ninth for the Cardinals) remembered hearing public address announcements in the ninth inning.[120]

No matter where one stands on the necessity for the forfeit, the call was very controversial because the Dodgers were in a tight race with the Colorado Rockies for first place in the National League West division. Indeed, at the time of this game, the Dodgers were just one game behind the first-place Rockies.[121] If the Dodgers had won this game, they would have entered into a tie for first place with the Rockies, who lost that night to the Florida Marlins.[122] Dodgers General Manager Fred Claire was very critical of the umpires for calling a forfeit in the midst of a tight pennant race. He said, "I've seen many disputes, many delays, many things taking place on the field. But all at once, in a close ballgame, when you're fighting for a pennant and first place, you've lost because an umpire made a ruling. I didn't like it then, I don't like it now, and I won't like it thirty years from now."[123] As things turned out, the Dodgers won the National League West Division by one game, so the forfeit did not affect which team came in first. The Dodgers were eventually swept by the Cincinnati Reds in the National League Division Series.[124]

Who was to blame? Some of those who commented simply blamed the fans. They said the fans acted alone in protesting what they saw as problematic umpiring, an umpire who missed balls and strikes calls and then threw out Dodgers who showed him up.[125] Lasorda said, "I'm disappointed in the [fans] who threw the balls, not the good fans."[126] Billy Ashley, left fielder for the Dodgers said, "It was ridiculous. The fans shouldn't be doing it in the first place, especially in a game like this where we had a chance to come back."[127] Cardinals coach Bob Gibson echoed Lasorda's concern about the fans that night: "Dodgers fans used to be among the best in baseball. I'm afraid you can't say that anymore."[128] Umpire Bob Davidson lamented, "People here are usually tremendous baseball fans. [Throwing the balls on the field] was disgraceful for Los Angeles and their fans. Very disgraceful."[129] According to the *Los Angeles Times*' Mike Downey, "Here, fans are best known for leaving early, if this is the way people tend to behave, please leave early."[130]

Eric Karros seemed to imply that Jim Quick was at fault. Several years later, the incident was still fresh in Karros' mind. He said, "Quick was [bleep] behind the plate, just having a bad night."[131] Consistent with this thinking, Lasorda would have been justified in coming onto the field to complain to Quick about his umpiring, leading to an uprising by the fans.

Umpire Bob Davidson blamed Lasorda for the shower of baseballs, arguing that his typically ardent, arm-flapping argument style "instigated the whole thing."[132] Cardinals catcher Tom Pagnozzi agreed.[133] To be fair to Lasorda, others said that he had previously acted in the same manner countless other times, and Dodgers fans never caused a stoppage in play.[134] Lasorda responded, "How did I instigate it? I was talking to Jim Quick. All I was asking was why he threw my players out.... If I don't come out and ask why my players are being thrown out, what kind of manager am I?[135] We didn't throw the balls."[136] Lasorda added, "[T]hat is a real crime, for those guys to put that blame on me."[137] Said Claire, "[Lasorda] didn't bump the umpire or anything. He manages with passion. That [argument] wasn't any different than Tommy's disputing any other near-play or call he didn't agree with. It's not as if a very mild manager went crazy."[138]

Truth be known: Both the fans and Lasorda acted in unison to cause the forfeit. As has been discussed, Lasorda cultivated a special relationship with the fans. Given their extraordinarily close relationship to Lasorda, who they saw not only as the team's manager but also as the Dodgers' principal fan, many of the fans in the stands that night didn't just agree with him but felt compelled to show that they had his back. When Lasorda got into Jim Quick's face, he wasn't just a manager expressing his dismay with the umpiring; rather, he was the primary fan channeling the anger and frustration of those in the stands. In so doing, he ignited a fan reaction that led to the forfeit. You may ask: If the fans had a longstanding special relationship with Lasorda, why didn't a forfeit happen before? Other times, only three ingredients were present: Lasorda's relationship to the fans, his combativeness, and reason to be displeased with the umpiring. In the past, when Lasorda argued with umpires, the fans had only their voices to show their support. This night, they had the souvenir balls and weren't deterred from flinging them.

POSTSCRIPT: Just two years later, in 1997, at a Milwaukee Brewers game, fans threw souvenir balls on the field, echoing fan behavior at the Dodgers' Souvenir Ball Night.[139] Although the game was not forfeited, the beloved sausage race had to be cancelled to ensure the safety of the racing sausages. De facto baseball commissioner Bud Selig happened to be at this game. After this fiasco, major league baseball decided that giveaways of baseballs or other throwable objects must occur as the fans are leaving the stadium or through a voucher system. This policy states: "In order to secure the safety and well-being of on-field personnel, and keep the field free of debris that could delay or cause the forfeit of a game, all in-stadium promotional giveaways that could be thrown on the field of play, such as baseballs, frisbees, etc., should be distributed to patrons as they exit the ballpark."[140] With this new policy, major league baseball teams were essentially instructed to give away to fans entering stadiums only items that are too floppy to throw onto the field, such as T-shirts and floppy hats; or items that fans cherish too much to throw on the field, such as bobbleheads.

Epilogue
The Thrill Is Gone

Yawn. I'm sorry. I was just reviewing major league baseball teams' promotional calendars for 2024 and, to say the least, they are underwhelming. Nothing like the inventive and innovative promotions we saw during the Era of the Barnums. With rare exception, it's the usual suspects in promotions. Lots of giveaways, mostly apparel and bobbleheads, with several other items thrown in for good measure. Then there are the tributes, usually to underrepresented communities, the military, and service professions. Teams are also staging promotions that seek to create awareness of diseases and illnesses. These tribute/awareness promotions are worthwhile, laudatory in their intent, and deserve fan support, but are hardly exciting. Virtually all teams sponsor events linked to popular media franchises, everything from Sesame Street to the Grateful Dead. Other than that, there is a hodgepodge of promotions designed to be safe, no matter how you think about them. I should note that teams sometimes add events to their promotion schedule during the course of the season.

The Rare Exception

Several major league baseball teams in 2024 staged light shows using drones. These promotions have the potential to be fascinating. In particular, the Los Angeles Angels staged a *Star Wars* light show using 800 drones. Courtesy of YouTube, I was able to watch this promotion. I must say that it was very impressive. With *Star Wars* music playing in the background, controllers managed to arrange 800 drones in the sky above Angel Stadium to create visuals of *Star Wars* characters and related images. One other team sponsored a promotion using 250 drones, and other teams used varying numbers.

Giveaways

The most popular major league promotion in 2024 was the giveaway. Teams often gave away away bobbleheads, usually depicting current baseball players, but also former players and sometimes characters from popular media franchises, such as the Peanuts cartoon and DC Super Villain characters. Teams also gave away apparel, including baseball caps, t-shirts, floppy hats, bucket hats, and replica baseball, basketball, hockey, and soccer jerseys. In addition, teams gave away a plethora of other items, such as beach totes and towels. Giveaways are safe promotions, as long as the items handed to fans can't be thrown onto the field. Teams feel safe giving away throwable bobbleheads because, as we've already noted, fans universally hang onto them. It seems that some teams were taking small risks with items such as cups, mugs, tumblers, and pickleball racquets. One team gave away replica baseball bats. As this list shows, teams gave away a very extensive, though unimaginative number of items.

Table 1: Major League Baseball 2024 Merchandise Giveaways

Action figures	Crossbody handbags	Replica baseball bats
Apparel	Cups	Replica championship rings
Aprons	Decals	
Backpacks	Dog leashes	Replica Oakland Coliseums
Baseball cards	Drawstring bags	
Baseball cards folios	Fanny packs	Replica World Series rings
Baseball gloves	Figurines	Rubik's cubes
Batting gloves	Growth charts	Sidewalk chalk
Beach totes	Hand puppets	Sliding gloves
Beach towels	Headbands	Slippers
Belt bags	Jigsaw puzzles	Snow globes
Blankets	Lunch boxes	Socks
Bobbleheads	Magnet schedules	Squishy pillows
Build-a-Bears	Mittens	Sticker sheets
Calendars	Nightlights	Sunglasses
Canvas prints	Pennants	Swim goggles
Children's books	Phone wallets	Team photos
Christmas sweaters	Pickleball racquets	Tote bags
Coffee mugs	Pins	Tumblers
Collectable miniatures	Plush dolls	Viewfinders
Comic Books	Posters	Wallets
Cookies	Power banks	Water bottles
Costume jewelry	Purses	
Coupon books	Rally monkey	

Source: MLB.com

As a personal aside, some years ago, I attended a Baltimore Orioles game at which the team gave away the ultimate non-throwable item. I knew prior to the game that I would receive an Adley Rutschman Rookie Season Digital Collectible non-fungible token (NFT). At the time, I had no idea what an NFT was, but it sounded great. I learned at the game that such an item does not exist in reality but only on a computer. Technically, an NFT is "a unique digital identifier that is recorded on a blockchain and is used to certify ownership and authenticity." These items cannot be copied, substituted, or subdivided, but they can be sold, meaning that they have value. I, and I assume others as well, were quite disappointed to be going home with nothing. At least, nothing I could hold in my hand or put in my pocket. My digital collectible still exists on the Internet. As far as I know, the Orioles never repeated the promotion.

Tribute Promotions

Major league teams also used promotions during the 2024 season to pay tribute to ethnic and other communities in the United States. As you can see from the following list, they worked very hard to ensure that no community was excluded. Often, the teams tied these tributes to giveaways. While these promotions are certainly laudatory and the communities involved appropriately take pride in being recognized by their major league baseball team, the promotions themselves appear unimaginative.

Table 2: Major League Baseball 2024 Ethnic and Other Community Tributes

African American/ Juneteenth	German	Native American
Asian Americans/ Pacific Islanders	Greek	Nicaraguan
	Haitian	Panamanian
Bahamian	Hispanic/Latino	Polish
Brazilian	Irish	Polynesian
Caribbean	Italian	Portuguese
Chinese	Jamaican	Puerto Rican
Colombian	Japanese	Scottish
Cuban	Jewish	Taiwanese
Dominican	Korean	Venezuelan
Filipino	LGBTQ+	
	Mexican	

Source: MLB.com

Major league teams also staged promotions to pay tribute to those in the military service, and in service and other professions. As with the ethnic and other community promotions, teams often sponsored giveaways in connection with these tributes.

Table 3: Major League Baseball 2024 Tributes to the Armed Forces, and Service and Other Professions

Agriculture	Law enforcement	U.S. Armed Forces/
Business	Meteorologist/Weather	Military
Firefighters	forecasters	Air Force
First responders	Nurses	Army
Health care	Teachers (including one	Coast Guard
	Math Day and one	Marine Corp
	STEM Day)	Navy
	Union workers	Space Force

Source: MLB.com

Teams also used promotions to honor, recognize, or otherwise single out the societal contributions of, among others:

- Former baseball players, notably those in the Negro Leagues, and former individual star players, including Jackie Robinson, Roberto Clemente, and Larry Doby. Also, Joe Mauer (to celebrate his recent induction into the Hall of Fame), Dwight Gooden (to retire his number), Daryl Strawberry (to retire his number), and Cole Hamels (to honor him after his retirement from baseball).
- Current non-baseball athletes, including all female athletes, Team USA, and one individual athlete—Kansas City Chiefs quarterback Patrick Mahomes.
- Other sports, such as aerobics/strength training, cricket, golf, hockey, football, Little League baseball, minor league baseball, NASCAR, pickleball, running, skateboarding, soccer, volleyball, yoga, and youth baseball & softball.
- Faith groups, including people of all faiths, and such individual faiths as Christians and Catholics.
- Fathers (usually on Father's Day), mothers (usually on Mother's Day), kids, women, and seniors.
- Boy Scouts and Girl Scouts.
- Colleges (students often get discounted entry prices), including community colleges, and historically black colleges and universities.

Awareness Promotions

Major league teams in 2024 also sponsored promotions to promote awareness of certain prominent illnesses, conditions, and disabilities. In addition to creating awareness, some of these promotions were aimed at supporting those who experience an illness, so that the name of the promotion was phrased in terms of "pride," such as "Disability Pride Night." Teams may give away items to fans in connection with these promotions.

Table 3: Major League Baseball 2024 Promotions to Create Awareness of Illnesses/Conditions

Alzheimer's disease	Cancer	Mental health
Amyotrophic Lateral Sclerosis (Lou Gehrig's Disease)	Colorectal cancer	Peanut allergies (Peanut control day at the park)
	Dental health	Pediatric cancer
	Disabilities	
Autism	Hearing impaired	Prostate cancer
Breast cancer	Hunger	Women's cancer

Source: MLB.com

As you might imagine, these were laudable but lowkey promotions.

Tie-In Promotions

In addition, major league teams sponsored promotions that tie in with popular media franchises. These often involved a giveaway related to the franchise, be it movies, television, music, or other forms of entertainment. These tie-in promotions were often entertaining. In case you were wondering, according to the White Sox promotional website, the World Wrestling Entertainment promotion did not involve any actual wrestling (or, for that matter, weddings).

Table 4: Major League Baseball 2024 Promotions That Tie in with Popular Media Franchises

Batman	Friends	Pixar
Bayou culture	Godzilla	Reggae
Bruce Lee	The Grateful Dead	Sesame Street
Country music	Happy Days	Star Wars
DC Comics	Harry Potter	World Wrestling Entertainment
Discovery Channel Shark Week	Hello Kitty	
	Jerry Garcia	Yacht Rock
	Margaritaville	
Elvis Presley	Peanuts	

Source: MLB.com

Remaining Promotions

Other 2024 promotions included among others:

- 5K races
- Baseball current player & alumni autographs
- Celebrations of ballpark and World Series championship anniversaries
- Days set aside for groups such as Camp Day, Family Day, and School Day
- Discount food and drink, including burgers & beer, brunch, Coca Cola, hot dogs, ice cream, salsa, tacos, and tequila
- Fan appreciation
- Fireworks
- Kids run the bases. Fans of all ages run the bases. Seniors stroll the bases. Seniors stroll the outfield warning track
- Old Timers Day (just the Yankees)
- Photo Day (fans can take pictures with players)
- Pre-game happy hours and post-game parties and concerts, including one Luau Weekend
- Ladies' Nights (sometimes called Girls Night Out or, in one case, Wine, Women & Baseball)
- Bark at the Park/Pups in the Park (patrons were permitted to bring dogs to the game), including one promotion which encouraged fans to dress up their pet
- Cat-urday (It's not what you think. Fans were *not* permitted to bring cats to the park. Rather, a portion of the proceeds was donated to the Humane Rescue Alliance)
- Team Hall of Fame inductions
- Throwback promotions (when players wore old-style uniforms)
- Work from Dome Day, a Toronto Blue Jays promotion, in which individuals or groups could play hooky from work and take in a game at the ballpark.

Conclusion

When the great Blues guitarist B.B. King sang "The Thrill Is Gone," he wasn't talking about major league baseball promotions, but he just as well may have. In the Era of the Barnums, fans no doubt were thrilled to view and, in one case, participate in the truly innovative and, sometimes outrageous, promotions staged at the ballparks. Who wouldn't be thrilled to see the only little person in the history of major league baseball take an at-bat, or actually manage their hometown team for a game? They must have been excited to win a car (even though it turned out to be a clunker) or watch Kiteman fly through the air. And yes, I have no doubt that the wet t-shirt contest caused a special kind of excitement for the spectators who witnessed it. Nowadays, major league baseball teams are careful to ensure that they don't stage promotions that upset baseball tradition or risk getting out of hand. I don't think anyone would consider the promotions cataloged in this epilogue, apart from the drone light shows, to be thrilling. Instead, they are routine, conventional, pedestrian, even humdrum. It is nice to receive a giveaway, see your community recognized at the ballpark, or know that your ballclub is spreading awareness of an illness that is touching your life. But are they truly memorable? Next time you go to a major league game, imagine that Bill Veeck owns your team, and you have no idea what crazy stunt he is going to pull, but you know that, at the least, it will be entertaining. Those were the good old days.

Appendix I

If You Give It Away, They Will Come

Outrageous Giveaways

You've probably noticed that none of the outrageous promotions discussed in this book were included solely because a giveaway item was outrageous. While no giveaways rose to the level of the *most* outrageous promotions in major league history, some can be considered outrageous because of the nature of the items given away. These range from synthetic sideburns to a chia pet to a bag of compost. Often, upon closer inspection, we find that the teams sponsoring these promotions have good reason to give away what at first appears to be an outrageous item. In one case, the item actually represents years of hard work towards a very laudatory goal. In another, the giveaway item represents a long-term nurturing relationship between a major league team and a child, who uses the confidence he gained to rise to fame, not in baseball, but in the music world.

◊ NEW YORK YANKEES/REGGIE BARS. On Opening Day 1978, the New York Yankees gave away Reggie Bars as a gameday promotion. This promotion was included in Jim Dunphy's list of "Worst Promotions in Baseball History," which also included such unmitigated disasters as Ten-Cent Beer Night and Disco Demolition Night.[1] Reggie Jackson was the baseball sensation who first plied his trade with the Oakland Athletics, until they traded him to the Baltimore Orioles where it became apparent in 1976 that he was going to seek free agency. Jackson decided not to re-sign with the small-market Orioles, choosing instead to play for the media circus New York Yankees, where he became a superstar. His superstar status as "Mr. October" was cemented when, in the 1977 World Series, Jackson hit three home runs on three consecutive pitches from three different pitchers.[2]

Jackson, who never lacked self-confidence, predicted that, if he ever played in New York, they would name a candy bar after him. The Curtiss Candy Company[3] made Jackson's prediction a reality when, following the 1977 season, the company introduced the Reggie Bar, named for the hero of the just-completed World Series. The Reggie Bar was round confection made of caramel and peanuts, covered in chocolate.[4] Many saw a candy bar named after a major league baseball player as outrageous. Catfish Hunter took the opportunity to mock Jackson's outsized ego when he said, "When you unwrap a Reggie Bar, it tells you how good it is."[5]

Some sought to moderate the criticism by pointing out that there was a precedent for naming a candy bar after a ballplayer; the Nestlé company decades earlier had marketed a candy bar called Baby Ruth, which many believed was named for the Sultan of Swat.[6] But upon closer inspection, that precedent evaporates. Turns out that, according to Nestlé, the candy bar was named after the eldest of President Grover Cleveland's daughters—Ruth Cleveland, who was known as "Baby Ruth."

Jackson didn't disappoint the fans on his big day (which, as Opening Day, should have been the team's big day). He hit a three-run homer in his first at-bat. And how did the Yankees fans celebrate this homer? How else: By throwing the candy bars on the field. The umpires had to stop play to give the grounds crew time to pick up all the discarded candy bars.[7] However, there was no forfeit. White Sox manager Bob Lemon (who would later manage the Yankees) expressed his dismay as he watched the grounds crew clear the field of the discarded Reggie Bars: "Let them throw them when he's in right field." He added, "People starving all over the world, and thirty billion calories are laying on the field."[8]

In 1981, the Curtiss Candy Company took the Reggie Bar off the market. Clark Candies, Inc. reintroduced the Reggie Bar in the 1990s, when Jackson was inducted into the Hall of Fame, but quickly took it off the market.[9] The Reggie Bar apparently made a comeback in 2022 to celebrate the 45th anniversary of Jackson's three home run heroics in the 1977 World Series. As of this writing, it is available on Amazon.com where $68.93 will buy you a box of 24 bars. All this begs the question: How many people seeing the ad on Amazon.com for the Reggie Bar 45 years after the fact would connect the bar to Reggie Jackson's World Series heroics or even know who Reggie Jackson was?

◊ Kansas City Royals/White Caps. In 1987, the Royals sponsored a promotion in which they gave white caps to fans. This giveaway was listed in sportswriter Chris Landers' article, "Each team's weirdest promotional item ever," which also included Charlie O. Finley's Automobile Industry Night.[10] That particular promotion did not make our list of outrageous promotions, but it was close. Now, why would anyone consider a white cap giveaway promotion outrageous? It turns out that fly balls would blend into the background of white caps worn by Kansas City fans in the stands. As a result, outfielders on several occasions were blinded as to the location of the ball as it hurtled toward them. Luckily, there were no reported injuries.[11] But in major league baseball, every fly ball should not be an adventure.

◊ MINNESOTA TWINS/JOE MAUER SIDEBURNS. In 2006, the Twins, in a game against the Toronto Blue Jays, hosted a promotion in which fans received synthetic sideburns that were the spitting image of those worn by Twins player Joe Mauer. This giveaway was listed in Chris Landers' article, "Each team's weirdest promotional item ever."[12] The sideburns were composed of synthetic hair with double-sided tape on the inside, which fans could use to attach the sideburns, presumably to the sides of their heads.[13]

Joe Mauer, as you might be aware, was the Minnesota Twins' Hall of Fame catcher and first baseman.[14] He was selected by the Twins as the first overall pick in the 2001 amateur draft. Mauer in his prime is considered by many to be the best contact hitter among catchers of his generation. He is the only catcher in major league history to win three batting titles and the only catcher to win a batting title in the American League. In 2009, Mauer won the American League Most Valuable Player award. He was inducted into the Hall of Fame in his first year of eligibility in 2024.

Mauer is no doubt worthy of recognition by the Twins. But why sideburns? Isn't that a little outrageous? Not really. Among his many attributes, Maurer was considered to have the most impressive sideburns in the major leagues. Why the Twins chose to recognize that attribute, I really can't say.

◊ FLORIDA MARLINS/VUVUZELAS. In 2009, the Florida Marlins gave away vuvuzela horns to fans entering the ballpark. This promotion was included in sportswriter Ray Tannock's article, "Top Ten Worst MLB Gameday Promotions Ever," which also included such cringeworthy promotions as the Dodgers' Souvenir Baseball Night, Wet T-Shirt Night, Ten-Cent Beer Night, and Disco Demolition Night.[15] Why would this giveaway constitute an outrageous promotion? When played, vuvuzelas, which are about 25 inches in length, emit a loud, dissonant sound. Some fans couldn't help but blow on their vuvuzelas throughout the game, annoying the players and those fans who would have liked to watch the contest without the sound of blaring horns.

◊ SEATTLE MARINERS/BAGS OF COMPOST. In 2011, on several occasions, the Seattle Mariners gave to fans entering Safeco Field (which in 2019 was renamed T-Mobile Park) bags of compost.[16] Jim Dunphy listed Seattle's compost giveaways as being among the already mentioned "Worst Promotions in Baseball."[17] This compost was composed of, among other things, decayed food waste, compostable food packaging material, drinking cups, and utensils.[18] The Mariners arranged for Cedar Grove Composting to transform this garbage into compost useful in the garden.[19] Essentially, the Mariners were returning to their fans in a biodegraded form the garbage they left behind. Pretty outrageous!

But the more we dig (pun intended) into the reasoning behind this promotion, the less outrageous it seems.[20] Throughout history, fans attending professional sporting events have seen one competitor win and one lose (unless the competition ended in a tie) and have left behind a mountain of trash for the venue to clean up and dispose of. For time immemorial, the trash fans left behind found its way into landfills. The Seattle Mariners franchise has been trying to change all that.

Since 2006, the Mariners have been leaders in bringing environmentally conscious practices to the management of sports arenas.[21] The Mariners sought to transform what was a "culture of waste" into a model of environmental stewardship; they devoted scarce resources to transform their stadium into a facility that recycles and composts a large portion of what would otherwise have been trash. What's more, by doing so, the Mariners influenced other professional sports teams to become environmentally conscious and go green.[22]

The Mariners set an ambitious sustainability goal for themselves—that is, being the first stadium to send zero waste to landfills.[23] As part of their sustainability efforts, the Mariners recycle or compost nearly all food waste, service ware, including "plates, knives, forks, cups, straws, and bottles," and grass clippings. They also have replaced garbage cans with compost and recycling bins[24] and installed signage to instruct fans on their use.[25] As of 2011, the year of the compost promotions, the Mariners' recycling efforts diverted an estimated 900,000 pounds of food, service ware, and grass clippings from the garbage stream.[26] What's more, the Mariners found, to their surprise, that their sustainability efforts saved the franchise money. For instance, they found that hauling what would have been garbage to the compost facility cost less than hauling it to the landfill.[27]

Through their efforts, the Mariners have inspired all 30 major league baseball teams to enact environmental efforts. Some teams, such as the Minnesota Twins and San Francisco Giants, have followed Seattle's lead and have taken major steps towards making their stadiums safe for the environment.[28]

In 2011, the Seattle Mariners joined with other environmentally conscious teams in the Pacific Northwest to form the Green Sports Alliance. Other founding members included the NFL's Seattle Seahawks, NBA's Portland Trailblazers, NHL's Vancouver Canucks, WNBA's Seattle

Storm, and MLS' Seattle Sounders FC. These teams sought to create a culture of conservation within the sports industry and reduce its negative impact on the environment.[29] This represents the first time teams from all six major American professional sports leagues joined together to pursue a common environmental agenda. Since its inception, the original members of the Green Sports Alliance have been joined by over 300 sports teams and venues from 20 different sports leagues in 14 countries.[30]

I wonder how many Mariners fans quizzically receiving their bag of compost realized the thought and effort that went into creating them and the hope for an environmentally cleaner world that they represented?

◊ OAKLAND ATHLETICS/MC HAMMER BOBBLEHEAD. In 2011, the Oakland Athletics sponsored a giveaway promotion in which fans received an MC Hammer bobblehead. MC Hammer[31] is a rap music impresario. He is a rapper, dancer, record producer and entrepreneur known for early-1990s hit songs such as "U Can't Touch This," "2 Legit 2 Quit," and "Pumps and a Bump."[32] This particular promotion was included in a blog by sports historian Roger Launius, titled "My Favorite Weird Baseball Promotions," that also included such outrageous promotions as the Eddie Gaedel Game and Ten-Cent Beer Night.[33] I guess it is considered outrageous because the giveaway was so random. What does MC Hammer have to do with major league baseball in general, and the Oakland Athletics in particular?

Well, upon closer inspection, it appears that MC Hammer's early life was interwoven with Athletics baseball.[34] In 1973, Charlie Finley, owner of the Oakland Athletics, happened upon a group of children entertaining themselves in the street. The story goes: One boy, named Stanley Burrell, caught Finley's eye. In Stanley's own words, he was "doing a dance with ten friends ... just being crazy." Finley approached the young man and told him that "he looks like Henry Aaron." Finley invited Stanley up to his stadium box. Finley tended to give people fanciful names, so he gave Stanley the nickname "Hammer," because of his uncanny resemblance to Hall of Fame slugger Henry Aaron.

Stanley became a fixture at the Athletics' front office and the dugout, where he would do odd jobs for various Athletics employees.[35] Stanley "helped the clubhouse managers, ran errands, and provided Finley with telephonic play-by-play broadcasts of the [Athletics] game back to his office in Chicago." Stanley was so useful that Finley gave him an honorary position as a club vice president.

Stanley hoped someday to play major league baseball,[36] but it never came to pass. So Stanley went into the entertainment business, where he adopted the moniker "MC Hammer" and, in time, became an international music superstar as an acrobatic singer and dancer. I'm sure that Stanley, doing odd jobs for the Athletics' front office, never dreamed that he would become the "forefather and pioneering innovator of pop rap ... and the first hip hop artist to achieve diamond status for one of his albums, 'Please Hammer Don't Hurt 'Em.'"[37]

When they distributed their MC Hammer bobbleheads, did the Athletics explain the history behind the giveaway or were curious fans in the dark as to his relationship with the team?

◊ Chicago White Sox/Roger Brossard Bobblehead. In 2011, the Chicago White Sox, in a game against the Oakland Athletics, gave away to the first 20,000 fans to enter Cellular Field a Roger Brossard bobblehead.[38] This giveaway was listed in Chris Landers' article, "Each team's weirdest promotional item ever." Who was Roger Brossard, you ask? He was the White Sox's head groundskeeper. It may sound outrageous to give away a groundskeeper bobblehead, but not in the case of Roger Brossard, who had been the team's groundskeeper since 1983. Anyone with that longevity in so difficult a job as being a groundskeeper in Chicago's sometimes extreme weather deserves some recognition. Why not a bobblehead?

◊ Tampa Bay Rays/The Zim Bear. In 2012, the Tampa Bay Rays wanted to pay homage to senior advisor and longtime major league baseball fixture, Don Zimmer. They staged a giveaway in which fans received a "Zim Bear"; that, is, a teddy bear in a Tampa Bay uniform with Don Zimmer's face. This giveaway was listed in Chris Landers' article, "Each team's weirdest promotional item ever."[39]

Don Zimmer worked for 65 years in minor league and major league baseball as a player, coach, manager, and front office executive. In a 12-year career as a major league player, during which Zimmer played for the Brooklyn/Los Angeles Dodgers, Chicago Cubs, New York Mets, Cincinnati Reds, and Washington Senators, he batted .235, with 91 home runs and 352 RBIs.[40] The highlights of Zimmer's managerial career include his stint in 1978 as skipper of the Boston Red Sox. That team surged to tie the Yankees for first place on the last day of the season, only to lose a one-game playoff when Bucky Dent hit a clutch home run to help the Yankees win the pennant. In 1984, Zimmer managed the Chicago Cubs to first place in the National League East. The Cubs won the first two games of the National League Championship Series, only to lose the next three games in San Diego to the Padres.[41]

Possibly, Zimmer achieved his greatest success in major league baseball from 1996 to 2003 as a coach for the New York Yankees, who were managed by Joe Torre.[42] In the eight years that Zimmer and Torre worked together, the Yankees won their division seven times, played in the World Series six times, and won the World Series four times. While Zimmer's tenure with the Yankees was overwhelmingly positive, it was marred by a confrontation with Boston pitcher Pedro Martinez who, in a bench-clearing brawl, pushed the much older Zimmer to the ground. Yet, as Derek Jeter later said, Zimmer's willingness to do battle with the Red Sox showed that, at 72 years of age, he was still a tough competitor.

Zimmer spent his last 10 years in major league baseball from 2004 to 2014 as a senior advisor to the Tampa Bay Rays,[43] which brings us back to the teddy bear with Zimmer's likeness. A teddy bear; really! No one lasts in professional baseball for over 60 years in various capacities who isn't a tough competitor. Those who knew Zimmer, who in his 70s was willing to fight much younger athletes to defend his team's honor, might see portraying him as a cuddly teddy bear to be just a bit … outrageous.

◊ Washington Nationals/Bryce Harper Chia Pet. In 2016, the Washington Nationals sponsored a promotion in which they gave fans a Bryce Harper Chia Pet. This giveaway was listed in Chris Landers' article, "Each team's weirdest promotional item ever."[44] No doubt, if you are reading this book, you are familiar with the baseball exploits of Bryce Harper, the superstar who was chosen by the Washington Nationals with the first selection in the 2010 amateur draft, was voted Rookie of the Year, and twice won the Most Valuable Player Award, once in 2015 with the Nationals, and again in 2021 with the Philadelphia Phillies.[45] You may not be familiar with the chia pet, which seems to have faded from public attention. A chia pet is a terracotta figurine, usually in the shape of a person or animal (in either case, real or imagined)—containing chia seeds, which grow into an annual herb in the mint family native to Mexico. When the chia plant grows, the plant takes on the appearance of the figurine's hair or fur. While Bryce Harper is well deserving of some form of recognition, a chia pet might seem outrageous. But then again, maybe not. In addition to his other attributes, Harper is reputed to have one of the most impressive heads of hair in major league baseball. Why the Nationals chose to recognize that aspect of Harper's notoriety, and not something more baseball-related, is anyone's guess.

Appendix II

Show Me the Money
The Demise of the Reserve Clause

Much to the chagrin of major league baseball players, the reserve clause continued to give owners the ability to dictate their salaries for decades after its institution in the early 1900s. The Major League Players Association (MLBPA), recognized in 1966 as a union whose leadership represented major league players in their relations with owners, sought to convince owners to at least modify the reserve clause, but to no avail.[1]

As recounted in Dan Epstein's book, *Big Hair and Plastic Grass*, Curt Flood, a star center fielder for the St. Louis Cardinals, initiated the first major attempt to remove the vise grip of the reserve clause on players' options.[2] In late 1969, the Cardinals sent Flood, as part of a multiplayer trade, to the Philadelphia Phillies. In a letter to Bowie Kuhn, the Commissioner of Baseball, Flood outlined his objections to being traded and asked Kuhn to declare him a free agent. In his public statements, Flood made clear his distaste for the reserve clause, which he declared gave owners the ability to "play God over other peoples' lives." He added that, after giving his all to the Cardinals through 12 seasons and three World Series, he deserved to be treated "better."

Once Kuhn denied his request, Flood, on January 16, 1970, with the support of the MLBPA, filed a $4.1 million civil lawsuit against Kuhn and Major League Baseball, alleging that the reserve clause, which Flood saw as an inequitable and antiquated aspect of the game, violated federal antitrust statutes.[3] Surprisingly, it appeared that public opinion veered against Flood. Some fans had difficulty feeling empathy for someone who earned $90,000 per year to play what they saw as a child's game. Even some other major league players, concerned that publicly supporting Flood would be detrimental to their careers, remained mute on the subject. Some actually thought free agency would ruin the game by driving up player salaries beyond what teams could reasonably afford. The district court dismissed Flood's lawsuit and, on April 7, 1971, the court of appeals upheld the dismissal. Not willing to give up his quest, Flood appealed to the Supreme Court, which on March 20, 1972, ruled in favor of Major League Baseball.

Jeff English, in his article "Catfish Hunter," explains how Charlie O. Finley, owner of the Oakland Athletics, set into motion the second major effort by a major league ballplayer to loosen the shackles of the reserve clause.[4] In January 1974, Finley entered into a contract with his star pitcher, Catfish Hunter, that required Finley to pay Hunter $100,000 for the upcoming season. The contract stipulated that Hunter would receive half his salary as a deferred payment. Finley, give his tendency to be tight-fisted, wanted to pay Hunter his entire salary during the contract year because he would not be able to write off the deferred $50,000 on his taxes until after the payment was made. Hunter charged Finley with breach of contract and threatened that, unless Finley ponied up the money as stipulated in the contract, he would declare himself a free agent. Finley refused to make the deferred payment. Rather than take his dispute to the courts, the MLBPA maneuvered it into the newly created major league baseball management-labor grievance system. On December 16, 1974, the grievance panel found in favor of Hunter, making him a free agent. Several teams competed for Hunter's services. He ultimately signed to play for the New York Yankees in return for more than $3 million over five years.

Seeing what Hunter could command on the open market, major league baseball players for the first time got a taste of what might happen if they too become free agents.[5] It was only a matter of time before they made a frontal assault on the reserve clause and placed it in a dustbin of history. With the support of the players' union, pitchers Dave McNally and Andy Messersmith challenged the holy grail of baseball owners—the reserve clause. Once again, this dispute was maneuvered into the management-labor grievance system. Much to everyone's surprise, the panel ruled in December 1975 that the reserve clause was invalid, meaning that every major league baseball player who plays out his contract is free to play for whatever team seeks their services.

Chapter Notes

Preface

1. "Sport Quotes," University of North Texas Center for Sport Psychology and Athlete Mental Health, accessed February 6, 2024, https://sportpsych.unt.edu/resources/sport-quotes.html.

Chapter 1

1. Bill Veeck with Ed Linn, *Veeck as in Wreck: The Autobiography of Bill Veeck* (Chicago: University of Chicago Press, 1962), 19.
2. John B. Lord, *Bill Giles & Baseball* (Philadelphia: Temple University Press, 2014), 1.
3. *Ibid.*, 1–2.
4. *Ibid.*, 2.
5. *Ibid.*
6. *Ibid.*
7. *Ibid.*
8. *Ibid.*
9. Jeff Obermeyer, "Baseball During World War II," *Society for American Baseball Research*, Accessed February 6, 2024, https://sabr.org/journal/article/the-business-of-baseball-during-world-war-II/.
10. Lord, *Bill Giles & Baseball*, 3.
11. *Ibid.*
12. *Ibid.*
13. Obermeyer, "Baseball During World War II."
14. Dave Brown and Jeff Rodimer, *Shadows of Glory* (Essex, CT: Lyons Press, 2024), 186.
15. "Major League Miscellaneous Averages and Totals," Baseball Reference, Accessed July 30, 2024, https://www.baseball-reference.com/leagues/majors/misc.shtml.
16. Lord, *Bill Giles & Baseball*, 3–4.
17. *Ibid.*, 4.
18. Obermeyer, "Baseball During World War II."
19. Lord, *Bill Giles & Baseball*, 5.
20. Obermeyer, "Baseball During World War II."
21. *Ibid.*
22. Lord, *Bill Giles & Baseball*, 7, 9.
23. *Ibid.*
24. *Ibid.*, 9.
25. "Former Chicago White Sox Owner Bill Veeck, the Baseball Barnum," United Press International, January 2, 1986, https://www.upi.com/Archives/1986/01/02/Former-Chicago-White-Sox-owner-Bill-Veeck-the-Baseball-Barnum/3964505026000.
26. Paul Dickson, *Bill Veeck: Baseball's Greatest Maverick* (New York: Walker Publishing, 2012), 9.
27. *Ibid.*, 10.
28. Veeck with Linn, *Veeck as in Wreck: The Autobiography of Bill Veeck*, 25.
29. *Ibid.*
30. Dickson, *Bill Veeck: Baseball's Greatest Maverick*, 21.
31. *Ibid*, 47.
32. Dickson, "Bill Veeck: The Maverick Who Changed Baseball," *American Heritage* (Summer 2017), https://www.americanheritage.com/bill-veeck-maverick-who-changed-baseball.
33. Bucky Fox, "Baseball's Bill Veeck Changed the Pitch of the National Pastime," *Investor's Business Daily*, June 11, 2016, https://investors.com/news/management/leaders-and-success/bill-veeck-brought-family-fun-out-to-the-ballgame.
34. Dickson, *Bill Veeck: Baseball's Greatest Maverick*, 47–49.

35. *Ibid.*, 55.
36. William Corbett, "Bill Veeck," *Society for American Baseball Research*, Accessed July 23, 2023, https://sabr.org/bioproj/person/bill-veeck.
37. William Barry Furlong, "The Veeck Impact on Chicago: Master of the Joyful Illusion," *Chicago Baseball Museum*, Accessed July 23, 2023, https://chicagobaseballmuseum.org/wp-content/uploads/CBM-Veeck-Impact-Joyful-Illusion-20120827.pdf.
38. Veeck with Linn, *Veeck as in Wreck: The Autobiography of Bill Veeck*, 49.
39. Furlong, "The Veeck Impact on Chicago: Master of the Joyful Illusion."
40. Dickson, *Bill Veeck: Baseball's Greatest Maverick*, 59.
41. *Ibid.*
42. *Ibid.*, 58.
43. *Ibid.*, 57.
44. *Ibid.*, 63.
45. *Ibid.*
46. Veeck with Linn, *Veeck as in Wreck: The Autobiography of Bill Veeck*, 49–50.
47. Dickson, *Bill Veeck: Baseball's Greatest Maverick*, 57–58.
48. Dan Vukelich, "The Great White Sox Hope," *Chicago Reader*, April 9, 1976, https://chicagoreader.com/news-politics/the-great-white-sox-hope/.
49. Dickson, *Bill Veeck: Baseball's Greatest Maverick*, 58.
50. Veeck with Linn, *Veeck as in Wreck: The Autobiography of Bill Veeck*, 104.
51. *Ibid.*, 117.
52. Veeck with Linn, *The Hustler's Handbook* (Chicago: Ivan R. Dee, 1965), 13.
53. Dickson, *Bill Veeck: Baseball's Greatest Maverick*, 68.
54. *Ibid.*
55. *Ibid.*
56. *Ibid.*
57. *Ibid.*
58. Veeck with Linn, *Veeck as in Wreck: The Autobiography of Bill Veeck*, 53.
59. *Ibid.*
60. Dickson, "Bill Veeck: The Maverick Who Changed Baseball."
61. Dickson, *Bill Veeck: Baseball's Greatest Maverick*, 68.
62. Veeck with Linn, *Veeck as in Wreck: The Autobiography of Bill Veeck*, 52.
63. Bill Veeck with Ed Linn, *The Hustler's Handbook*, 19.
64. *Ibid.*
65. Dickson, *Bill Veeck: Baseball's Greatest Maverick*, 63.
66. *Ibid.*, 63–64.
67. *Ibid.*, 64.
68. *Ibid.*, 85.
69. Furlong, "The Veeck Impact on Chicago: Master of the Joyful Illusion."
70. Dickson, *Bill Veeck: Baseball's Greatest Maverick*, 85.
71. *Ibid.*
72. *Ibid.*
73. *Ibid.*
74. *Ibid.*
75. *Ibid.*
76. Veeck with Linn, *Veeck as in Wreck: The Autobiography of Bill Veeck,* 54.
77. Dickson, *Bill Veeck: Baseball's Greatest Maverick*, 87.
78. *Ibid.*
79. *Ibid.*
80. *Ibid.*
81. *Ibid.*
82. Thomas Boswell, "Bill Veeck," *Washington Post*, May 31, 1981, https://washingtonpost.com/archives/sports1981/05/31/bill-veeck/6e41714f-5043-4a2e-be3a-fa7beb86d946.
83. Dickson, *Bill Veeck: Baseball's Greatest Maverick*, 87.
84. Craig Muder, "Veeck Brought Fun Back to Baseball," *National Baseball Hall of Fame*, Accessed July 23, 2023, https://baseball.org/discover/inside-pitch-veeck-brought-fun-back-to-baseball.
85. Dickson, *Bill Veeck: Baseball's Greatest Maverick*, 66.
86. *Ibid.*, 87.
87. *Ibid.*, 88.
88. *Ibid.*, 89.
89. *Ibid.*, 95.
90. *Ibid.*
91. *Ibid.*
92. *Ibid.*, 95–96.
93. *Ibid.*, 96.
94. *Ibid.*, 99.
95. Furlong, "The Veeck Impact on Chicago: Master of the Joyful Illusion."
96. Dickson, *Bill Veeck: Baseball's Greatest Maverick*, 99.
97. "Former Chicago White Sox Owner Bill Veeck, the Baseball Barnum."
98. "Ex-Baseball Owner Bill Veeck: Used Clowns, Giveaways and Midgets to Spice Up Sport," *Los Angeles Times*, January 2, 1986, https://www.latimes.com/

articles/la-xpm-1986-01-02-mn-23473-story.html.
99. Dickson, *Bill Veeck: Baseball's Greatest Maverick*, 104.
100. Veeck with Linn, *Veeck as in Wreck: The Autobiography of Bill Veeck*, 80.
101. Nick Acocella, "Baseball's Showman," *Entertainment and Sports Programming Network*, Accessed July 24, 2023, https://www.espn.com/classic/veeckbill000816.html.
102. Dickson, *Bill Veeck: Baseball's Greatest Maverick*, 106.
103. "Baseball's P.T. Barnum," *The Attic*, April 8, 2021, https://www.theattic.space/home-page-blogs/2021/4/8/baseball's-wild-showman.
104. Dickson, *Bill Veeck: Baseball's Greatest Maverick*, 106.
105. Furlong, "The Veeck Impact on Chicago: Master of the Joyful Illusion."
106. Ibid.
107. "Cleveland Guardians Attendance, Stadiums, and Park Factors," *Baseball Reference*, Accessed January 4, 2024, https://www.baseball-reference.com/teams/CLE/attend.shtml.
108. Veeck with Linn, *Veeck as in Wreck: The Autobiography of Bill Veeck*, 105.
109. Ibid., 155.
110. Dickson, *Bill Veeck: Baseball's Greatest Maverick*, 114.
111. Ibid., 115.
112. Ibid., 151–152.
113. "Veeck, William (Bill) L.," *Case Western Reserve University, Encyclopedia of Cleveland*, Accessed July 23, 2023, https://case.edu/ech/articles/v/veeck-william-bill-l.
114. Dickson, *Bill Veeck: Baseball's Greatest Maverick*, 154.
115. Ibid., 154–155.
116. Ibid.
117. Ibid., 155.
118. Ibid.
119. Ibid., 175.
120. Ibid., 174–76.
121. Corbett, "Bill Veeck."
122. Dickson, *Bill Veeck: Baseball's Greatest Maverick*, 178–179.
123. Ibid., 186.
124. Ibid., 188.
125. Ibid., 187.
126. Veeck with Linn, *Veeck as in Wreck: The* Autobiography *of Bill Veeck*, 215.
127. Ibid., 216.
128. Dickson, *Bill Veeck: Baseball's Greatest Maverick*, 187.
129. Veeck with Linn, *Veeck as in Wreck: The Autobiography of Bill Veeck*, 219.
130. Corbett, "Bill Veeck."
131. Dickson, *Bill Veeck: Baseball's Greatest Maverick*, 208.
132. Furlong, "The Veeck Impact on Chicago: Master of the Joyful Illusion."
133. Dickson, *Bill Veeck: Baseball's Greatest Maverick*, 209.
134. Ibid., 210, 214.
135. Furlong, "The Veeck Impact on Chicago: Master of the Joyful Illusion."
136. Dickson, *Bill Veeck: Baseball's Greatest Maverick*, 216.
137. "1951 St. Louis Browns Statistics," *Baseball Reference*, Accessed January 4, 2024, https://www.baseball-reference.com/teams/SLB/1951.shtml.
138. Dickson, *Bill Veeck: Baseball's Greatest Maverick*, 227–228.
139. "Chicago White Sox Attendance, Stadiums, and Park Factors," *Baseball Reference*, Accessed January 4, 2024, https://www.baseball-reference.com/teams/CHW/attend.shtml.
140. Ibid.
141. Veeck with Linn, *Veeck as in Wreck: The* Autobiography *of Bill Veeck*, 341.
142. Dickson, *Bill Veeck: Baseball's Greatest Maverick*, 231.
143. Veeck with Linn, *Veeck as in Wreck: The Autobiography of Bill Veeck*, 343.
144. Individuals would collect S&H Green Stamps at participating stores in accordance with how much they spent and then cash them in at redemption centers for household items.
145. Dickson, *Bill Veeck: Baseball's Greatest Maverick*, 231.
146. Veeck with Linn, *Veeck as in Wreck: The Autobiography of Bill Veeck*, 341.
147. Dickson, *Bill Veeck: Baseball's Greatest Maverick*, 232.
148. Gary Livacari, "Al Smith," *Society for American Baseball Research*, Accessed December 14, 2023, https://sabr.org/bioproj/person/al-smith-4/.
149. Veeck with Linn, *Veeck as in Wreck: The Autobiography of Bill Veeck*, 342, 345.
150. Ibid., 345.
151. Ibid., 342–343.

152. Dickson, *Bill Veeck: Baseball's Greatest Maverick*, 240.
153. Furlong, "The Veeck Impact on Chicago: Master of the Joyful Illusion."
154. Veeck with Linn, *Veeck as in Wreck: The Autobiography of Bill Veeck*, 345.
155. Dickson, *Bill Veeck: Baseball's Greatest Maverick*, 242.
156. *Ibid.*, 186, 245.

Chapter 2

1. Alex Coffey and Alec Lewis, "Remembering Charlie-O the mule, the A's mascot inspired by Charles O. Finley," *The Athletic*, May 8, 2020, https://theathletic.com/1801465/2020/05/08/remembering-charlie-o-the-mule-the-mascot-inspired-by-charlie-o-finley.
2. "1961 Kansas City Athletics Statistics," *Baseball Reference*, Accessed January 4, 2024, https://www.baseball-reference.com/teams/KCA/1961.shtml.
3. G. Michael Green and Roger Launius, *Charlie Finley: The Outrageous Story of Baseball's Super Showman* (New York: Walker & Company, 2010), 28.
4. Mark Armour, "Charlie Finley," *Society for American Baseball Research*, Accessed October 18, 2023, https://sabr.org/bioproj/person/charlie-finley.
5. Roger Launius, "Good Charlie/Bad Charlie: What Made Charlie Finley Tick?" *Roger Launius' Blog*, June 19, 2015, https://launiusr.wordpress.com/2015/06/19/good-charliebad-charlie-what-made-charlie-finley-tick%20priorities,activities,%20 virtually%20everyone%20recognized%20 it.
6. Green and Launius, *Charlie Finley: The Outrageous Story of Baseball's Super Showman*, 18–19.
7. Ron Fimrite, "Charlie O. Eyes a Pennant or Three," *Sports Illustrated*, October 9, 1972, https://vault.si.com/vault/1972/10/09/charlie-o-eyes-a-pennant-or-three.
8. Launius, "Good Charlie/Bad Charlie: What Made Charlie Finley Tick?"
9. Armour, "Charlie Finley."
10. Green and Launius, *Charlie Finley: The Outrageous Story of Baseball's Super Showman*, 41, 49.
11. *Ibid.*, 51–52.
12. *Ibid.*, 53.
13. *Ibid.*, 54.
14. *Ibid.*, 70.
15. Launius, "Good Charlie/Bad Charlie: What Made Charlie Finley Tick?"
16. Herbert Michelson, *Charlie O: Charles Oscar Finley vs. the Baseball Establishment* (Indianapolis: Bobbs-Merrill, 1975), 129.
17. Launius, "Good Charlie/Bad Charlie: What Made Charlie Finley Tick?"
18. Green and Launius, *Charlie Finley: The Outrageous Story of Baseball's Super Showman*, 61–62.
19. *Ibid.*, 70.
20. *Ibid.*, 63–77.
21. *Ibid.*, 70.
22. *Ibid.*, 55.
23. Bill Libby, *Charlie O. and the Angry A's* (Garden City, NY: Doubleday, 1975), 64.
24. Green and Launius, *Charlie Finley: The Outrageous Story of Baseball's Super Showman*, 167.
25. *Ibid.*, 58.
26. Libby, *Charlie O. and the Angry A's*, 64.
27. Green and Launius, *Charlie Finley: The Outrageous Story of Baseball's Super Showman*, 58.
28. Armour, "Charlie Finley."
29. *Ibid.*
30. Green and Launius, *Charlie Finley: The Outrageous Story of Baseball's Super Showman*, 86.
31. *Ibid.*, 89.
32. Norm King, "Charlie-O," *Society for American Baseball Research*, Accessed August 18, 2023, https://sabr-org/bioproj/topic/charlie-o/.
33. Armour, "Charlie Finley."
34. Green and Launius, *Charlie Finley: The Outrageous Story of Baseball's Super Showman*, 93.
35. *Ibid.*, 113.
36. *Ibid.*, 114.
37. Nick Acocella, "Finley Entertained and Enraged," *ESPN Classic*, Accessed October 16, 2023, https://www.espn.com/classic/biography/s/Finley_Charles.html.
38. Green and Launius, *Charlie Finley: The Outrageous Story of Baseball's Super Showman*, 78.
39. "Oakland Athletics Attendance, Stadiums, and Park Factors," *Baseball Reference*, Accessed January 4, 2024, https://

Notes—Chapter 2

www.baseball-reference.com/tools/share.fcgi?id=ox7BH.

40. Green and Launius, *Charlie Finley: The Outrageous Story of Baseball's Super Showman*, 133.

41. *Ibid.*, 141.

42. *Ibid.*, 148.

43. *Ibid.*, 152.

44. Doug Miller, "TBT: 72 A's Hold Memorable 'Mustache Day,'" *Major League Baseball*, Accessed August 18, 2023, https://www.mlb.com/news/tbt-72-as-hold-memorable-mustache-day/c-131407816.

45. Green and Launius, *Charlie Finley: The Outrageous Story of Baseball's Super Showman*, 164.

46. D.L. Nelson, "The Reign of Finley," *Athletics Nation*, August 1, 2013, https://www.athleticsnation.com/2013/8/1/4576930/the-reign-of-finley.

47. Acocella, "Finley Entertained and Enraged."

48. Green and Launius, *Charlie Finley: The Outrageous Story of Baseball's Super Showman*, 207.

49. Fimrite, "Charlie O. Eyes a Pennant or Three."

50. Green and Launius, *Charlie Finley: The Outrageous Story of Baseball's Super Showman*, 230.

51. *Ibid.*, 241.

52. Acocella, "Finley Entertained and Enraged."

53. Nelson, "The Reign of Finley."

54. *Ibid.*

55. Green and Launius, *Charlie Finley: The Outrageous Story of Baseball's Super Showman*, 293.

56. Bill Giles with Doug Myers, *Pouring Six Beers at a Time: Stories from a Lifetime in Baseball* (Chicago: Triumph Books, 2007), 85–86.

57. *Ibid.*, 86, 89.

58. John B. Lord, *Bill Giles & Baseball* (Philadelphia: Temple University Press, 2014), 227.

59. "Philadelphia Phillies Attendance, Stadiums, and Park Factors," *Baseball Reference*, Accessed January 4, 2024, https://www.baseball-reference.com/teams/PHI/attend.shtml.

60. Giles with Myers, *Pouring Six Beers at a Time: Stories from a Lifetime in Baseball*, 88.

61. Larry Shenk, "1972 Rewind," *Phillies Insider*, Accessed November 8, 2023, https://philliesinsider.mlblogs.com/1972-rewind-4a8da68a2fc2.

62. Giles with Myers, *Pouring Six Beers at a Time: Stories from a Lifetime in Baseball*, 92.

63. *Ibid.*, 92–93.

64. Larry Shenk, *If These Walls Could Talk: Philadelphia Phillies* (Chicago: Triumph Books, 2014), 59.

65. *Ibid.*, 158.

66. Matt Rappa, "Phillies: Celebrating 50th Anniversary of Veterans Stadium," *Fanside*, April 10, 2021, https://thatballsoutahere.com/2021/04/10/phillies-veterans-stadium-50-years/.

67. Giles with Myers, *Pouring Six Beers at a Time: Stories from a Lifetime in Baseball*, 98.

68. *Ibid.*, 1.

69. *Ibid.*, 99.

70. *Ibid.*

71. Rich Westcott, *Veterans Stadium, Field of Memories* (Philadelphia: Temple University Press, 2005), 90.

72. Shenk, "1972 Rewind."

73. Giles with Myers, *Pouring Six Beers at a Time: Stories from a Lifetime in Baseball*, 103.

74. Westcott, *Veterans Stadium, Field of Memories*, 88.

75. Giles with Myers, *Pouring Six Beers at a Time: Stories from a Lifetime in Baseball*, 103–104.

76. *Ibid.*, 108–109.

77. *Ibid.*, 113–114.

78. *Ibid.*, 104–105.

79. *Ibid.*, 105.

80. Westcott, *Veterans Stadium, Field of Memories*, 94.

81. Giles with Myers, *Pouring Six Beers at a Time: Stories from a Lifetime in Baseball*, 105–106.

82. *Ibid.*, 106–107.

83. *Ibid.*, 107.

84. "Bill Giles (baseball)," *Wikipedia*, Accessed December 18, 2023, https://en.wikipedia.org/wiki/Bill_Giles_(baseball).

85. Bob Hope, *We Could've Finished Last Without You* (Atlanta: Longstreet Press, 1991), 9–10.

86. *Ibid.*, 83–88.

87. Ted Turner with Bill Burke, *Call Me Ted* (New York: Grand Central Publishing, 2008), 113.

88. Hope, *We Could've Finished Last Without You*, 99, 193.

89. "Atlanta Braves Attendance, Stadiums, and Park Factors," *Baseball Reference*, Accessed January 4, 2024, https://www.baseball-reference.com/teams/ATL/attend.shtml.
90. Hope, *We Could've Finished Last Without You*, 105.
91. Ibid., 106.
92. Ibid., 122.
93. Robert Ashley Fields, *Take Me Out to the Crowd: Ted Turner and the Atlanta Braves* (Huntsville, AL: Strode Publishers, 1977), 153.
94. Ibid., 153.
95. Hope, *We Could've Finished Last Without You*, 119.
96. Ibid., 99.
97. Ibid., 99–100.
98. Ibid., 101.
99. Ibid., 102.
100. Fields, *Take Me Out to the Crowd: Ted Turner and the Atlanta Braves*, 154–159.
101. Ibid., 158–159.
102. Hope, *We Could've Finished Last Without You*, 123.
103. Ibid., 108–110.
104. Ibid., 110.
105. Ibid., 105, 113–115, 122, 168.
106. Ibid., 119.
107. Ibid., 120.
108. Ibid.
109. Ibid., 162–167.
110. Ibid., 167–169.
111. Ibid., 195–209.
112. Warren Corbett, "Bill Veeck," *Society for American Baseball Research*, Accessed July 23, 2023, https://sabr.org/bioproj/person/bill-veeck.
113. Paul Dickson, *Bill Veeck: Baseball's Greatest Maverick* (New York: Walker & Company, 2012), 285.
114. Ibid., 288.
115. Ibid., 291.
116. Bill Veeck with Ed Linn, *Veeck as in Wreck: The Autobiography of Bill Veeck* (Chicago: University of Chicago Press, 1962), 383.
117. Dickson, *Bill Veeck: Baseball's Greatest Maverick*, 297.
118. Ibid., 300.
119. Ibid., 299.
120. Ibid., 314.
121. Craig Muder, "Veeck Brought Fun Back to Baseball," *Baseball Hall of Fame*, Accessed July 23, 2023, https://baseballhall.org/discover/inside-pitch/veeck-brought-fun-back-to-baseball.
122. Joseph Durso, "Bill Veeck, Baseball Innovator, Dies," *New York Times*, January 3, 1986, https://www.nytimes.com/1986/01/03/obituaries/bill-veeck-baseball-innovator-dies.html.
123. "White Sox History: The Days of 'Sport Shirt Bill Veeck,'" *Sox at 35th*, April 25, 2022, https://www.soxon35th.com/white-sox-history-the-days-of-sport-shirt-bill-veeck.
124. Nick Acocella, "Baseball's Showman," *ESPN Classic*, Accessed July 24, 2023, www.espn.com/classic/veeckbill000816.html.

Chapter 3

1. Dennis Pajot and Greg Erion, "St. Louis Browns Team Ownership History," *Society for American Baseball Research*, Accessed November 27, 2023, https://sabr.org/bioproj/topic/st-louis-browns-team-ownership-history/.
2. Ibid.
3. "Branch Rickey, Executive," *National Baseball Hall of Fame*, Accessed November 27, 2023, https://baseballhall.org/hall-of-famers/rickey-branch.
4. Bill Giles with Doug Myers, *Pouring Six Beers at a Time: Stories from a Lifetime in Baseball* (Chicago: Triumph Books, 2007), 21.
5. Dave Brown and Jeff Rodimer, *Shadows of Glory* (Essex, CT: Lyons Press, 2024), 93.
6. Pajot and Erion, "St. Louis Browns Team Ownership History."
7. Ibid.
8. "History of the St. Louis Cardinals (1920–1952)," *Wikipedia*, Accessed January 11, 2024, https://en.wikipedia.org/wiki/History_of_the_St._Louis_Cardinals_(1920%E2%80%931952).
9. Peter Golenbock, *The Spirit of St. Louis: A History of the St. Louis Cardinals and Browns* (New York: Avon Books, 2000), 270.
10. "St. Louis Browns Yearly Records and Games," *Back to Baseball*, Accessed February 13, 2024, https://www.backtobaseball.com/teams/st-louis-browns/.
11. Pajot and Erion, "St. Louis Browns Team Ownership History."
12. Golenbock, *The Spirit of St. Louis*:

Notes—Chapter 3

A History of the St. Louis Cardinals and Browns, 270.

13. Ibid., 273.
14. Ibid., 280.
15. Ibid., 285.
16. Pajot and Erion, "St. Louis Browns Team Ownership History."
17. Golenbock, *The Spirit of St. Louis: A History of the St. Louis Cardinals and Browns*, 280–281.
18. Brown and Rodimer, *Shadows of Glory*, 87.
19. Golenbock, *The Spirit of St. Louis: A History of the St. Louis Cardinals and Browns*, 281.
20. Pajot and Erion, "St. Louis Browns Team Ownership History."
21. Golenbock, *The Spirit of St. Louis: A History of the St. Louis Cardinals and Browns*, 285.
22. "St. Louis Browns Yearly Records and Games."
23. Golenbock, *The Spirit of St. Louis: A History of the St. Louis Cardinals and Browns*, 286–287.
24. "St. Louis Browns Yearly Records and Games."
25. Ibid.
26. "1944 St. Louis Browns Statistics," *Baseball Reference*, Accessed November 27, 2023, https://www.baseball-reference.com/teams/SLB/1944.shtml.
27. Pajot and Erion, "St. Louis Browns Team Ownership History."
28. Ibid.
29. Brown and Rodimer, *Shadows of Glory*, 88.
30. Pajot and Erion, "St. Louis Browns Team Ownership History."
31. Ibid.
32. "St. Louis Browns Yearly Records and Games."
33. Pajot and Erion, "St. Louis Browns Team Ownership History."
34. Golenbock, *The Spirit of St. Louis: A History of the St. Louis Cardinals and Browns*, 320.
35. Ibid.
36. Ibid., 321.
37. "St. Louis Browns Yearly Records and Games."
38. Golenbock, *The Spirit of St. Louis: A History of the St. Louis Cardinals and Browns*, 321.
39. Pajot and Erion, "St. Louis Browns Team Ownership History."
40. Norm King, "August 24, 1951: Browns Fans Manage to Get It Right in Veeck Promotion," *Society for American Baseball Research*, Accessed August 29, 2023, https://sabr.org/gamesproj//game/august-24-1951-st-louis-browns-fans-manage-to-get-it-right-in-veeck-promotion.
41. Paul Dickson, *Bill Veeck: Baseball's Greatest Maverick* (New York: Walker & Company, 2012), 188.
42. Ibid., 198, 205.
43. Ibid., 187.
44. Bill Veeck with Ed Linn, *Veeck as in Wreck: The Autobiography of Bill Veeck* (Chicago: University of Chicago Press, 1962), 223–229.
45. Ibid., 11.
46. Ibid.
47. Ibid., 11–12.
48. Dickson, *Bill Veeck: Baseball's Greatest Maverick*, 191.
49. Ibid., 193–194.
50. Ibid., 194.
51. Ibid., 16.
52. Veeck with Linn, *Veeck as in Wreck: The Autobiography of Bill Veeck*, 12.
53. Ibid.
54. Dickson, *Bill Veeck: Baseball's Greatest Maverick*, 191.
55. Ibid.
56. Veeck with Linn, *Veeck as in Wreck: The Autobiography of Bill Veeck*, 13–14.
57. Ibid., 14.
58. Ibid.
59. Dickson, *Bill Veeck: Baseball's Greatest Maverick*, 191.
60. Ibid., 113.
61. Veeck with Linn, *Veeck as in Wreck: The Autobiography of Bill Veeck*, 17.
62. Norm King, "Zack Taylor," *Society for American Baseball Research*, Accessed January 7, 2024, https://sabr.org/bioproj/person/zack-taylor/.
63. Dickson, *Bill Veeck: Baseball's Greatest Maverick*, 191.
64. Brian McKenna, "Eddie Gaedel," *Society for American Baseball Research*, Accessed August 7, 2023, https://sabr.org/bioproj/person/eddie-gaedel/.
65. Veeck with Linn, *Veeck as in Wreck: The Autobiography of Bill Veeck*, 15.
66. Dickson, *Bill Veeck: Baseball's Greatest Maverick*, 192.
67. Veeck with Linn, *Veeck as in Wreck: The Autobiography of Bill Veeck*, 15–16.
68. Ibid., 16.

69. *Ibid.*, 17.
70. *Ibid.*
71. *Ibid.*, 12.
72. Dickson, *Bill Veeck: Baseball's Greatest Maverick*, 192.
73. McKenna, "Eddie Gaedel."
74. Ryan Turnquist, "Bill Veeck, Eddie Gaedel and the Birth of a Legend," *National Baseball Hall of Fame*, Accessed July 23, 2023, https://baseballhall.org/discover-more-stories/inside-pitch/bill-veeck-eddie-gaedel-and-the-birth-of-a-legend.
75. Dickson, *Bill Veeck: Baseball's Greatest Maverick*, 192.
76. McKenna, "Eddie Gaedel."
77. Dickson, *Bill Veeck: Baseball's Greatest Maverick*, 193.
78. Veeck with Linn, *Veeck as in Wreck: The Autobiography of Bill Veeck*, 19–20.
79. Kitty Feld, "Son of Legendary Sportswriter Vincent X. Flaherty Sells Off Collectibles to Run for Congress," *89.3KPCC*, March 15, 2014, https://archive.kpcc.org/blogs/politics/2014/03/15.
80. King, "August 24, 1951: St. Louis Browns Fans Manage to Get It Right in Veeck Promotion."
81. Veeck with Linn, *Veeck as in Wreck: The Autobiography of Bill Veeck*, 21.
82. Dickson, *Bill Veeck: Baseball's Greatest Maverick*, 195.
83. Veeck with Linn, *Veeck as in Wreck: The Autobiography of Bill Veeck*, 21.
84. Dickson, *Bill Veeck: Baseball's Greatest Maverick*, 193.
85. Veeck with Linn, *Veeck as in Wreck: The Autobiography of Bill Veeck*, 22.
86. Dickson, *Bill Veeck: Baseball's Greatest Maverick*, 193.
87. *Ibid.*, 195.
88. Ed Wulf, "Vote, Vote, Vote for the Home Team," *ESPN*, September 16, 2014, https://www.espn.com,mlb/story/_/page/FansourceVeeck/bill-veeck-birth-fansourcing.
89. Veeck with Linn, *Veeck as in Wreck: The Autobiography of Bill Veeck*, 23.
90. Eric Robinson, "The Peculiar Professional Baseball Career of Eddie Gaedel," *Society for American Baseball Research*, Accessed August 7, 2023, https://sabr.org/journal/article/the-peculiar-professional-baseball-career-of-eddie-gaedel/.
91. Dickson, *Bill Veeck: Baseball's Greatest Maverick*, 194.
92. William Corbett, "Bill Veeck," *Society for American Baseball Research*, Accessed July 23, 2023, https://sabr.org/bioproj/person/bill-veeck/.
93. Dickson, *Bill Veeck: Baseball's Greatest Maverick*, 189.
94. King, "August 24, 1951: St. Louis Browns Fans Manage to Get It Right in Veeck Promotion."
95. Alex Coffey, "Veeck Holds 'Grandstand Managers Night,'" *National Baseball Hall of Fame*, Accessed July 23, 2023, https://baseballhall.org/discover-more/stories/inside-pitch/grandstand-managers-night.
96. Veeck with Linn, *Veeck as in Wreck: The Autobiography of Bill Veeck*, 219–220.
97. *Ibid.*
98. Dickson, *Bill Veeck: Baseball's Greatest Maverick*, 190.
99. King, "August 24, 1951: St. Louis Browns Fans Manage to Get It Right in Veeck Promotion."
100. *Ibid.*
101. *Ibid.*
102. Veeck with Linn, *Veeck as in Wreck: The Autobiography of Bill Veeck*, 220.
103. King, "August 24, 1951: St. Louis Browns Fans Manage to Get It Right in Veeck Promotion."
104. Eric Chesterton, "In 1951, Bill Veeck Let the Fans Manage the St. Louis Browns on Grandstand Managers Night," *Major League Baseball*, August 24, 2017, https://www.mlb.com/cut4/in-1951-bill-veeck-let-the-fans-manage-the-st-louis-browns-on-grandstanbd-managers-night.
105. Veeck with Linn, *Veeck as in Wreck: The Autobiography of Bill Veeck*, 220.
106. Wulf, "Vote, Vote, Vote for the Home Team."
107. Dickson, *Bill Veeck: Baseball's Greatest Maverick*, 195.
108. Veeck with Linn, *Veeck as in Wreck: The Autobiography of Bill Veeck*, 219.
109. Dickson, *Bill Veeck: Baseball's Greatest Maverick*, 195.
110. King, "August 24, 1951: St. Louis Browns Fans Manage to Get It Right in Veeck Promotion."
111. *Ibid.*
112. Veeck with Linn, *Veeck as in Wreck: The Autobiography of Bill Veeck*, 220.

113. *Ibid.*
114. *Ibid.*, 220–221.
115. Ed Wulf, "Vote, Vote, Vote for the Home Team."
116. King, "August 24, 1951: St. Louis Browns Fans Manage to Get It Right in Veeck Promotion."
117. Wulf, "Vote, Vote, Vote for the Home Team."
118. *Ibid.*
119. *Ibid.*
120. King, "August 24, 1951: St. Louis Browns Fans Manage to Get It Right in Veeck Promotion."
121. Coffey, "Veeck Holds 'Grandstand Managers Night.'"
122. Wulf, "Vote, Vote, Vote for the Home Team."
123. Coffey, "Veeck Holds 'Grandstand Managers Night.'"
124. King, "August 24, 1951: St. Louis Browns Fans Manage to Get It Right in Veeck Promotion."
125. Veeck with Linn, *Veeck as in Wreck: The Autobiography of Bill Veeck*, 221.
126. Wulf, "Vote, Vote, Vote for the Home Team."
127. *Ibid.*

Chapter 4

1. G. Michael Green and Roger Launius, *Charlie Finley: The Outrageous Story of Baseball's Super Showman* (New York: Walker & Company, 2010), 18.
2. Leonard Koppett, "Charles O. Finley, Baseball Team Owner Who Challenged Traditions, Dies at 77," *New York Times*, February 20, 1966, https://www.nytimes.com/1996/02/20/sports/charles-o-finley-baseball-team-owner-who-challenged-traditions-diesat-77.html.
3. Bill Libby, *Charlie O. and the Angry A's* (Garden City, NY: Doubleday), 39.
4. Koppett, "Charles O. Finley, Baseball Team Owner Who Challenged Traditions, Dies at 77."
5. Herbert Michelson, *Charlie O: Charles Oscar Finley vs. the Baseball Establishment* (New York: Bobbs-Merrill, 1975), 23.
6. Ron Fimrite, "Charlie O. Eyes a Pennant or Three," *Sports Illustrated*, September 10, 1972, https://vault.si.com/vault/1972/10/09/charlie-o-eyes-a-pennant-or-three.
7. Koppett, "Charles O. Finley, Baseball Team Owner Who Challenged Traditions, Dies at 77."
8. Green and Launius, *Charlie Finley: The Outrageous Story of Baseball's Super Showman*, 23–24.
9. Fimrite, "Charlie O. Eyes a Pennant or Three."
10. Green and Launius, *Charlie Finley: The Outrageous Story of Baseball's Super Showman*, 25–26.
11. Donald Marquez, "The Charlie Finley Story, Part 1 (or 'The Movie That Should Have Been')," *Athletics Nation*, November 18, 2010, https://www.athleticsnation.com/2010/11/18/1821764/the-charlie-finley-story-part-1-or-the-movie-that-should-have-been.
12. Green and Launius, *Charlie Finley: The Outrageous Story of Baseball's Super Showman*, 27.
13. "Will Harridge, Executive," *National Baseball Hall of Fame*, Accessed October 11, 2023, https://baseballhall.org/hall-of-famers/harridge-will.
14. Libby, *Charlie O. and the Angry A's*, 45.
15. Marquez, "The Charlie Finley Story, Part 1 (or 'The Movie That Should Have Been')."
16. Green and Launius, *Charlie Finley: The Outrageous Story of Baseball's Super Showman*, 27–35.
17. Alex Coffey and Alec Lewis, "Remembering Charlie-O the Mule, the A's Mascot Inspired by Charles O. Finley," *The Athletic*, May 8, 2020, https://theathletic.com/1801465/2020/05/08/remembering-charlie-o-the-mule-the-as-mascot-inspired-by-charles-o-finley.
18. Bill Libby, *Charlie O. and the Angry A's*, 39.
19. Green and Launius, *Charlie Finley: The Outrageous Story of Baseball's Super Showman*, 43–44.
20. *Ibid.*, 51.
21. *Ibid.*, 44.
22. Michelson, *Charlie O: Charles Oscar Finley vs. the Baseball Establishment*, 128.
23. "Kansas City Municipal Stadium," *Ballparks of Baseball*, Accessed August 30, 2024, https://www.ballparksofbaseball.com/ballparks/kansas-city-municipal-stadium/.

24. Green and Launius, *Charlie Finley: The Outrageous Story of Baseball's Super Showman*, 45–46.
25. Mark Armour, "Charlie Finley," *Society for American Baseball Research*, Accessed October 16, 2023, https://sabr.org/bioproj/person/charlie-finley/.
26. Koppett, "Charles O. Finley, Baseball Team Owner Who Challenged Traditions, Dies at 77."
27. Mark Armour, "Charlie Finley."
28. Green and Launius, *Charlie Finley: The Outrageous Story of Baseball's Super Showman*, 46.
29. Michelson, *Charlie O: Charles Oscar Finley vs. the Baseball Establishment*, 124.
30. Green and Launius, *Charlie Finley: The Outrageous Story of Baseball's Super Showman*, 42, 49.
31. D.L. Nelson, "The Reign of Finley," *Athletics Nation*, August 1, 2013, https://www.athleticsnation.com/2013/8/1/4576930/the-reign-of-finley.
32. Fimrite, "Charlie O. Eyes a Pennant or Three."
33. Green and Launius, *Charlie Finley: The Outrageous Story of Baseball's Super Showman*, 38.
34. *Ibid.*, 38, 53, 59.
35. Roger Launius, "The Beatles Come to Kansas City, Fifty Years Ago," *Wordpress*, September 15, 2014, https://launiusr.wordpress.com/2014/09/15/the-beatles-and-charles-o-finley-owner-of-the-kansas-city-as-in-the-1960s/.
36. Green and Launius, *Charlie Finley: The Outrageous Story of Baseball's Super Showman*, 48–49.
37. Libby, *Charlie O. and the Angry A's*, 59.
38. Green and Launius, *Charlie Finley: The Outrageous Story of Baseball's Super Showman*, 55.
39. *Ibid.*, 57–58.
40. Libby, *Charlie O. and the Angry A's*, 64.
41. Green and Launius, *Charlie Finley: The Outrageous Story of Baseball's Super Showman*, 55–59.
42. Libby, *Charlie O. and the Angry A's*, 66.
43. Green and Launius, *Charlie Finley: The Outrageous Story of Baseball's Super Showman*, 61.
44. *Ibid.*, 61–62.
45. Michelson, *Charlie O: Charles Oscar Finley vs. the Baseball Establishment*, 125.
46. Green and Launius, *Charlie Finley: The Outrageous Story of Baseball's Super Showman*, 65, 67.
47. Libby, *Charlie O. and the Angry A's*, 69.
48. Green and Launius, *Charlie Finley: The Outrageous Story of Baseball's Super Showman*, 65–66.
49. *Ibid.*, 67.
50. *Ibid.*, 68.
51. Coffey and Lewis, "Remembering Charlie-O the Mule, the A's Mascot Inspired by Charlie O. Finley."
52. Green and Launius, *Charlie Finley: The Outrageous Story of Baseball's Super Showman*, 72.
53. Armour, "Charlie Finley."
54. Libby, *Charlie O. and the Angry A's*, 66.
55. Green and Launius, *Charlie Finley: The Outrageous Story of Baseball's Super Showman*, 70–72.
56. Armour, "Charlie Finley."
57. Aaron Krerowicz, "Charlie Finley," *Beatles Blog*, Accessed January 18, 2024, https://www.arronkrerowicz.com/beatles-blog/charlie-finley.
58. Jeff Cochran, "John Lennon on Charlie Finley: 'I Just Didn't Particularly Like Him,'" *Seamheads.com*, November 1, 2014, https://seamheads.com/blog/2014/11/01/john-lennon-on-charlie-finley-ijust-didn't-particularly-like-him/.
59. "Can't Buy Him Love," *K.C. History.org*, Accessed January 18, 2024, https://kchistory.org/week-kansas-city-history/can't-buy-him-love.
60. Cochran, "John Lennon on Charlie Finley: 'I Just Didn't Particularly Like Him.'"
61. Krerowicz, "Charlie Finley."
62. Cochran, "John Lennon on Charlie Finley: 'I Just Didn't Particularly Like Him.'"
63. Krerowicz, "Charlie Finley."
64. *Ibid.*
65. Launius, "The Beatles Came to Kansas City, Fifty Years Ago."
66. "Can't Buy Him Love."
67. *Ibid.*
68. Cochran, "John Lennon on Charlie Finley: 'I Just Didn't Particularly Like Him.'"
69. "The Beatles Concert Setlist at

Kansas City Municipal Stadium," *setlist. com*, Accessed January 18, 2024, https://www.setlist.fm/setlist/the-beatles/1964/kansas-city-municipal-stadium-kansas-city-mo-7bdae244.html.

70. Green and Launius, *Charlie Finley: The Outrageous Story of Baseball's Super Showman*, 77.

71. Krerowicz, "Charlie Finley."

72. *Ibid.*

73. Green and Launius, *Charlie Finley: The Outrageous Story of Baseball's Super Showman*, 86.

74. Dan Vukelich, "The Great White Sox Hope," *Chicago Reader*, Accessed January 20, 2024, https://chicagoreader.com/news-politics/the-great-white-sox-hope.

75. Nelson, "The Reign of Finley."

76. Green and Launius, *Charlie Finley: The Outrageous Story of Baseball's Super Showman*, 87.

77. *Ibid.*, 87–88.

78. *Ibid.*, 88.

79. Norm King, "Charlie-O," *Society for American Baseball Research*, Accessed January 13, 2024, https://sabr-org/bioproj/topic/charlie-o/.

80. *Ibid.*

81. Green and Launius, *Charlie Finley: The Outrageous Story of Baseball's Super Showman*, 88–89.

82. *Ibid.*, 89.

83. Michael Murphy, "Charlie-O—Baseball's Favorite Mule," *Medium*, Accessed January 13, 2024, https://medium.com/stmaryssports/charlie-o-baseball's-favorite-mule-76c34bf4e5bd.

84. Norm King, "Charlie-O."

85. Green and Launius, *Charlie Finley: The Outrageous Story of Baseball's Super Showman*, 89.

86. *Ibid.*

87. *Ibid.*, 89–90.

88. *Ibid.*, 90.

89. *Ibid.*

90. *Ibid.*, 90–92.

91. Libby, *Charlie O. and the Angry A's*, 76.

92. Green and Launius, *Charlie Finley: The Outrageous Story of Baseball's Super Showman*, 90.

93. King, "Charlie-O."

94. Green and Launius, *Charlie Finley: The Outrageous Story of Baseball's Super Showman*, 90.

95. *Ibid.*, 90–91.

96. Libby, *Charlie O. and the Angry A's*, 76.

97. Green and Launius, *Charlie Finley: The Outrageous Story of Baseball's Super Showman*, 91.

98. *Ibid.*, 91–92.

99. Libby, *Charlie O. and the Angry A's*, 76.

100. Green and Launius, *Charlie Finley: The Outrageous Story of Baseball's Super Showman*, 91–92.

101. Libby, *Charlie O. and the Angry A's*, 76.

102. Green and Launius, *Charlie Finley: The Outrageous Story of Baseball's Super Showman*, 86.

103. Coffey and Lewis, "Remembering Charlie-O the Mule, the A's Mascot Inspired by Charlie O. Finley."

104. Libby, *Charlie O. and the Angry A's*, 76.

105. Coffey and Lewis, "Remembering Charlie-O the Mule, the A's Mascot Inspired by Charlie O. Finley."

106. Libby, *Charlie O. and the Angry A's*, 76.

107. Green and Launius, *Charlie Finley: The Outrageous Story of Baseball's Super Showman*, 92.

108. King, "Charlie-O."

109. Murphy, "Charlie-O—Baseball's Favorite Mule."

110. Coffey and Lewis, "Remembering Charlie-O the Mule, the A's Mascot Inspired by Charlie O. Finley."

111. King, "Charlie-O."

112. *Ibid.*

113. Murphy, "Charlie-O—Baseball's Favorite Mule."

Chapter 5

1. Bill Giles with Doug Myers, *Pouring Six Beers at a Time: Stories from a Lifetime in Baseball* (Chicago: Triumph Books, 2007), 30.

2. *Ibid.*, 19.

3. *Ibid.*, 30.

4. *Ibid.*

5. *Ibid.*, 30–31.

6. *Ibid.*, 30.

7. *Ibid.*, 26.

8. *Ibid.*, 31–32.

9. *Ibid.*, 33.

10. *Ibid.*, 34.

11. *Ibid.*, 35.
12. *Ibid.*, 35–36.
13. *Ibid.*, 25.
14. *Ibid.*, 14.
15. *Ibid.*, 37.
16. *Ibid.*, 42.
17. *Ibid.*, 72–73.
18. *Ibid.*, 73.
19. *Ibid.*, 85–86.
20. *Ibid.*, 86, 89.
21. *Ibid.*, 91.
22. *Ibid.*, 89.
23. "Shibe Park, Philadelphia, Pennsylvania," *This Great Game*, Accessed August 26, 2023, https://thisgreatgame.com/ballparks-shibe-park/.
24. James Lincoln Ray, "Connie Mack Stadium (Philadelphia)," *Society for American Baseball Research*, Accessed January 21, 2024, https://sabr.org/park/connie-mack-stadium-philadelphia/.
25. *Ibid.*
26. "Shibe Park, Philadelphia, Pennsylvania."
27. *Ibid.*
28. Ray, "Connie Mack Stadium (Philadelphia)."
29. *Ibid.*
30. "Shibe Park, Philadelphia, Pennsylvania."
31. Ray, "Connie Mack Stadium (Philadelphia)."
32. "Shibe Park, Philadelphia, Pennsylvania."
33. *Ibid.*
34. Ray, "Connie Mack Stadium (Philadelphia)."
35. "Shibe Park, Philadelphia, Pennsylvania."
36. *Ibid.*
37. Ray, "Connie Mack Stadium (Philadelphia)."
38. *Ibid.*
39. *Ibid.*
40. "Shibe Park, Philadelphia, Pennsylvania."
41. *Ibid.*
42. Ray, "Connie Mack Stadium (Philadelphia)."
43. *Ibid.*
44. Giles with Myers, *Pouring Six Beers at a Time: Stories from a Lifetime in Baseball*, 90.
45. David White, "The Graveyard of Baseball: October 1, 1970, Was a Day That Will Live in Infamy," *Order of the Jackalope*, Accessed August 26, 2023, https://order-of-the-jackalope.com/the-graveyard-of-baseball/.
46. "Philadelphia Phillies Attendance, Stadiums, and Park Factors," *Baseball Reference*, Accessed January 25, 2024, https://www.baseball-reference.com/PHI/attendance-stadiums-and-park-factors/.
47. John B. Lord, *Bill Giles & Baseball* (Philadelphia: Temple University Press, 2014), 227.
48. Giles with Myers, *Pouring Six Beers at a Time: Stories from a Lifetime in Baseball*, 88.
49. Larry Shenk, "1972 Rewind," *Phillies Insider*, Accessed November 8, 2023, https://philliesinsider.mlblogs.com/1972-rewind-4a8da68a2fc2.
50. Rich Westcott, *Veterans Stadium, Field of Memories* (Philadelphia: Temple University Press, 2005), 86.
51. Ray, "Connie Mack Stadium (Philadelphia)."
52. *Ibid.*
53. White, "The Graveyard of Baseball: October 1, 1970, Was a Day That Will Live in Infamy."
54. *Ibid.*
55. Giles with Myers, *Pouring Six Beers at a Time: Stories from a Lifetime in Baseball*, 93.
56. Larry Shenk, "End of an Era," *Major League Baseball*, September 30, 2020, https://www.mlb.com/news/phillies-alumni-end-of-an-era.
57. White, "The Graveyard of Baseball: October 1, 1970, Was a Day That Will Live in Infamy."
58. *Ibid.*
59. *Ibid.*
60. *Ibid.*
61. Matthew Frank, "Only in Philadelphia: A Look Back on the Day Eagles Fans Booed Santa at Franklin Field," *The Daily Pennsylvanian*, December 1, 2020, https://www.thedp.com/article/2020/12/penn-football-franklin-field-eagles-santa.
62. White, "The Graveyard of Baseball: October 1, 1970, Was a Day That Will Live in Infamy."
63. *Ibid.*
64. *Ibid.*
65. Giles with Myers, *Pouring Six Beers at a Time: Stories from a Lifetime in Baseball*, 93.
66. *Ibid.*, 94.

67. "Shibe Park, Philadelphia, Pennsylvania."
68. Shenk, "End of an Era."
69. Larry Shenk, *If These Walls Could Talk: Stories from the Philadelphia Phillies Dugout, Locker Room, and Press Box* (Chicago: Triumph Books, 2014), 59.
70. Giles with Myers, *Pouring Six Beers at a Time: Stories from a Lifetime in Baseball*, 93.
71. Jack McCafferty, "All of 50 Years Later, Bowa and Vankowski Can't Forget Phillies' Final Hours at Connie Mack Stadium," *Delco Times*, July 5, 2020, https://www.delcotimes.com/2020/07/05/all-of-50-years-later-bowa-and-vankowski-can't-forget-phillies-final-hours-at-connie-mack-stadium/.
72. Giles with Myers, *Pouring Six Beers at a Time: Stories from a Lifetime in Baseball*, 93.
73. White, "The Graveyard of Baseball: October 1, 1970, Was a Day That Will Live in Infamy."
74. *Ibid.*
75. *Ibid.*
76. *Ibid.*
77. *Ibid.*
78. *Ibid.*
79. *Ibid.*
80. *Ibid.*
81. *Ibid.*
82. *Ibid.*
83. "Shibe Park, Philadelphia, Pennsylvania."
84. *Ibid.*
85. Rich Westcott, *Veterans Stadium: Field of Memories*, 91.
86. Giles with Myers, *Pouring Six Beers at a Time: Stories from a Lifetime in Baseball*, 8.
87. *Ibid.*, 1.
88. *Ibid.*, 2.
89. *Ibid.*
90. *Ibid.*
91. *Ibid.*
92. *Ibid.*, 2–4.
93. Westcott, *Veterans Stadium: Field of Memories*, 90–91.
94. "Year by Year Results/Philadelphia Phillies," *Major League Baseball*, Accessed August 20, 2024, https://www.mlb.com/phillies/history/year-by-year-results.

Chapter 6

1. J. Scott Shaffer and Millard Fisher, "Ted Turner," *Society for American Baseball Research*, Accessed March 10, 2024, https://sabr.org/bioproj/person/ted-turner/.
2. Ted Turner with Bill Burke, *Call Me Ted* (New York: Grand Central, 2008), 7.
3. Shaffer and Fisher, "Ted Turner."
4. Turner with Burke, *Call Me Ted*, 6–7.
5. *Ibid.*, 3.
6. *Ibid.*, 4.
7. *Ibid.*
8. *Ibid.*, 4–5.
9. *Ibid.*, 5.
10. *Ibid.*, 8.
11. *Ibid.*, 9.
12. *Ibid.*, 11–12.
13. *Ibid.*, 17–18.
14. Shaffer and Fisher, "Ted Turner."
15. Turner with Burke, *Call Me Ted*, 26–27.
16. Shaffer and Fisher, "Ted Turner."
17. Turner with Burke, *Call Me Ted*, 30–31.
18. *Ibid.*, 33–38.
19. *Ibid.*, 39–40.
20. *Ibid.*, 50–52.
21. *Ibid.*, 54.
22. Shaffer and Fisher, "Ted Turner."
23. Turner with Burke, *Call Me Ted*, 55–58.
24. *Ibid.*, 69–71.
25. *Ibid.*, 72–74.
26. *Ibid.*, 72, 91.
27. *Ibid.*, 79–84.
28. *Ibid.*, 91–93.
29. *Ibid.*, 95–96.
30. *Ibid.*, 91.
31. Shaffer and Fisher, "Ted Turner."
32. Turner with Burke, *Call Me Ted*, 97.
33. *Ibid.*, 94.
34. *Ibid.*, 97–103.
35. *Ibid.*, 105.
36. *Ibid.*, 110–111.
37. *Ibid.*, 112.
38. Robert Ashley Fields, *Take Me Out to the Crowd: Ted Turner and the Atlanta Braves* (Huntsville, AL: Strode Publishers, 1977), 56.
39. *Ibid.*, 34.
40. Turner with Burke, *Call Me Ted*, 115.
41. Shaffer and Fisher, "Ted Turner."
42. Turner with Burke, *Call Me Ted*, 116.

43. Bob Hope, *We Could've Finished Last Without You* (Atlanta: Longstreet Press, 1991), 10.
44. Robert Ashley Fields, *Take Me Out to the Crowd: Ted Turner and the Atlanta Braves*, 88.
45. "Year by Year Results/Atlanta Braves," *Major League Baseball*, Accessed August 5, 2024, https://www.mlb.com/braves/history/year-by-year-results.
46. Hope, *We Could've Finished Last Without You*, 10.
47. Fields, *Take Me Out to the Crowd: Ted Turner and the Atlanta Braves*, 85–90.
48. Ibid., 85.
49. Ibid.
50. Ibid.
51. Hope, *We Could've Finished Last Without You*, 32.
52. Fields, *Take Me Out to the Crowd: Ted Turner and the Atlanta Braves*, 85–87.
53. Hope, *We Could've Finished Last Without You*, 32.
54. Fields, *Take Me Out to the Crowd: Ted Turner and the Atlanta Braves*, 87.
55. Hope, *We Could've Finished Last Without You*, 32.
56. Fields, *Take Me Out to the Crowd: Ted Turner and the Atlanta Braves*, 87–88.
57. Ibid., 88.
58. Ibid., 90–91.
59. Turner with Burke, *Call Me Ted*, 117.
60. Ibid.
61. Ibid.
62. Ibid.
63. Ibid., 121–122.
64. Ibid., 122.
65. Ibid., 119–120.
66. Ibid., 122.
67. Ibid.
68. Ibid.
69. Ibid.
70. Doug Williams, "The Night Ted Turner Managed the Braves," *ESPN*, May 23, 2013, https://www.espn.com/blog/playbook/fandom/post/_/id/22066/the-night-ted-turner-managed-the-braves.
71. Ibid.
72. Turner with Burke, *Call Me Ted*, 123.
73. Ibid.
74. Williams, "The Night Ted Turner Managed the Braves."
75. Turner with Burke, *Call Me Ted*, 123.
76. Hope, *We Could've Finished Last Without You*, 32.
77. Fields, *Take Me Out to the Crowd: Ted Turner and the Atlanta Braves*, 158.
78. Hope, *We Could've Finished Last Without You*, 123.
79. Ibid.
80. Fields, *Take Me Out to the Crowd: Ted Turner and the Atlanta Braves*, 159.
81. Hope, *We Could've Finished Last Without You*, 123.
82. Ibid.
83. Ibid., 92–93.
84. Ibid., 123–124.
85. Ibid., 124.
86. Fields, *Take Me Out to the Crowd: Ted Turner and the Atlanta Braves*, 159.
87. Ibid.
88. Ibid.
89. Hope, *We Could've Finished Last Without You*, 125.
90. Dan Epstein, *Stars and Strikes* (New York: Thomas Dunne, 2014), 210.
91. Fields, *Take Me Out to the Crowd: Ted Turner and the Atlanta Braves*, 159.
92. Hope, *We Could've Finished Last Without You*, 162–163.
93. Ibid., 163.
94. Ibid.
95. Ibid.
96. Ibid.
97. Ibid.
98. G. Michael Green and Roger D. Launius, *Charlie Finley: The Outrageous Story of Baseball's Super Showman* (New York: Walker & Company, 2010), 164.
99. Hope, *We Could've Finished Last Without You*, 163.
100. Jim Dunphy, "Worst Promotions in Baseball History," *Slideplayer*, Accessed July 23, 2023, https://player.slideplayer.com/104/17579561.
101. Hope, *We Could've Finished Last Without You*, 163.
102. Dunphy, "Worst Promotions in Baseball History."
103. Hope, *We Could've Finished Last Without You*, 164.
104. Dunphy, "Worst Promotions in Baseball History."
105. Hope, *We Could've Finished Last Without You*, 164.
106. Ibid.
107. Ibid., 164–166.
108. Ibid., 166.

Notes—Chapter 7

109. Dunphy, "Worst Promotions in Baseball History."
110. Hope, *We Could've Finished Last Without You*, 166.
111. Ibid.
112. Dunphy, "Worst Promotions in Baseball History."
113. Hope, *We Could've Finished Last Without You*, 167.
114. Dunphy, "Worst Promotions in Baseball History."
115. Hope, *We Could've Finished Last Without You*, 167.

Chapter 7

1. "40 Years Ago, Disco Demolition Night Stirred Culture War Still Being Fought," *freep.com*, July 12, 2019, https://www.freep.com/story/sports/mlb/tigers/2019/07/12/detroit-tigers-disco-demolition-chicago-white-sox-lgbtq/1682439001.
2. 2 "Disco Demolition Night," *Major League Sports Fandom*, Accessed May 29, 2022, https://about:reader?url=https://-majpr-league-sports.fandom.com/wiki/Disco-Demolition-Night.
3. Alexis Petridis, "Disco Demolition: The Night They Tried to Crush Black Music," *The Guardian*, July 19, 2019, https://www.theguardian.com/music/2019/jul/19/all.
4. Jacob Kornhauser, "Moment #96: Disco Demolition Night Goes Awry: MLB's ALL-TIME MOMENTS," *Baseball FYI*, Accessed May 21, 2021, https://www.baseball.fyi/posts/moment/96-disco-dmolition-night-goes-awry-mlbs-all-time-moments.
5. Gary Waleik, "Forty Years Later, Disagreement About Disco Demolition Night," *WBUR.org*, July 12, 2019, https://www.ubur.org/onlyagame/2019/07/disco-demolition-dahl-veeck-chicago-white-sox.
6. Petridis, "Disco Demolition: The Night They Tried to Crush Black Music."
7. Waleik, "Forty Years Later, Disagreement About Disco Demolition Night."
8. "Disco Demolition Night."
9. Ibid.
10. Petridis, "Disco Demolition: The Night They Tried to Crush Black Music."
11. Lyndsey Parker, "'Let's Blow Up This Black Music!' The Ugliness and Unrest of 1979's Disco Demolition Night," *Yahoo.com*, Accessed May 21, 2021, https://www.yahoo.com/now/lets-blow-up-this-black-music-the-ugliness-and-unrest-of-1979-s-disco-demolition-night.
12. "Disco Demolition Night."
13. Alice Echols, *Hot Stuff: Disco and the Remaking of American Culture* (New York: W.W. Norton, 2010), 195.
14. Ibid., 206.
15. "Disco Demolition Night."
16. Echols, *Hot Stuff: Disco and the Remaking of American Culture*, 206.
17. Ibid., 213.
18. Ibid., 204.
19. Ibid., 205.
20. Ibid., 212–213.
21. Ibid., 213.
22. Ibid.
23. Dan Epstein, *Big Hair and Plastic Grass* (New York: Thomas Dunne, 2010), 241.
24. Echols, *Hot Stuff: Disco and the Remaking of American Culture*, 214.
25. Christopher J. Young, "When Fans Wanted to Rock, the Baseball Stopped: Sports, Promotions, and the Demolition of Disco on Chicago's South Side," *Society for American Baseball Research*, Accessed September 21, 2022, https://sabr.org/journal/article/when-fans-wanted-to-rock-the-baseball-stopped-sports-promotions-and-the-demolition-of-disco-on-chicagos-south-side/.
26. Echols, *Hot Stuff: Disco and the Remaking of American Culture*, 205.
27. Ibid., 195.
28. Ibid., 196.
29. "Disco Demolition Night."
30. Ibid.
31. Echols, *Hot Stuff: Disco and the Remaking of American Culture*, 199.
32. Ibid., 197.
33. Ibid.
34. Steve Dahl, with Dave Hoekstra and Paul Natkin, *Disco Demolition: The Night Disco Died*, e-book edition (Chicago: Curbside Splendor Publishing, 2016), 89. (Please note: E-book pagination may be different on different devises. I used an Apple iPhone to view this E-book.)
35. Ibid.
36. Echols, *Hot Stuff: Disco and the Remaking of American Culture*, 198.
37. Ibid.
38. Ibid., 199.

39. *Ibid.*
40. *Ibid.*, 199–200.
41. *Ibid.*, 201.
42. Petridis, "Disco Demolition: The Night They Tried to Crush Black Music."
43. Echols, *Hot Stuff: Disco and the Remaking of American Culture*, 201.
44. *Ibid.*
45. Parker, "'Let's Blow Up This Black Music!' The Ugliness and Unrest of 1979's Disco Demolition Night."
46. Echols, *Hot Stuff: Disco and the Remaking of American Culture*, 201.
47. *Ibid.*
48. Epstein, *Big Hair and Plastic Grass*, 245.
49. *Ibid.*, 201.
50. Echols, *Hot Stuff: Disco and the Remaking of American Culture*, 202.
51. "Disco Demolition Night."
52. Kornhauser, "Moment #96: Disco Demolition Night Goes Awry: MLB's ALL-TIME MOMENTS."
53. Echols, *Hot Stuff: Disco and the Remaking of American Culture*, 206.
54. "Disco Demolition Night."
55. "40 Years Ago, Disco Demolition Night Stirred Culture War Still Being Fought."
56. "Disco Demolition Night."
57. *Ibid.*
58. Epstein, *Big Hair and Plastic Grass*, 242.
59. "40 Years Ago, Disco Demolition Night Stirred Culture War Still Being Fought."
60. Interestingly, the White Sox Held a "Disco Night" at Comiskey Park in 1977.
61. Dave Hoekstra, "The Night Disco Died," *chicagomag.com*, July 2016, https://www.chicagomag.com/Chicago-Magazine/July-2016/the-night-disco-died.
62. Jake Rossen, "When Disco Demolition Night Nearly Demolished Chicago's Comiskey Park." *mentalfloss.com*, December 5, 2019, https://www.mentalfloss.com/article/609062/disco-demolition-night-comiskey-park.
63. Mike Fisk, "MLB History: Disco Demolition Night at Comiskey Park," *OvertimeHeroics.net*, January 23, 2021, https://www.overtimeheroics.net/2021/01/31/mlb-history-disco-demolition.
64. Dahl, with Hoekstra and Natkin, *Disco Demolition: The Night Disco Died*, 26.
65. Epstein, *Big Hair and Plastic Grass*, 186.
66. "Disco Demolition Night."
67. Kornhauser, "Moment #96: Disco Demolition Night Goes Awry: MLB's ALL-TIME MOMENTS."
68. "Disco Demolition Night."
69. Hoekstra, "The Night Disco Died."
70. Mike Huber, "July 12, 1979: Chicago's Disco Demolition Night Results in White Sox Loss and Forfeit," *Society for American Baseball Research*, Accessed September 21, 2022, https://sabr.org/gamesproj/game/July-12-1979-chicagos-disco-demolition-night-doubleheader-results-in-loss-and-forfeit/.
71. Derek John, "July 12, 1979: 'The Night Disco Died'—Or Didn't," *National Public Radio*, July 16, 2016, https://www.npr.org/2016/07/16/485873750/the-night-disco-died-or-didn't#.
72. Dahl, with Hoekstra and Natkin, *Disco Demolition: The Night Disco Died*, 26.
73. Rossen, "When Disco Demolition Night Nearly Demolished Chicago's Comiskey Park."
74. "Disco Demolition Night."
75. Epstein, *Big Hair and Plastic Grass*, 242.
76. *Ibid.*
77. David Nemec and Eric Miklich, *Forfeits and Successfully Protested Games in Major League Baseball, A Complete Record, 1871–2013* (Jefferson, NC: McFarland, 2014), 148.
78. Hoekstra, "The Night Disco Died."
79. *Ibid.*
80. "Disco Demolition Night."
81. Dahl, with Hoekstra and Natkin, *Disco Demolition: The Night Disco Died*, 9.
82. Huber, "July 12, 1979: Chicago's Disco Demolition Night Results in White Sox Loss and Forfeit."
83. "Disco Demolition Night."
84. Epstein, *Big Hair and Plastic Grass*, 242.
85. *Ibid.*, 241.
86. Young, "When Fans Wanted to Rock, the Baseball Stopped: Sports, Promotions, and the Demolition of Disco on Chicago's South Side."
87. "Disco Demolition Night."
88. *Ibid.*
89. Young, "When Fans Wanted to Rock, the Baseball Stopped: Sports,

Promotions, and the Demolition of Disco on Chicago's South Side."
90. Ibid.
91. Hoekstra, "The Night Disco Died."
92. Young, "When Fans Wanted to Rock, the Baseball Stopped: Sports, Promotions, and the Demolition of Disco on Chicago's South Side."
93. Ibid.
94. "Disco Demolition Night."
95. Echols, *Hot Stuff: Disco and the Remaking of American Culture*, 207.
96. Hoekstra, "The Night Disco Died."
97. Epstein, *Big Hair and Plastic Grass*, 243.
98. Hoekstra, "The Night Disco Died."
99. Waleik, "Forty Years Later, Disagreement About Disco Demolition Night."
100. Ibid.
101. Ibid.
102. Dahl with Hoekstra and Natkin, *Disco Demolition: The Night Disco Died*, 232.
103. "The Night Disco Died."
104. Rossen, "When Disco Demolition Night Nearly Demolished Chicago's Comiskey Park."
105. Waleik, "Forty Years Later, Disagreement About Disco Demolition Night."
106. Dahl, with Hoekstra and Natkin, *Disco Demolition: The Night Disco Died*, 25.
107. Hoekstra, "The Night Disco Died."
108. Waleik, "Forty Years Later, Disagreement About Disco Demolition Night."
109. "Disco Demolition Night."
110. "Super Disco Demolition: The 40th Anniversary Compilation (1979)," YouTube, youtube.com/watch?v=kqDkBM9vxw8.
111. Nemec and Miklich, *Forfeits and Successfully Protested Games in Major League Baseball, A Complete Record, 1871–2013*, 149.
112. "Disco Demolition Night."
113. Waleik, "Forty Years Later, Disagreement About Disco Demolition Night."
114. Hoekstra, "The Night Disco Died."
115. "Disco Demolition Night."
116. Epstein, *Big Hair and Plastic Grass*, 242.
117. Hoekstra, "The Night Disco Died."
118. Ibid.
119. "Disco Demolition Night."
120. "40 Years Ago, Disco Demolition Night Stirred Culture War Still Being Fought."
121. "Disco Demolition Night."
122. Hoekstra, "The Night Disco Died."
123. "40 Years Ago, Disco Demolition Night Stirred Culture War Still Being Fought."
124. Dahl, with Hoekstra and Natkin, *Disco Demolition: The Night Disco Died*, 262.
125. "Disco Demolition Night."
126. "40 Years Ago, Disco Demolition Night Stirred Culture War Still Being Fought."
127. Hoekstra, "The Night Disco Died."
128. "Flashback: 'Disco Demolition Night' at Chicago's Comiskey Park," *vermillioncountyfirst.com*, Accessed May 21, 2021, https://vermilioncountyfirst.com/2020/07/09/flash-disco-demolition-night-at-chicago-comiskey-park.
129. "Disco Demolition Night."
130. "On This Day: "Disco Demolition Night" Causes Riot at Chicago White Sox Game," *findingDulcinea.com*, Accessed May 21, 2021, https://www.findingdulcinea.com/news/on-this-day/July-August-08/On-this-Day---Disco-Demolition-Night-Ruins-Chicago-White-Sox-Game.html.
131. Young, "When Fans Wanted to Rock, the Baseball Stopped: Sports, Promotions, and the Demolition of Disco on Chicago's South Side."
132. "Disco Demolition Night."
133. Fisk, "MLB History: Disco Demolition Night at Comiskey Park."
134. "40 Years Ago, Disco Demolition Night Stirred Culture War Still Being Fought."
135. Nemec and Miklich, *Forfeits and Successfully Protested Games in Major League Baseball, A Complete Record, 1871–2013*, 149.
136. Huber, "July 12, 1979: Chicago's Disco Demolition Night Results in White Sox Loss and Forfeit."
137. "Disco Demolition Night."
138. "Disco Demolition Night."
139. Young, "When Fans Wanted to Rock, the Baseball Stopped: Sports, Promotions, and the Demolition of Disco on Chicago's South Side."
140. Ibid.
141. Hoekstra, "The Night Disco Died."
142. "Disco Demolition Night."
143. Huber, "July 12, 1979: Chicago's

Disco Demolition Night Results in White Sox Loss and Forfeit."

144. Young, "When Fans Wanted to Rock, the Baseball Stopped: Sports, Promotions, and the Demolition of Disco on Chicago's South Side."

145. Kornhauser, "Moment #96: Disco Demolition Night Goes Awry: MLB's ALL-TIME MOMENTS."

146. Rossen, "When Disco Demolition Night Nearly Demolished Chicago's Comiskey Park."

147. Luke Saunders, "Disco Demolition Night: Why Your Taste Doesn't Matter and Never Will," *happymagtv.com*, Accessed May 21, 2021, https://happymag.tv/disco-demolition-night-and-why-your-taste-doesnt-matter-and-never-will.

148. Echols, *Hot Stuff: Disco and the Remaking of American Culture*, 209.

149. Petridis, "Disco Demolition: The Night They Tried to Crush Black Music."

150. Parker, "'Let's Blow Up This Black Music!' The Ugliness and Unrest of 1979's Disco Demolition Night."

151. Petridis, "Disco Demolition: The Night They Tried to Crush Black Music."

152. Michelle Kim, "Chicago White Sox Giving Away 'Disco Demolition Night' T-Shirts for 40th Anniversary," *pitchfork.com*, Accessed May 21, 2021, https://pitchfork.com/news/chicago-white-sox-giving-away-disco-demolition-night-t-shirts-for-40th-anniversary.

153. "40 Years Ago, Disco Demolition Night Stirred Culture War Still Being Fought."

154. Dahl, with Hoekstra and Natkin, *Disco Demolition: The Night Disco Died*, 20.

155. Petridis, "Disco Demolition: The Night They Tried to Crush Black Music."

156. "40 Years Ago, Disco Demolition Night Stirred Culture War Still Being Fought."

157. Dahl, with Hoekstra and Natkin, *Disco Demolition: The Night Disco Died*, 20.

158. Parker, "'Let's Blow Up This Black Music!' The Ugliness and Unrest of 1979's Disco Demolition Night."

159. Rossen, "When Disco Demolition Night Nearly Demolished Chicago's Comiskey Park."

160. Petridis, "Disco Demolition: The Night They Tried to Crush Black Music."

161. Paul Natkin, "Disco Demolition Night Was a Disgrace, and Celebrating It Is Worse," *vice.com*, Accessed January 21, 2021, https://www.vice.com/en/article/8xzke5/disco-demolityion-night-was-a-disgrace-ans-celebrating-it-is-worse.

162. Parker, "'Let's Blow Up This Black Music!' The Ugliness and Unrest of 1979's Disco Demolition Night."

163. *Ibid.*

164. John, "July 12, 1979: 'The Night Disco Died'—Or Didn't."

165. Petridis, "Disco Demolition: The Night They Tried to Crush Black Music."

166. "Disco Is Dealt Death Blow by Fans of the Chicago White Sox," *History.com*, Accessed January 21, 2021, https://www.history.com/this-day-in-history/disco-is-dealt-death-blow-by-fans-of-the-chicago-white-sox.

167. Echols, *Hot Stuff: Disco and the Remaking of American Culture*, 213.

168. *Ibid.*, 208.

169. *Ibid.*, 213.

170. *Ibid.*, 208.

171. *Ibid.*

172. *Ibid.*, 211.

173. Saunders, "Disco Demolition Night: Why Your Taste Doesn't Matter and Never Will."

174. Petridis, "Disco Demolition: The Night They Tried to Crush Black Music."

175. Echols, *Hot Stuff: Disco and the Remaking of American Culture*, 207.

176. *Ibid.*, 209.

177. Petridis, "Disco Demolition: The Night They Tried to Crush Black Music."

178. Natkin, "Disco Demolition Night Was a Disgrace, and Celebrating It Is Worse."

179. Parker, "'Let's Blow Up This Black Music!' The Ugliness and Unrest of 1979's Disco Demolition Night."

180. John, "July 12, 1979: 'The Night Disco Died'—Or Didn't."

181. Echols, *Hot Stuff: Disco and the Remaking of American Culture*, 216–232.

Chapter 8

1. "Boston Braves vs. Brooklyn Dodgers Box Score: September 25, 1942," *Baseball Reference*, Accessed February 27, 2024, https://www.baseball-reference.com/boxscores/1942/September-25-1942.

Notes—Chapter 8

2. Jim Kaplan, "Warren Spahn," *Society for American Baseball Research*, Accessed February 28, 2024, https://sabr.org/bioproj/person/warren-spahn/.

3. "Material Drives on the World War II Home Front," *National Park Service*, Accessed September 2, 2023, https://www.nps.gov/articles/000/material-drives-on-the-world-war-ii-home-front.htm.

4. *Ibid.*

5. *Ibid.*

6. Richard Keller, "World War II: Recycling and Patriotism," *Baltimore County Government*, Accessed August 20, 2023, https://www.baltimorecountymd.gov/public-works/solid-waste/recycling/theresource/world-war-ii-recycling-and-patriotism.

7. "Material Drives on the World War II Home Front."

8. Keller, "World War II: Recycling and Patriotism."

9. "Material Drives on the World War II Home Front."

10. Ronald Baily, "Iron Will: Scrapping History," *Historynet.com*, November 27, 2017, https://www.historynet.com/iron-0will-scrapping-history/.

11. "Salvage for Victory: World War II & Now," *National World War II Museum*, January 11, 2022, https://www.nationalww2museum.org/war/articles/salvage-for-victory-world-war-ii.

12. Baily, "Iron Will: Scrapping History."

13. Cecil Adams, "Were WWII Scrap Drives Just a Ploy to Boost Morale?" *The Straight Dope*, May 31, 2002, https://www.straightdope.com/21343531/were-wwii-scrap-drives-just-a-ploy-to-boost-morale.

14. Sarah Sundin, "Make It Do—Scrap Drives in World War II," *Sarah Sundin*, Accessed August 20, 2023, htttps://www.sarahsundin.com/make-it-do-scrap-drives-in-world-war-ii.

15. *Ibid.*

16. "Material Drives on the World War II Home Front."

17. *Ibid.*

18. *Ibid.*

19. Sundin, "Make It Do—Scrap Drives in World War II."

20. *Ibid.*

21. "Material Drives on the World War II Home Front."

22. Baily, "Iron Will: Scrapping History."

23. *Ibid.*

24. *Ibid.*

25. *Ibid.*

26. "Material Drives on the World War II Home Front."

27. *Ibid.*

28. *Ibid.*

29. Sundin, "Make It Do—Scrap Drives in World War II."

30. "Material Drives on the World War II Home Front."

31. *Ibid.*

32. *Ibid.*

33. *Ibid.*

34. *Ibid.*

35. *Ibid.*

36. Sundin, "Make It Do—Scrap Drives in World War II."

37. "Material Drives on the World War II Home Front."

38. *Ibid.*

39. *Ibid.*

40. *Ibid.*

41. Steve Bullock, "Playing for Their Nation: The American Military and Baseball During World War II," *Journal of Sport History*, Vol. 27, No. 1, Spring 2000, https://www.jstor.org/stable/8b6c2e30-627c-8479-673864723c94?readnow=1&seq=1.

42. Matt Cox, "Keep Baseball Going," *National Baseball Hall of Fame*, Accessed August 20, 2023, https://baseballhall.org/discover-more/stories/short-stops/keep-baseball-going.

43. Gerald Bazer and Steven Culbertson, "When FDR Said 'Play Ball,'" *National Archives*, Spring 2002, https://www.archives.gov/publications/prologue/2002/spring/greenlight.html.

44. Craig Muder, "President Roosevelt Gives 'Green Light' to Baseball," *Baseball Hall of Fame*, Accessed February 28, 2024, https://baseballhall.org/roosevelt-sends-green-light-letter-to-baseball.

45. Cox, "Keep Baseball Going."

46. Gary Bedingfield, "Baseball in World War II," *Baseball in Wartime*, Accessed August 20, 2023, https://www.baseballinwartime.com/baseball_in_wwii/baseball_in_wwii.htm.

47. Cox, "Keep Baseball Going."

48. James C. Roberts, "Baseball Goes to War: The National Pastime in World

War II," *American Veterans Center*, Accessed September 2, 2023, https://www.americanveteralscenter.org/avc-media/magazine/wwiichronicles/wwii-chronicles-issue-xxxix/baseball-goes-to-war-the-national-pastime-in-world-war-ii.

49. Bullock, "Playing for Their Nation: The American Military and Baseball During World War II."
50. Roberts, "Baseball Goes to War: The National Pastime in World War II."
51. Bazer and Culbertson, "When FDR Said 'Play Ball.'"
52. Roberts, "Baseball Goes to War: The National Pastime in World War II."
53. *Ibid.*
54. Bullock, "Playing for Their Nation: The American Military and Baseball During World War II."
55. *Ibid.*
56. Bazer and Culbertson, "When FDR Said 'Play Ball.'"
57. Bullock, "Playing for Their Nation: The American Military and Baseball During World War II."
58. Roberts, "Baseball Goes to War: The National Pastime in World War II."
59. Kaplan, "Warren Spahn."
60. *Ibid.*
61. *Ibid.*
62. Bullock, "Playing for Their Nation: The American Military and Baseball During World War II."
63. *Ibid.*
64. *Ibid.*
65. *Ibid.*
66. *Ibid.*
67. "Harry O'Neill (catcher)," *Wikipedia*, Accessed February 23, 2023, https:/en.wikipedia.org/wiki/harry_o'neill_(catcher).
68. "Elmer Gedeon," *Wikipedia*, Accessed February 23, 2023, https://en.wikipedia.org/wiki/elmer_gedeon.
69. Bullock, "Playing for Their Nation: The American Military and Baseball During World War II."
70. Roberts, "Baseball Goes to War: The National Pastime in World War II."
71. *Ibid.*
72. "Bert Shepherd," *Wikipedia*, Accessed February 22, 2024, https://en.wikipedia.org/wiki/Bert_Shepard.
73. Bazer and Culbertson, "When FDR Said 'Play Ball.'"
74. Bullock, "Playing for Their Nation: The American Military and Baseball During World War II."
75. *Ibid.*
76. *Ibid.*
77. *Ibid.*
78. *Ibid.*
79. *Ibid.*
80. David Nemec and Eric Miklich, *Forfeits and Successfully Protested Games in Major League Baseball: A Complete Record, 1871–2013* (Jefferson, NC: McFarland, 2014), 139.
81. *Ibid.*
82. Women and children rarely attended baseball games.
83. Nemec and Miklich, *Forfeits and Successfully Protested Games in Major League Baseball, A Complete Record, 1871–2013*, 139–140.
84. Thomas E. Merrick, "September 23, 1942: Larry French Nearly Perfect, as Patriotic Dodgers Collect Scrap Metal, Keep Pennant Hopes Alive," *Society for American Baseball Research*, Accessed February 27, 2024, https://sabr.org/gamesproj/game/september-23-1942-larry-french-nearly-perfect-aspatriotic-dodgers-collect-scrap-metal-keep-pennant-hopes-alive/.
85. *Ibid.*
86. James Forr, "September 26, 1942: Braves Win by Forfeit Behind Rookie Warren Spahn at Polo Grounds," *Society for American Baseball Research*, Accessed August 20, 2023, https://sabr.org/gamespro/game/september-26-1942-braves-win-by-forfeit-behindrookie-warren-spahn-at-polo-grounds/.
87. Jim Kaplan, "Warren Spahn."
88. Forr, "September 26, 1942: Braves Win by Forfeit Behind Rookie Warren Spahn at Polo Grounds."
89. *Ibid.*
90. *Ibid.*
91. Nemec and Miklich, *Forfeits and Successfully Protested Games in Major League Baseball, A Complete Record, 1871–2013*, 139–140.
92. Forr, "September 26, 1942: Braves Win by Forfeit Behind Rookie Warren Spahn at Polo Grounds."
93. Nemec and Miklich, *Forfeits and Successfully Protested Games in Major League Baseball, A Complete Record, 1871–2013*, 140.
94. Forr, "September 26, 1942: Braves

Win by Forfeit Behind Rookie Warren Spahn at Polo Grounds."
95. *Ibid.*
96. *Ibid.*
97. Nemec and Miklich, *Forfeits and Successfully Protested Games in Major League Baseball, A Complete Record, 1871–2013,* 140.
98. Forr, "September 26, 1942: Braves Win by Forfeit Behind Rookie Warren Spahn at Polo Grounds."
99. *Ibid.*
100. Nemec and Miklich, *Forfeits and Successfully Protested Games in Major League Baseball, A Complete Record, 1871–2013,* 140.
101. Forr, "September 26, 1942: Braves Win by Forfeit Behind Rookie Warren Spahn at Polo Grounds."

Chapter 9

1. Shirley Povich, "The Senators' Final Game," *Washington Post,* October 1, 1971, www.washingtonpost.com/wp-srv/sports/longterm/general/povich/launch/senators2.htm.
2. Timothy Dwyer, "The (Forfeited) Last Game of the Washington Senators in 1971," *WordPress,* June 10, 2010, https://miscbaseball.wordpress.com/2010/10/06/-the-forfeited-last-game-of-the-washington-senators-in-1971/.
3. *Ibid.*
4. Art Audley, "This Date in Washington Senators History—The Final Game," *DC Baseball History,* September 2020, https://dcbaseballhistory.com/2020/09/this-date-in-washington-senators-history-the-final-game.
5. Dwyer, "The (Forfeited) Last Game of the Washington Senators in 1971."
6. Myra McPherson and Tom Huth, "Rowdy Fans Hand Senators Final Loss," *Washington Post,* October 1, 1971, www.washingtonpost.com/wpsrv/sports/redskins/history/rfk/articles/baseball.htm.
7. Dwyer, "The (Forfeited) Last Game of the Washington Senators in 1971."
8. Shelby Whitfield, *Kiss It Goodbye* (New York: Abelard-Schuman, 1973), 245.
9. "Why the Washington Nationals Were Once Known as the Senators," *U.S. Senate,* Accessed August 17, 2021, www.senate.gov/artandhistory/history/minute/washington_nationals_once_known_as_senators.htm.
10. *Ibid.*
11. Andrew Sharp, "Washington Senators II Team Ownership History," *Society for American Baseball Research,* Accessed August 17, 2021, sabr.org/bioproj//topic/-Washington-senators-ii-team-ownership-history.
12. Whitfield, *Kiss It Goodbye,* 4, 17.
13. *Ibid.,* 13.
14. *Ibid.,* 15.
15. Bert Kalmar and Harry Ruby, "Hello, I Must Be Going," sung by Groucho Marx and Margaret Dumont in the movie, *Animal Crackers,* Directed by Victor Heerman, written by George S. Kaufman, Morrie Ryskind, and Bert Kalmar (Hollywood, CA: Paramount Pictures Corporation, 1930).
16. Sharp, "Washington Senators II Team Ownership History."
17. Whitfield, *Kiss It Goodbye,* 218.
18. *Ibid.*
19. *Ibid.*
20. Sharp, "Washington Senators II Team Ownership History."
21. Whitfield, *Kiss It Goodbye,* 225–226.
22. *Ibid.,* 218.
23. *Ibid.,* 223.
24. Sharp, "Washington Senators II Team Ownership History."
25. Dan Epstein, *Big Hair and Plastic Grass* (New York: Thomas Dunne Books, 2010), 7–8.
26. Dave Brown and Jeff Rodimer, *Shadows of Glory* (Essex, CT: Lyons Press, 2024), 232.
27. Sharp, "Washington Senators II Team Ownership History."
28. Whitfield, *Kiss It Goodbye,* 120.
29. Sharp, "Washington Senators II Team Ownership History."
30. Whitfield, *Kiss It Goodbye,* 220.
31. Sharp, "Washington Senators II Team Ownership History."
32. Whitfield, *Kiss It Goodbye,* 191.
33. *Ibid.,* 233.
34. Epstein, *Big Hair and Plastic Grass,* 33.
35. Sharp, "Washington Senators II Team Ownership History."
36. Epstein, *Big Hair and Plastic Grass,* 33.
37. Whitfield, *Kiss It Goodbye,* 216.
38. *Ibid.,* 225.

39. Sharp, "Washington Senators II Team Ownership History."
40. Whitfield, *Kiss It Goodbye*, 217.
41. Ibid., 233.
42. Ibid., 217.
43. Ibid., 219–220.
44. Ibid., 221.
45. Ibid., 224.
46. Ibid., 225.
47. Sharp, "Washington Senators II Team Ownership History."
48. Whitfield, *Kiss It Goodbye*, 222.
49. Sharp, "Washington Senators II Team Ownership History."
50. Whitfield, *Kiss It Goodbye*, 222–223.
51. Ibid., 233.
52. Ibid., 238.
53. Ibid., 233.
54. Ibid.
55. Ibid., 234.
56. Ibid., 238.
57. Ibid., 237.
58. Ibid.
59. Dwyer, "The (Forfeited) Last Game of the Washington Senators in 1971."
60. Epstein, *Big Hair and Plastic Grass*, 33.
61. Whitfield, *Kiss It Goodbye*, 218.
62. Ibid., 238.
63. Ibid.
64. Ibid., 240.
65. Sharp, "Washington Senators II Team Ownership History."
66. Frederic J. Frommer, "A Chaotic Closing Act," *Washington Post*, September 29, 2021, D1.
67. Sharp, "Washington Senators II Team Ownership History."
68. Jeff Kallman, "September 30, 1971: Senators Forfeit Final Home Game in Washington, DC," *Society for American Baseball Research*, Accessed August 17, 2021, https://sabr.org/gamesproj/game/-September-30-1971-senators-forfeit-final-home-game-in-washington-dc/.
69. Epstein, *Big Hair and Plastic Grass*, 42.
70. Frommer, "A Chaotic Closing Act," D5.
71. Ibid.
72. Kallman, "September 30, 1971: Senators Forfeit Final Home Game in Washington, DC."
73. Frommer, "A Chaotic Closing Act," D1.
74. Kallman, "September 30, 1971: Senators Forfeit Final Home Game in Washington, DC."
75. Frommer, "A Chaotic Closing Act," D1.
76. Ibid., D5.
77. Dwyer, "The (Forfeited) Last Game of the Washington Senators in 1971."
78. Frommer, "A Chaotic Closing Act," D5.
79. Audley, "This Date in Washington Senators History—The Final Game."
80. McPherson and Huth, "Rowdy Fans Hand Senators Final Loss."
81. Povich, "The Senators' Final Game."
82. Dwyer, "The (Forfeited) Last Game of the Washington Senators in 1971."
83. Kallman, "September 30, 1971: Senators Forfeit Final Home Game in Washington, DC."
84. McPherson and Huth, "Rowdy Fans Hand Senators Final Loss."
85. Audley, "This Date in Washington Senators History—The Final Game."
86. Dwyer, "The (Forfeited) Last Game of the Washington Senators in 1971."
87. Frommer, "A Chaotic Closing Act," D5.
88. Audley, "This Date in Washington Senators History—The Final Game."
89. Kallman, "September 30, 1971: Senators Forfeit Final Home Game in Washington, DC."
90. Ibid.
91. McPherson and Huth, "Rowdy Fans Hand Senators Final Loss."
92. Povich, "The Senators' Final Game."
93. Audley, "This Date in Washington Senators History—The Final Game."
94. Kallman, "September 30, 1971: Senators Forfeit Final Home Game in Washington, DC."
95. Frommer, "A Chaotic Closing Act," D5.
96. Kallman, "September 30, 1971: Senators Forfeit Final Home Game in Washington, DC."
97. Ibid.
98. Ibid.
99. Ibid.
100. Audley, "This Date in Washington Senators History—The Final Game."
101. Ibid.
102. Povich, "The Senators' Final Game."
103. Audley, "This Date in Washington Senators History—The Final Game."

104. Dwyer, "The (Forfeited) Last Game of the Washington Senators in 1971."
105. Audley, "This Date in Washington Senators History—The Final Game."
106. David Nemec and Eric Miklich, *Forfeits and Successfully Protested Games in Major League Baseball, A Complete Record, 1871-201* (Jefferson, NC: McFarland, 2014), 143.
107. Frommer, "A chaotic closing act," D5.
108. Dwyer, "The (Forfeited) Last Game of the Washington Senators in 1971."
109. Nemec and Miklich, *Forfeits and Successfully Protested Games in Major League Baseball, A Complete Record, 1871-2013*, 143.
110. Ibid.
111. Dwyer, "The (Forfeited) Last Game of the Washington Senators in 1971."
112. Povich, "The Senators' Final Game."
113. Nemec and Miklich, *Forfeits and Successfully Protested Games in Major League Baseball, A Complete Record, 1871-2013*, 144.
114. Frommer, "A Chaotic Closing Act," D5.
115. Dwyer, "The (Forfeited) Last Game of the Washington Senators in 1971."
116. Audley, "This Date in Washington Senators History—The Final Game."
117. Povich, "The Senators' Final Game."
118. Kallman, "September 30, 1971: Senators Forfeit Final Home Game in Washington, DC."
119. Dwyer, "The (Forfeited) Last Game of the Washington Senators in 1971."
120. Audley, "This Date in Washington Senators History—The Final Game."
121. Dwyer, "The (Forfeited) Last Game of the Washington Senators in 1971."
122. Frommer, "A Chaotic Closing Act," D5.
123. McPherson and Huth, "Rowdy Fans Hand Senators Final Loss."
124. Povich, "The Senators' Final Game."
125. Ibid.
126. Dwyer, "The (Forfeited) Last Game of the Washington Senators in 1971."
127. Kallman, "September 30, 1971: Senators Forfeit Final Home Game in Washington, DC."
128. Ibid.
129. McPherson and Huth, "Rowdy Fans hand Senators Final Loss."
130. Audley, "This Date in Washington Senators History—The Final Game."
131. Frommer, "A Chaotic Closing Act," p. D5.
132. Dwyer, "The (Forfeited) Last Game of the Washington Senators in 1971."
133. Kallman, "September 30, 1971: Senators Forfeit Final Home Game in Washington, DC."
134. Audley, "This Date in Washington Senators History—The Final Game."
135. Frommer, "A Chaotic Closing Act," D5.
136. Ibid.
137. Ibid.
138. Jeff Kallman, "September 30, 1971: Senators Forfeit Final Game in Washington, D.C."

Chapter 10

1. Bill Lubinger, "The Strange Tale of the Ten Cent Beer Night," *Ohio Magazine*, June 2014, http://www.ohiomagazine.com/ohio-life/article/brawl-game.
2. Daniel R. Grimes, *Ten-Cent Beer Night and the 1974 Baseball Season*. E-book ed. (Daniel R. Grimes, 2014), 65. (Please note: E-book pagination may be different on different devises. I used an Apple iPhone to view this E-book.)
3. Martin Gitlin, *Ultimate Cleveland Indians Time Machine Book* (Guilford, CT: Lyons Press, 2019), 99.
4. "Cleveland Guardians Attendance Data," *Baseball Almanac*, Accessed August 11, 2021, https://baseball almanac.com/teams/cleiatte.shtml.
5. Grimes, *Ten-Cent Beer Night and the 1974 Baseball Season*, 22.
6. Dan Coughlin, *Crazy, with the Papers to Prove It* (Cleveland: Gray & Company, 2010), 67.
7. Paul Jackson, "The Night Beer and Violence Bubbled Over in Cleveland," *ESPN*, June 4, 2008, https://espn.com/espn/page2/story?page=beernight/080604&sportCat=mlb.
8. Grimes, *Ten-Cent Beer Night and the 1974 Baseball Season*, 18.
9. Michael Rotman, "Cuyahoga River Fire," *Cleveland Historical*, https://clevelandhistorical.org/items/show/63.
10. Jackson, "The Night Beer and Violence Bubbled Over in Cleveland."

11. "Demographics of Cleveland," *Wikipedia*, Accessed February 8, 2021, https://en.wikipedia.org/wiki/Demographics_of_Cleveland.

12. Gitlin, *Ultimate Cleveland Indians Time Machine Book*, 93.

13. "Slam for Stunning Steve Dunning: On This Day in Cleveland Indians History," *Cleveland.com*, May 11, 2020, https://www.cleveland.com/tribe/2020/05/slam-for-stunning-steve-dunning-this-day-in-cleveland-indians-history.

14. Grimes, *Ten-Cent Beer Night and the 1974 Baseball Season*, 34.

15. Craig Calcaterra, "Today in Baseball History: Indians Hold Infamous Ten Cent Beer Night," *NBC Sports*, June 4, 2020, https://mlb.nbcsports.com/2020/06/04/today-in-baseball-history-indians-hold-infamous-ten-cent-beer-night/.

16. Grimes, *Ten-Cent Beer Night and the 1974 Baseball Season*, 34.

17. Jackson, "The Night Beer and Violence Bubbled Over in Cleveland."

18. *Ibid.*

19. Grimes, *Ten-Cent Beer Night and the 1974 Baseball Season*, 10.

20. Gitlin, *Ultimate Cleveland Indians Time Machine Book*, 93–94.

21. Dan Epstein, *Big Hair and Plastic Grass* (New York, Thomas Dunne Books, 2010), 235.

22. Grimes, *Ten-Cent Beer Night and the 1974 Baseball Season*, 42, 68.

23. *Ibid.*, 8.

24. *Ibid.*, 37–40.

25. Coughlin, *Crazy, with the Papers to Prove It*, 67.

26. Grimes, *Ten-Cent Beer Night and the 1974 Baseball Season*, 38.

27. "Cleveland Indians' Ten Cent Beer Night: The Worst Idea Ever," *Bleacher Report*, March 21, 2009, https://bleacherreport.com/articles/142952-ten-cent-beer-night-the-worst-idea-ever.

28. Mike Shropshire, *Seasons in Hell* (Lincoln: University of Nebraska Press, 1996), 170.

29. Frederick C. Bush, "June 4, 1974: 10-cent beer night at Cleveland stadium leads to riot," *Society for American Baseball Research*, Accessed September 21, 2022, https://sabr.org/gamesproj/game/june-4-1974-10-cent-beer-riot-at-cleveland-stadium-leads-to-beer-riot/.

30. Shropshire, *Seasons in Hell*, 170.

31. *Ibid.*

32. *Ibid.*, 170–171.

33. Grimes, *Ten-Cent Beer Night and the 1974 Baseball Season*, 40.

34. Gitlin, *Ultimate Cleveland Indians Time Machine Book*, 94.

35. Jackson, "The Night Beer and Violence Bubbled Over in Cleveland."

36. Coughlin, *Crazy with the Papers to Prove It*, 67.

37. Anthony Castrovince, "Forty Years Ago, 10-Cent Beer Makes Memories," *MLB News*, June 4, 2014, https://www.mlb.com/news/anthony-castrovince-forty-years-ago-10-cent-beer-makes-memorgies-c78045480.

38. Bush, "June 4, 1974: 10-Cent Beer Night at Cleveland Stadium Leads to Riot."

39. Michael Heaton, "It Was a Hot and Thirsty Night: Looking Back at 10-Cent Beer Night," *Cleveland.com*, June 3, 2012, https://www.cleveland.com/pdq/2012/06/it_was_a_hot_and_thristy_night.html.

40. *Ibid.*

41. Grimes, *Ten-Cent Beer Night and the 1974 Baseball Season*, 41.

42. Kyle Dalton, "Beer, Bombs, and Brawls: 10-Cent Beer Night with Cleveland Indians Devolves Into Riot," *Sportscasting*, June 5, 2020, https://www.sportscasting.com/beer-bombs-and-brawls-ten-cent-beer-night-with-cleveland-indians-devolves-into-riot.

43. Coughlin, *Crazy, with the Papers to Prove It*, 66.

44. Castrovince, "Forty Years Ago, 10-Cent Beer Makes Memories."

45. Grimes, *Ten-Cent Beer Night and the 1974 Baseball Season*, 46.

46. Wayne Scanlan, "10-Cent Beer Night: June 4, 1974, in Cleveland," *WordPress*, October 26, 2009, https://miscbaseball.https://wordpress.com/2009/10/26/10-cent-beer-night-june-4-1974-in-cleveland.

47. Grimes, *Ten-Cent Beer Night and the 1974 Baseball Season*, 47.

48. Matt Schlichting, "Happy 45th Anniversary, 10 Cent Beer Night!," *Let's Go Tribe*, June 4, 2019, httpds://letsgotribe.com/2019/6/4/18652095/10-cent-beer-night-45th-anniversary-rangers-indians-baseball-forfeits-june-4-1974.

49. Dan Culberson, "Tonight Is a Historic Night for Cleveland Sports and It Has Nothing to Do with the NBA Finals,"

Notes—Chapter 10

Civilized, June 4, 2016, https://www.civilized.life/articles/ten-cent-cleveland.

50. Coughlin, *Crazy, with the Papers to Prove It*, 67.

51. Culberson, "Tonight Is a Historic Night for Cleveland Sports and It Has Nothing to Do with the NBA Finals."

52. Grimes, *Ten-Cent Beer Night and the 1974 Baseball Season*, 47.

53. Heaton, "It Was a Hot and Thirsty Night: Looking Back at 10-Cent Beer Night."

54. Grimes, *Ten-Cent Beer Night and the 1974 Baseball Season*, 65.

55. Shropshire, *Seasons in Hell*, 173.

56. Grimes, *Ten-Cent Beer Night and the 1974 Baseball Season*, 63.

57. Dalton, "Beer, Bombs, and Brawls: 10-Cent Beer Night with Cleveland Indians Devolves into Riot."

58. Grimes, *Ten-Cent Beer Night and the 1974 Baseball Season*, 48.

59. Coughlin, *Crazy, with the Papers to Prove It*, 69.

60. Michael Heaton, "It Was a Hot and Thirsty Night: Looking Back at 10-Cent Beer Night."

61. Shropshire, *Seasons in Hell*, 171.

62. Grimes, *Ten-Cent Beer Night and the 1974 Baseball Season*, 48.

63. Jackson, "The Night Beer and Violence Bubbled Over in Cleveland."

64. Dalton, "Beer, Bombs, and Brawls: 10-Cent Beer Night with the Cleveland Indians Devolves into Riot."

65. Grimes, *Ten-Cent Beer Night and the 1974 Baseball Season*, 49.

66. Dalton, "Beer, Bombs, and Brawls: 10-Cent Beer Night with the Cleveland Indians Devolves into Riot."

67. Gitlin, *Ultimate Cleveland Indians Time Machine Book*, 95–96.

68. Grimes, *Ten-Cent Beer Night and the 1974 Baseball Season*, 49.

69. Bush, "June 4, 1974: 10-Cent Beer Night at Cleveland Stadium Leads to Riot."

70. Grimes, *Ten-Cent Beer Night and the 1974 Baseball Season*, 49.

71. Ibid.

72. Jackson, "The Night Beer and Violence Bubbled Over in Cleveland."

73. Bush, "June 4, 1974: 10-Cent Beer Night at Cleveland Stadium Leads to Riot."

74. Coughlin, *Crazy, with the Papers to Prove It*, 68.

75. Bush, "June 4, 1974: 10-Cent Beer Night at Cleveland Stadium Leads to Riot."

76. Coughlin, *Crazy, with the Papers to Prove It*, 68.

77. Grimes, *Ten-Cent Beer Night and the 1974 Baseball Season*, 51.

78. Shropshire, *Seasons in Hell*, 173.

79. Bush, "June 4, 1974: 10-Cent Beer Night at Cleveland Stadium Leads to Riot."

80. Grimes, *Ten-Cent Beer Night and the 1974 Baseball Season*, 51.

81. Gitlin, *Ultimate Cleveland Indians Time Machine Book*, 95.

82. Grimes, *Ten-Cent Beer Night and the 1974 Baseball Season*, 51.

83. Ibid.

84. Coughlin, *Crazy, with the Papers to Prove It*, 68–69.

85. Grimes, *Ten-Cent Beer Night and the 1974 Baseball Season*, 53.

86. Ibid., 54.

87. Coughlin, *Crazy, with the Papers to Prove It*, 69.

88. Grimes, *Ten-Cent Beer Night and the 1974 Baseball Season*, 53.

89. Coughlin, *Crazy, with the Papers to Prove It*, 69.

90. Grimes, *Ten-Cent Beer Night and the 1974 Baseball Season*, 52.

91. Ibid., 55.

92. Ibid.

93. Ibid.

94. David Nemec and Eric Miklich, *Forfeits and Successfully Protested Games in Major League Baseball, A Complete Record, 1871–2013* (Jefferson, NC: McFarland, 2014), 145.

95. Coughlin, *Crazy, with the Papers to Prove It*, 69.

96. Jackson, "The Night Beer and Violence Bubbled Over in Cleveland."

97. Grimes, *Ten-Cent Beer Night and the 1974 Baseball Season*, 62.

98. Jackson, "The Night Beer and Violence Bubbled Over in Cleveland."

99. Grimes, *Ten-Cent Beer Night and the 1974 Baseball Season*, 53.

100. Coughlin, *Crazy, with the Papers to Prove It*, 66.

101. Bush, "June 4, 1974: 10-Cent Beer Night at Cleveland Stadium Leads to Riot."

102. Gitlin, *Ultimate Cleveland Indians Time Machine Book*, 96.

103. Culberson, "Tonight Is a Historic Night for Cleveland Sports and It Has Nothing to Do with the NBA Finals."

104. Grimes, *Ten Cent Beer Night and the 1974 Baseball Season*, 76.

105. *Ibid.*, 75–76.
106. Dalton, "Beer, Bombs, and Brawls: 10-Cent Beer Night with the Cleveland Indians Devolves into Riot."
107. Craig Calcaterra, "Today in Baseball History: Indians Hold Infamous Ten Cent Beer Night."
108. Grimes, *Ten-Cent Beer Night and the 1974 Baseball Season*, 76.
109. Bush, "June 4, 1974: 10-Cent Beer Night at Cleveland Stadium Leads to Riot."
110. Jackson, "The Night Beer and Violence Bubbled Over in Cleveland."
111. Gitlin, *Ultimate Cleveland Indians Time Machine Book*, 96.
112. "10-Cent Beer Night: June 4, 1974, in Cleveland," *Misc. Baseball*, October 26, 2009, https://miscbaseball.wordpress.com/2009/10/26/10-cent-beer-night-june-4-1974-in-cleveland/.
113. Grimes, *Ten-Cent Beer Night and the 1974 Baseball Season*, 57.
114. *Ibid.*, 63.
115. *Ibid.*, 57.
116. Epstein, *Big Hair and Plastic Grass*, 236.
117. Gitlin, *Ultimate Cleveland Indians Time Machine Book*, 57.
118. Coughlin, *Crazy, with the Papers to Prove It*, 70.
119. Joe Noga, "Fans Riot on 10-Cent Beer Night: On This Day in Cleveland Indians History," *Cleveland.com*, June 4, 2020, https://cleveland.com/tribe/2020/06/fans-riot-on-10-cent-beer-night-on-this-day-in-cleveland-indians-history.html#:text=Fans%2.
120. Jackson, "The Night Beer and Violence Bubbled Over in Cleveland."
121. Coughlin, *Crazy, with the Papers to Prove It*, 69–70.
122. Grimes, *Ten-Cent Beer Night and the 1974 Baseball Season*, 57.
123. *Ibid.*, 58.
124. Lubinger, "The Strange Tale of Ten Cent Beer Night."
125. Epstein, *Big Hair and Plastic Grass*, 236.
126. Grimes, *Ten-Cent Beer Night and the 1974 Baseball Season*, 79.
127. Ian O'Connor, "Keeping Score," *USA Today*, April 17, 2003, https://usatoday.com/sports/columnist/oconnor/23003-04-17-ian_x.htm.
128. Jackson, "The Night Beer and Violence Bubbled Over in Cleveland."
129. Coughlin, *Crazy, with the Papers to Prove It*, 70.
130. Heaton, "It Was a Hot and Thirsty Night: Looking Back at Ten-Cent Beer Night."
131. Shropshire, *Seasons in Hell*, 177.
132. Lubinger, "The Strange Tale of the Ten Cent Beer Night."
133. Dalton, "Beer, Bombs, and Brawls: 10-Cent Beer Night with Cleveland Indians Devolves into Riot."
134. Grimes, *Ten-Cent Beer Night and the 1974 Baseball Season*, 81.
135. Noga, "Fans Riot on 10-Cent Beer Night: On This Day in Cleveland Indians History."
136. Bush, "June 4, 1974: 10-Cent Beer Night at Cleveland Stadium Leads to Riot."
137. Schlichting, "Happy 45th Anniversary," 10 Cent Beer Night."
138. Grimes, *Ten-Cent Beer Night and the 1974 Baseball Season*, 60.
139. Bush, "June 4, 1974: 10-Cent Beer Night at Cleveland Stadium Leads to Riot."
140. "Ten Cent Beer Night," *Wikipedia*, Accessed January 5, 2021, https//en.wikipedia.org/wiki/Ten_Cent_Beer_Night.
141. Lubinger, "The Strange Tale of the Ten Cent Beer Night."
142. Shropshire, *Seasons in Hell*, 176.
143. "Ten Cent Beer Night,"
144. Lubinger, "The Strange Tale of the Ten Cent Beer Night."
145. Castrovince, "Forty Years Ago, 10-Cent Beer Makes Memories."
146. Grimes, *Ten-Cent Beer Night and the 1974 Baseball Season*, 58.
147. *Ibid.*, 58.
148. "10-Cent Beer Night: June 4, 1974, in Cleveland."
149. Shropshire, *Seasons in Hell*, 175.
150. Jackson, "The Night Beer and Violence Bubbled Over in Cleveland."
151. Bush, "June 4, 1974: 10-Cent Beer Night at Cleveland Stadium Leads to Riot."
152. Calcaterra, "Today in Baseball History: Indians Hold Famous Ten Cent Beer Night."
153. Herschel Nissenson, "Umpire Chylak Admits Fear in Seeing Crowd Go Wild," *Paducah Sun*, June 5, 1974, https://www.newspapers.com/June/5/1974/umpire-chylak-admits-fear-in-seeing-crowd-go-wild.
154. O'Connor, "Keeping Score."
155. Jackson, "The Night Beer and Violence Bubbled Over in Cleveland."
156. Shropshire, *Seasons in Hell*, 174.

157. O'Connor, "Keeping Score."
158. Calcaterra, "Today in Baseball History: Indians Hold Famous Ten Cent Beer Night."
159. Jackson, "The Night Beer and Violence Bubbled Over in Cleveland."
160. Coughlin, *Crazy, with the Papers to Prove It*, 72.
161. *Ibid.*
162. Grimes, *Ten-Cent Beer Night and the 1974 Baseball Season*, 68.
163. Gitlin, *Ultimate Cleveland Indians Time Machine Book*, 99.

Chapter 11

1. "Tommy Lasorda MLB Career and Early Life," *Diamond Mind Online*, Accessed September 25, 2022, https://imaginesports.com/news/tommy-lasorda-mlb-career-and-early-life.
2. Richard Goldstein, "Tommy Lasorda, a Dodger from His Cleats to His Cap, Dies at 93," *New York Times*, January 8, 2021, https://www.nytimes.com/2021/01/08/sports/baseball/tommy-lasorda-dead.html.
3. "Tommy Lasorda MLB Career and Early Life."
4. *Ibid.*
5. Cary Osborne, "What Tommy Lasorda Lived and Loved By," *Dodger Insider*, Accessed September 25, 2022, https://dodgers.mlblogs.com/what-tommy-lasorda-lived-and-loved-by-38acf24c10fb.
6. Joe Comporeale, "Tommy Lasorda Biography & Los Angeles Dodgers Career," *Dodger Blue*, Accessed November 8, 2021, https://dodgerblue.com/tommy-lasorda-biography-los-angeles-dodgers-career.
7. *Ibid.*
8. "Tommy Lasorda MLB Career and Early Life."
9. Goldstein, "Tommy Lasorda, a Dodger from His Cleats to His Cap, Dies at 93."
10. "Tommy Lasorda," *National Baseball Hall of Fame*, Accessed September 25, 2022, https://baseballhall.org/hall-of-famers/lasorda-tommy.
11. Osborne, "What Tommy Lasorda Lived and Loved By."
12. Comporeale, "Tommy Lasorda Biography & Los Angeles Dodgers Career."
13. Colin Gunderson, *Tommy Lasorda: My Way* (Chicago: Triumph Books, 2015), 62–63.
14. Osborne, "What Tommy Lasorda Lived and Loved By."
15. "Tommy Lasorda Stats," *Baseball Almanac*, Accessed November 28, 2021, https://baseball Almanac.com/players/player.php?p=lasorto01.
16. Osborne, "What Tommy Lasorda Lived and Loved By."
17. "Tommy Lasorda MLB Career and Early Life."
18. *Ibid.*
19. *Ibid.*
20. Osborne, "What Tommy Lasorda Lived and Loved By."
21. "Tommy Lasorda MLB Career and Early Life."
22. "Hall of Fame Los Angeles Dodgers Manager Tommy Lasorda Dies at 93," *ESPN News Service*, January 8, 2021, https://www.espn.com/mlb/story/_/30674374/hasll-of-famr-dodgers-manager-tommy-lasorda-dies-93.
23. "Hall of Fame Los Angeles Dodgers Manager Tommy Lasorda Dies at 93."
24. Osborne, "What Tommy Lasorda Lived and Loved By."
25. "Tommy Lasorda MLB Career and Early Life."
26. Osborne, "What Tommy Lasorda Lived and Loved By."
27. Gunderson, *Tommy Lasorda: My Way*, 166.
28. "Legendary Dodgers Manager Tommy Lasorda Dies at 93 of a Heart Attack," *Los Angeles Times*, January 8, 2021, https://www.latimes.com/obituaries/2021-01-08/dodgers-legendary-manager-tom-lasorda-dies-at-age-93-heart-attack.
29. Gunderson, *Tommy Lasorda: My Way*, 162–163.
30. Osborne, "What Tommy Lasorda Lived and Loved By."
31. "Legendary Dodgers Manager Tommy Lasorda Dies at 93 of a Heart Attack."
32. Osborne, "What Tommy Lasorda Lived and Loved By."
33. "Tommy Lasorda MLB Career and Early Life."
34. "Walter Alston Managerial Stats," *Baseball Reference*, Accessed November 28, 2021, https://baseball-reference.com/managers/alstowa01.shtml.
35. "Legendary Dodgers Manager Tommy Lasorda Dies at 93 of a Heart Attack."

36. Goldstein, "Tommy Lasorda, a Dodger from His Cleats to His Cap, Dies at 93."
37. *Ibid.*
38. "Hall of Fame Los Angeles Dodgers Manager Tommy Lasorda Dies at 93."
39. "Tommy Lasorda Managerial Stats."
40. "Tommy Lasorda MLB Career and Early Life."
41. "Tommy Lasorda."
42. Goldstein, "Tommy Lasorda, a Dodger from His Cleats to His Cap, Dies at 93."
43. "Legendary Dodgers Manager Tommy Lasorda Dies at 93 of a Heart Attack."
44. *Ibid.*
45. "Tommy Lasorda MLB Career and Early Life."
46. *Ibid.*
47. *Ibid.*
48. Goldstein, "Tommy Lasorda, a Dodger from His Cleats to His Cap, Dies at 93."
49. *Ibid.*
50. "Hall of Fame Los Angeles Dodgers Manager Tommy Lasorda Dies at 93."
51. Gunderson, *Tommy Lasorda: My Way*, 64.
52. Osborne, "What Tommy Lasorda Lived and Loved By."
53. "Tommy Lasorda MLB Career and Early Life."
54. Osborne, "What Tommy Lasorda Lived and Loved By."
55. "Tommy Lasorda MLB Career and Early Life."
56. "Legendary Dodgers Manager Tommy Lasorda Dies at 93 of a Heart Attack."
57. *Ibid.*
58. Gunderson, *Tommy Lasorda: My Way*, 27.
59. *Ibid.*, 35–36.
60. *Ibid.*, 70.
61. *Ibid.*, 41.
62. *Ibid.*, 86.
63. *Ibid.*, 55.
64. *Ibid.*
65. "Legendary Dodgers Manager Tommy Lasorda Dies at 93 of a Heart Attack."
66. *Ibid.*
67. "Hall of Fame Los Angeles Dodgers Manager Tommy Lasorda Dies at 93."
68. Osborne, "What Tommy Lasorda Lived and Loved By."
69. "Hall of Fame Los Angeles Dodgers Manager Tommy Lasorda Dies at 93."
70. Goldstein, "Tommy Lasorda, a Dodger from His Cleats to His Cap, Dies at 93."
71. "Tommy Lasorda Managerial Stats."
72. Goldstein, "Tommy Lasorda, a Dodger from His Cleats to His Cap."
73. "Legendary Dodgers Manager Tommy Lasorda Dies at 93 of a Heart Attack."
74. "Hall of Fame Los Angeles Dodgers Manager Tommy Lasorda Dies at 93."
75. Goldstein, "Tommy Lasorda, a Dodger from His Cleats to His Cap, Dies at 93."
76. Gunderson, *Tommy Lasorda: My Way*, 170.
77. Chris Baker, "Three Strikes and Dodgers Forfeit Baseball: Game Is Called After Fans Throw Balls on the Field with One Out in the Ninth. Nomo Overshadowed," *Los Angeles Times,* August 11, 1995, https://www.latimes.com/archives/la-xpm-1995-08-11-sp-34067-story.html.
78. 77 Anthony Castrovince, "The Crazy Story Behind MLB's Last Forfeit," *Major League Baseball,* August 29, 2019, https://www.mlbnews.com/featured/-dodgers-cardinals-last-mlb-forfeit1995.
79. "How Cardinals Won by Forfeit at Dodger Stadium," *RetroSimba*, October 6, 2012, https://retrosimba.com/2012/10/06/braves-fans-behavior-recalls-dodgers-forfeit-to-cards.
80. Sam Miller, "25 Years Ago Tonight, MLB Had Its Last Forfeit," *ESPN*, Accessed November 8, 2021, https://www.espn.com/mlb/story/_/id/29614065/25-years-ago-tonight-mlb-had-last-forfeit-los-angeles-dodgers-st-louis-cardinals-game.
81. These included Raul Mondesi (1994), Mike Piazza (1993), Eric Karros (1992), Steve Sax (1982), Fernando Valenzuela (1981), Steve Howe (1980), Rick Sutcliffe (1979), Ted Sizemore (1969), Jim Lefebvre (1965), Frank Howard (1960), Jim Gilliam (1953), Joe Black (1952), Don Newcombe (1949), and Jackie Robinson (1947).
82. Castrovince, "The Crazy Story Behind MLB's Last Forfeit."
83. *Ibid.*
84. Andrew Simon, "How Nomo Changed MLB Forever," *Major League*

Notes—Chapter 11

Baseball, February 12, 2024, https://www.mlb.com/news/hideo-nomo-pioneered-path-to-mlb-in-1995.
85. *Ibid.*
86. *Ibid.*
87. Neil Paine, "Hideo Nomo Paved the Way for a Generation of Damn Good Japanese Ballplayers," *FiveThirtyEight*, Accessed March 30, 2024, https://fivethirtyeoght.com/ features/hideo-nomo-paved-the-way-for-a-generation-of-damn-good-japanese-ballplayers.
88. Castrovince, "The Crazy Story Behind MLB's Last Forfeit."
89. Miller, "25 Years Ago Tonight, MLB Had Its Last Forfeit."
90. David Nemec, and Eric Miklich, *Forfeits and Successfully Protested Games in Major League Baseball, A Complete Record, 1871–2013* (Jefferson, NC: McFarland, 2014), 150.
91. Chris Baker, "Three Strikes and Dodgers Forfeit: Baseball: Game Is Called After Fans Throw Balls on the Field with One Out in the Ninth. Nomo Overshadowed."
92. Castrovince, "The Crazy Story Behind MLB's Last Forfeit."
93. Nemec and Miklich, *Forfeits and Successfully Protested Games in Major League Baseball, A Complete Record, 1871–2013*, 150.
94. Castrovince, "The Crazy Story Behind MLB's Last Forfeit."
95. Nemec and Miklich, *Forfeits and Successfully Protested Games in Major League Baseball, A Complete Record, 1871–2013*. 150.
96. Castrovince, "The Crazy Story Behind MLB's Last Forfeit."
97. "How Cardinals Won by Forfeit at Dodger Stadium."
98. Castrovince, "The Crazy Story Behind MLB's Last Forfeit."
99. *Ibid.*
100. *Ibid.*
101. "Fans Force Dodgers to Forfeit Game," *Washington Post*, August 11, 1995, https://www.washingtonpost.com/archive/sports/1995/08/11/fans-force-dodgers-to-forfeit-game/1ba90d0c-1fc9-4923-90cd-1ca681e3fa24/.
102. "How Cardinals Won by Forfeit at Dodger Stadium."
103. Castrovince, "The Crazy Story Behind MLB's Last Forfeit."
104. "Fans Force Dodgers to Forfeit Game."
105. Miller, "25 Years Ago Tonight, MLB Had Its Last Forfeit."
106. Baker, "Three Strikes and Dodgers Forfeit: Baseball: Game Is Called After Fans Throw Balls on the Field with One Out in the Ninth. Nomo Overshadowed."
107. *Ibid.*
108. Castrovince, "The Crazy Story Behind MLB's Last Forfeit."
109. *Ibid.*
110. *Ibid.*
111. *Ibid.*
112. Baker, "Three Strikes and Dodgers Forfeit: Baseball: Game Is Called After Fans Throw Balls on the Field with One Out in the Ninth. Nomo Overshadowed."
113. *Ibid.*
114. "How Cardinals Won by Forfeit at Dodger Stadium."
115. *Ibid.*
116. Miller, "25 Years Ago Tonight, MLB Had Its Last Forfeit."
117. *Ibid.*
118. Castrovince, "The Crazy Story Behind MLB's Last Forfeit."
119. Baker, "Three Strikes and Dodgers Forfeit: Baseball: Game Is Called After Fans Throw Balls on the Field with One Out in the Ninth. Nomo Overshadowed."
120. Castrovince, "The Crazy Story Behind MLB's Last Forfeit."
121. *Ibid.*
122. Baker, "Three Strikes and Dodgers Forfeit: Baseball: Game Is Called After Fans Throw Balls on the Field with One Out in the Ninth. Nomo Overshadowed."
123. Castrovince, "The Crazy Story Behind MLB's Last Forfeit."
124. *Ibid.*
125. "Fans Force Dodgers to Forfeit Game."
126. Baker, "Three Strikes and Dodgers Forfeit: Baseball: Game Is Called After Fans Throw Balls on the Field with One Out in the Ninth. Nomo Overshadowed."
127. *Ibid.*
128. "How Cardinals Won by Forfeit at Dodger Stadium."
129. Baker, "Three Strikes and Dodgers Forfeit: Baseball: Game Is Called After Fans Throw Balls on the Field with One Out in the Ninth. Nomo Overshadowed."
130. "How Cardinals Won by Forfeit at Dodger Stadium."

131. Castrovince, "The Crazy Story Behind MLB's Last Forfeit."
132. Ibid.
133. "How Cardinals Won by Forfeit at Dodger Stadium."
134. Castrovince, "The Crazy Story Behind MLB's Last Forfeit."
135. Jason Foster, "Aug. 10, 1995: When Fans Threw Balls on the Field and the Dodgers Forfeited." *Sporting News*, August 10, 2017, https://www.sportingnew.com/us/author/jason-foster.
136. Ibid.
137. Ibid.
138. Castrovince, "The Crazy Story Behind MLB's Last Forfeit."
139. Miller, "25 Years Ago Tonight, MLB Had Its Last Forfeit."
140. Ibid.

Appendix I

1. Jim Dunphy, "Worst Promotions in Baseball History," *Slideplayer*, Accessed July 23, 2023, https://player/slideplayer.com/104/17579561/.
2. Ibid.
3. Brian Kachejian, "History of the Baby Ruth Bar and Reggie Bar," *Classic-NewYorkHistory.com* Accessed April 8, 2024, https://classicnewyorkhistory.com/history-of-the-baby-ruth-bar-and-reggie-bar.
4. Dunphy, "Worst Promotions in Baseball History."
5. Ibid.
6. Ibid.
7. Ibid.
8. Ibid.
9. Kachejian, "History of the Baby Ruth Bar and Reggie Bar."
10. Chris Landers, "Each Team's Weirdest Promotional Item Ever," *Major League Baseball*, May 18, 2020, https://www.mlb.com/news/weirdest-mlb-promotions-ever.
11. Ibid.
12. Ibid.
13. "All Star Look: Twins Offer Mauer Sideburns Promotion," *ESPN*, July 18, 2006, https://www.espn.com/mlb/news/story/all-star-look-twins-offer-mauer-sideburns-promotion.
14. "Joe Maurer," *Wikipedia*, Accessed April 7, 2024, https://en.wikipedia.org/wiki/Joe_Mauer.

15. Ray Tannock, "Top Ten Worst MLB Gameday Promotions Ever," *Bleacher-Report.com*, Accessed August 6, 2023, https://bleacherreport.com/articles/-846519-top-ten-worst-mlb-gameday-promotions-ever.
16. "Like Bobbleheads, Seattle Sports Fans? Try Free Compost Night," *Seattle Times*, March 21, 2011, https://www.seattletimes.com/seattle-news/like-bobbleheads-seattle-sports-fans-try-free-compost-night/.
17. Dunphy, "Worst Promotions in Baseball History."
18. "Like Bobbleheads, Seattle Sports Fans? Try Free Compost Night."
19. "*Ibid.*
20. Ross Zelen, "Seattle Mariners Go Green: Time to Give Praise to Those Who Take Responsibility," *Bleacher-Report*, Accessed April 3, 2024, https://bleacherreport.com/articles/993831-seattle-mariners-go-green-thime-to-give-praise-to-those-who-take-responsibility.
21. "Mariners Sustainability," *Major League Baseball*, Accessed April 3, 2024, https://www.mlb.com/mariners/ballpark/information/sustainability.
22. Zelen, "Seattle Mariners Go Green: Time to Give Praise to Those Who Take Responsibility."
23. "Seattle Mariners Recycle/Compost 80% of Waste," *SustainableBusiness.com*, September 2011, https://www.sustainablebusiness.com/2011/09/seattle-mariners-recyclecompost-80-of-waste-49627/.
24. "Mariners Sustainability,"
25. Zelen, "Seattle Mariners Go Green: Time to Give Praise to Those Who Take Responsibility."
26. "Seattle Mariners Recycle/Compost 80% of Waste."
27. Zelen, "Seattle Mariners Go Green: Time to Give Praise to Those Who Take Responsibility."
28. Ibid.
29. "Like Bobbleheads, Seattle Sports Fans? Try Free Compost Night."
30. "Mariners Sustainability."
31. Roger Launius, "My Favorite Weird Baseball Promotions," *Wordpress*, May 15, 2017, https://launiusr.wordpress.com/2017/05/15/my-favorite-weird-baseball-promotions/.
32. "MC Hammer," *Wikipedia: The Free*

Encyclopedia, Accessed April 5, 2024, https://en.Wikipedia.org/wiki/MC_Hammer.
  33. Launius, "My Favorite Weird Baseball Promotions."
  34. *Ibid.*
  35. *Ibid.*
  36. *Ibid.*
  37. "MC Hammer."
  38. Landers, "Each Team's Weirdest Promotional Item Ever."
  39. *Ibid.*
  40. "Don Zimmer," *Baseball Reference*, Accessed April 9, 2024, https://www.baseball-reference.com/don-zimmer. baseball-refernce.com/don-zimmer.
  41. Bob Hurte, "Don Zimmer," *Society for American Baseball Research*, Accessed April 9, 2024, https://sabr.org/bioproj/person/don-zimmer/.
  42. *Ibid.*
  43. *Ibid.*
  44. Landers, "Each Team's Weirdest Promotional Item Ever."
  45. "Bryce Harper," *Wikipedia*, Accessed April 7, 2024, https://en.wikipedia.org/wiki/Bryce_Harper.

Appendix II

  1. Dan Epstein, *Big Hair and Plastic Grass* (New York: Thomas Dunne Books, 2010), 9.
  2. *Ibid.*
  3. *Ibid.*, 9–10.
  4. Jeff English, "Catfish Hunter," *Society for American Baseball Research*, Accessed October 31, 20243 https://sabr.org/bioproj/person/catfish-hunter.
  5. G. Michael Green and Roger Launius, *Charlie Finley: The Outrageous Story of Baseball's Super Showman* (New York: Walker & Company, 2010), 241.

Bibliography

Books

Brown, Dave, and Jeff Rodimer. *Shadows of Glory* (Essex, CT: Lyons Press, 2024).
Coughlin, Dan. *Crazy, with the Papers to Prove It* (Cleveland: Gray & Company, 2010).
Dahl, Steve, with Dave Hoekstra and Paul Natkin. *Disco Demolition: The Night Disco Died*, E-book edition (Chicago: Curbside Splendor, 2016).
Dickson, Paul. *Bill Veeck: Baseball's Greatest Maverick* (New York: Walker, 2012).
Echols, Alice. *Hot Stuff: Disco and the Remaking of American Culture* (New York: W.W. Norton, 2010).
Epstein, Dan. *Big Hair and Plastic Grass* (New York: Thomas Dunne Books, 2010).
_____. *Stars and Strikes* (New York: Thomas Dunne Books, 2014).
Fields, Robert Ashley. *Take Me Out to the Crowd: Ted Turner and the Atlanta Braves* (Huntsville, AL: Strode Publishers, 1977).
Giles, Bill, with Doug Myers. *Pouring Six Beers at a Time: Stories from a Lifetime in Baseball* (Chicago: Triumph Books, 2007).
Gitlin, Martin. *Ultimate Cleveland Indians Time Machine Book* (Guilford, CT: Lyons Press, 2019).
Golenbock, Peter. *The Spirit of St. Louis: A History of the St. Louis Cardinals and Browns* (New York: Avon Books, 2000).
Green, G. Michael, and Roger Launius. *Charlie Finley: The Outrageous Story of Baseball's Super Showman* (New York: Walker, 2010).
Grimes, Daniel R. *Ten-Cent Beer Night and the 1974 Baseball Season*, E-book edition (Daniel R. Grimes, 2014).
Gunderson, Colin. *Tommy Lasorda: My Way* (Chicago: Triumph Books, 2015).
Hope, Bob. *We Could've Finished Last Without You* (Atlanta: Longstreet Press, 1991).
Libby, Bill. *Charlie O. and the Angry A's* (Garden City, NY: Doubleday, 1975).
Lord, John B. *Bill Giles & Baseball* (Philadelphia: Temple University Press, 2014).
Michelson, Herbert. *Charlie O: Charles Oscar Finley vs. the Baseball Establishment* (Indianapolis: Bobbs-Merrill, 1975).
Nemec, David, and Eric Miklich. *Forfeits and Successfully Protested Games in Major League Baseball, A Complete Record, 1871–2013* (Jefferson, NC: McFarland, 2014).
Shenk, Larry. *If These Walls Could Talk: Philadelphia Phillies* (Chicago: Triumph Books, 2014).
Shropshire, Mike. *Seasons in Hell* (Lincoln: University of Nebraska Press, 1996).
Turner, Ted, with Bill Burke. *Call Me Ted* (New York: Grand Central Publishing, 2008).
Veeck, Bill, with Ed Linn. *Veeck as in Wreck: The Autobiography of Bill Veeck* (Chicago: University of Chicago Press, 1962).
Westcott, Rich. *Veterans Stadium, Field of Memories* (Philadelphia: Temple University Press, 2005).
Whitfield, Shelby. *Kiss It Goodbye* (New York: Abelard-Schuman, 1973).

Newspaper Articles

Frommer, Frederic J. "A chaotic closing act." *Washington Post*, September 29, 2021.

Internet Sources

Acocella, Nick. "Baseball's Showman." *ESPN Classic*, Accessed July 24, 2023, https://www.espn.com/classic/veeckbill000816.html.

———. "Finley Entertained and Enraged." *ESPN Classic*, Accessed October 16, 2023, https://www.espn.com/classic/biography/s/Finley_Charles.html.

Adams, Cecil. "Were WWII Scrap Drives Just a Ploy to Boost Morale?" *The Straight Dope*, May 31, 2002, https://www.straightdope.com/21343531/were-wwii-scrap-drives-just-a-ploy-to-boost-morale.

"All Star look: Twins Offer Mauer Sideburns Promotion." *ESPN*, July 18, 2006, https://www.espn.com/mlb/news/story/all-star-look-twins-offer-maurer-sideburns-promotion.

Armour, Mark. "Charlie Finley." *Society for American Baseball Research*, Accessed October 18, 2023, https://sabr.org/bioproj/person/charlie-finley.

"Atlanta Braves Attendance, Stadiums, and Park Factors." *Baseball Reference*, Accessed January 4, 2024, https://www.baseball-reference.com/ATL/attendance-stadiums-and-park-factors.

Audley, Art. "This Date in Washington Senators History—The Final Game." *DC Baseball History*, September 2020, https://dcbaseballhistory.com/2020/09/this-date-in-washington-senators-history-the-final-game.

Baily, Ronald. "Iron Will: Scrapping History." *Historynet.com*, November 27, 2017, https://www.historynet.com/iron-0will-scrapping-history/.

Baker, Chris. "Three Strikes and Dodgers Forfeit: Baseball Game Is Called After Fans Throw Balls on the Field with One Out in the Ninth. Nomo Overshadowed." *Los Angeles Times*, August 11, 1995, https://www.latimes.com/archives/la-xpm-1995-08-11-sp-34067-story.html.

"Baseball's P.T. Barnum." *The Attic*, April 8, 2021, https://www.theattic.space/home-page-blogs/2021/4/8/baseball's-wild-showman.

Bazer, Gerald, and Steven Culbertson. "When FDR Said 'Play Ball.'" *National Archives*, Spring 2002, https://www.archives.gov/publications/prologue/2002/spring/greenlight.html.

"The Beatles Concert Setlist at Kansas City Municipal Stadium." *setlist.com*, Accessed January 18, 2024, https://www.setlist.fm/setlist/the-beatles/1964/kansas-city-municipal-stadium-kansas-city-mo-7bdae244.html.

Bedingfield, Gary. "Baseball in World War II." *Baseball in Wartime*, Accessed August 20, 2023, https://www.baseballinwartime.com/baseball_in_wwii/baseball_in_wwii.htm.

"Bert Shepard." *Wikipedia*, Accessed February 22, 2024, https://en.wikipedia.org/wiki/Bert_Shepard.

"Bill Giles (baseball)." *Wikipedia*, Accessed December 18, 2023, https://en.wikipedia.org>wiki>Bill_Giles_(bsseball).

"Boston Braves vs. Brooklyn Dodgers Box Score: September 25, 1942." *Baseball Reference*, Accessed February 27, 2024, https://www.baseball-reference.com/boxscores/1942/September-25-1942.

Boswell, Thomas. "Bill Veeck." *Washington Post*, May 31, 1981, https://washingtonpost.com/archives/sports1981/05/31/bill-veeck/6e41714f-5043-4a2e-be3a-fa7beb86d946.

"Branch Rickey, Executive." *Major League Baseball Hall of Fame*, Accessed November 27, 2023, https://baseballhall.org/hall-of-famers/rickey-branch.

"Bryce Harper." *Wikipedia*, Accessed April 7, 2024, https://en.wikipedia.org>wiki>Bryce_Harper.

Bullock, Steve. "Playing for Their Nation: The American Military and Baseball During World War II." *Journal of Sport History*, Vol. 27, No. 1, Spring 2000, https://www.jstor.org/stable/8b6c2e30-627c-8479-673864723c94?readnow=1&seq=1.

Bush, Frederick C. "June 4, 1974: 10-Cent Beer Night at Cleveland Stadium Leads to Riot." *Society for American Baseball Research,* Accessed September 21, 2022, https://sabr.org/gamesproj/game/june-4-1974-10-cent-beer-riot-at-cleveland-stadium-leads-to-beer-riot/.

Calcaterra, Craig. "Today in Baseball History: Indians Hold Infamous Ten Cent Beer Night." *NBC Sports,* June 4, 2020, https://mlb.nbcsports.com/2020/06/04/today-in-baseball-history-indians-hold-infamous-ten-cent-beer-night/.

"Can't Buy Him Love." *K.C. History.org,* Accessed January 18, 2024, https://kchistory.org/week-kansas-city-history/can't-buy-him-love.

Castrovince, Anthony. "The Crazy Story Behind MLB's Last Forfeit." *Major League Baseball,* August 29, 2019, https://www.mlbnews.com/featured/dodgers-cardinals-last-mlb-forfeit1995.

———. "Forty Years Ago, 10-Cent Beer Makes Memories." *MLB News,* June 4, 2014, https://www.mlb.com/news/anthony-castrovince-forty-years-ago-10-cent-beer-makes-memories-c78045480.

Chesterton, Eric. "In 1951, Bill Veeck Let the Fans Manage the St. Louis Browns on Grandstand Managers Night." *Major League Baseball,* August 24, 2017, https://www.mlb.com/cut4/in-1951-bill-veeck-let-the-fans-manage-the-st-louis-browns-on-grandstanbd-managers-night.

"Chicago White Sox Attendance, Stadiums, and Park Factors." *Baseball Reference,* Accessed January 4, 2024, https://www.baseball-reference.com/CWS/attendance-stadiums-and-park-factors.

"Cleveland Guardians Attendance Data." *Baseball Almanac,* August 11, 2021, https://baseballalmanac.com/teams/cleiatte.shtml.

"Cleveland Guardians Attendance, Stadiums, and Park Factors." *Baseball Reference,* Accessed January 4, 2024, https://www.baseballreference.com/CLE/attendance-stadiums-and-park-factors.

"Cleveland Indians' Ten Cent Beer Night: The Worst Idea Ever." *Bleacher Report,* March 21, 2009, https://bleacherreport.com/articles/142952-ten-cent-beer-night-the-worst-idea-ever.

Cochran, Jeff. "John Lennon on Charlie Finley: 'I Just Didn't Particularly Like Him.'" *Seamheads.com,* November 1, 2014, https://seamheads.com/blog/2014/11/01/john-lennon-on-charlie-finley-ijust-didn't-particularly-like-him/.

Coffey, Alex. "Veeck Holds 'Grandstand Managers Night.'" *National Baseball Hall of Fame,* Accessed July 23, 2023, https://baseballhall.org/discover-more/stories/inside-pitch/grandstand-managers-night.

Coffey, Alex, and Alec Lewis. "Remembering Charlie-O the Mule, the A's Mascot Inspired by Charles O. Finley." *The Athletic,* May 8, 2020, https://theathletic.com/1801465/2020/05/08/remembering-charlie-o-the-mule-the-as-mascot-inspired-by-charles-o-finley.

Comporeale, Joe. "Tommy Lasorda Biography & Los Angeles Dodgers Career." *Dodger Blue,* Accessed November 8, 2021, https://dodgerblue.com/tommy-lasorda-biography-los-angeles-dodgers-career.

Corbett, Warren. "Bill Veeck." *Society for American Baseball Research,* Accessed July 23, 2023, https://sabr.org/bioproj/person/bill-veeck.

Cox, Matt. "Keep Baseball Going." *National Baseball Hall of Fame,* Accessed August 20, 2023, https://baseballhall.org/discover-more/stories/short-stops/keep-baseball-going.

Culberson, Dan. "Tonight Is a Historic Night for Cleveland Sports and It Has Nothing to Do with the NBA Finals." *Civilized,* June 4, 2016, https://www.civilized.life/articles/ten-cent-cleveland.

Dalton, Kyle. "Beer, Bombs, and Brawls: 10-Cent Beer Night with Cleveland Indians Devolves Into Riot." *Sportscasting,* June 5, 2020, https://www.sportscasting.com/beer-bombs-and-brawls-10-cent-beer-night-with-cleveland-indians-devolves-into-riot.

"Demographics of Cleveland." *Wikipedia,* Accessed February 8, 2021, https://en.wikipedia.org/wiki/Demographics_of_Cleveland.

Dickson, Paul. "Bill Veeck: The Maverick Who Changed Baseball." *American Heritage,*

Summer 2017, https://www.americanheritage.com/bill-veeck-maverick-who-changed-baseball.

"Disco Demolition Night." *Major League Sports Fandom*, Accessed May 29, 2022, https://about:reader?url=https://majpr-league-sports.fandom.com/wiki/Disco-Demolition-Night.

"Disco Is Dealt Death Blow by Fans of the Chicago White Sox." *History.com*, Accessed January 21, 2021, https://www.history.com/this-day-in-history/disco-is-dealt-death-blow-byfans-of-the-chicago-white-sox.

"Don Zimmer." *Baseball Reference*, Accessed April 9, 2024, https://www.baseball-reference.com/players/z/zimmedo01.shtml.

Dunphy, Jim. "Worst Promotions in Baseball History." *Slideplayer*, Accessed July 23, 2023, https://player.slideplayer.com/104/17579561.

Durso, Joseph. "Bill Veeck, Baseball Innovator, Dies." *New York Times*, January 3, 1986, https://www.nytimes.com/1986/01/03/obituaries/bill-veeck-baseball-innovator-dies.html.

Dwyer, Timothy. "The (Forfeited) Last Game of the Washington Senators in 1971." *WordPress*, June 10, 2010, https://miscbaseball.wordpress.com/2010/10/06/the-forfeited-last-game-of-the-washington-senators-in-1971/.

"Elmer Gedeon." *Wikipedia*, Accessed February 23, 2023, https://en.wikipedia.org/wiki/elmer_gedeon.

English, Jeff. "Catfish Hunter." *Society for American Baseball Research*, Accessed October 31, 2023, https://sabr.org/bioproj/person/catfish-hunter.

"Ex-Baseball Owner Bill Veeck: Used Clowns, Giveaways and Midgets to Spice Up Sport." *Los Angeles Times*, January 2, 1986, https://www.latimes.com/articles/la-xpm-1986-01-02-mn-23473-story.html.

"Fans Force Dodgers to Forfeit Game." *Washington Post*, August 11, 1995, https://www.washingtonpost.com/archive/sports/1995/08/11/fans-force-dodgers-to-forfeit-game/1ba90d0c-1fc9-4923-90cd-1ca681e3fa24/.

Feld, Kitty. "Son of Legendary Sportswriter Vincent X. Flaherty Sells Off Collectibles to Run for Congress." *89.3KPCC*, March 15, 2014, https://archive.kpcc.org/blogs/politics/2014/03/15.

Fimrite, Ron. "Charlie O. Eyes a Pennant or Three." *Sports Illustrated*, October 9, 1972, https://vault.si.com/vault/1972/10/09/charlie-o-eyes-a-pennant-or-three.

Fisk, Mike. "MLB History: Disco Demolition Night at Comiskey Park." *OvertimeHeroics.net*, January 23, 2021, https://www.overtimeheroics.net/2021/01/31/mlb-history-disco-demolition.

"Flashback: 'Disco Demolition Night' at Chicago's Comiskey Park." *vermillioncountyfirst.com*, https://vermilioncountyfirst.com/2020/07/09/flash-disco-demolition-night-at-chicago-comiskey-park.

"Former Chicago White Sox Owner Bill Veeck, the Baseball Barnum." *United Press International*, January 2, 1986, htps://www.upi.com/Archives/1986/01/02/Former-Chicago-White-Sox-owner-Bill-Veeck-the-Baseball-Barnum/3964505026000.

Forr, James. "September 26, 1942: Braves Win by Forfeit Behind rookie Warren Spahn at Polo Grounds." *Society for American Baseball Research*, Accessed August 20, 2023, https://sabr.org/gamespro/game/september-26-1942-braves-win-by-forfeit-behindrookie-warren-spahn-at-polo-grounds/.

"40 Years Ago, Disco Demolition Night Stirred Culture War Still Being Fought." *freep.com*, July 12, 2019, https://www.freep.com/story/mlb/tigers/2019/07/12/detroit-tigers-disco-demolition-chigago-white sox-lgbtq/1682439001.

Foster, Jason. "Aug. 10, 1995: When Fans Threw Balls on the Field and the Dodgers Forfeited." *Sporting News*, August 10, 2017, https://www.sportingnew.com/us/author/jason-foster.

Fox, Bucky. "Baseball's Bill Veeck Changed the Pitch of the National Pastime." *Investor's Business Daily*, June 11, 2016, https://investors.com/news/management/leaders-and-success/bill-veeck-brought-family-fun-out-to-the-ballgame.

Frank, Matthew. "Only in Philadelphia: A Look Back on the Day Eagles Fans Booed Santa at Franklin Field." *The Daily Pennsylvanian*, December 1, 2020, https://www.thedp.com/article/2020/12/fans-boo-santa.

Bibliography

Furlong, William Barry. "The Veeck Impact on Chicago: Master of the Joyful Illusion." *Chicago Baseball Museum*, Accessed July 23, 2023, https://chicagobaseballmuseum.org/upload/chicago-special-features>the-veeck-impact-on-chicago-master-of-the-joyful-illusion.

Goldstein, Richard. "Tommy Lasorda, a Dodger from His Cleats to His Cap, Dies at 93." *New York Times*, January 8, https://www.nytimes.com/2021/01/08/sports/baseball/tommy-lasorda-dead.html.

"Hall of Fame Los Angeles Dodgers Manager Tommy Lasorda Dies at 93." *ESPN News Service*, January 8, 2021, https://www.espn.com/mlb/story/_/30674374/hasll-of-famr-dodgers-manager-tommy-lasorda-dies-93.

"Harry O'Neill (catcher)." *Wikipedia*, Accessed February 23, 2023, https:/en.wikipedia.org/wiki/harry_o'neill_(catcher).

Heaton, Michael. "It Was a Hot and Thirsty Night: Looking Back at 10-Cent Beer Night." *Cleveland.com*, June 3, 2012, https://www.cleveland.com/pdq/2012/06/it_was_a_hot_and_thristy_night.html.

"History of the St. Louis Cardinals (1920–1952)." *Wikipedia*, Accessed January 11, 2024, https://en.wikipedia.org/wiki/history-of-the-st-louis-cardinals-(1920-1952).

Hoekstra, Dave. "The Night Disco Died." *chicagomag.com*, July 2016, https://www.chicagomag.com/Chicago-Magazine/July-2016/the-night-disco-died.

"How Cardinals Won by Forfeit at Dodger Stadium." *RetroSimba*, October 6, 2012, https://retrosimba.com/2012/10/06/braves-fans-behavior-recalls-dodgers-forfeit-to-cards.

Huber, Mike. "July 12, 1979: Chicago's Disco Demolition Night Results in White Sox Loss and Forfeit." *Society for American Baseball Research*, Accessed September 21, 2022, https:// sabr.org/gamesproj/game/July-12-1979-chicagos-disco-demolition-night-doubleheader-results-in-loss-and-forfeit/.

Hurte, Bob. "Don Zimmer." *Society for American Baseball Research*, Accessed April 9, 2024, https://sabr.org/bioproj/person/don-zimmer/.

Jackson, Paul. "The Night Beer and Violence Bubbled Over in Cleveland." *ESPN*, June 4, 2008, https://espn.com/espn/page2/story?page=beernight/080604&sportCat=mlb.

"Joe Mauer." *Wikipedia*, Accessed April 7, 2024, https://en.wikipedia.org/wiki/Joe_Maurer.

John, Derek. "July 12, 1979: 'The Night Disco Died'—Or Didn't." *National Public Radio*, July 16, 2016, https://www.npr.org/2016/07/16/485873750/the-night-disco-died-or-didn't#.

Kachejian, Brian. "History of the Baby Ruth Bar and Reggie Bar." *ClassicNewYorkHistory.com*, Accessed April 8, 2024, https://classicnewyorkhistory.com/history-of-the-baby-ruth-bar-and-reggie-bar.

Kallman, Jeff. "September 30, 1971: Senators Forfeit Final Home Game in Washington, D.C." *Society for American Baseball Research*, Accessed August 17, 2021, https://sabr.org/gamesproj/game/September-30-1971-senators-forfeit-final-home-game-in-washington-dc/.

Kalmar, Bert, and Harry Ruby. "Hello, I Must Be Going," sung by Groucho Marx and Margaret Dumont, in *Animal Crackers*, directed by Victor Heerman, written by George S. Kaufman, Morrie Ryskind, and Bert Kalmar (Hollywood: Paramount Pictures Corporation, 1930).

"Kansas City Municipal Stadium." *Ballparks of Baseball*, Accessed August 30, 2024, https://www.ballparksofbaseball.com/ballparks/kansas-city-municipal-stadium.

Kaplan, Jim. "Warren Spahn." *Society for American Baseball Research*, Accessed February 28, 2024, https://sabr.org/bioproj/person/warren-spahn/.

Keller, Richard. "World War II: Recycling and Patriotism." *Baltimore County Government*, Accessed August 20, 2023, https://www.baltimorecountymd.gov/public-works/solid-waste/recycliing/theresource/world-war-ii-recycling-and-patriotism.

Kim, Michelle. "Chicago White Sox Giving Away 'Disco Demolition Night' T-Shirts for 40th Anniversary." *pitchfork.com*, Accessed May 21, 2021, https://pitchfork.com/news/chicago-white-sox-giving-away-disco-demolition-night—t-shirts-for-40th-anniversary.

King, Norm. "August 24, 1951: Browns Fans Manage to Get It Right in Veeck Promotion."

Society for American Baseball Research, Accessed August 29, 2023, https://sabr.org/gamesproj//game/august-24-1951-st-louis-browns-fanes-manage-to-get-it-right-in-veeck-promotion.

———. "Charlie-O." *Society for American Baseball Research,* Accessed August 18, 2023, https://sabr-org/bioproj/topic/charlie-o/.

———. "Zack Taylor." *Society for American Baseball Research,* Accessed January 7, 2024, https://sabr.org/bioproj/person/zack-taylor.

Koppett, Leonard. "Charles O. Finley, Baseball Team Owner Who Challenged Traditions, Dies at 77." *The New York Times,* February 20, 1966, https://www.nytimes.com/1996/02/20/sports/charles-o-finley-baseball-team-owner-who-challenged-traditions-diesat-77.html.

Kornhauser, Jacob. "Moment #96: Disco Demolition Night Goes Awry: MLB's ALL-TIME MOMENTS." *Baseball FYI,* Accessed May 21, 2021, https://www.baseball.fyi/posts/moment/96-disco-dmolition-night-goes-awry-mlbs-all-time-moments.

Krerowicz, Aaron. "Charlie Finley." *Beatles Blog,* Accessed January 18, 2024, https://www.arronkrerowicz.com/beatles-blog/charlie-finley.

Landers, Chris. "Each Team's Weirdest Promotional Item Ever." *Major League Baseball,* May 18, 2020, https://www.mlb.com/news/weirdest-mlb-promotions-ever.

Launius, Roger. "The Beatles Come to Kansas City, Fifty Years Ago." *Wordpress,* September 15, 2014, https://launiusr.wordpress.com/2014/09/15/the-beatles-and-charles-o-finley-owner-of-the-kansas-city-as-in-the-1960s/.

———. "Good Charlie/Bad Charlie: What Made Charlie Finley Tick?" *Roger Launius' Blog,* June 19, 2015, https://launiusr.wordpress.com/2015/06/19/good-charliebad-charlie-what-made-charlie-finley-tick%20priorities, activities,%20virtually%20everyone%20recognized%20it.

———. "My Favorite Weird Baseball Promotions." *Wordpress,* May 15, 2017, https://launiusr.wordpress.com/2017/05/15/my-favorite-weird-baseball-promotions/.

"Legendary Dodgers Manager Tommy Lasorda Dies at 93 of a Heart Attack." *Los Angeles Times,* January 8, 2021, https://www.latimes.com/obituaries/2021-01-08/dodgers-legendary-manager-tom-lasorda-dies-at-age-93-heart-attack.

"Like Bobbleheads, Seattle Sports Fans? Try Free Compost Night." *Seattle Times,* March 21, 2011, https://www.seattletimes.com/seattle-news/like-bobbleheads-seattle-sports-fans-try-free-compost-night/.

Livacari, Gary. "Al Smith." *Society for American Baseball Research,* Accessed December 14, 2023, https://sabr.org/bioproj/person/al.smith-4.

Lubinger, Bill. "The Strange Tale of the Ten Cent Beer Night." *Ohio Magazine,* June 2014, http://www.ohiomagazine.com/ohio-life/article/brawl-game.

"Major League Miscellaneous Averages and Totals." *Baseball Reference,* Accessed July 30, 2024, https://www.baseballreference.com/Leagues/major-leagues-miscellaneous-year-by-year-averages-and-totals.

"Mariners Sustainability." *Major League Baseball,* Accessed April 3, 2024, https://www.mlb.com/mariners/ballpark/information/sustainability.

Marquez, Donald. "The Charlie Finley Story, Part 1 (or 'The Movie That Should Have Been')." *Athletics Nation,* November 18, 2010, https://www.athleticsnation.com/2010/11/18/1821764/the-charlie-finley-story-part-1-or-the-movie-that-should-have-been.

"Material Drives on the World War II Home Front." *National Park Service,* Accessed September 2, 2023, https://www.nps.gov/articles/000/material-drives-on-the-world-war-ii-home-front.htm.

"MC Hammer." *Wikipedia: The Free Encyclopedia,* Accessed April 5, 2024, https://en.Wikipedia.org/wiki/MC_Hammer.

McCafferty, Jack. "All of 50 years later, Bowa and Vankowski can't forget Phillies' final hours at Connie Mack Stadium." *Delco Times,* July 5, 2020, https://www.delcotimes.com/2020/07/05/all-of-50-years-later-bowa-and-vankowski-can't-forget-phillies-final-hours-at-connie-mack-stadium/.

McKenna, Brian. "Eddie Gaedel." *Society for American Baseball Research,* Accessed August 7, 2023, https://sabr.org/bioproj/person/eddie-gaedel/.

McPherson, Myra, and Tom Huth. "Rowdy Fans Hand Senators Final Loss." *Washington Post*, October 1, 1971, www.washingtonpost.com/wpsrv/sports/redskins/history/rfk/articles/baseball.htm.

Merrick, Thomas E. "September 23, 1942: Larry French Nearly Perfect, as Patriotic Dodgers Collect Scrap Metal, Keep Pennant Hopes Alive." *Society for American Baseball Research*, Accessed February 27, 2024, https://sabr.org/gamesproj/game/september-23-1942-larry-french-nearly-perfect-aspatriotic-dodgers-collect-scrap-metal-keep-pennant-hopes-alive/.

Miller, Doug. "TBT: 72 A's Hold Memorable 'Mustache Day.'" *Major League Baseball*, Accessed August 18, 2023, https://www.mlb.com/news/tbt-72-as-hold-memorable-mustache-day/c-131407816.

Miller, Sam. "25 Years Ago Tonight, MLB Had Its Last Forfeit." *ESPN*, Accessed November 8, 2021, https://www.espn.com/mlb/story/_/id/29614065/25-years-ago-tonight-mlb-had-last-forfeit-los-angeles-dodgers-st-louis-cardinals-game.

Muder, Craig. "President Roosevelt Gives 'Green Light' to Baseball." *Baseball Hall of Fame*, Accessed February 28, 2024, https://baseballhall.org/roosevelt-sends-green-light-letter-to-baseball.

———. "Veeck Brought Fun Back to Baseball." *The National Baseball Hall of Fame*, Accessed July 23, 2023, https://baseball.org/discover/inside-pitch-veeck-brought-fun-back-to-baseball.

Murphy, Michael. "Charlie-O—Baseball's Favorite Mule." *Medium*, Accessed January 13, 2024, https://medium.com/stmaryssports/charlie-o-baseball's-favorite-mule-76c34bf4e5bd.

Natkin, Paul. "Disco Demolition Night Was a Disgrace, and Celebrating It Is Worse." *vice.com*, Accessed January 21, 2021, https://www.vice.com/en/article/8xzke5/disco-demolityion-night-was-a-disgrace-ans-celebrating-it-is-worse.

Nelson, D.L. "The Reign of Finley." *Athletics Nation*, August 1, 2013, https://www.athleticsnation.com/2013/8/1/4576930/the-reign-of-finley.

"1951 St. Louis Browns Statistics." *Baseball Reference*, Accessed January 4, 2024, https://www.baseball-reference.com/teams/SLB/1951-st-louis-browns-statistics.

"1944 St. Louis Browns Statistics." *Baseball Reference*, Accessed November 27, 2023, https://www.baseball-reference.com/teams/SLB/1944.

"1961 Kansas City Athletics Statistics." *Baseball Reference*, Accessed January 4, 2024, https://www.baseball-reference.com/KCA.

Nissenson, Herschel. "Umpire Chylak Admits Fear in Seeing Crowd Go Wild." *The Paducah Sun*, June 5, 1974, https://www.newspapers.com/June/5/1974/umpire-chylak-admits-fear-in-seeing-crowd-go-wild.

Noga, Joe. "Fans Riot on 10-Cent Beer Night: On This Day in Cleveland Indians History." *Cleveland.com*, June 4, 2020, https://cleveland.com/tribe/2020/06/fans-riot-on-10-cent-beer-night-on-this-day-in-cleveland-indians-history.html#:text=Fans%2.

"Oakland Athletics Attendance, Stadiums, and Park Factors." *Baseball Reference*, Accessed January 4, 2024, https://www.baseball-reference.com/OAK/attendance-stadiums-and-park-factors.

Obermeyer, Jeff. "Baseball During World War II." *Society for American Baseball Research*, Accessed February 6, 2024, https://sabr.org/journal/article/the-business-of-baseball-during-world-war-II/.

O'Connor, Ian. "Keeping Score." *USA Today*, April 17, 2003, https://usatoday.com/sports/columnist/oconnor/23003-04-17-ian_x.htm.

"On This Day: 'Disco Demolition Night' Causes Riot at Chicago White Sox Game." *FindingDulcinea.com*, Accessed May 21, 2021, https://www.findingdulcinea.com/news/-on-this-day/July-August-08/On-this-Day---Disco-Demolition-Night-Ruins-Chicago-White-Sox-Game.html.

Osborne, Cary. "What Tommy Lasorda Lived and Loved By." *Dodger Insider*, Accessed September 25, 2022, https://dodgers.mlblogs.com/what-tommy-lasorda-lived-and-loved-by-38acf24c10fb.

Paine, Neil. "Hideo Nomo Paved the Way for a Generation of Damn Good Japanese

Ballplayers." *FiveThirtyEight*, Accessed March 30, 2024, https://fivethirtyeoght.com/features/hideo-nomo-paved-the-way-for-a-generation-of-damn-good-japanese-ballplayers.

Pajot, Dennis, and Greg Erion. "St. Louis Browns Team Ownership History." *Society for American Baseball Research*, Accessed November 27, 2023, https://sabr.org/bioproj/topic/st-louis-browns-team-ownership-history/.

Parker, Lyndsey. "'Let's Blow Up This Black Music!' The Ugliness and Unrest of 1979's Disco Demolition Night." *Yahoo.com*, Accessed May 21, 2021, https://www.yahoo.com/now/lets-blow-up-this-black-music-the-ugliness-and-unrest-of-1979-s-disco-demolition-night.

Petridis, Alexis. "Disco Demolition: The Night They Tried to Crush Black Music." *The Guardian*, July 19, 2019, https://www.theguardian.com/music/2019/jul/19/all.

"Philadelphia Phillies Attendance, Stadiums, and Park Factors." *Baseball Reference*, Accessed January 4, 2024, https://www.baseball-reference.com/PHI/attendance-stadiums-and-park-factors.

Povich, Shirley. "The Senators' Final Game." *Washington Post*, October 1, 1971, www.washingtonpost.com/wp-srv/sports/longterm/general/povich/launch/senators2.htm.

Rappa, Matt. "Phillies: Celebrating 50th Anniversary of Veterans Stadium." *Fanside*, April 10, 2021, https://thatballsoutahere.com/2021/04/10/phillies-veterans-stadium-50-years/.

Ray, James Lincoln. "Connie Mack Stadium (Philadelphia)." *Society for American Baseball Research*, Accessed January 21, 2024, https://sabr.org/park/connie-mack-stadium-philadelphia/.

Raymond, Dave. "Kiteman!" *Dave Raymond Speaks*, March 16, 2023, https://daveraymondspeaks.com/2023/03/16/kite-man/.

Roberts, James C. "Baseball Goes to War: The National Pastime in World War II." *American Veterans Center*, Accessed September 2, 2023, https://www.americanveteralscenter.org/avc-media/magazine/wwiichronicles/wwii-chronicles-issue-xxxix/baseball-goes-to-war-the-national-pastime-in-world-war-ii.

Robinson, Eric. "The Peculiar Professional Baseball Career of Eddie Gaedel." *Society for American Baseball Research*, Accessed August 7, 2023, https://sabr.org/journal/article/the-peculiar-professional-baseball-career-of-eddie-gaedel/.

Rossen, Jake. "When Disco Demolition Night Nearly Demolished Chicago's Comiskey Park." *mentalfloss.com*, December 5, 2019, https://www.mentalfloss.com/article/609062/disco-demolition-night-comiskey-park.

Rotman, Michael. "Cuyahoga River Fire." *Cleveland Historical*, https://clevelandhistorical.org/items/show/63.

"St. Louis Browns Yearly Records and Games." *Back to Baseball*, Accessed February 13, 2024, https://www.backtobaseball.com/teams/st.-louis-browns.

"Salvage for Victory: World War II & Now." *National World War II Museum*, January 11, 2022, https://www.nationalww2museum.org/war/articles/salvage-for-victory-world-war-ii.

Saunders, Luke. "Disco Demolition Night: Why Your Taste Doesn't Matter and Never Will." *Happymagtv.com*, Accessed May 21, 2021, https://happymag.tv/disco-demolition-night-and-why-your-taste-doesn't-matter-and-never-will.

Scanlan, Wayne. "10-Cent Beer Night: June 4, 1974 in Cleveland." *WordPress*, October 26, 2009, https://miscbaseball. https://wordpress.com/2009/10/26/10-cent-beer-night-june-4-1974-in-cleveland.

Schlichting, Matt. "Happy 45th Anniversary, 10 Cent Beer Night!" *Let's Go Tribe*, June 4, 2019, https://letsgotribe.com/2019/6/4/18652095/10-cent-beer-night-45th-anniversary-rangers-indians-baseball-forfeits-june-4-1974.

"Seattle Mariners Recycle/Compost 80% of Waste." *SustainableBusiness.com*, September 2011, https://www.sustainablebusiness.com/2011/09/seattle-mariners-recyclecompost-80-of-waste-49627/

Shaffer, J. Scott, and Millard Fisher. "Ted Turner." *Society for American Baseball Research*, Accessed March 10, 2024, https://sabr.org/bioproj/person/ted-turner/.

Sharp, Andrew. "Washington Senators II Team Ownership History." *Society for*

Bibliography

American Baseball Research, Accessed August 17, 2021, sabr.org/bioproj//topic/Washington-senators-ii-team-ownership-history.

Shenk, Larry. "End of an Era." *Major League Baseball,* September 30, 2020, https://www.mlb.com/news/phillies-alumni-end-of-an-era.

———. "1972 Rewind." *Phillies Insider,* Accessed November 8, 2023, https://philliesinsider.mlblogs.com/1972-rewind-4a8da68a2fc2.

"Shibe Park, Philadelphia, Pennsylvania." *This Great Game,* Accessed August 26, 2023, https://thisgreatgame.com/ballparks-shibe-park/.

Simon, Andrew. "How Nomo Changed MLB Forever." *Major League Baseball,* February 12, 2024, https://www.mlb.com/news/hideo-nomo-pioneered-path-to-mlb-in-1995.

"Slam for Stunning Steve Dunning: On this Day in Cleveland Indians History." *Cleveland.com,* May 11, 2020, https://www.cleveland.com/tribe/2020/05/slam-for-stunning-steve-dunning-this-day-in-cleveland-indians-history.

"Sport Quotes." *University of North Texas Center for Sport Psychology and Athlete Mental Health,* Accessed February 6, 2024, https://sportpsych.unit.edu/sport-quotes.

Sundin, Sarah. "Make It Do—Scrap Drives in World War II." *Sarah Sundin,* Accessed August 20, 2023, https://www.sarahsundin.com/make-it-do-scrap-drives-in-world-war-ii.

"Super Disco Demolition: The 40th Anniversary Compilation (1979)." *YouTube,* youtube.com/watch?v=kqDkBM9vxw8.

Tannock, Ray. "Top Ten Worst MLB Gameday Promotions Ever." *BleacherReport.com,* Accessed August 6, 2023, https://bleacherreport.com/articles/846519-top-ten-worst-mlb-gameday-promotions-ever.

"10-Cent Beer Night: June 4, 1974 in Cleveland." *Misc. Baseball,* October 26, 2009, https://miscbaseball.wordpress.com/2009/10/26/10-cent-beer-night-june-4-1974-in-cleveland/.

"Ten Cent Beer Night." *Wikipedia,* Accessed January 5, 2021, https//en.wikipedia.org/wiki/Ten_Cent_Beer_Night.

"Tommy Lasorda." *National Baseball Hall of Fame,* Accessed September 25, 2022, https://baseballhall.org/hall-of-famers/lasorda-tommy.

"Tommy Lasorda Managerial Stats." *Baseball Reference,* Accessed November 28, 2021, https:www.baseball.reference.com/managers/lasorto01.shtml.

"Tommy Lasorda MLB Career and Early Life." *Diamond Mind Online,* Accessed September 25, 2022, https://imaginesports.com/news/tommy-lasorda-mlb-career-and-early-life.

"Tommy Lasorda Stats." *Baseball Almanac,* Accessed November 28, 2021. https://baseballAlmanac.com/players/player.php?p=lasorto01.

Turnquist, Ryan. "Bill Veeck, Eddie Gaedel and the Birth of Legend." *National Baseball Hall of Fame,* Accessed July 23, 2023, https://baseballhall.org/discover-more-stories/inside-pitch/bill-veeck-eddie-gaedel-and-the-birth-of-a-legend.

"Veeck, William (Bill) L." *Case Western Reserve University,* Encyclopedia of Cleveland, Accessed July 23, 2023, https://case.edu/ech/articles/v/veeck-william-bill-l.

Vukelich, Dan. "The Great White Sox Hope." *Chicago Reader,* April 9, 1976, https://chicagoreader.com/news-politics/the-great-white-sox-hope/.

Waleik, Gary. "Forty Years Later, Disagreement About Disco Demolition Night." *WBUR.org,* July 12, 2019, https://www.ubur.org/onlyagame/2019/07/disco-demolition-dahl-veeck-chicago-white-sox.

"Walter Alston Managerial Stats." *Baseball Reference,* baseball reference.com/managers/alstowa01.shtml.

White, David. "The Graveyard of Baseball: October 1, 1970, Was a Day That Will Live in Infamy." *Order of the Jackalope,* Accessed August 26, 2023, https://order-of-the-jackalope.com/the-graveyard-of-baseball/.

"White Sox History: The Days of 'Sport Shirt Bill Veeck.'" *Sox at 35th,* April 25, 2022, https://www.soxon35th.com/white-sox-history-the-days-of-sport-shirt-bill-veeck.

"Why the Washington Nationals Were Once Known as the Senators." *U.S. Senate,* Accessed August 17, 2021, www.senate.gov/artandhistory/history/minute/washington_nationals_once_known_as_senators.htm.

"Will Harridge, Executive." *Baseball Hall of Fame,* Accessed October 11, 2023, https://baseballhall.org/hall-of-famers/harridge-will.

Williams, Doug. "The Night Ted Turner Managed the Braves." *ESPN*, May 23, 2013, https://www.espn.com/blog/playbook/fandom/post/_/id/22066/the-night-ted-turner-managed-the-braves.

Wulf, Ed. "Vote, Vote, Vote for the Home Team." *ESPN*, September 16, 2014, https://www.espn.com,mlb/story/_/page/FansourceVeeck/bill-veeck-birth-fansourcing.

"Year by Year Results/Atlanta Braves." *Major League Baseball,* Accessed August 5, 2024, https://www.mlb.com/braves/history/year-by-year-results.

"Year by Year Results/Philadelphia Phillies." *Major League Baseball,* Accessed August 20, 2024, https://www.mlb.com/phillies/history/year-by-year-results.

Young, Christopher J., "When Fans Wanted to Rock, the Baseball Stopped: Sports, Promotions, and the Demolition of Disco on Chicago's South Side." *Society for American Baseball Research,* Accessed September 21, 2022, https://sabr.org/journal/article/when-fans-wanted-to-rock-the-baseball-stopped-sports-promotions-and-the-demolition-of-disco-on-chicagos-south-side/.

Zelen, Ross. "Seattle Mariners Go Green: Time to Give Praise to Those Who Take Responsibility." *BleacherReport,* Accessed April 3, 2024, https://bleacherreport.com/articles/993831-seattle-mariners-go-green-thime-to-give-praise-to-those-who-take-responsibility.

Index

Abdul the Butcher (a.k.a. the Madman from the Sudan) 102
AC/DC 110
Acosta, Julio 13
Aker, Jack 62, 72, 148
Alevizos, John 99
Alexander, Grover Cleveland 129
Allyn, Arthur 21
Allyn, Arthur, Jr. 21, 71, 72
Alou, Felipe 149
Alston, Walter 168–170
American League 5, 6, 16, 19, 22, 25, 26, 38, 44, 45, 47, 49, 51, 52, 59, 60, 62, 64, 70, 72, 79, 80, 113, 118, 134, 139, 142, 145, 147, 152, 153, 155, 159, 164, 175, 189
Anderson, Sparky 118
Anheuser-Busch Brewery 18, 46
Arco Go-Patrol Helicopter 31, 83, 86
Arft, Hank 56, 58
Arlington Stadium 155
Armory Board 143–145
Ashburn, Richie 32, 47
Ashby, Alan 160
Ashley, Billy 76
Aspromonte, Ken 155, 159, 161, 164
Astrodome 76–78
Asylum Records 121
Atlanta Braves 22, 34–38, 91, 94–105
Atlanta Christian Council 103
Atlanta-Fulton County Stadium 100, 104
Automobile Industry Night promotion (Kansas City Athletics) 26, 188
Avondale Public School 92

Baez, Joan 112
Bags of Compost giveaway (Seattle Mariners) 189–191
Baker, Dan 89
Baker, Frank 147
Baker Bowl 80
Ball, Phil 43
Baltimore Orioles 23, 139, 146, 175, 181, 187

Baltimore Terrapins 6
Barnes, Donald 44, 45
Barnet, Jim 101
Barnum, P.T. 1
Bartell, Dick 136
Baseball Nose Push promotion (Atlanta Braves) 36, 37
Bateman, John 85
Battle of Guadalcanal 14, 125
Batts, Matt 56
Beatles promotion (Kansas City Athletics) 2, 25, 59, **65**–67, 118
Bee Gees 112
Belle, Albert 172
Bender, Albert "Chief" 80
Benjamin, Howard 69
Benny the Bomb promotion (Philadelphia Phillies) 31
Benson, Vern 99
Berna, Babe 136
Bernadino, Johnnie 57
Berra, Yogi 130
Bert Campaneris Night promotion (Kansas City Athletics) 26
The B.F. Goodrich Company 128
Billings, Rick 148
Black, Dan 15
Black Sox Scandal 6
Blanchard, Tully 102
Blind Date Night promotion (Atlanta Braves) 38
Blondie 112
Bonda, Ted 162–164
Bonifay, Peter 90
Borchert Field 10, 11, 13, 14
Borowy, Hank 133
Bosman, Dick 146, 147, 163
Boston Braves 125, 134–136
Boston Red Sox 43, 45, 52, 79, 99, 131, 139, 154, 192, 193
Bougainville 14
Bowman, Joe 64

239

Index

Boy Scouts of America 127
Breadon, Sam 43
breakfast baseball promotion (Milwaukee Brewers/minor league) 12
Brinkman, Ed 142, 163
Brinkman, Joe 163
Bristol, Dave 99
Broeg, Bob 49, 52
Brohamer, Jack 155, 158
Brooklyn Dodgers 80, 125, 135, 167
Brossard, Roger 192
Brown University 93
Bryant, Anita 109
Bryce Harper Chia Pet giveaway (Washington Nationals) 193
Burroughs, Jeff 148, 157, 159–163
Bush, President George W. 151

C&P Telephone Company 144
Cain, Bob 51, 53, 54
Caine, Marty 48
Callahan, Paul 33, 89, 90
Cannizzaro, Chris 99
Capote, Truman 111
Caray, Harry 39, 118
Cardinal Dougherty High School Band 84
Carpenter, Bob 136
Carpenter, Bob Ruly 29, 77, 81, 105, 106
Carroll, Parke 62
Cash Scramble promotion (Atlanta Braves) 36
Cash Scramble promotion (Philadelphia Phillies) 32
Cey, Ron 170
Chaney, Darrel 96
Charlie Quinn's Deep Right Field Café 83
Charlie-O the Mule 59, **68**–73
Chic 121
Chicago Cubs 8, 9, 19, 48, 104, 105, 192
Chicago Evening American 8
Chicago Whalers 6
Chicago White Sox 4, 6, 11, 19–22, 25, 38, 39, 71, 72, 96, 112–116, 118, 119, 151, 152, 183, 188, 192
Children's Mercy Hospital 66, 67
Cincinnati, Ohio 30, 87, 92
Cincinnati Reds 74–76, 95, 98, 176, 192
Claire, Fred 172, 175–177
Clarke, Horace 138, 149
Clay, Otis 120
Cleveland, Ohio 153
Cleveland Indians 4, 15–17, 130, 152–164
Cleveland-Marshall College of Law 156
Cleveland Plain Dealer 156
Cochrane, Mickey 80
Coleman, Joe 142

Coleman, Leonard 174
Colleti, Ned 169
Comiskey Park 71, 72, 107, 113, 114, 117, 118, 120, 121
Comiskey Rigney, Dorothy 19
Concord Weavers 166
Conlin, Bill 32
Connie Mack Stadium/Shibe Park 29, 30, 74, 77, **78**–87, 136
contacting aliens promotion (Atlanta Braves) 37
Continental Army soldiers promotion (Chicago White Sox) 39
Copland, Aaron 56
Cosell, Howard 70
Coughlin, Dan 156, 160, 162
Cowan, Wayne 102
cricket match promotion (Chicago White Sox) 20
Cristiani Bros. Circus promotion (Chicago White Sox) 20
Cronin, Joe 145
Crosby, Bing 51, 126, 133
Crosby, Ed 160
Cullen, Tim 149
Curse of the Bambino 43
Curse of Branch Rickey 43
Cuyahoga River 153

Dahl, Steve 108–113, 116–120
Daly, Ed 145
Danzansky, Joe 145
Davidson, Bob 174–177
Davidson, Donald 96, 97
Davis, Tyrone 120
Dean, "Dizzy" 43
Delahanty, Ed 5
Deliverance Evangelistic Church 87
Dell, John 87
Delsing, Jim 51, 53, 58
DeMars, Billy 86
Denver Bears 167
Depeche Mode 122
Detroit Rockers Engaged in the Abolition of Disco 110
DeWitt, Bill 44–46, 51
DeWitt, Charlie 46
Dickey, Bill 45
DiMaggio, Dom 45, 133
DiMaggio, Joe 45, 130, 132
Disco Demolition Night promotion (Chicago White Sox) 39, 107, 108, 113–**115**, 119–121, 136, 175, 187, 189
Doby, Larry 52, 113, 182
Dodger Stadium 172, 174
Donahue, Dan 94, 95
Donnelly, Jackie 84

Index

D'Ortona, Councilman Paul 83
Dropo, Walt 52
Dryden, Charlie 139
duck race promotion (Philadelphia Phillies) 32
Duncan, Dave 155
Dunn, Tommy 136
Dunning, Steve 153, 154
Durney, Bill 50
Durslag, Melvin 97
Dykes, Jimmy 57

Easter egg hunt promotion (Atlanta Braves) 36
Easter egg hunt promotion (Philadelphia Phillies) 33
Ebbets Field 135, 167
Eckersley, Dennis 170
Eddie Gaedel Game promotion (St. Louis Browns) 18–20, 42, 48–54, 191
Ehlers, Arthur 55
Electra Records 121
Ellis, John 147, 148, 155
Ellis, Ryan W. 17
Elson, Bob 62
Emory University Sigma Phi Fraternity 35
Encarnación, Angelo 175
Epstein, Brian 65, 66
Epstein, Mike 142
Era of the Barnums 1, 38, 107, 179, 185
Erectus, Dennis 110
Ernie Mehl Appreciation Day promotion (Kansas City Athletics) 25, 63
Etten, Nick 135
Evansville Braves 135

Fain, Ferris 57
Falstaff Brewery 47, 49–51
Falwell, Jerry 109
Fanning, Jim 31
Farewell to Connie Mack Stadium promotion (Philadelphia Phillies) 30, 83
Farrah Fawcett Look-Alike Contest promotion (Atlanta Braves) 38
Fazio, Carl 157, 162, 163
Federal League 6, 79, 80
Feeney, Chub 100
Feller, Bob 51, 130–132
Fernandez, Frank 142
Ferrone, Frank 163
Finley, Charlie O. 1, 22, 39, 59, 60, 188, 191, 195; and the Beatles 65–67; and Charlie-O the Mule 67–73; with Kansas City Athletics 22, **23**–26, 61–65; with Oakland Athletics 26–29

Firestone Tire and Rubber Company 128
Fishel, Bob 48, 57, 58
Fisk, Carlton 73
Flag Day promotion (Houston Astros) 77
Flaherty, Vincent X. 52
Flood, Curt 113, 142, 194, 195
Forster, Terry 170
Foucault, Steve 159, 160, 162
Foxx, Jimmy 80
Franklin, Pete 156
Fregosi, Jim 155, 158
French, Larry 135
Frick, Commissioner Ford 18, 63
Frisch, Frankie 133
Funeral for the 1948 Pennant Flag promotion (Cleveland Indians) 16

Gaedel, Eddie 48–54, 191
Gamble, Oscar 85, 86, 158
Garver, Ned 54, 57, 58
Garvey, Steve 170
Gashouse Gang 44
Gavin, Tom 63
Gaye, Marvin 120
Gehrig, Lou 82, 168
Georgia Championship Wrestling 101
Georgia Military Academy 92
Get in the Scrap 126
Gibbs, C.M. 55
Gibson, Bob 176
Gibson, Kirk 170
Gideon, Elmer 132
Gifford, Frank 70
Giles, Bill 1, 22, **30**, 35, 74–77, 81, 82; and Farewell to Connie Mack Stadium 82–87; and Kiteman 87–90; with the Philadelphia Phillies 29–33
Girl Scouts of America 127, 129, 182
giveaway promotions 11, 15, 20, 49, 144, 165, 177, 179–182, 187, 189
Gleason, Bill 119
golfing trick shot expert promotion (Houston Astros) 77
Gomez, Vernon "Lefty" 133
Good Old Joe Earley Night promotion (Cleveland Indians) 15, 16
The Goodyear Tire and Rubber Company 128
Gordon, Joe 24, 62
Gore, Martin 122
Grable, Betty 133
Graham, Billy 82
Grammy Awards ceremony 112, 121
Grandstand Managers Night promotion (St. Louis Browns) 19, 42, 55–58
Gray, Pete 132

242 Index

Great Depression 7, 80
Great Mattress Stacking Championship promotion (Atlanta Braves) 35
"Green Light" letter 7, 129
Green Sports Alliance 190, 191
Greenberg, Hank 130, 132, 133, 145
Grieve, Tom 155, 157, 158
Grimm, Charles 13
Grizzard, Lewis 103
Grove, Lefty 80
Grzenda, Joe 149, 151
Gutteridge, Don 44
Gwynn, Tony 172

Haas, Walter 29, 73
Hahn, Gilbert 144
Hammer, M.C. (a.k.a. Stanley Burrell) 191–192
Hanks, Tom 146
Hannan, Jim 142
Hansen, Dave 173
Hardy, J.J. 175
Hargrove, Mike 157, 158, 161, 163
Hargrove, Sharon 162
Harper, "Skinny" Bobby 37
Harrah, Toby 158
Harrelson, Ken "Hawk" 70–72
Harridge, Will 22, 49, 52, 53, 60
Harris, Bucky 139, 146
Harry Caray Appreciation Night promotion (Chicago White Sox) 39
Hartford Chiefs 135
Harvey, the Mechanical Rabbit 61
Hayworth, Rita 126
Hearnes, Governor Warren 69
Henderson, Ken 96, 98
Hendrick, George 159, 160
Henke, Tom 173, 176
Hershiser, Orel 170
Herzog, Whitey 72
Highest Jumping Bunny promotion (Philadelphia Phillies) 33
Highway Beautification Act 93
Hilgendorf, Tom 161, 162
Hiroshima 26
History.com 121
Hitchcock, Billy 46
Hochberg, Phil 146
Holmes, Judge Oliver Wendell 6
Honochick, Jim 150
Hooton, Burt 170
Hoover, John O. 87
Hope, Bob 1, 22, 91, 96, 97, 100; with Atlanta Braves 34–38; and Wedlock and Headlock Night 100–102; and Wet T-Shirt Day 102–106
Hornsby, Rogers 43

Hot Pants Day promotion (Oakland Athletics) 28, 103
Hot Pants Patrol (Philadelphia Phillies) 32
Houk, Ralph 167
Houston Astros 74–77
Howard, Frank "Hondo" 147, 148
Howard, Fred 114
Hubbell, Carl 135
Hubert, William 5
Hughes, Charles E. 56, 57
Human League 122
Hunter, Jim "Catfish" 27, 188, 195
Hurley, Ed 51
Hyland, Frank 97

Ian, Janice 112
Inglehart, Joe 23
Insane Coho Lips 109

Jackson, Reggie 27, 187, 188
Jackson, "Shoeless" Joe 7
Jenkins, Ferguson 158, 159
The Jersey Standard Tire Company 128
Jeter, Derek 193
Joe Maurer Sideburns giveaway (Minnesota Twins) 189
Johnson, Arnold 61, 81
Johnson, Ban 5
Johnson, Lady Bird 93
Johnson, Richard 88, 89
Johnson, Walter 132, 139
Jones, Chipper 172
Jones, Grace 122
Jordan, Brian 173, 175

Kalas, Harry 32
Kaline, Al 117, 118
Kansas City Athletics 22, 24–26, 59, 61–66, 68–72, 167
Kansas City Star 25, 62, 66
Kansas City Times 62
Karl Wallenda promotion (Philadelphia Phillies) 31, 32
Karl Wallenda Skywalk promotion (Atlanta Braves) 36
Karros, Eric 170, 173, 176
Keeler, Wee Willie 53
Kekich, Mike 142, 148
Kell, George 117
Kenyon College 9
KIIS-FM 112
Kinder, Ellis 45
King, B.B. 184
King, Dr. Martin Luther, Jr. 143
Kirkpatrick, Ed 26
Kiss 112

Index

Kiteman promotions (Philadelphia Phillies) 31, 74, 88–90, 185
Knowles, Darold 142
KOMR 110
Koufax, Sandy 75, 82, 167
Kramer, Jackie 45
Krausse, Lew 24
Krebs, Kris 100, 101
Kuhn, Bowie 99, 100, 106, 145, 146, 194
Kuntz, Ron 161

Lacey, Lee 96
Ladies' Day 9
Lajoie, Nap 5
Landis, Judge Kenesaw Mountain 6, 7, 129
Lane, Frank "Trader" 62
Lasorda, Tommy 1, 165, **166**–171, 174–177
Lawrence, Vince 120, 121
Lazzeri, Tony 168
A League of Their Own 132
leap into pool of ice cream promotion (Atlanta Braves) 37
Lee, Leron 158
Lefebvre, Joe 171
Lehigh University 33
Lennon, John 66
Liberty University 109
Lindblad, Paul 142
Little Blowhard 62
Litwiler, Dan 133
Lofton, Kenny 172
Logan, Dave 113
Lollar, Sherm 56, 58
Loney, James 171
Los Angeles Dodgers 1, 96, 165–177, 189, 192
Lotspeich School 92
Lowenstein, John 155, 160
Luchessi, Frank 85, 86
Lupica, Charlie 16, 17
Lurie, Bob 99

Mabry, John 173–176
Mack, Connie 56, 57, 78–81, 169
Mack, Earle 81
Mack, Roy 81
MacPhail, Lee 118, 152
Maddox, Elliott 148
Maddux, Greg 172
Madonna 122
Majewski, Hank 57
Manilow, Barry 112
Mapes, Chris 58
Maranville, "Rabbit" 129
Maris, Roger 61
Marsh, Dave 119
Martin, Billy 152, 156–160, 162, 163

Martinez, Edgar 172
Martinez, Pedro 193
Marx Brothers 140
Mathewson, Christy 129
Matthews, Gary 99
Matthews, T.J. 173
mattress stacking promotion (Philadelphia Phillies) 33
Mauch, Gene 85
Mauer, Joe 189
Mayfield, Curtis 120
M.C. Hammer Bobblehead giveaway (Oakland Athletics) 191–192
McCallie Military Academy 92, 93
McCarver, Tim 85, 86
McCoy, Benny 133
McCoy, Van 109
McGraw, John 48, 81, 169
McGraw, Tommy 148
McGraw, Tug 37
McLain, Denny 142
McNally, Dave 195
Mead, Bill 45
Mehl, Ernie 25, 62–64, 66
Meier, Greg 108, 116
Menchine, Ron 138, 139, 147, 148, 150
Merman, Ethel 112
Merrill, Durwood 115
Messersmith, Andy 36, 95, 97, 99, 195
Miles, Clarence 19
Miller, Freddie 101
Millie the Queen of the Air promotion (St. Louis Browns) 18
Milwaukee Brewers (major league) 154, 177
Milwaukee Brewers (minor league) 4, 8–15, 154, 177
Mincher, Don 142, 148
Minnesota Twins 139, 153, 189, 190
Mr. Wrestling II 102
Mitze, Clark 56–58
Mize, Johnny 44, 136
Mondesi, Raul 173, 174
"The Monster" exploding scoreboard promotion (Chicago White Sox) 20
Montanez, Willie 96
Montreal Expos 30, 31, 82, 85
Montreal Royals 167
Morales, Jerry 115
Moran, Eddie 48
Muckerman, Richard 45, 46
Mulcahy, Hugh "Losing Pitcher" 130, 131
Mulhearn, Pat 31
Municipal Stadium (Cleveland) 16, 17, 153, 154
Municipal Stadium (Kansas City) 25, 61, 63–66, 69, 72

Munson, Thurman 148
Murakami, Masanori 172
Murcer, Bobby 105, 147, 149
Murray, Jim 23
Musial, Stan "The Man" 44, 130, 133
Mustache Day promotion (Oakland Athletics) 28

Nashville Volunteers 74, 76
National Agreement of 1903 5
National Association of Professional Baseball Players 4
National Baseball Hall of Fame and Museum 39, 54, 169, 182, 188, 189
National Dairy Week promotion (Chicago White Sox) 20
National League 5, 6, 43, 44, 75, 79, 80, 82, 95, 100, 168, 169, 172, 174, 176, 192
National Public Radio 120
Negro Leagues 82, 132, 182
Nelson, Dave 147
New York Daily News 70
New York Giants 48, 81, 96, 99, 124, 125, 129, 134–136, 169, 172, 190
New York Yankees 44, 45, 52, 61, 70, 95, 138, 139, 147–150, 154, 167–169, 171, 184, 187, 188, 192, 193, 195
Niedenfuer, Tom 171
Niekro, Phil 100
Nixon, President Richard M. 142, 151
Nomo, Hideo 172, 173
Northern Virginia Community College 147

Oakland Athletics 26–28, 103, 169, 170, 187, 191, 192, 195
Oakley, Phillip 122
Oates, Ted 102
Offerman, Jose 173
O'Neill, Harry 132
Opening Day attendance promotion (Milwaukee Brewers/minor league) 12
Oriole Park at Camden Yards 78
ostrich race promotion (Atlanta Braves) 37
ostrich race promotion (Philadelphia Phillies) 32
Ott, Mel 135
Outlar, Jesse 102

Pagnozzi, Tom 177
Paige, Satchel 50, 113
Parachute Man promotion (Philadelphia Phillies) 31
Parrish, Lance 115
Passeau, Claude 84

Patkin, Max 49, 50
Paul, Gabe 75, 76
Pearl Harbor 7, 44, 124–126, 128, 130
Pennock, Herb 80
Percy Faith Orchestra 112
Pesky, Johnny 45
Peters, Hank 24, 27
Peterson, Fritz 157
Philadelphia Athletics 55–58, 75, 77, 79, 80–82, 132, 169
Philadelphia Eagles 82
Philadelphia Hospital for Contagious Diseases 77
Philadelphia Phillies 22, 29–33, 36, 37, 47, 74, 77, 80–90, 105, 130, 131, 135, 166, 167, 193, 194
Philley, Dave 57
Phillips, Dave 115, 118
Piazza, Mike 173
Pittsburgh Pirates 99, 134, 174
Plank, Eddie 80
Please Hammer Don't Hurt 'Em 192
Pocatello Chiefs 168
Polo Grounds 129, 133–135
Portland Trailblazers 190
Povich, Shirley 146, 149, 150
Powers, Doc 79
Princess Aloha Orchid Night (Cleveland Indians) 16
Pryor, Greg 114
Putnam, Ed 116

Queen 112
Quick, Jim 165, 173, 174, 176, 177

Ragland, Tom 147
Randle, Lenny 155
Rau, Doug 171
Reese, Pee Wee 53, 135
Reggie Bars giveaway (New York Yankees) 187, 188
Reilly, Police Lieutenant Robert 118
Reinsdorf, Jerry 39
reserve clause 5, 6, 28, 29, 39, 113, 142, 194, 195
Reuss, Jerry 171
Rickey, Branch 42, 43
Ringling Brothers Circus 82
Ripken, Cal, Jr. 53
Rizzo, Police Chief Frank 89
Rizzuto, Phil 45, 52, 53, 130, 133
Roberge, Skippy 136
Robert F. Kennedy Memorial Stadium 138, 142–144
Roberts, Tony 150
Robinson, Brooks 75
Robson Field 43

Index

Rocket Man promotion (Houston Astros) 76
Rodriguez, Aurelio 142
Roger Brossard Bobblehead giveaway (Chicago White Sox) 192
Roosevelt, President Franklin Delano 7, 126, 127, 129
Roosevelt, President Theodore 66
Rose, Pete 75
Rosie the Riveter early morning game promotion (Milwaukee Brewers/minor league) 13
Rosney, Joan 83, 86
Royal Canadian Mounted Police 31
Royster, Jerry 96
Ruffing, Red 45
Russert, Tim 156
Ruth, Babe 53, 132, 133
Ryan, Ellis W. 17
Ryan, "Irish" Mike 31

Saigh, Frank 18, 46, 145
St. Louis Browns 4, 17–19, 21, 42–58, 132
St. Louis Cardinals 17, 18, 42–44, 46, 75, 89, 135, 142, 145, 167, 172–177, 194
St. Louis Globe-Democrat 55
Salenger, Oscar 14
Salsoul Records 121
Salvage for Victory 126
Salvation Army Band 87
Saturday Night Fever 111
Saucier, Frank 51, 53, 57
Schaaf, Jim 66, 68–72
Schenectady Blue Jays 166
Schwartz, Jeff 113
Scioscia, Mike 170
Score, Herb 158, 161
Scrap Metal Day promotion (New York Giants) 134, 135
Sears, Ziggy 136
Seattle Seahawks 190
Seattle Sounders FC 191
Seattle Storm 190–191
Seghi, Phil 163
The Selective Training and Service Act 130
Selig, Bud 177
Sewell, Luke 44
Shark, Lorelei 114, 116
Shepherd, Bert 132
Shibe, Benjamin Franklin 77–80
Short, Bob 139–149, 151
Short, Chris 84
Short, Ed 71
Shropshire, Mike 163
Simmons, Al 80, 82
Sims, Duke 161
Slaughter, Enos 134

Smith, Al 20
Smith, Kate 133
Smith, Marjie 144
Sohesky, Joseph 83
Southern Ocean Racing Conference 94
Souvenir Baseball Night promotion (Los Angeles Dodgers) 172
Spahn, Warren 124, 125, 130, 131, 135–137
Spanish Flu 6
Spikes, Charlie 158
The Sporting News 47, 58, 64, 133, 175
Sportsman's Park 43–46, 49, 52, 56
Stanford University 153
Stasiak, Stan 102
Stengel, Casey 135
Stephens, Vern 44, 45
Stewart, Rod 109, 112
Stone, Ron 85
Stoneham, Horace 136
Studio 54 111
Suder, Pete 58
Sulphur Dell 76
Summers, Bill 57
Summers, Donna 121
Sundberg, Jim 158
Sweeney, Mark 173
Swift, Bob 51, 53
Symington, Senator Stuart, III 26

Tait, Joe 156, 161–163
Take Me Out to the Ballgame 39, 118, 162, 176
Taylor, Ben 56
Taylor, Zack 49, 51, 55–57
Tebbetts, "Birdie" 134
Teenage Radiation 109
Temple University Hospital 83, 86
Ten-Cent Beer Night promotion (Cleveland Indians) 83, 136, 147, 152, 156, 163, 164, 175, 187, 189, 191
Tepley, Paul 161
Texas Rangers 152, 154–159, 161–163
The Thrill Is Gone 184
Thurber, James 47
Torres, Rusty 116, 147, 160
Tovar, Cesar 158
Tramps Discotheque 111
Travis, Cecil 131
Travolta, John 111
Trout, "Dizzy" 51
Turner, Ted **34**, 35–38, 91–100; and Wedlock and Deadlock Day 101, 102; and Wet T-Shirt Night 102–104, 106

Underwood, Pat 114
U.S. Army Golden Knights promotion (Philadelphia Phillies) 31

Index

U.S. Coast Guard 93
U.S. government 124, 126, 126–128
U.S. Military Academy at West Point 127
U.S. Navy Leap Frogs promotion (Philadelphia Phillies) 31
Unser, Del 143, 148

Valo, Elmer 57
Vancouver Canucks 190
Van Halen 110
Van Wieren, Peter 36
Veeck, Bill, Jr. 1, 2, 4, **8**–10, 14, 22, 25, 29, 30, 67, 68, 71, 74, 81, 185; with Chicago White Sox (first ownership) 19–21; with Chicago White Sox (second ownership) 22, 38, 39; with Cleveland Indians 15–17; and Disco Demolition Night **108**, 112–114, 118, 119, 121; and the Eddie Gaedel Game 46–54; and the Grandstand Managers promotion 54–58; with Milwaukee Brewers 9, **10**–14; with St. Louis Browns 17–19, 42, 46
Veeck, Mary Frances 51, 56, 57
Veeck, Mike 58, 112–114, 116, 119
Veeck, William, Sr. 8, 9
Veterans Stadium 29–33, 74, 77, 81–83, 87–89
Vida Blue appreciation promotion (Oakland Athletics) 27, 28
Voice of America 112
Vuvuzelas giveaway (Florida Marlins) 189

Walker, Fred "Dixie" 133
Wagner, Charlie 131
Waner, Paul 136
War Production Board 124, 126
Warner Records 121
Washington, D.C. 111, 139, 140, 142–146, 151
Washington, Walter 151
Washington Nationals 151, 193
Washington Redskins 144
Washington Senators 132, 133, 136, 138–151, 163, 176, 192
Washington Senators Last Game promotion 136, 138
Washington University in St. Louis 56
WBOS 112
WDAI 108, 109, 111

Wedlock and Headlock Day promotion (Atlanta Braves) 36, 92, 100
Weeghman, Charles 6
Weisman, Max "Lefty" 15
Western League 5
Wet T-Shirt Night promotion (Atlanta Braves) 38, 92, 100, 102–106, 185, 189
Wheaton College 93
White, Roy 147
White Caps giveaway (Kansas City Royals) 188–189
White Sox don shorts promotion 39
Wilcox, Milt 155
Williams, Joe 52
Williams, Ted 45, 52, 53, 82, 130, 132, 140, 143
Wilson, Bill 86
Wilson, Hack 53
WJRJ 94
WLBL 112
WLUP 108, 109, 113, 114, 120
Wolfe, Art 85
Wonder, Stevie 120
Wood, Ken 58
World Series 9, 15, 28, 35, 43, 79, 80, 99, 125, 139, 142, 146, 168–171, 187, 188, 193, 194
World War I 6, 68, 129
World War II 7, 8, 14, 42, 45, 56, 60, 126, 127, 129–132
WRIF 110
Wrigley, William, Jr. 8
Wrigley Field 9, 39
WTCG 94
WTOP-TV 143
WWDC 143
WWWE 156
WWWW 110
Wynn, Jimmy 96

Yerkic, Terry 160, 161
York, Jackie 164
Young, Babe 136
Young, Cy 53, 125
Young, Delmon 175

Zernial, Gus 57
Zim Bear giveaway (Florida Marlins) 193
Zureick, Hank 75

www.ingramcontent.com/pod-product-compliance
Ingram Content Group UK Ltd.
Pitfield, Milton Keynes, MK11 3LW, UK
UKHW041937140426
5217IPUK00014B/528